D0935550

PRESCRIPTION FOR FAILURE

SOCIAL
PHILOSOPHY
& POLICY CENTER

PRESCRIPTION
FOR FAILURE

Race Relations
in the
Age of Social Science

BYRON M. ROTH

transaction

Transaction Publishers
New Brunswick (USA) and London (UK)

Published by the Social Philosophy and Policy Center and by Transaction Publishers 1994

Copyright © by the Social Philosophy and Policy Center

Library of Congress Cataloging-in-Publication Data

Roth, Byron M. (Byron Mitchell)
  Prescription for failure : race relations in the age of social science / by Byron M. Roth.
    p.   cm.—(Studies in social philosophy & policy ; no. 18)
  Includes bibliographical references and index.
  ISBN 1-56000-161-5 (cloth).—ISBN 1-56000-739-7 (paper)
  1. United States—Race relations.   2. Racism—United States.
I. Title.   II. Series.
E185.615.R62   1994
305.8′00973—dc20   93-42745
                                                                          CIP

Cover Design: Colin Moore

To the memory of my parents
Abraham and Sophie Roth

Series Editor: Ellen Frankel Paul
Series Managing Editor: Harry Dolan

The Social Philosophy and Policy Center, founded in 1981, is an interdisciplinary research institution whose principal mission is the examination of public
policy issues from a philosophical perspective. In pursuit of this objective, the
Center supports the work of scholars in the fields of political science,
philosophy, law, and economics. In addition to this book series, the Center
hosts scholarly conferences and edits an interdisciplinary professional journal,
Social Philosophy & Policy. For further information on the Center, write to:
Social Philosophy and Policy Center, Bowling Green State University,
Bowling Green, OH 43403.

Contents

Acknowledgments

Since this book is the product of over thirty years of thinking about the roots of human conflict, there is no way that I can possibly acknowledge all that I owe to the teachers, students, colleagues, and family members who have contributed to my views over the years. Similarly, the debt I owe to the vast number of scholars who have struggled with similar ideas must go largely unpaid. I submit my own efforts in partial fulfillment of the many obligations I bear.

Some people, however, have been particularly influential in helping to bring this book to fruition and should not go unmentioned. My wife, Doris Ernst Roth, has, over the years, with keen insight and considerable good humor, helped me to avoid many of the more dangerous pitfalls of intellectual fashion. Her contribution to this work, both as perceptive critic and demanding editor, was particularly important. My daughters, Erica Palim and Ilana Roth, have, in numerous ways, helped me to overcome the personal and generational limitations of perception which often distort understanding. My son-in-law, Mark Palim, a new immigrant to America, has, with good nature, corrected many of the provincialisms under which I mistakenly labored.

Edward Stern of Bethesda, Maryland, a wise and steadfast friend, and one possessed of a lively and penetrating intellect, read an early version of this book, and made many useful and important suggestions for its improvement even, and especially, in regard to those arguments with which he was unsympathetic. As important, his encouragement at an early stage fortified my resolve to move this work ahead. I would also be remiss not to mention my colleagues at Dowling College, in particular John D. Mullen and James O. Tate, with whom I have had long discussions on this and related topics, and who have critiqued various parts of this book. While they have not always agreed with my views, they have encouraged me in my efforts and offered important insights and advice.

I do not think this book could have been written were it not for the open and collegial atmosphere which prevails at Dowling College where I work. Like any academic institution, it suffers from its peculiar maladies, but its tolerance of dissenting opinion marks it as an especially healthy and robust institution. Dowling's president, Victor P. Meskill, must be given considerable credit for preserving that spirit of tolerance during some often difficult times for the institution. I must also thank Dowling College for the considerable support, both financial and in the form of released time, which enabled me to bring this manuscript to completion. Let me not forget to acknowledge, in addition, the many Dowling students who have, over the years, encouraged me, very often against my wishes, to clarify and substantiate ideas and principles with which I had become overly comfortable. I hope that they have benefited as much as I from our long association.

I am pleased to thank the Social Philosophy and Policy Center at Bowling Green State University, which provided financial support for this work and oversaw its publication. I am particularly indebted to Dr. Ellen Frankel Paul, Deputy Director of the Center, and my editor on this book. She undertook the arduous task of helping me transform a rough manuscript into a finished product. If what follows is clear, to the point, well-substantiated, and free of intellectual rancor and polemics, it is largely the result of Dr. Paul's strenuous, if not always successful, efforts to that effect. She helped me to clarify, strengthen, and where necessary, rethink and modify, many of the premises and arguments put forward in the following pages. Harry Dolan, the Center's Managing Editor, read the manuscript closely and with much discernment, and made many useful suggestions for its improvement in both content and style.

I would also like to pay a debt of gratitude to Thomas Sowell, whom I have never met, but whose penetrating analyses in numerous publications served to stimulate my own ideas on the troubling issues of racial and ethnic conflict. Much of what follows rests on a foundation laid by him.

Of course, I alone am responsible for the errors, confusions, and outright follies which the reader will no doubt discover. I hope that these do not detract overmuch from whatever value this work may have.

I have dedicated this book to my parents, and I have done so as a way of acknowledging a special debt I owe them above and beyond those which any child owes diligent and loving parents. That debt results from their unwavering devotion to personal honesty and intellectual integrity. I was instructed by them to tell the truth, no matter how painful and unpopular the truth might be, and in word and deed they fortified that instruction daily. Such a proud legacy I would not squander.

Introduction

In 1962, the distinguished social scientist Arnold Rose commented on the great strides America had made toward racial equality and racial harmony during the preceding two decades. So great was his optimism that he predicted that over the next three decades racial enmity would decline to ''the minor order of Catholic-Protestant'' prejudice as it then existed.[1] Rose was not alone; many Americans at the time, perhaps most, shared his optimism.

The history of the past three decades suggests, however, that this earlier view may have been overly optimistic. There can be no doubt that life for large numbers of black Americans has vastly improved since World War II. On the other hand, the widespread deterioration of inner-city black neighborhoods during recent decades has meant that life has grown worse for many blacks. Furthermore, the gradual improvement in race relations in the early days of the civil rights movement seems to have stagnated and been replaced by a growing unease about the future of those relations. On the nation's college campuses and in its largest cities, there are troubling reports of new tensions and animosities between blacks and other groups. Prominent black Americans reflect pessimistically on the pervasiveness of white racism, while civil rights advocates argue for more-strenuous efforts to overcome the effects of that racism. It is my purpose in what follows to examine the sources of this unease and to attempt to discover why progress in civil rights for black Americans does not appear to have been matched, at least in recent years, by equal progress in social harmony.

In the chapters that follow I argue that a considerable part of our present racial difficulties are the result of commonly expressed understandings that are deeply flawed. I argue that the flaws in those understandings can only be

1

corrected if social scientists are more forthright in their reporting of social science research. Much of that research, contrary to widespread belief, does not support but rather contradicts many of the opinions, expressed by civil rights advocates and government spokesmen, that dominate the discussion of race in the popular media.

It was about fifty years ago that America began the task of correcting the historic wrongs visited on black Americans by pervasive discrimination in the laws and customs of American society that continued long after the shameful chapter of American slavery had been brought to a close. The injustices that blacks suffered were particularly egregious in light of the American attachment to fair play and open opportunity. The enormous contradiction between those values and America's treatment of its black citizens was brought to the fore by the events of World War II. It is noteworthy that the generation that came of age in that terrible period of history was the one that embarked upon the momentous task of dismantling the legal and social apparatus that kept black Americans from achieving their rightful place in American society.

The task seemed relatively straightforward. Black Americans lagged behind white Americans socially and economically because of widespread discrimination and prejudice. If that discrimination and prejudice were eliminated, blacks would, in due course, rise to the same level as whites. As Arnold Rose's comments make clear, the first two decades of those efforts had been remarkably successful. Government-sponsored segregation was largely dismantled, and strenuous educational efforts were undertaken to reduce racial prejudice and discriminatory social customs. By the 1960s, black Americans were indeed moving into the mainstream, albeit slowly but nonetheless steadily.

For many people, the slow and gradual nature of black progress was to be expected due to the fact that blacks had so much to overcome and so far to go. The transformation of a whole race of people from the status of a despised caste in society to that of equal participants could not, in this view, occur overnight. The prejudicial attitudes and discriminatory behaviors that white Americans had acquired over centuries would require time to overcome; in some places this might require the actual passing of one or more generations of people who were too fixed in their ways to adjust to new realities. Blacks too would have to make difficult adjustments. They would have to develop new skills in order to take advantage of new opportunities. They would have to acquire new habits of thought and shed attitudes that centuries of slavery and injustice had imposed. All of these changes would require time, perhaps decades, before they could be thoroughly assimilated by all Americans. The development of a new accommodation between the races, made possible by legal equality, could not, in this view, be imposed by law, but could only evolve naturally over time as new realities took hold. Progress toward racial equality, accordingly, would not be measured in years, but rather in generations, much as had the progress of various immigrant groups who established themselves in America after very humble beginnings. For those who held this view, the removal of legal discrimination was a necessary first step toward eventual social equality, the actual attainment of which would necessarily be halting and gradual, however much one may have wished to speed the process.

For others, however, the lumbering pace toward racial equality in the two decades following World War II seemed to promise once again, in Langston Hughes's poignant phrase, ''a dream deferred.''[2] To people of this view, the real but modest success of government efforts during the previous decades suggested that more-strenuous government efforts could and should be made to bring about equality sooner. How, these people asked, could one ask black Americans to wait generations after all they had suffered at the hands of a cruel and indifferent America? Such people argued for radical change to correct past injustices.

This argument over the pace of progress in the 1960s was won, in large measure, by those who argued for more-radical government action. A wide range of policies were implemented in that decade and since then to eliminate segregation and speed the assimilation of black Americans. Affirmative action guidelines were instituted to assure that blacks were fairly represented in the workplace and in the universities. Compensatory education programs, such as Head Start, were initiated. Educational programs in the schools and in the media were undertaken to stamp out prejudice. A wide range of legal changes were implemented to reduce discrimination in the criminal justice system and in other areas of life.

The more-strenuous efforts undertaken since the 1960s have had decidedly mixed results. On the one hand, blacks have continued in greater numbers to move into the mainstream of middle-class American life. Paralleling this progress, however, has been the growth of an increasingly troubled black underclass and the decay of the central cities where many blacks live. As I will attempt to demonstrate in the pages that follow, it is the growth of the black underclass that represents the greatest impediment to black progress and racial harmony today. I will explore the extent to which the growth of the underclass since the 1960s is related to many of the civil rights policies designed to speed black assimilation that were implemented in that decade. It is important to examine these policies with special scrutiny since few were supported by sound social science research, but were based rather, as I said earlier, on erroneous popular understandings. Perhaps the most important contribution of this book will be the demonstration that there never was any sound basis in social science research for many of the policies on race that have been followed during the past three decades. This is not to deny that social scientists overwhelmingly supported these policies, as they surely did; the point is that the social science evidence did not.

The above may come as a surprise to the general reader, but is unlikely to be surprising to the relatively small group of scholars who are most intimately familiar with the research relating to race. In fact, a wide gap has grown up between what the educated layman and the scientific specialist understand about the nature of such things as poverty, crime, and educational failure, all of which have important ramifications for understanding racial matters. The purpose of this book is to review the social science research on a variety of such issues, especially in psychology and sociology, in the hope that improved understanding can allow for a more thoughtful discussion of race relations than has hitherto taken place.

A thorough analysis of the social science literature will reveal that most of the problems blacks face in America today are directly attributable to patterns of behavior that have become common in black underclass communities. Underclass neighborhoods are plagued by welfare dependency, crime, illegitimacy, and educational failure, all of which seriously undercut black economic and social advancement, and in addition serve to undermine efforts to facilitate racial integration. The common charge by civil rights advocates that disapproval of underclass behavior patterns is a cover for racist sentiment, a charge often construed as an attempt to justify those behavior patterns, serves mainly to widen the gap between blacks and whites.

The above understanding, of course, runs counter to the common understanding espoused by the media and by government bureaucrats, for whom the problems of black Americans, including the growth of the underclass, are usually explained in terms of an endemic white racism and the discrimination it fosters. In the pages that follow I make the case that the continuing attempt to counter the purported racism of white Americans may be largely counterproductive today and, insofar as it obstructs dealing with the real sources of black difficulties, serves to exacerbate them. Why has the scientific literature of which I speak had so little impact on popular understanding and government policy? A thorough answer to this question will not be attempted here; in later chapters a rather complete answer will, I think, emerge. A few thoughts, however, are in order. Modern democracies, owing in large measure to modern communications media, have become far more responsive to public opinion, and to an increasing degree, public opinion is shaped by the mass media and those who control the media. Information on racial problems is filtered through a media establishment whose members share with each other common preconceptions and understandings, especially on issues relating to race. In addition, the information the media receives about the social scientific study of race comes from a relatively small number of influential academics at the nation's elite universities. People in the media, generally, share the same world-view as leading academics.[3] Consequently, they are often not as critical as they should be in their handling of the information they receive from academics, who are often reluctant to speak plainly on issues of race.

The reasons for the lack of candor on racial issues are many and varied and will be explored at some length in later chapters. For now, it is enough to point out what is probably the most important reason: social scientists are acutely sensitive to the possibility that they might contribute to the acceptance of doctrines of racial superiority or inferiority. The history of twentieth-century American social science cannot be understood without an understanding of this sensitivity. It derives from the fact that the social sciences were very much influenced by evolutionary theory in the late nineteenth and early twentieth centuries. Early social science was not uncomfortable with the notion that cultural differences reflected biological differences among human groups, or with the notion that some groups had made more progress up the evolutionary ladder than had others. As an example, IQ tests, developed by psychologists early in this century, were sometimes cited in explaining why some ethnic groups lagged behind others in assimilating into the mainstream.

This is not to suggest there was no disagreement on questions of group differences. To the contrary, the nature-nurture issue was, in fact, hotly debated in the early decades of this century.[4] World War II and the Nazi racial atrocities, however, put an end to that debate, and served moreover to cast it in moral terms. Those who had argued in favor of biological explanations for group differences were viewed not merely as wrong, but as grotesquely immoral for having paved the way for racial genocide.[5]

The fear of being in league with the devil continues to haunt most thoughtful social scientists and has had a pervasive influence on their contributions to the current civil rights debate. This is especially so with regard to their treatment of alternatives to the prevailing view that black difficulties are rooted in white prejudice and discrimination. The most obvious alternative to that view is the common-sense view that people's failures and successes, including the failures and successes of blacks, are in large measure the result of their own behaviors and values. That is the argument made most notably by the well-known black economist Thomas Sowell.[6] The problem, however, with accepting this argument is that it opens up the possibility that the differences in behaviors and values between blacks and whites may be related in some more basic way to native differences between the races. In other words, perhaps blacks have educational and economic difficulties because they lack the same level of abilities as whites? Perhaps the higher incidence of violent criminal behavior among blacks is the result of more-fundamental differences in aggressiveness or in impulse control between the races? It is not at all an exaggeration to say that the social science discussion of race relations is conditioned by a desire to avoid even the possibility of lending support to such explanations of black problems.

Even when it is patently clear that a pattern of behavior among blacks is a direct cause of black poverty, as is clear in the case of illegitimacy, social scientists hesitate to emphasize the need to change behavior, and look rather for the causes of that behavior in white discrimination. The very possibility of seeming to buttress doctrines of racial inferiority is, understandably, so abhorrent to the vast majority of academics that any evidence that *seems* to lend any support to such a thesis tends to be dismissed or ignored. The aversion to addressing the negative impact of many black patterns of behavior forces the social sciences into a mental straitjacket, as it were, requiring all black problems to be viewed as rooted in white racism. Research that contradicts the prevailing view is dismissed or, where possible, ignored. When contrary research cannot be dismissed or ignored, it is often rendered impotent by the charge that it was motivated by racist intent. The net result is that the full and damaging consequences of many underclass behaviors for black economic advancement remain poorly understood. For that reason, policy proposals designed to change those behavior patterns and reduce, for instance, single parenthood and delinquency are rarely taken seriously.

The highly respected research sociologist James Coleman has written that the pressure to conform to prevailing views leads to a "self-suppression" that "prevents many relevant research questions from being raised." He explains: "We hesitate to ask research questions that might lead to results that would elicit disapproval by those colleagues we see regularly. We monitor our own activities, and suppress those that do not meet this criterion. When there is a strong consensus among these colleagues, we redirect our behavior accordingly." [7] Coleman was recently honored by election to a term as president of the American Sociological Association. Perhaps more social scientists will come to agree with him on the dangers of suppressing unpopular points of view. To date, however, people of Coleman's view are a distinct minority and have had only modest effect.

Coleman is expressing more than a vague personal impression. In Chapter 1, I will examine evidence that strongly suggests there is a surprising homogeneity of opinion among social scientists that effectively suppresses research into controversial areas. Moreover, when controversial work is done, as it sometimes is, if it produces findings that contradict prevailing views, those findings are also likely to be suppressed. While that research is often known among specialists close to specific research areas, it rarely reaches the public through the popular media or through standard college texts. Social scientists, no less than other professionals, look askance at telling tales out of school. [8]

Abetting this self-censorship is the fact that even among social scientists, relatively few are familiar in an intimate way with the evidence contradictory to prevailing views. Many are in fact often not much better informed than the general public in this regard. The social sciences have become so specialized in recent years that social scientists are often unfamiliar with large areas of knowledge even in their own disciplines. They are as likely, therefore, as laymen to accept conventional views out of a plain lack of information in subject matters with which they do not have intimate familiarity.

A similar insularity prevails among members of the mainstream media. Even when contrary ideas on race reach members of the media, they have a difficult time assimilating them into their understanding. It should be remembered that influential members of the media were educated alongside of, and share a similar world-view with, influential academicians. In particular, they share the prevailing view relating black problems to white racism, and this causes them to practice their own brand of self-censorship when events contradict their understanding.[9]

A recent case in point is instructive. In November 1992, in Florida, a group of four young black men hijacked a car in which were riding three young white men and a black woman. The car was driven to a remote field where the white men were forced to strip off their clothes and lie facedown on the ground. While the black woman watched, all three men were shot, execution style, in the back of the head. Two died and the third survived by playing dead. The black woman was left unhurt, but was taunted for consorting with white men. The *New York Times* article reporting on this incident appeared in the back pages under the heading ''Woman Forced to Watch as 2 Friends are Killed.''[10] There was no follow-up on the story in the following weeks, and in fact there was a virtual blackout on the incident in the major media in the New York City area.[11]

There can be no question that had the races of the participants been reversed, the story would have been headline news confirming that racism in America continues to inspire the most vile lynchings, especially against black men who have the temerity to befriend white women. Perhaps the New York news media played down the story because they thought it might further inflame racial tensions that were already raw in the New York City area following the riot in Crown Heights. Such an explanation doesn't square, however, with the active and continuing reporting of racial incidents in which the victims are black. The general rule for reporting on interracial crime seems premised on the assumption that when blacks commit crimes against whites, they, for reasons of poverty and lack of opportunity, act almost exclusively with pecuniary intent, whereas when whites commit crimes against blacks, they, for reasons of racism, act primarily with bigoted intent. Stories that contradict this general view of things seem difficult for the media to assimilate. Following this logic, the Florida murders were reported as a routine instance of a "carjacking" meriting extensive local coverage, to be sure, but not the sort of national coverage that is appropriate for "racial incidents," as in cases of white gangs attacking black victims.

I am not suggesting any active conspiracy in all of this. Rather, I am suggesting that such things can be understood to result from the fairly mundane fact of life that when the vast majority of people in a community share a common set of assumptions about the nature of the world, it is difficult for them to view clearly any evidence, including that produced by reputable scholars, which challenges the soundness of those assumptions. In effect, I am arguing, and will demonstrate in the pages which follow, that an orthodoxy reigns among academics and among media professionals that blinds them to the scientific facts about race relations today. As we will see in Chapter 1, those social scientists who are familiar with the facts are generally reluctant to challenge the prevailing view for fear of ostracism and condemnation. The result is that the free exchange of ideas that characterizes healthy science, and that should inform social policy, is missing in the current discussion of race.

I. Some Difficulties with the Prevailing View

Consider the following comments on prejudice presented in a popular textbook on social psychology:

> In the United States, racial prejudice against blacks by whites has been a tenacious social problem. It has resulted in an enormous catalog of social ills, ranging from the deterioration and near bankruptcy of large cities, to poverty, shorter life expectancy, high levels of crime and drug abuse, and human misery of all kinds among blacks themselves.[12]

In a similar vein the distinguished black psychologist Kenneth Clark (a past president of the American Psychological Association)—whose research was cited by the Supreme Court in the 1954 school-desegregation decision—gave the following explanation for black-white differences in SAT scores in a 1982 op-ed piece in the *New York Times*:

> Black children are educationally retarded because the public schools they are required to attend are polluted with racism. Their low scores reflect the racial segregation and inferiority of these schools. These children are perceived and treated as if they were uneducable. From the earliest grades they are programmed for failure. Throughout their lives, they are classic examples of the validity of the concept of victimization by self-fulfilling prophecy.[13]

The above statements are fairly representative of the views of social scientists commonly heard in the popular media. Under the prevailing view, white America is endemically racist and racism is the primary cause of the problems that blacks confront. Racism is claimed as the primary, almost exclusive cause of poverty, crime, illegitimacy, drug abuse, and educational failure among blacks. In fact, it is the assumption of widespread racism which is the justification for most of the laws and policies associated with the civil rights movement—laws and policies that a large majority of social scientists support.

But even modest reflection must give one pause. It is simply not reasonable to attribute *all* black problems to the single cause of white racism. In fact, it is almost always the case that complex social phenomena are caused and influenced by a multitude of factors. It is of course true and indisputable that, in the ultimate sense, everything about blacks in America today can be traced to the racism of the white Europeans who enslaved their ancestors. In addition, it is probably true that historical black responses to centuries of abuse have played a prominent, perhaps determinative, role in many of the responses of blacks today. But to say that is by no means to outline in precisely what ways past racist practices shaped the behavior patterns common today. Nor is it clear what impact current white attitudes have upon blacks in the very different circumstances of the late twentieth century. These are questions of great importance for blacks and whites and the future of America, and it is unlikely that the answers to them will be simple. At the very least, we should examine the empirical evidence with great scrutiny before accepting this or that answer as if it were a foregone conclusion.

For instance, it is a reasonable hypothesis to assert that the educational difficulties blacks face may be due to the fact that historically blacks were denied the fruits of educational success by racist practices. But that is a very different hypothesis from one that suggests that these educational problems are the result of current white racism. Indeed, these hypotheses are radically different and would lead to very different policy prescriptions for improving black educational performance. The historical-racism hypothesis would recommend an effort to change the attitudes of black children about the current opportunities that educational success can provide. The hypothesis that current racism is to blame would suggest attempts to eliminate racism among whites, especially those in the schools. There are, however, many reasons to question the impact of current racism on black children today. It is by no means clear how the racism of some white teachers—I doubt that even the supporters of the white-racism hypothesis would argue that all white teachers are racist—undermines the education of black children in Atlanta, Georgia, where, according to Abigail Thernstrom, "white teachers have almost disappeared from the school system."[14] Even more unclear is how the attitudes of white teachers could have affected children in the earlier segregated schools of the South when virtually all teachers in segregated black schools were themselves black and were given considerable freedom in what and how they taught.[15]

Certainly the segregationist practices in the South of the past may have demoralized black children and interfered with their motivation to learn, but that is very different from arguing that America today denies educated blacks fair opportunities. The latter is merely an assertion and one that runs counter to everyday experience and to the evidence that will be presented in later chapters.

Illegitimacy in the black community, to take another example, is a very serious problem. Some 64 percent of all black children are born to unmarried women.[16] It is certainly a reasonable hypothesis to suggest that discrimination against black men leads to unemployment among them and thereby contributes to high rates of unwed motherhood due to the scarcity of men able to support a family. But this hypothesis must also account for the fact that the illegitimacy rate was less than one-third of today's rate in the 1950s when, by all accounts, discrimination against black men was more severe than it is today.[17] The point is that reasonable hypotheses are not the same as sound scientific explanations. In fact, it is not at all clear what factors contribute to high rates of illegitimacy among blacks. It is very clear, however, that so long as the rate of unwed motherhood remains high, so will poverty among black women and children. Policies to improve the economic prospects for blacks would do well to aim at reducing the illegitimacy rate, whatever the ultimate causes. Attributing the problem to white prejudice, even if that were the case, would not solve the problem, since it is unclear how white prejudice could be more effectively dealt with than it is today.

A very serious problem with the white-racism explanation is the fact that large numbers of blacks have done very well in recent decades. It is difficult to explain why a pattern of discrimination that is said to be so pervasive has been relatively ineffective in thwarting the ambitions of the many blacks who perform well in school and the many who succeed in highly desirable occupations. The large number of successful blacks argues against the notion that they are merely "tokens" to assuage white guilt. It is interesting that among the 2.4 million blacks who are Catholic (9 percent of all blacks) the high school dropout rate is lower than that of white Americans. Black Catholics are 40 percent more likely to be college graduates than other blacks. In fact, among forty- to fifty-year-olds, more black Catholics (26 percent) have college degrees than do other blacks (15 percent) and more even than whites (24 percent).[18]

Such statistics force us to question the white-discrimination hypothesis, since it is unreasonable to suppose that whites make distinctions about blacks on the basis of religion. Similar questions arise when we are confronted with statistics comparing black Americans of Caribbean descent to those whose ancestors were born in America. Blacks of Caribbean background have higher rates of employment in professional occupations than American-born blacks and higher rates of such employment even than Americans in general.[19]

Further reflection leads to other questions regarding the white-racism hypothesis. How is it possible for racism to be so virulent after all these years of educational and media efforts to reduce it? Have these efforts been ineffective, and if so, why? We have all been witness in recent years to highly publicized incidents of physical assaults on black individuals, and numerous reports of racial incidents on college campuses. Are these incidents newsworthy because they represent only the tip of the iceberg, as it were, or are they newsworthy because they are so atypical in America today? Perhaps the incidents receive the coverage they do because they seem consistent with the prevailing view that racism is widespread among white Americans.

It is important to stress the point that questioning the hypothesis that white racism is the primary source of black problems is not the same as denying the existence of white racism. There can be little doubt that there are people who openly express antagonism to blacks, and probably many others who secretly share their antagonism. But it is simply not clear how many white Americans are avowed racists. Nor is it clear what proportion of racists there are in positions of influence who can in any major way affect what happens to blacks. So long as such questions remain unanswered, it is unwise and perhaps counterproductive to accept many common assertions as to the sources of black difficulties. I do not think it is useful to argue that many blacks fare poorly in school because American education is polluted with racism, when no evidence for such a claim can be brought forward.

On its face such a charge seems extremely dubious in light of the fact that college professors and public school teachers are generally known to be liberal on racial matters. Similar reasoning undermines the frequent claim that a disproportionate number of blacks have criminal records because of the racism endemic to the criminal justice system, when no evidence is brought forward to show that racism is common among judges, lawyers, or police officers. There are, to be sure, anecdotal reports of police misconduct and highly publicized accounts of incidents of police brutality such as the Rodney King beating, but these hardly substitute for sound evidence of widespread racism within the system. If anything, the public outcry against such incidents tends to suggest that such misconduct is, in fact, unrepresentative of the system as a whole. Also questionable is the charge that blacks suffer disproportionate health problems because racism taints American medicine. Doctors and nurses are among the least likely candidates upon whom to pin the label of bigotry.

In other words, the claim that black Americans suffer the problems they do because of the racism of white Americans requires considerable scrutiny before it is accepted as a sound explanation. On its face it seems unreasonable to assume that large numbers of white Americans, including the best educated and most influential, are as bigoted and mean-spirited as were many uneducated whites earlier in the century. If American bigotry is in fact still the primary source of black problems, then the future of black Americans is grim indeed, since it is hard to see how further efforts to eradicate bigotry can be more successful than have been those of the past four decades. Unfortunately, the prevailing orthodoxy, if closely analyzed, leads inexorably to such an unhappy conclusion. Perhaps it is time to cast aside the current view and look for alternative explanations that may produce a more useful and less pessimistic conclusion.

II. An Overview

A fundamental assumption underlying what follows is that one is unlikely to solve problems if one lacks a clear understanding of the nature of those problems. In the case of the problems facing black Americans, I think this simple truth has often been overlooked, and as a consequence, many of the policy prescriptions designed to aid blacks have, in the end, proved counter-productive.

Chapter 1 of Part I examines the current scene in the social sciences and outlines the reasons why social scientists have, in the main, resisted coming to terms with much of the evidence that contradicts the conventional wisdom on race. This resistance is explained to a large extent by the ideological biases common to social scientists, biases which make it difficult for them to accept the thesis that blacks and other ethnic groups may have difficulties whose origins have little to do with the attitudes of whites. It is no exaggeration to call this view an orthodoxy; its treatment of dissent certainly adds credence to that characterization. A consequence is that serious research devoted to finding sound explanations for black problems has been limited and constrained. Without a foundation in research findings, civil rights policy has, in the main, been based on unsubstantiated conjecture.

This chapter also explores the moral obligations of scientists. In particular, it deals with the question of why the doctrine of value-free or politically neutral social science has fallen in repute among social scientists, and has been replaced instead by ideologically driven theory and research. In addition, the difficulties which serious scientists confront on ''politically correct'' campuses are examined, especially in light of the way these difficulties hinder necessary and useful research on issues relating to race.

Chapter 2 of Part I explores the attitudes of whites today and the current economic status of blacks in America in an attempt to determine if the white-racism hypothesis can be substantiated. Widespread polling data casts substantial doubt on the hypothesis that white Americans continue to hold racist attitudes toward blacks, and suggests that the educational efforts to reduce bigotry seem to have been largely successful. Furthermore, a close inspection of census data reveals that blacks have made remarkable strides economically, especially those who live in stable two-parent families. An attempt is made to pinpoint in what precise ways blacks as a group face economic difficulties and what the sources of those difficulties are.

Part II outlines the origins of the conventional view on race relations and traces its evolution to the present. A consensus began to take shape in the 1930s and was crystallized in Gunnar Myrdal's extremely influential book on race relations, *An American Dilemma: The Negro Problem and Modern Democracy,* published in the early 1940s.[20] In Myrdal's view, which is outlined in Chapter 3 of Part II, white discrimination forced blacks into demeaning roles and behaviors that, when viewed by whites, seemed to confirm whites' negative opinions of blacks. This "vicious circle," as Myrdal called it, could only be broken by concerted efforts on the part of government to end discrimination against blacks, who were not themselves in a position to better their lot in the face of overwhelming white resistance, especially in the South. Myrdal's view became the prevailing one among social scientists and among most intellectuals and continues to prevail some fifty years after it was so effectively put forward.

Chapter 4 of Part II looks at the research on prejudice as it evolved in the aftermath of World War II. Research efforts undertaken during this period played a role almost equal to that of Myrdal's in shaping the way the social sciences approached questions of race. The most ambitious of these efforts resulted in the publication of *The Authoritarian Personality,* which dealt with the nature of prejudice and the personality characteristics of people who held prejudiced views.[21] An important element of this and other studies of prejudice was a tendency for researchers to discount rational explanations of any generalized beliefs people might hold about this or that ethnic group. Human rationality was out of favor with psychologists at the time, and they were more inclined to see behavior in terms of the Freudian model of unconscious motivation or the behaviorist model of automatic habit-formation, both of which allow little room for rational thought. Anthropologists and sociologists, for their part, were enamored of Marxist relativism, which tends to view human understanding as distorted by class or group interests. A consequence of this was that almost any belief about a group, even a benign generalization, was characterized as irrational. It was seen as indicative of a neurotic or disturbed personality, or as motivated by a desire to preserve some class or racial advantage. Beliefs about groups, often clearly based in empirical reality, were therefore usually mistaken for and confused with prejudice and hostility.

Another important element of this work on prejudice was a hypothesized relationship between free-market values and bigotry. From that purported association, the traditional American values dealing with self-reliance and individualism, law and order, family stability, and national pride were often characterized as forms of racial bias in disguise. For instance, the common American belief that able people should take care of themselves and not rely on government support was characterized as expressing covert hostility to blacks and a callous failure to acknowledge how blacks' problems justified their need for government assistance.

Chapter 5 of Part II reviews more-recent work on prejudice, much of which continues to be influenced by the assumptions established in the earlier period, including the assumption of an association between traditional American values and racism. This chapter explores the possibility that this association may have contributed to the undercutting of traditional values (e.g., the work ethic, individual responsibility, attachment to the traditional family, etc.) in America. It also explores the possibility that the association of those values with racism may have contributed to the rise of the social problems which plague inner-city neighborhoods.

Part III introduces the reader to recent thinking on the evolution of human social behavior. This may at first appear to be a detour, but this material is, in fact, central to a sound understanding of the problems which plague America's inner cities. Chapter 6 of Part III discusses the contribution of evolutionary thinking as it relates to human development, especially during the critical period of adolescence. Much of the failure to deal with underclass pathology is the result of an inadequate theoretical base for understanding adolescent development, and much of that inadequacy can be traced to an unwillingness to take evolutionary explanations seriously. For instance, psychologists and sociologists have left few stones unturned in their attempt to find the social and environmental factors that would explain why young unmarried women get pregnant and young men engage in physical conflicts, but their efforts have not proved particularly fruitful. Had they turned to the substantial body of work in modern evolutionary theory they might have been more successful. Evolutionary theory makes clear that these adolescent behaviors do not require much explaining at all, since they are perfectly natural. From the perspective of evolutionary theory, physical competition between males, especially for the favors of females, and the desire to reproduce on the part of both sexes are among the most powerful forces influencing human conduct. Such behaviors and desires do not have to be actively taught, any more than people need to be taught to eat and drink.

Chapter 7 of Part III explores the contribution of evolutionary thinking to a clearer understanding of ethnic relations and ethnic conflict. For instance, the study of the evolution of social behavior casts doubt on the common assumption that prejudice and discrimination have to be taught. Research on kinship recognition and kinship favoritism in animals suggests that animals are predisposed to be altruistic to those closely related to them, but just as predisposed to competition and aggression against those less closely related.

Considerable psychological research provides convincing evidence that similar patterns are common among humans. That research suggests that the tendency to divide the world into an "us" and a "them," into an in-group and an out-group, is something to which human beings are very much predisposed. The notion that bigotry and prejudice may be natural human proclivities does not mean that bigotry is inevitable, but does suggest that much difficult work must be done to prevent it and to prevent the strife that so often accompanies it. The failure to understand the nature of human altruism and human hatred has had tragic consequences. Clearer insight in these matters may well be the most important contribution of evolutionary thinking to the social sciences.

Part IV reviews in depth the literature on what I call the "debilitating triad," made up of crime, school failure, and illegitimacy, and the truly disastrous consequences these problems have for black aspirations and racial harmony. Chapter 8 of Part IV, which deals with crime and delinquency, offers a concrete example of the aforementioned gap between informed public opinion and expert opinion in the social sciences. The notion that crime and delinquency are the product of poverty and discrimination is not much supported by the scholarly literature. To be sure, poverty and crime are related, but not in any simple cause-and-effect way. The experts are almost unanimous, however, in attributing crime to an individual's alienation from the larger community. This chapter reviews prominent criminological theories in an attempt to understand how crime has come to spiral out of control in the nation's cities. It also explores the profoundly negative effect of crime on black economic and social aspirations, as well as the impact that high crime rates among blacks have on the attitudes and behavior of whites.

Chapter 9 of Part IV reviews the extensive and often convoluted literature on the educational problems of black children and demonstrates that much popular opinion is not supported by expert judgment. For instance, a review of the literature on the impact of teacher expectations on student performance suggests that, contrary to popular views, teacher expectations have only limited impact on how well children perform in school, and may have no impact at all. The chapter reviews the extensive literature on school achievement in order to attempt to understand why black children exhibit higher rates of school failure than most other ethnic groups. The chapter also explores the ramifications of black educational weakness on black economic and social progress, and in addition, the impact which educational weakness has on the attempt to assure blacks proportional representation in various professions.

Chapter 10 of Part IV explores the causes and consequences of illegitimacy in the black community, where today about two out of every three children are born to single women. This chapter drives home the undeniable fact that so long as black women opt, or are forced to opt, for single-parent status, there is virtually no possibility that black family income will ever achieve parity with white family income. The chapter examines the various explanations for high rates of single parenthood. Among the hypotheses explored are those that attribute illegitimacy to a lack of potential husbands. It reviews evidence suggesting that there has been a historical tendency in the urban North for black women to outnumber black men in the marriage pool. In addition, young black men have such high rates of incarceration and school failure that the marriage prospects for young black women appear bleak. Also examined is the impact of cultural factors and government policies which may play a role in biasing black women in the direction of single parenthood.

Chapter 10 also looks at the impact of single parenthood on children and adults. The impact of illegitimacy on educational attainment is fairly clear. Its impact on delinquency, contrary to popular opinion, is far from resolved by the evidence gathered to date. While it is undoubtedly the case that delinquency is very high in underclass neighborhoods where illegitimacy is also very high, it is unclear whether it is the illegitimacy per se that causes the delinquency, rather than the combination of conditions common in underclass neighborhoods.

Taken as a whole, the chapters in Part IV raise troubling questions about the direction of current government policies designed to assist blacks. Especially troubling is the widespread reluctance among authorities to tackle crime, inadequate schooling, and illegitimacy, which, taken together, represent such powerful impediments to black economic and social advancement. Even if one accepts the argument that these problems are at base the result of racism, this does not obviate the need to attack the problems head on, whatever one does in the way of reducing white racism. The point is that even if racism were reduced to a nullity, the life of most blacks would not be improved appreciably if the debilitating conditions of life in the underclass were not ameliorated. On the other hand, if crime, school failure, and illegitimacy can be curtailed, white racism in its current form is unlikely to hold blacks back either socially or economically.

III. A Troubling Prognosis

The concluding chapter of the book attempts a prognosis of the future of race relations should current trends and current policies continue. While the black middle class probably will continue to grow, there is little reason to suppose that the problems of the underclass will abate.[22] Such a prognosis is not heartening, and is even less so when one drops the unreasonable assumption that current trends will continue unchanged.

In this final chapter I explore the possibility that the problems plaguing blacks in the inner cities may well lead to increased tensions between the races that, in turn, may make it more difficult to address the problems blacks confront in trying to achieve economic and social progress. It is therefore essential to understand the causes of those problems and find ways to reduce them. Failure to do so now may preclude doing so in the future. If white racism is the true source of those problems, then new and more effective ways of reducing that racism must be found. On the other hand, if white racism is not the primary cause of those problems, then continuing to rely on that explanation seriously undermines the search for the real causes and thereby postpones, perhaps indefinitely, the implementation of solutions.

It is important to allow for the possibility that the attitudes toward blacks among whites could well turn very negative if crime and illegitimacy continue to spiral out of control in black underclass neighborhoods. The seriousness of this problem was highlighted by Senator Bill Bradley (Democrat from New Jersey) on the floor of the U.S. Senate:

> In a kind of ironic flip of fate, the fear of brutal white repression felt for decades in the black community and the seething anger it generated now appear to be mirrored in the fear whites have of random attack from blacks and the growing anger it fuels.
>
> Today many whites responding to a more violent reality, heightened by sensational news stories, see young black men traveling in groups, cruising the city, looking for trouble, and they are frightened. Many white Americans, whether fairly or unfairly, seem to be saying to some young black males, ''You litter the street and deface the subway, and no one, white or black, says stop. . . . You snatch a purse, crash a concert, break open a telephone box, and no one, black or white, says stop. You rob a store, rape a jogger, shoot a tourist, and when they catch you . . . you cry racism. And nobody, white or black, says stop.''[23]

Thus does Senator Bradley, one of the most respected members of the Senate, characterize the views of many of his constituents, and there is little reason to question his assessment of their views. Nor is there any reason to suppose that middle-class whites in New Jersey are unique in their attitudes. What these white perceptions and feelings, which are surely growing more common, portend for black-white harmony and for black social advancement is unclear, but they are hardly a positive development. To suggest that these views are racist and can be changed by the further education of whites rather than by reducing criminal behavior among black adolescents is plainly less than helpful.[24]

To date, the common response of middle-class whites has been to retreat in the face of underclass pathology. All too often this has been confused with a fear of racial integration, when it appears rather to be motivated largely by fear of crime and civic decay. But whatever its motivation, major cities like Detroit have been emptied of their middle-class citizens and face fiscal and social bankruptcy as a result. Many cities are increasingly becoming black enclaves, large sections of which are dominated by the underclass, where anarchy and disorder reign. Surrounding these cities are middle-class suburbs whose inhabitants' sympathies for urban dwellers and willingness to provide financial support for them wane with every passing year.

Furthermore, if underclass criminal behavior spills over into middle-class suburbs, as it has most noticeably in the recent spate of "carjackings," suburban indifference may turn to hostility. Such hostility may create a desire to quarantine the members of the underclass, who are clearly viewed as the carriers of social pathologies that middle-class people, both black and white, find repellent.

An additional complicating factor is the increased immigration to America of people from Asia and West Asia. The success of these groups both academically and economically, and the absence of serious social pathology among them, clearly invites invidious comparison with the behavior of underclass blacks. The generally receptive welcome these groups, even those who are racially distinct, receive from white Americans makes the charge of endemic white racism difficult to sustain. Furthermore, the open and growing hostility to successful ethnics common in black communities, as evidenced by the open attacks on Jews in New York City and Koreans in Los Angeles and elsewhere, threatens to deprive blacks of the general sympathy of the white middle class that has, to date, largely tempered majority disdain for underclass behavior.[25]

Any reading of history demonstrates that it is difficult at best to maintain harmony in multiethnic and multiracial societies, for reasons that will be explored in later pages. It is hardly helpful, however, for leaders to allow false and potentially explosive information to circulate without correction. A recent poll conducted by the *New York Times* asked, among other things, whether people agreed with the statement "Some people say the Government deliberately makes sure that drugs are easily available in poor black neighborhoods in order to harm black people." Twenty-five percent of the black respondents thought the statement true, and 35 percent thought it "might possibly be true." On a question dealing with AIDS, 29 percent of black respondents thought it was either true or might possibly be true that ". . . AIDS was deliberately created in a laboratory in order to infect black people."[26] Race relations are not improved when few people raise their voices to denounce these beliefs for the dangerous untruths they are.

Such views of American society among substantial numbers of blacks are unlikely to foster racial harmony and racial integration. In fact, if whites come to believe that these views are seriously held by many blacks, they are likely to resist integration on perfectly rational grounds. One doesn't easily feel comfortable with a person who actually believes you support a conspiracy to turn his child into a drug addict or infect him with AIDS.

The dangers to social harmony are exacerbated when differences of race and ethnicity are compounded by differences in important values and allegiances. That is why current efforts to magnify group cultural differences may be misguided. Equally problematic in this regard are attempts to debunk and devalue American cultural heroes such as the founding fathers for their hypocrisy in ratifying the Constitution while blacks remained in slavery. All children need to be taught about the ugly history of the slave trade and the utter brutality with which it was carried out. They must be made aware of the fact that the discovery of America opened new possibilities of fulfillment to Europeans, but only centuries of sorrow for Africans. They must be made aware that slavery made a mockery of the claim in the Declaration of Independence that all men were equal in their right to "Life, Liberty and the pursuit of Happiness."

Children must not be spared the harsh truths about the settling of the Americas and the compromised nature of the United States' founding. However, they should also come to understand that the founding fathers had to struggle with an institution entrenched in America during the previous 150 years. The ineradicable stain of slavery cannot be removed from American history, but it is less than a fair portrayal of history to suggest that many of the founding fathers were not deeply disturbed by the moral implications of that evil practice. The northern states never fully embraced slavery and were led to compromise on the issue, perhaps too readily, by their need for unity during the War of Independence, and afterward in their desire to create a unified, potentially continental nation. In any case, the compromise failed and the descendants of the founders died by the hundreds of thousands because of that failure. Whatever one's views on this issue, it is hard to deny that racial harmony is made more difficult if black children are taught to hold Washington, Jefferson, and Madison in contempt while white children are taught to revere those same figures.

Just as surely, such teachings do little to overcome the behavioral pathologies endemic in underclass communities that are so troubling to middle-class people of all ethnic groups. There is a very real danger that if black inner-city communities continue to exhibit high rates of crime, school failure, and illegitimacy because of a failure to address their true causes, old stereotypes and prejudices will be revived, even as ever-greater numbers of blacks achieve middle-class status themselves. It takes a peculiar blindness to history to fail to see the potential for serious racial enmity in these diverging patterns of behavior and belief.

Black Americans have made great strides since the barriers of legal discrimination were dismantled in the 1950s and 1960s. It is much less clear whether the policies instituted after the 1960s have been helpful. Since the 1960s, guided by the assumption that America is endemically hostile to members of ethnic and racial minorities, nearly every institution in America has undergone revision of one sort or another. Educational standards have been revised and school disciplinary codes relaxed in order to counteract the purported bias and unfairness of teachers and school administrators. The criminal justice system has been reshaped to prevent the purported bias of police and judges. Vagrancy laws and curfews have been curtailed or eliminated because of the claim that they were being used in a discriminatory fashion. The concept of merit in job and educational advancement has been vitiated, sometimes openly, more often covertly, with various sorts of formulas and quotas. The American values of individualism and self-reliance have been disparaged on the grounds that their invocation is designed to demean blacks. Voting procedures, voting districts, and legislative bodies have been ruled unconstitutional on the grounds that they do not allow fair representation for minorities.

Many of these things may have helped blacks economically and socially and may have speeded black assimilation into middle-class lives. Certainly large numbers of blacks are better off today than they were in the past, and while it is not certain that their progress might not have come about in the absence of those efforts, it is reasonable to attribute some of the progress to those programs and efforts. On the other hand, the pathologies associated with the inner cities have grown much worse during this same period, and at least part of that negative outcome must in turn be associated with those same efforts. Perhaps a better mix of policies would have promoted progress and avoided the emergence of a large and troubled black underclass whose growth now threatens to undermine racial harmony.

Of all the things that government may do in order to help blacks achieve their rightful place in American society, the single most important is the restoration of public order to the streets of underclass neighborhoods. Orderly and crime-free neighborhoods are essential for the healthy development of children and for the expression of the creative impulses that provide economic progress and personal pride of accomplishment. Order is necessary for the gradual accretion of material and spiritual capital that human foresight allows and on which communities thrive. The Hobbesian streets inhabited by the urban underclass allow for none of these, and reward rather the most destructive impulses in human nature. Anything else government may do will come to nought if government continues to desist, out of misguided concerns and sensitivities, from providing the order that only it can enforce and that in the end is its most important domestic responsibility. If the government can muster the will to assure order, a task that most societies accomplish as a matter of routine, then black Americans and the cause of racial harmony will be the most immediate beneficiaries. If the American government fails in this task, the prognosis for race relations is problematic at best.

The emergence of the social sciences in the last century has created great possibilities for social betterment. Good social science can allow a democratic people to formulate policy options in a truly informed and therefore responsible way, since good science makes clear the likely consequences of various policy options. The growth of the social sciences, therefore, allows us to adopt a reasonable optimism that our communal life can be made richer and more rewarding.

That optimism, however, is utterly dependent on the integrity of the social sciences. Scientific statements are given a high degree of veracity by most people because they are viewed as the product of verifiable research performed with great professional integrity and supported by a community of disinterested scholars whose task is to seek a clear understanding of the way things work. Any deviation from a devotion to that task, no matter how admirable otherwise, compromises the value of the social sciences for human understanding and for the formulation of sound policy. Too often in recent decades, social scientists have departed from their scientific mission and, in the understandable desire to ease the plight of black Americans and improve race relations, have encouraged policies that are prescriptions for failure.

Whether the tensions between blacks and whites diminish or grow worse will depend on many things. Social scientists can play an important role in providing clear and honest explanations of the causes of ethnic hostility and the reasons for the economic and social disparities between blacks and whites. Social scientists can aid in providing clear and verifiable explanations for why the inner cities have deteriorated so badly in recent decades, and they can aid in the formulation of policies to recreate inner-city neighborhoods where children can thrive and families can prosper. Whether the United States has the will to act on an honest understanding of these things will surely test the very fabric of our nationhood. Future generations are unlikely to forgive our temporizing at what, in retrospect, may well be seen as a fateful moment in our history.

Part I

The Current Scene

The prevailing view of race relations which guides social policy in the United States is now fifty years old. The world is a very different place in the 1990s than it was in the early 1940s when Gunnar Myrdal was putting the finishing touches on *An American Dilemma,* the book that served so well as a guide for civil rights policies in the decades immediately following its publication.[1] Many of the assumptions that serious social scientists made in the 1940s were at the time self-evident, as were the policies flowing from them. Those assumptions may no longer be valid, and if they are not, then the policies derived from them may now be counterproductive or at best impotent to solve problems whose causes have changed over the years.

It is obvious, I think, that one ought to have the clearest and most accurate assessment possible about the nature of a problem one wishes to solve. It is equally important to understand the likely consequences and side effects of any proposed solution, especially in the case of social problems. Social systems are inherently more complex and dynamic than most physical systems. So many things co-vary that even in the simplest social systems it is often difficult to pin down just which factors are important and which merely coincidental. Even if one gets a clear picture of what is causing what, it is not always easy to create worthwhile interventions. Due to the dynamic nature of social systems, even the most thoughtful and careful interventions sometimes have unintended consequences of a harmful nature.

Social systems are organic structures that evolve over generations. It is often not clear why a particular set of conventional social practices have come into being or exactly how they function. It is equally unclear what the impact might be if they were to be altered or discarded. For example, in the 1960s and 1970s, many people came to believe that with the advent of the birth-control pill and safe and legal abortions, the traditional restraints on sexual behavior could be relaxed without any great effect. Not many people at the time imagined that removing restraints on sexuality would produce a dramatic rise in illegitimacy, especially among black Americans. Most people at the time assumed that young women would continue to take steps to prevent pregnancies before marriage. Of course, many factors played a part in the rise of illegitimacy, which will be examined in due course. For now, it is enough to point out that an unanticipated chain of events was initiated in the 1960s that led to a change in mores relating to premarital sex. One result of this was a dramatic rise in out-of-wedlock births among all women, which has had an especially devastating consequence for black women.

It is extremely important, therefore, when we undertake to examine the problems of black Americans that we think long and clearly before we propose remedies. One must be particularly cautious in racial matters since errors in this area can produce explosive and undesirable results.

Since much of our understanding about race relations comes from the social sciences, it is important to understand how social scientists have approached this topic. Chapter 1 explores the question of why much of the research evidence that casts doubt on current policies has had relatively little impact on the debate about those policies.

Part of the reason, discussed in the Introduction, is that social scientists are very sensitive to the potential misuse of their theories and research findings. An often-expressed fear is that the study of racial differences might, for instance, produce results which will reinforce white prejudices, or be misused by those with malevolent motives. Such questions about the misuse of science are not limited to social scientists, of course. Virologists and physicists and computer scientists are surely aware that their findings might be put to unsavory use by undemocratic regimes. Should scientists be held accountable for the evil uses of the knowledge they uncover? Should they resist areas of research that seem especially vulnerable to misuse? In most cases physical scientists answer such questions in the negative, arguing that knowledge is a positive good and worth pursuing even if it can, in the wrong hands, cause much harm.

Social scientists on the whole have not been as comfortable with this response. In recent years much discussion has taken place about the need for social scientists to be conscious of the larger ramifications of their research, and some have questioned the ethical standing of those social scientists who have chosen to pursue their research independent of such considerations. Chapter 1 explores the question of whether and to what extent such concerns may have inhibited the open search for knowledge in racial matters and whether this has reduced the potential value of the social sciences for the formulation of social policy. Policy formulated without a sound basis in scientific evidence is unlikely to be fully effective and may well prove counterproductive.

Chapter 2 explores the fundamental assumptions that drive so much of social policy today. The first of these is that large numbers of white Americans have prejudicial and bigoted attitudes toward the members of minority groups and hold them in varying degrees of contempt. Since so many important policy implications hang on whether this assumption is true, it is essential that we have a proper understanding of the nature of the attitudes of white Americans. If in fact Americans are still full of prejudice and enmity toward minority groups, then one must question the value of much of what we have been doing over the years to reduce white prejudice. On the other hand, if those efforts have been successful and whites are not in great numbers bigoted, then one must question many current civil rights strategies. Chapter 2 reviews data from a wide variety of polls in an attempt to determine the extent of white prejudice toward blacks.

A second fundamental question important to social policy on race is whether white prejudices, even if they have not decreased, are as important today as they were in the past for an understanding of black difficulties. This is a separate question from whether whites are prejudiced against blacks. It is also separate from the question of whether whites engage in discriminatory behavior. Whites may be prejudiced and may discriminate, but those things may not, in any important way, be the true cause of black difficulties today.

Fifty years ago, it would have seemed unreasonable and callous to question the relationship between black problems and white discrimination. Most blacks lived in the South and suffered under oppressive government-sponsored restrictions that clearly limited blacks' possibilities for economic and social advancement. Today, however, it is important to assess this purported relationship. Almost all forms of racial discrimination by the government and many forms of private discrimination are now illegal and have been so since the 1960s. Today almost half of all blacks live in the North. In many large cities in both the North and the South, blacks have considerable political power, and they often control the government and other important public institutions in those cities.

These represent massive changes in American society, and it is important to get a firm grasp on how these changes have influenced black economic fortunes. An examination of income statistics is undertaken in Chapter 2 to assess the economic progress blacks have made and provide insight into why blacks still lag behind whites. These statistics may also provide insight as to whether white discrimination is still as important a factor as it once was in thwarting black aspirations. If white prejudice is no longer the primary source of black difficulties, then it is clearly essential to rethink many current policies designed to bring about racial equality. Some policies which were sound and effective in the past may be unsound today and therefore ineffective or even harmful to the cause of racial equality.

1

Social Science and Social Responsibility

I. Introduction

Sound scientific evaluation of social policy is crucial to the success of any program designed to benefit individuals or groups. For that reason, scientists must maintain a certain independence of mind so that they can objectively critique popular views and government policies. Unfortunately, many social scientists, in recent years, have lost that objectivity. Too many have become committed to the current civil rights agenda and, rather than offering independent analysis, have instead become uncritical supporters of current policies.[1]

This commitment may not be surprising in light of the prominent role played by social scientists in the formulation and implementation of those very policies. It does, however, deprive policy makers and the general public of the sort of independent scientific information and analysis important for sound judgment.

For instance, any reasonable scientific explanation of the current status of blacks in America would have to examine a host of factors likely to have a significant influence. One can surely make a case, as have a handful of social scientists—Thomas Sowell, Charles Murray, and William Julius Wilson come readily to mind—that the formulation which attributes all black problems to the racism of whites is grossly exaggerated and grossly oversimplified.[2] Surely there are other factors besides racism that play a role in some of the difficulties confronting blacks. Perhaps there are cultural patterns in black communities that have an adverse effect and contribute to the problems blacks face. Blacks are, after all, only one of many identifiable ethnic and racial groups in

America. Members of various groups exhibit marked differences from each other, and from the majority white population, in income and other measures of social success—differences that are difficult to explain on the basis of racism or differential treatment by the white majority.

The point is that there are many factors that are important to individual success. If the members of some ethnic groups perform better educationally or fare better economically, perhaps it is because of the values or habits they acquire through the socialization common to their group. Understanding how different types of socialization influence individual success might prove extremely useful in the formulation of policy to improve the lot of those currently not doing so well. Perhaps some methods and some cultural patterns work better in America than others. Thomas Sowell is one of the few who have studied the impact of culture on the economic fate of individuals. He has argued widely and persuasively that cultural influences do, in fact, make an important difference in individual success.[3]

Improved understanding here could be valuable in helping to develop and guide sound policy for improving education, curtailing crime, improving marital relations, etc. What is it, for instance, about Asian children or their upbringing which leads them, on average, to outperform others in mathematics? A valid answer to this question might help guide the development of programs aimed at improving the mathematical performance of children in general.

The differing economic experiences of various minority groups, including once despised groups such as the Japanese in California, throw doubt on the idea that there is a simple linkage between discrimination and economic performance.[4] Perhaps the cultural responses of some ethnic groups to discrimination are as important in determining their economic fate as is the discrimination itself.

At first blush, the desire to answer the above questions about ethnicity and economic and educational success would appear eminently reasonable. It seems innocent enough to seek answers to these questions out of a simple faith that sound knowledge often proves helpful. It certainly seems reasonable to suppose that the closer we get to the truth in the analysis of any problem, the more likely we are to devise sound solutions. This would hardly need saying if there were not strong voices, especially in the social sciences, which express a contrary view.

Such voices, the voices of orthodoxy as it were, argue that knowledge can be dangerous when discussing group differences since that knowledge may be used to reinforce negative and faulty stereotypes. In our Asian example, for instance, research might produce results suggesting that Asians' success in mathematics has a genetic basis. That might reinforce the assertion that genetics plays a part in group differences, an assertion that many people find offensive, and that many label racist.[5]

But where does that leave the researcher who is really interested in finding the answers to questions that are, when all is said and done, interesting and important? If he is honest, he has to accept the possibility that his research may produce answers that are offensive to many. Suppose, for instance, that in the course of researching the question as to why fewer women than men enter the physical sciences, the researcher comes to the conclusion that it is due to a lack of interest in mechanical things and that this difference between the sexes appears to be, at least in part, innate. Such a finding could be said to reinforce prevailing stereotypes harmful to women, and for that reason, some argue, that type of research ought not to be pursued.[6] Those who make this argument claim that, even if the assertion were true, the harm it causes women cannot be compensated by the value, dubious at best, that some attach to the *truth*. Put another way, socially responsible science requires that we take into account the consequences of our ideas when deciding whether to make them known to the general public.

It is important to note here that the finding of sex differences is assumed, on its face, to be harmful to women. This assumption is routinely asserted although there is no empirical evidence for such harm. In fact, just the opposite may be true. If one lacks an interest in a subject area, the discovery that this may be due to genetics and in that sense may be "natural" could have a salutary effect; one can stop trying to develop the interest and move on to more productive things. I will explore this point further, but for now it is enough to stress the fact that the purported harm caused by findings of group differences is not based on empirical research. Yet based on such assumed harm, researchers have been urged to avoid certain lines of research if that research might produce findings that might be put to harmful effect by those inclined to do so.

II. Value-Free versus Socially Conscious Science

The issues raised above have come into wider public view in the recent debate on the influence of "politically correct" thinking on American campuses. In few other academic areas has the politically correct mentality had more impact than in the social sciences. Much social science research is now guided as much by the purported social impact of research on the fate of minority groups and women as it is by a desire to determine the truth. This socially conscious approach to social science is clearly at variance with the, by now, much maligned traditional belief in what used to be called "value-free," or politically neutral, social science. In the traditional value-free approach, based in large part on the thinking of John Stuart Mill, the nineteenth-century social philosopher, it was simple arrogance for the social scientist to imagine that he had special insight into what kinds of knowledge could be used for good and what kinds for ill.[7] The scientist, as scientist, had to resist that arrogance and diligently pursue the truth in the faith that, in the long run, honest answers would be his most worthwhile contribution to the general good, however defined. Such a faith, which I think needs restoring, rests on a loose pragmatism. Good ideas eventually drive out bad ones because they work better—that is, they prove more effective in solving intellectual and practical problems.

In this view, all understandings must be allowed to compete freely in the hope and expectation that honest scientists will respect the evidence and that, in the end, the better ideas will prevail and will, in fact, be closer to the truth than those rejected. While such a method is hardly foolproof, it has traditionally been viewed as better than any attempt to forestall open debate in favor of received or majority opinion. Needless to say, there will be periods, sometimes long periods, when false ideas gain ascendancy, but such errors seem a necessary corollary to free and unfettered research. Eventually, though it may take some time, the truer vision usually triumphs. Whatever the dangers in such a method, it has proved a far more potent engine of human betterment than methods based on tradition, popular opinion, or received wisdom.

In the value-free view, once a person gains admission to a community of scholars or scientists by demonstrating his professional competence, he is free to make a case for his ideas so long as he honestly believes them to be correct and adheres to the methodological canons of his discipline. The training of a scientist is designed to provide him with clear guidelines so as to avoid the more obvious errors common in his field. In the social sciences, for instance, students are extensively trained in the handling and interpretation of statistical and other empirical data, and the need to control for the effects of extraneous factors. They are also trained to avoid common errors in logic and to adhere to common rules governing the communication of research findings. They are trained to become aware of their biases and preferences, which are especially troublesome in social research, so as to avoid having them color or distort their efforts. Such training cannot eliminate errors or biases, but when faithfully adhered to can significantly limit the impact of these failings.

In the social sciences this ''value-free'' orientation is now much despised and, in the discussion of group differences in income and academic achievement, is rejected as disingenuous and mean-spirited. The value-free approach has, to a remarkable degree, been replaced by a relativistic perspective. From the perspective of relativism there is no ''god's eye'' view of the truth; all knowledge is relative to a particular place or time, or to a society, or a class within a society. There can be no doubt that the attempt to clarify how the particularities of place and time and social position affect human understanding (the area of study known as the ''sociology of knowledge'') has provided important insights.[8] Extreme relativism, however, which denies the very possibility of common understanding (that is, of truth), has little to recommend it as a guide for science.

In psychology, for instance, extreme relativism has led some to assert that there can be no culture-free definition of insanity; insanity is claimed to be merely a "social definition," and what is defined as insane in one time and place will be seen as normal in another.[9] Similar reasoning has lead sociologists and anthropologists to question the objective status of any definition of criminality.[10] A similar questioning of the objective basis to legal interpretation is undertaken by advocates of what in law schools is called "critical legal studies."[11] In literary studies, the relativistic perspective is pursued by those who engage in the "deconstruction" of texts and who argue that all interpretations of literary meaning are equally valid, or invalid, as the case may be.[12]

The relativistic perspective is derived, at least in part, from the Marxist view that all knowledge is based in class interest—that is, is created by elites and serves to protect the interests of elites. In this view the canons of value-free science are really legitimations for those who benefit from the status quo, and the scientists who support a value-free view are merely agents, either consciously or not, of those who so benefit. Since there can be no objective science, and since all science must serve some interest, the relativist asserts that he is free to choose whose interests he serves. Marxist theory argues that elites invariably owe their advantage to the oppression and exploitation of the powerless; for that reason, many relativists argue that the only ethical science is one that serves the interests of the exploited and oppressed.[13]

In effect, relativists with this Marxist slant have redefined science as a species of propaganda. When engaging in propaganda, the only serious question is whether you are on the right side; adhering to canons of objective truthfulness necessarily takes second place to the rightness of the cause. Unfortunately, scientists who adopt this view, as do many in the social sciences, do not reveal their perspective to the general public. Consequently, readers have no way of knowing that the scientific reports they have read about in newspapers were prepared by people with very little respect for objective and disinterested research.[14] Edward O. Wilson, the Harvard biologist, for example, came under concerted attack on the occasion of the publication of his groundbreaking work on sociobiology because he argued that human social behavior is not immune to the laws of evolution.[15] Wilson argued against the assertion that the human mind is a blank slate and argued instead that it is necessary to take into account genetic factors when trying to understand human nature—in other words, that there is some merit to the *nature* side of the nature-nurture controversy in psychology.

Those who take a critical attitude toward evolutionary theory often do so from a Marxist perspective, since evolution contradicts their assumption of cultural determinism and undercuts the claim that human nature is purely the product of social class conditioning. The attack on Wilson was led by the aptly named Sociobiology Study Group of Science for the People, which included many well-known scientists, including Harvard's Stephen Jay Gould and Richard Lewontin.[16] The group argued that evolutionary explanations survive because, in their words, "they consistently tend to provide a genetic justification of the *status quo* and of existing privileges for certain groups according to class, race or sex." In addition, they argued that such theories "led to the establishment of gas chambers in Nazi Germany."[17]

The Sociobiology Study Group was not content to suggest merely that Wilson's work may be used by "powerful countries or ruling groups" to maintain and extend their power, but felt it necessary to attack Wilson personally. They argued that Wilson's book betrays "the personal and social class prejudice of the author" and went on to argue that he joins a "long parade" of those "whose work has served to buttress the institutions of their society by exonerating them from responsibility for social problems."[18]

This attack on Wilson does not merely charge that his interpretations are incorrect, but that they are unsavory and self-serving. Such *ad hominem* attacks on people's motives and decency are quite common in the social sciences today.

Of course, many of those who have attacked Wilson's ideas have done so for reasons that have nothing to do with Marxism. Many thought, incorrectly, that his ideas might buttress racial theories of group superiority or inferiority. But the attacks on him, whatever their motivation, were markedly at variance with normal intellectual civility. Wilson was hounded for many years by student demonstrators, no doubt influenced by views such as those expressed by the Sociobiology Study Group. He was even on occasion prevented by demonstrators from speaking before university audiences that he had been invited to address. Arthur Fisher, science editor of *Popular Science,* reports that at the 1978 meeting of the American Association for the Advancement of Science, "[a]ntagonists commandeered the podium as Wilson was scheduled to speak, delivered a five-minute diatribe against him and his works, and concluded by pouring a pitcher of water over him. . . ."[19] Such behavior is perhaps not surprising among those who have been taught that civility is merely a cover for indifference to oppression, and science merely a justification of the status quo.

What is surprising and troubling, however, is the extent to which such abusive tactics and *ad hominem* argument-by-epithet have come to dominate much discourse in the civil rights debate. Many seem to think that labeling an idea as racist has, by the mere act of applying the label, the effect of discrediting the idea. One is reminded that nobody really tried to prove Galileo wrong about his idea that the earth went around the sun, it was sufficient to brand his ideas blasphemous, which at the time they surely were.

The current wisdom among vast numbers of social scientists is that while differential success among *individuals* may be explained by differences in individual abilities and proclivities, such an explanation for group differences is unacceptable. If groups differ in average income or school performance, or almost any other index, it is taken as given that those average differences must be due to differential treatment by society. Group differences, in this orthodoxy, are the result of racism or ethnocentrism or sexism, etc. Those who disagree are not merely attacked for being wrong, but are charged with going beyond the bounds of legitimate scientific inquiry, and are further charged with acting as spokesmen, either consciously or unconsciously, for the racist and sexist status quo. They are charged, in short, with blasphemy.[20]

The fear of dangerous and blasphemous ideas helps to explain the unreasonable and personal attacks on Arthur Jensen for his arguments that differences in school performance can be explained by IQ differences between groups, and that such differences may be in large part genetically caused and not merely the result of environmental factors.[21] Sandra Scarr, a highly respected research psychologist, hardly overestimates when she remarks that "from 1969 to the 1980s Arthur Jensen was harassed, threatened, and driven virtually into protective custody by colleagues, students, and other radicals who resented his hypothesis." In Scarr's view, people found Jensen's views so threatening that he became, in her words, "a prime target for unconscionable abuse in public and in private."[22]

A similar "storm of protest" greeted Harvard psychologist Richard J. Herrnstein, according to well-known psychologist Ernest Hilgard, for "writing a fairly conventional article . . . on the evidence for a hereditary contribution to intelligence—conventional from the academic point of view of what had been appearing in our textbooks for years."[23] Hilgard was making the point that the routine and uncontroversial discussion of genetic factors in IQ that normally appeared in introductory textbooks in the past had, by the late 1960s, become so controversial that open discussion of the topic had become an invitation for severe personal abuse.

Scarr explained the problem in the *American Psychologist* in the following way: "If one purposely examines racial or gender variation in psychology, one is likely to be suspected of reactionary politics or malevolence toward socially disadvantaged groups." The consequence of this, according to Scarr, is to put oneself "in danger of ostracism or worse from one's . . . well-intentioned colleagues." The net result of this social pressure is that psychologists have, in recent years, tended to avoid studies of racial and sexual differences even though, as Scarr points out, "good psychologists are aware of the enormous research literature on race differences on nearly every behavioral measure and gender differences on many measures.''[24] The research literature of which Scarr speaks is somewhat dated now, since research on racial differences has become much constrained since the late 1960s, and is unlikely to be brought up to date in the current atmosphere.

It is not only, or even especially, findings of possible genetic differences between groups that are seen as offensive and potentially dangerous. Even those who have asserted that cultural differences influence social success have been characterized as ethnocentric and mean-spirited. Thomas Sowell, for instance, has come under repeated attack for arguing that cultural (rather than genetic) differences between groups account for much of the variation in education and income among them. Sowell correctly points out that there is a ''poisonous atmosphere surrounding any attempt to debate issues involving race and ethnicity. . . .''[25] Those who criticize Sowell argue that almost any examination of group differences is likely to have negative consequences. To hypothesize, for instance, that Asians' academic success might be due to the effort expended by Asian parents in regulating and assisting their children, might be thought demeaning to parents in other ethnic groups whose children do not perform as well.

The experience of Sandra Scarr and Richard A. Weinberg is particularly ironic. Their research on the environmental influences on IQ is among the strongest evidence available against the argument that racial differences in IQ are genetic. Scarr and Weinberg found that black children adopted by middle-class white parents had higher average IQ scores than black children in general.[26] Nevertheless, Scarr and Weinberg came under severe attack by Chester W. Oden, Jr. and W. Scott MacDonald because their article focused on black child-rearing rather than on discrimination. Oden and MacDonald, then at the University of Minnesota, charged Scarr and Weinberg with denigrating black culture because their findings implied that ''family atmosphere is the cause of black children'' scoring lower on IQ exams than white children.[27] They went on to argue that IQ tests are culturally biased and therefore that asking blacks to adjust their family life to improve black children's performance is unreasonable. They claimed that ''the alteration of black culture and traditions appears a grisly price to pay'' to satisfy white cultural expectations.[28]

Oden and MacDonald argue that it is inappropriate to apply white middle-class standards to black children, but they do not explain how they expect black children to achieve social advancement if they fail to meet the educational standards expected of middle-class society. In rejecting the cultural-deficit explanation for IQ differences, Oden and MacDonald are left with either the genetic explanation or an explanation which places responsibility for these differences on the nature of white society. Since the genetic explanation is widely viewed as racist, the only option left open to them is to blame the larger society for the IQ difference, which, not surprisingly, they do.

Stephen Ceci, Douglas Peters, and Jonathan Plotkin investigated the impact these sorts of attacks have on research funding in the social sciences.[29] All research involving human subjects funded by the federal government is required to meet the approval of an Institutional Review Board at the researcher's home university. These boards, composed of faculty, are supposed to review research in order to protect human subjects from physical and mental harm. Ceci, Peters, and Plotkin found, however, that political factors played an important part in the approval process.

In their experiment, the researchers submitted various fake, but seemingly legitimate, research proposals to 157 review boards and discovered a consistent tendency for the boards to reject proposals that were politically sensitive when compared with those that were not, even though the proposals were almost identical in all other respects.[30]

The authors comment that even though it was contrary to federal guidelines, "it was clear that the IRBs [Institutional Review Boards] *did* consider the sociopolitical consequences of the proposed research. . . ." The authors were particularly surprised by the fact that many Institutional Review Boards "stated their sociopolitical objections so openly in the reasons for nonapproval." Ceci, Peters, and Plotkin express the fear that the review process could be corrupted by political concerns "under the guise of objective scientific standards." Proposals may ostensibly be rejected on scientific grounds when their "real offense might be their social and political distastefulness to IRB members."[31]

The net result of these social and institutional pressures to avoid sensitive research is predictable. Sandra Graham, a fellow at the Center for Advanced Study in the Behavioral Sciences at Stanford University, reporting on a survey of major psychological journals, wrote in the *American Psychologist* that "methodologically sound empirical articles on Blacks have all but vanished from the pages of major APA [American Psychological Association] journals." Graham found this to be the case for a broad spectrum of journals, including those dealing with both basic and applied research.[32]

This is especially surprising in light of the fact that, as Graham explained, many researchers would normally be drawn to the study of black Americans out of social concern with the many problems they face. There is hardly a dearth of topics to engage the interested researcher. Graham suggests that psychologists may wish to "investigate intelligence because of the chronic school failure of many African-American children; aggression due to the higher incidence of violent crimes among urban black males; helping behavior, given the negative consequences associated with welfare dependency; and so on."[33]

Unfortunately, these topics are rarely dealt with, according to Graham, because of the "ethical and moral risks associated with studying the psychological functioning of African-Americans." Rather than deal with the almost certain controversy that "unpopular findings" might arouse, most researchers seem to have given up the psychological study of black Americans.[34]

An important consequence of this reticence to do serious research on racially sensitive topics is that many popular social science explanations for black problems turn out, upon close inspection, to be mainly conjectural and lacking in substantive empirical support.

In the current atmosphere anyone who advances explanations, even cultural explanations, for group differences contrary to the view that all such differences are completely explained by racism is likely to come under severe personal attack. The error of such individuals, according to the current wisdom, is not so much that they are wrong but that they are grossly insensitive to the harm their ideas purportedly cause. The new orthodoxy turns the traditional view of science on its head: whereas formerly ideas were seen as dangerous because they were wrong, now they are seen as wrong because they are dangerous.

III. The Dangers of the *Ad Hominem* Fallacy

The controversies surrounding questions of evolution and genetics are not instances to be seen in isolation, but rather reflect a broader tendency to cast any disagreement with current views on race relations as somehow implying antipathy to civil rights per se, as if there were only one legitimate and decent way to promote greater equality. Those who do not agree, for instance, that American institutions are polluted with a racism that oppresses minorities are cast in the role of supporting the oppression of minorities. Such *ad hominem* attacks are common and serve to seriously jeopardize open discussion of the many troubling issues surrounding race today. It is well worth considering just why these sorts of attacks lead to difficulties.

The *ad hominem* fallacy is a well-known rhetorical device in which the logic of an argument is discounted by impugning the motives or the character of the person making the argument. It is useful as a debating trick but often leads to faulty judgment. For instance, it is obviously in the interests of landlords to prevent the imposition of rent controls. But pointing out someone's status as a landlord is no refutation of that person's argument against rent control. An argument can only be refuted by attacking its logic or its premises, not the motivation for making it. Nevertheless, the good rhetorician can move an audience to discount the landlord's argument by a mere assertion of a potential conflict of interest.

In a similar vein, it would be improper to discount a black person's argument in favor of affirmative action by suggesting that he thinks the way he does because he has something to gain from affirmative action programs. It is similarly incorrect to discount the argument of a male who challenges the legal merit of *Roe v. Wade* on the grounds that his understanding of abortion, and by extension his logic, is tainted by the fact that as a male he need never deal with an unwanted pregnancy.

Yet social scientists often discount the arguments of whites who oppose affirmative action on the grounds that as whites they have an interest in doing so.[35] Equally common is the argument that a black who opposes affirmative action must be an Uncle Tom trying to ingratiate himself with the white power-structure, as was suggested of Supreme Court Justice Clarence Thomas during his nomination hearings.[36]

This is not to suggest that there is anything wrong with attempting to determine the source of a person's views. It may well be the case that landlords support arguments against rent control because they have a pecuniary interest at stake. Blacks may well support arguments in favor of affirmative action policies because they believe they will benefit from them. In fact, much of the reason for this book derives from an attempt to understand why social scientists have adopted the particular theories about race relations that have guided public policy over the last quarter-century. It is important and valuable to trace the origins and motivations of beliefs and scientific theories, whether to improve understanding of those theories or to see clearly why they might be misguided. One does not commit the *ad hominem* error by citing motives or conflicts of interest, but one does make the error if one dismisses out of hand a theory on the basis of motives or conflicts of interest alone. One compounds the error if, as is so commonly done, one merely asserts a base motive or conflict of interest to those with contrary views, without any other independent confirmation of a base motive. Black conservatives like Clarence Thomas may be dissembling to obtain white approval, as is so often charged, but how is anyone to know? The charge is merely gratuitous mudslinging if there is no independent evidence of obsequious conduct. And even if the charge were true, it would not, by itself, say anything about the truth or falsity of the views Justice Thomas expresses.

In the debate on current policies relating to race, the *ad hominem* device is all too commonly used. All those who attempt to locate some of the causation for black difficulties in black behavioral patterns are said to "blame the victim" out of base and mean-spirited motivations, or out of vaguely neurotic motivations. William Ryan, in his widely read *Blaming the Victim,* argues that those who engage in victim-blaming are generally self-satisfied, middle-class whites who are guilt-ridden over the status of the poor and of blacks in America. According to Ryan, such a person is "acutely aware of poverty, racial discrimination, exploitation, and deprivation, and, moreover, he wants to do something concrete to ameliorate the condition of the poor, the black and the disadvantaged.''[37]

But in Ryan's view, these well-intentioned people are, at base, dishonest since they wish to help the disadvantaged without any real cost to themselves. In particular, "[t]hey cannot bring themselves to attack a system that has been so good to them" even though they really do wish to help "the victims of racism and economic injustice."[38] Such people hit upon a "brilliant compromise," according to Ryan. They direct their attention to how the victim was damaged by past injustice, and so avoid any concern with current injustice. The past injustice has determined the victim's current behavior and attitudes, so that it is now those things that are the cause of his problems, and not any current victimization. In other words, people who disagree with the current wisdom on racial matters do not do so out of logic or familiarity with empirical evidence but as an unconscious and neurotic way of avoiding the guilt of their own complicity in the injustices perpetrated by America's economic system. "They are all unconsciously passing judgment on themselves and bringing in the unanimous verdict of Not Guilty."[39]

Explaining black problems in terms of troublesome cultural patterns or in terms of family instability is merely avoiding the real culprits, which are, in Ryan's view, the "corporation-dominated economy" and "the pervasive racism that informs and shapes and distorts our every social institution."[40]

In short, if you do not agree with Ryan that America is dominated by corporations bent on exploiting the poor and minorities, or if you doubt that "every social institution" in America is infested with racism, then you are, in his interpretation, suffering a neurotic and unconscious delusion. In the strange world of this Freudian-like analysis, there is no defense against such a charge. You are guilty if you accept the interpretation and guilty if you deny it, since denial is evidence of your inability to come to terms with your unconscious motivations.

Unfortunately, far too many social scientists allow this sort of rhetoric to pass for logic. Reasoning in this way is not uncommon in social science writing, nor is it uncommon among those who have joined the burgeoning ranks of the politically correct. As will become apparent, the "damned if you do and damned if you don't" argument is employed quite often to discredit those who challenge prevailing views on civil rights. Ryan's book is very popular and is regularly assigned to undergraduates as required reading in sociology and psychology courses. This would be fine if students were exposed to alternative views; unfortunately they rarely are. The lack of balance on racial matters perhaps explains why students so often misinterpret the views of scholars such as Edward O. Wilson and attack them with such incivility.

The thoughts of James Coleman, a recent president of the American

Sociological Association, are instructive here. Coleman argues that there is a general consensus that arguments over public policy reflect moral differences "between those with good intentions, who want to help the disadvantaged, and those who are selfish and opposed to any aid to those less fortunate."[41] Public policies, according to Coleman, "that have the property that they stem from benevolent intentions" toward those less fortunate have widespread support among social scientists. Since such policies are assumed to be altogether benevolent, any research that might undercut those policies "is subject to disapproval and attack."[42]

The danger in all of this, of course, is that "intentions do not equal consequences." All too often policies derived from good intentions end badly. Of course, without full discussion and open debate over policy options, it is difficult to avoid negative, but unintended, outcomes. Unfortunately, as Coleman makes clear, "so long as there is a consensus among academics on [these] policies . . . self-suppression will prevent serious questioning."[43]

IV. Rationality and Human Conduct

The general acceptance of Ryan's perspective is better understood if one considers the fact that a good deal of modern social science, especially in psychology and sociology, has taken the form of an extended critique of the Enlightenment. European Enlightenment thinking took form in the seventeenth and eighteenth centuries and championed science and reason as guides to action above faith and authority. A crucial principle of the Enlightenment was that people were essentially rational and could be expected to act in ways to forward their long-term interests. The Constitution of the United States was written by people fully committed to the principles of the Enlightenment. The assumption or faith, if you will, in the rationality of the average citizen serves as the primary logical justification for popular democracy and universal suffrage.

Modern social science, on the other hand, from Marx to Durkheim in sociology and from Freud to Skinner in psychology, has questioned human rationality. These seminal thinkers developed theories and perspectives in which human beings are depicted as driven by forces (societal and unconscious) that are beyond their control or even their comprehension and awareness. How can a person act in his own interest(s) if those interests cannot be known because they are unconscious? How can a person act in his own interests if his understanding of the world is shaped by a false consciousness imposed on him by his capitalist masters?

One modern outgrowth of the Enlightenment perspective is decision theory, which examines the logic and limitations of human rationality. Most decision theorists assume that, within broad limits, human action is based on more or less rational choice.[44] Rational action, according to decision theory, requires that people know what they want and act in ways consistent with their abilities and with their understanding of the way the world works. If a person knows his interests, is correct in his assessment of his abilities, and has an accurate understanding of the world, then according to decision theory, his actions are likely to be such as to increase his overall well-being. If, on the other hand, a person's truest desires are unconscious, as psychoanalysts assert, how can he formulate rational behaviors to obtain those desires? If a person's understanding of the world is fundamentally flawed because it is guided by his class interests or the interests of elites, as relativists assert, how can he hope to act in sensible ways?

All too often social scientists, in following popular theories, fail to accept the possibility that people often *do* know what is in their interests and often *do* have a clear understanding of the way the world works. Too often social scientists look for hidden meanings in what people say and do, and refuse to take the reasons people give at face value. This is especially the case in discussions of race relations. When, for instance, people reject policies of racial quotas on the grounds that quotas violate the American value of fair play, many social scientists claim that this argument is merely a rationalization for an unconscious desire to deny blacks equal treatment. When people express a concern with crime and demand greater efforts to maintain public order, many social scientists insist that this is a cover, perhaps unconscious, for justifying hostility to blacks. When people express adherence to the work ethic and express disapproval of reliance on welfare, this too is taken as a way of denigrating blacks.[45]

The failure of many social scientists to take human rationality seriously often leads them to underestimate the dangers that false descriptions of reality can generate. The theory of rational action assumes that people will act on the basis of what they believe to be true about the world. That is why inaccurate understandings are so dangerous and why sound education is so important. If, for instance, young blacks come to accept the depiction of American society as hopelessly racist, then it is hardly irrational for them to suppose that working hard and postponing gratification are unlikely to produce desirable results. If they come to believe that no matter what values they adopt, white Americans will continue to despise them, then it is hardly irrational for them to view those blacks who adopt white middle-class standards as somehow betraying their own group and taking on the role of ''Uncle Toms.'' For similar reasons, black students who take education seriously are sometimes condemned by their classmates for ''acting white.''[46]

The very real danger, here, is that if black adolescents accept this view of reality, they are likely to act in ways almost guaranteed to confirm their worst suspicions about whites—ways that, in addition, will tend to confirm the negative views held by many whites. To expect that the charge of virulent racism in American society, made so often by people in positions of authority, will have no effect on the attitudes and behavior of young blacks is at the least irresponsible and almost certainly incorrect. Thomas Sowell, quoted in a *Wall Street Journal* editorial, put it aptly:

> Is it possible to din into the heads of a whole generation that their problems are all other people's fault; that the world owes them an enormous debt; that everything they have yet to achieve is an injustice; that violence is excusable when the world is flawed—and yet to expect it all to have no effect on attitudes? Is the arduous process of acquiring skills and discipline supposed to be endured for years by people who are told, by word and deed, that skills are not the real issue?[47]

V. Conclusion

The current view, which Sowell has aptly named the "civil rights vision," claims that the racism of American society accounts for all group differences in achievement, and anyone who argues otherwise is assumed to support and condone that racism, or to be so hopelessly naive as to be unaware of the harm such ideas can cause.[48] But is this received wisdom correct? Are large and important numbers of white Americans racist? Do large numbers of influential whites conspire to thwart the ambitions of blacks and other minority groups? In other words, is racism still the problem today that it was thirty or forty years ago? Is suggesting otherwise either dangerous or naive? It is my contention that the received wisdom in this area is incorrect and has little scientific evidence to support it. Furthermore, I believe that continued reliance on this faulty view is far more harmful than the ideas it attempts to banish. The historical record unambiguously supports the position that knowledge based on sound evidence, however dangerous or painful it may seem, is invariably the best basis upon which societies can build sound policy and the best way for individuals to craft productive and meaningful lives. The current wisdom on race is, in view of this historical reality, particularly dangerous because it is so thoroughly incorrect.

There is a curious inconsistency, furthermore, in the rejection of the idea that black problems are rooted in black patterns of behavior. Many of the conventional arguments made to explain black economic and social difficulties, for instance, trace the sources of those difficulties to the legacy of slavery, in addition to current ongoing racism. Now it may well be the case that blacks reacted to the particular experiences of slavery by adopting a set of mechanisms and preferred behavioral patterns that enabled them to cope with the cruelties and injustices they experienced as slaves. For instance, in the South during slavery and afterward, the police and the courts were used to enforce the slave system and the subsequent system of racial separation and debasement that followed the Civil War and lasted well into the 1960s. In such a setting, betraying a fellow black to the police or courts was looked upon, quite correctly, as treasonous and despicable.[49] It would be surprising if distrust of the criminal justice system were not found among many blacks today, given that a substantial majority of blacks either experienced that past southern discrimination personally or had parents who did.[50]

Similar legacies of past injustice undoubtedly have an impact today. But those legacies can only affect today's blacks if they have taken the form of institutional or preferred behavioral patterns that are still at work, today, within black communities. It would seem reasonable to conclude that if those institutional and behavioral patterns cause problems today, then those patterns need changing, whatever one thinks about white racism or about the past justification for those patterns. Unfortunately, this conclusion is usually rejected on the basis that it wrongly locates the problem in the black community, and blames the victim, rather than the oppressor. The rejection of this conclusion is not merely inconsistent, but seems to deny the possibility of historical change. Even if most of the problems confronting blacks in the past were caused by white oppression, it is not automatically the case that most still are today.

Recognition of past wrongs, and the assignment of communal guilt, are not substitutes for reasoned analysis of current dilemmas, nor are they likely to lead to productive solutions to those dilemmas. In any case, it is a simple lapse in logic to argue that slavery left a legacy that creates problems for blacks, and at the same time deny that any aspect of that legacy is identifiable today. Either slavery left a legacy that creates behavioral or attitudinal patterns that affect the way blacks operate today, or there are no such patterns today and hence no such legacy; but it cannot, logically, be had both ways.

None of the above is meant to deny the reality of bigotry. I wish to be very clear on this. I do not argue that racism is nonexistent. There are, in fact, far too many Americans who harbor racist ideas and engage in discriminatory behavior. There are also, to be sure, institutional practices in unions and corporations, and in municipalities large and small, that do in fact unfairly impede blacks and other minorities.[51] What I am saying is that the importance of racism today for an understanding of black problems should not be taken as a foregone conclusion, especially since so much empirical research suggests that racism is not as serious a problem as it once was. There are now, as I will attempt to demonstrate, far more potent factors operating to hinder black advancement that have at most only a tangential relation with racism. Continuing to rely on outmoded understandings that divert us from the critical analysis of current sources of difficulties has the effect of postponing into the indefinite future efforts to overcome such difficulties.

It is unreasonable to expect that the resources of a society are infinite, and that choices need not be made. Only so much societal time and energy and wealth can be assigned to any particular problem. Time and money spent trying to eliminate racism in schools cannot be used to improve education. Money spent to bus children in search of some ideal racial balance is money not spent to bus children to museums and scientific exhibits. Energies expended to root out racism in the criminal justice system cannot be used to reduce crime in black communities. Individual passions devoted to uncovering racism in American business are passions that are not devoted to educating people in the skills and attitudes critical to business success. If racism is widespread and causing serious harm, then of course efforts to eliminate it are necessary and worthwhile. But if we overestimate the damage caused by racism, we misdirect vital resources and vital energies from where they are likely to do the most good.

2

White Attitudes and Black Economic Status Today

I. Introduction

The social science model that underpins modern civil rights policies is based on three related assumptions. It is assumed, first, that white Americans harbor prejudice against most minority groups. Second, it is assumed that prejudice leads, both directly and indirectly, to discriminatory actions. And finally, it is assumed that such discriminatory actions are the main cause of the economic difficulties that minority groups face. In light of this model, any effort to assist minority groups in achieving economic parity with whites must include intense efforts to change the attitudes of white Americans and, where necessary, to overcome the effects of discrimination through legal means and through programs of affirmative action. This model was first formulated a half-century ago by Gunnar Myrdal, the Swedish economist who oversaw the research and writing of *An American Dilemma,* a book that played an extraordinarily influential role in shaping post–World War II policies on race relations.[1]

Much has happened during the past fifty years, and much has been learned about race relations; yet the Myrdal model remains the guiding vision among most civil rights advocates and social scientists, if not among the general public.

Whether or not that model continues to be a valid guide for social policy, after the changes and experiences of the last fifty years, is a question rarely asked. I think it should be asked. On every count, the model can and should be tested for empirical validity. Are Americans prejudiced, and if so, to what extent? Does that prejudice lead to discriminatory action? And finally, are the economic disparities among ethnic groups the result of the discrimination imputed to whites?

As Thomas Sowell has repeatedly stressed, discrimination may not lead to economic failure. The Jews in Europe and the ethnic Chinese in Southeast Asia have both been the subject of severe state-sponsored discrimination and have nonetheless flourished economically in most instances.[2] In America the Japanese bore the brunt of considerable discrimination and yet have outperformed whites economically.[3] The obvious failure of the civil rights model to account for Asians' economic success in America is either overlooked or dismissed on the grounds that American prejudicial attitudes toward blacks and Hispanics are much more pervasive and debilitating than prejudice against Asians. But is that true? American anti-Japanese propaganda during World War II was demeaning and unsparing. The internment of Japanese Americans during the war, protested at the time by few Americans, led to considerable economic losses from the forced sale of homes and businesses, yet the Japanese managed to achieve remarkable economic success in the postwar period.

The argument that Hispanics suffer from discrimination ignores the vast differences among the people labeled ''Hispanic.'' The Cubans, for instance, have been noticeably more successful economically than either Puerto Ricans or Mexicans. To advocates of the civil rights model, Cuban success is explained as resulting from selective migration. They argue that Castro's accession to power drove out the more successful Cubans who would have done well anywhere. But more recent arrivals from Cuba had no such advantage and yet are doing well.[4] Mexican Americans, about half of whom are recent immigrants, are having problems typical among immigrant groups. Native-born Mexican Americans, however, appear to be assimilating into the mainstream as did the children of earlier immigrants from Europe.[5] Puerto Ricans in New York City are the only group of Hispanics who seem to be failing to follow the standard immigrant pattern, but it is not clear why.[6] Dominicans, very recent arrivals to New York, are a group with a racial makeup similar to Puerto Ricans, and they appear to be thriving.[7]

The fact that Hispanic groups, with the possible exception of Puerto Ricans, seem to be following the pattern of earlier European immigrant groups is sometimes dismissed on the basis that prejudice against blacks is far more pernicious than that against Hispanics.

In fact, it is generally assumed by those who adopt the discrimination hypothesis that white Americans have a special animus toward blacks that causes, in one way or another, all of the disparities in income, education, and social pathology between blacks and other ethnic groups. The bulk of civil rights policies hang upon this assumption. If Americans hold no particular animus against blacks, most current remedies lose their justification. Furthermore, these remedies are not likely to solve problems that have their sources elsewhere. This point is underscored by the important and often overlooked experience of West Indian or Caribbean blacks who have immigrated to this country in large numbers over the years. The term "black," like the term "Hispanic," covers a variety of people with very different cultural backgrounds. There are blacks whose ancestors lived in the North as freemen before the Civil War. There are blacks whose ancestors migrated to the North shortly after the Civil War and others whose ancestors migrated North in the years before and after World War II. Recently blacks have migrated directly from Africa and the Caribbean. Each of these groups has had different historical experiences which may influence how its members approach problems today.

West Indian blacks migrated, and continue to migrate, to the United States from the Caribbean islands of Jamaica, Haiti, the U.S. Virgin Islands, and similar places. They have the same African origin as blacks born in America and are indistinguishable from them in physical appearance. Yet members of this group have managed to do well in America in spite of their race and immigrant status. Sowell reports that "West Indian family incomes are 94 percent of the U.S. national average, while the family incomes of blacks as a group are only 62 percent of the national average." Sowell also reports that West Indians' employment in "professional occupations is double that of [other] blacks, and slightly *higher* than that of the U.S. population as a whole."[8] Sowell rejects the argument sometimes made that West Indians are treated better than other blacks because of their foreign accents, since second-generation West Indians do not generally have accents and they also do well. Sowell concludes that the most reasonable explanation for the difference between West Indians and other blacks lies in the cultural differences between them rather than in any differential treatment by white Americans.[9]

The evidence, therefore, that Americans are uniformly hostile to minority groups, and that such hostility impedes their economic success, is at best problematic. Are Americans really as ethnocentric as they are thought to be? Are they any more or less ethnocentric than, say, the French or the Canadians? Given recent news reports they certainly appear less ethnocentric than the Germans.[10] Why is the experience of different ethnic groups so different in the face of the imputed widespread ethnocentrism of Americans?

Put another way, even if we suppose that white Americans are ethnocentric, why is it that some individuals manage to cope with that ethnocentrism and prosper, while others tend to lag behind? If white Americans are uniformly ethnocentric toward all groups, then ethnocentrism cannot explain the differences in economic success among various minority groups. If whites are not uniformly hostile to other ethnic groups, then it is important to understand why.

II. White American Attitudes Today

Since it is common to attribute black difficulties to white racism, it is important to get some estimate of the extent of that racism. Racism is a relatively new word. According to the *Oxford English Dictionary,* it first came into use during the 1930s. It is defined as the "theory that distinctive human characteristics and abilities are determined by race." Racism was a newer form of the word "racialism," which came into use early in the twentieth century. Racialism is defined as a belief "in the superiority of a particular race leading to prejudice and antagonism toward people of other races. . . ."[11]

While the notion that different races have different attributes and qualities is as old as man, modern attitudes about race were informed primarily by evolutionary theory. During the nineteenth century it became commonplace to hypothesize that various races could be assigned degrees of advancement and complexity in an evolutionary hierarchy. The eugenics movement, which proposed to improve human "stock" by selective breeding, had numerous followers, some of whom saw miscegenation (interracial marriage) as an antidote to inbreeding, but many of whom saw it as diluting the supposed superior virtues of this or that race or ethnic group. The southern states in America found in such thinking a justification for their practices, both before and after emancipation. Superior races could and should, it was thought, regulate the behavior of those they claimed were inferior. The barbarities committed by the Nazi regime in their campaign of racial murder were rationalized on similar grounds.

By the 1950s, racism came to be defined as a belief in the genetic inferiority of a particular racial group and a willingness to discriminate against that group by a denial of rights or privileges on the basis of its assumed inferiority. This is the definition currently endorsed in *A Common Destiny: Blacks and American Society,* a major 1989 research report sponsored by the National Research Council of the National Academy of Sciences. The authors of that study reserve the term racism "for patterns of belief and related actions that overtly embrace the notion of genetic or biological differences between human groups." They point out that the term is used in a variety of ways, and think it "unfortunate that a single analytic concept has so many different meanings."[12]

Are white Americans racist according to the above definition? Do they believe that blacks, for instance, are genetically inferior to whites, and do they display overt patterns of behavior premised on such a belief? Almost all polling data suggests that they do not. Surveys of white Americans' attitudes toward blacks do not indicate that they believe blacks to be genetically inferior to whites, nor do they indicate any desire to restrict black opportunities or rights. White Americans are more likely to attribute black difficulties to situational and motivational factors rather than to genetic factors.

The empirical support for the above statements comes from a variety of public-opinion surveys. Perhaps the most comprehensive of these is a series of public-opinion polls undertaken almost every year going back to 1942 by the National Opinion Research Center. The data gathered in these polls, on a wide range of topics, is published in a series of General Social Surveys that allow for the analysis of trends in attitudes over time.[13] It is important for the reader to be aware that many of the questions asked in the General Social Surveys were asked intermittently over the years. Some questions were asked only in earlier years and were dropped in the 1960s and 1970s. Other questions were not introduced until more recent years.

One question asked fairly regularly in early polls dealt with whites' attitudes about black intelligence, a question that would seem to be critical to the question of white racism. If whites do not think blacks are less intelligent than whites, it would seem inappropriate to apply the label "racist" to them, at least according to the general understanding of that term. Respondents were asked: "In general, do you think that Negroes are as intelligent as white people—that is, can they learn things just as well if they are given the same education and training?" In the early 1940s, only about 47 percent of respondents agreed with that statement. However, by 1956, the percentage of whites endorsing a belief in the equal intelligence of blacks had grown to 80 percent. That percentage remained unchanged until this question was dropped from the survey after 1968.[14] Interestingly, in a survey of the attitudes of Princeton undergraduates taken in 1932, which would seem to reflect elite opinion, only 22 percent chose "stupid" as a trait common to blacks. By 1950, that figure had dropped to 10 percent.[15]

In more recent polls, the General Social Survey included the question, "On the average, blacks have worse jobs, income, and housing than white people. Do you think these differences exist mainly because most blacks have less in-born ability to learn?" In 1986, 21 percent of whites responded affirmatively to this question, a percentage consistent with the data gathered in the 1950s and 1960s. Surprisingly, 18 percent of blacks gave this explanation for the black-white income gap. Whites are more likely to explain the income gap as resulting from a lack of motivation and willpower on the part of blacks. Sixty-four percent of whites and 38 percent of blacks endorsed this motivational explanation. Blacks, on the other hand, are much more likely to blame discrimination. Fully 74 percent of blacks, but only 40 percent of whites, saw discrimination as the cause of black economic difficulties. Substantial numbers from both races, 51 percent of whites and 65 percent of blacks, thought a lack of educational opportunities contributed to the black-white income gap.[16]

It should be noted that younger individuals are less likely to attribute black problems to a lack of ability. Furthermore, as respondents' education and income increase, they are also less like to give the "less in-born ability" explanation.[17] In summary, approximately 80 percent of white Americans, when asked, express disagreement with the idea that blacks have less native ability. Of course, it is possible that people believe blacks are intellectually inferior, but refrain from expressing that belief. However, all these surveys promise people anonymity, and are known to honor that commitment. Perhaps whites think blacks are intellectually inferior, but are embarrassed to admit such a belief to the person questioning them? Perhaps they are unwilling even to admit to themselves that they hold that belief, because it is inconsistent with their basic values? There is no way to answer these questions. However, even if these data merely reflect the fact that Americans are now unwilling to reveal what they secretly believe, that is a significant change from the past and suggests that it is no longer socially acceptable to argue for black inferiority. On the other hand, it is not unreasonable to conclude that many, perhaps most, of these people are responding honestly. While these results cannot prove in any absolute sense that Americans reject theories of black genetic inferiority, they provide no evidence that sizable numbers of whites endorse such theories.

Shouldn't we be troubled, however, by the finding that, even today, approximately 20 percent of Americans continue to believe blacks are intellectually inferior? What is one to make of the finding that this view is shared by an almost equal proportion of blacks? Are these people, black and white, racist because they hold such a view? It is of course reasonable to assume that many of these 20 percent are racist in the generally understood sense. But, on the other hand, many may hold that belief out of an innocent, though socially offensive, way of understanding the well-publicized gap in IQ and SAT test scores between whites and blacks, and the continued public discussion of black school difficulties. If such people do not endorse oppressive or discriminatory treatment of blacks, then it is difficult to fairly label them racist. Whatever the motivation of the people who answer in this way, their numbers hardly support the contention that Americans are in large measure racist.[18]

As important, perhaps more important, to the question of American racism is whether whites support blacks' right to equal treatment. Here the evidence is even more positive. In 1944, when asked whether blacks should have equal opportunities to get "any kind of job," only 45 percent of respondents thought blacks should have equal opportunities. By 1963, that percentage had climbed to 85 percent, and it reached 97 percent in 1972, when this question was last included in the General Social Survey.[19]

In the area of school integration there has also been a massive shift in attitude. In 1942, only 32 percent of respondents thought blacks and whites should attend the same schools. That figure climbed to 65 percent in the mid-1960s and climbed steadily until it reached 90 percent in the middle of the 1980s, when this question was last asked.[20]

A question about public accommodations asked respondents whether blacks "should have the right to use the same parks, restaurants and hotels as white people." When this question was first asked in 1963, 73 percent agreed. When it was last asked in 1970, 88 percent of the respondents answered affirmatively.[21]

This data suggests that overwhelming majorities of white Americans endorse equal employment and educational opportunities and equal access to public facilities for blacks.

In questions relating to integrated housing there has been somewhat less progress. In response to the statement "White people have a right to keep blacks out of their neighborhoods if they want to and blacks should respect that right," some 21 percent responded that they strongly agreed or slightly agreed with the statement when asked in 1989. Surprisingly, some 11 percent of blacks even in the 1980s agreed that whites should have the right to maintain segregated neighborhoods.[22] This is, however, a major shift, since in 1963, some 60 percent of respondents thought whites should have the right to maintain residential segregation. Part of the sentiment on this issue may relate to questions of class rather than race. When respondents were asked in the late 1970s if a black "with the same income and education as you have, moved into your block, would it make any difference to you," only 14 percent responded that they "would not like it. . . ."[23]

A different version of the "keep blacks out" question seems to confirm the economic-motivation explanation. Respondents were asked to choose between the following: "White people have the right to keep black people out of their neighborhoods if they want to, or, black people have the right to live wherever *they can afford to,* just like anybody else" (emphasis added). In the late 1970s, fully 88 percent of respondents chose the statement that blacks should have the right to live where they can afford to live.[24] In the area of intimate relations, especially marriage, fewer people express integrationist sentiments. As recently as 1989, some 21 percent of white respondents thought that "there should be laws against marriages between blacks and whites." Interestingly, almost 10 percent of blacks also thought that interracial marriage should be illegal.[25] When asked in the 1970s about interracial marriage, some 73 percent of respondents reported that they would be very uneasy or somewhat uneasy about a close relative planning to marry someone of a different race.[26] Part of this uneasiness may be explained by the fact that 87 percent of respondents agreed with the statement "you can expect special problems with marriages between blacks and whites."[27]

It is well to point out that the major changes in white attitudes took place in the 1940s and 1950s. By the middle of the 1960s, 75 to 90 percent (depending on the question) of white Americans rejected policies of discrimination in public accommodations, education, employment, and housing.[28] The evidence strongly suggests that, at least in the responses they are prepared to give pollsters, whites in large majorities endorse equal treatment for blacks and have done so for some time. It is also important to note that while southern respondents are more likely to express intolerant views than northerners, regional differences have declined significantly. For instance, by 1980, there was only a small north-south difference in support for integrated education, with most of the difference explained by opposition on the part of those southern whites with limited schooling. On the question of equal job opportunities there is virtually no difference between the responses of northerners and southerners.[29] As the South begins to approach other regions in terms of education and living standards, regional differences in racial attitudes are likely to decline even further.

In a recent (1992) article on trends in racial attitudes, Charlotte Steeh and Howard Schuman of the University of Michigan express dismay that the evidence of declining prejudice is often ignored by commentators who claim that "a resurgence of racism occurred in the United States in the late 1980s." Highly publicized racial incidents on college campuses and in cities, "especially among working-class youth," are sometimes cited as evidence of this resurgence of racism. Steeh and Schuman point out that "to scholars who use national surveys to study racial attitudes these examples of racial strife seem to conflict with [the] broader empirical evidence." They add: "Over the last 25 years, the attitudes of the general population of white adults have steadily become more supportive of black advancement on most, although not all, issues." After reviewing the data for the 1980s, Steeh and Schuman report that there is no evidence for a "decline in racial liberalism."[30]

Nevertheless, we continue to hear many civil rights advocates and numerous government spokesmen arguing that greater efforts must be made to overcome the racism of white Americans. The evidence suggests that much progress has been made. In fact, the percentage of Americans who oppose equal treatment of blacks in education and employment is very small and declining. Since racial liberalism is greater among the younger cohorts and among the better educated, it may well be that support for racial discrimination will whither away by attrition as older individuals pass from the scene. Few would deny the value of continuing to educate against prejudice, but one can reasonably question the value of some current efforts such as multicultural programs and sensitivity seminars designed to reduce racism on college campuses.[31] These efforts are unlikely to be of much benefit if they teach lessons that, according to all the polls, have already been learned. And they may have the effect of misleading black students into thinking that whites are more prejudiced than the evidence suggests.

It is important to note that many social scientists question the polling evidence cited above. They argue that Americans still harbor prejudice, but are less likely to admit it due to changes in public perception of what constitutes acceptable opinion. In addition, they argue that there are now new, more subtle forms of racism and prejudice which Americans express without conscious awareness. These new expressions of prejudice take the form of "symbolic racism" or "unconscious racism," which are difficult to detect, but are just as damaging to blacks as the older "redneck racism" of the past.[32] To understand the basis of this claim requires an inquiry into how social scientists have formulated the problem of racism and how they have changed their thinking over the years. Such an inquiry is undertaken in Part II, where I attempt to demonstrate that these claims of new forms of racism are of dubious merit.

III. Income Disparities between Blacks and Whites

Whether or not white Americans hold stereotyped and prejudiced views about blacks is a separate question from whether or not American whites discriminate against blacks. The question of discrimination is, in turn, separate from whether discrimination is effective. In general, the polling evidence supports the respected sociologist Rodney Stark when he says: "Again and again, researchers [have] found that the more education and income a person has, the less likely a person is to be prejudiced against other racial and ethnic groups."[33] This suggests that those whites who express open hostility toward blacks, whatever their exact percentage, may not be in a position to hurt them, since they are likely to be concentrated among the least influential whites in society. If prejudiced whites do not hold positions of significant influence or power in American life, then they are not likely to be in a position to cause blacks economic or social harm. Of course, ignorant and prejudiced whites can cause blacks considerable emotional harm and can sometimes cause physical harm when they engage in violent criminal behavior. Nevertheless, it is difficult to see how this prejudiced minority can today do real and lasting economic damage to blacks.

Some have argued that it is not so much that whites are prejudiced, but rather that American society has such a long history of racial separation and intolerance that institutions and practices that were put in place in support of separatism, continue to exist, and make black success difficult. It is further argued that these institutions and practices are often so subtle as to be hard for either whites or blacks to detect. It is this "institutional" racism, some argue, rather than unconscious or symbolic racism on the part of individual whites, which holds blacks back.

The sheer magnitude of the income gap between blacks and whites is often cited to bolster this and other arguments for the existence of pervasive discrimination against blacks. The median income of black households in 1990 amounted to 58 percent of median white household income.[34] This figure is almost unchanged from what it was in 1950, when black families had 54 percent of the median income of white families. The figure rose to 61 percent in 1970, but since then has dropped back to the 58 percent figure cited above, close to what it had been in 1950.[35] The gap, therefore, between the incomes of black and white households is substantial and long-standing; it is a very large difference, and it is important to understand why it exists. It is especially important to understand why, given all the effort to eliminate discrimination against blacks, the gap in family income has hardly changed at all in over forty years. To argue that this gap may be due to continuing discrimination is a hypothesis worth examining and testing. To assume, however, as do many, that the household incomes of blacks and whites would not differ at all were it not for the effects of discrimination, and to assume that other factors play no role, is, on its face, unreasonable. A scientific approach requires that we attempt to tease out all the factors and their relative importance, and not prematurely assign all the weight to this or that potential contributor.

In order to make a legitimate scientific claim that discrimination causes economic hardship, one has first to satisfy what is known as the *ceteris paribus* assumption, the assumption that everything else is equal. For instance, if I claim that the income gap between male attorneys and female attorneys is due to discrimination, I must first control for other relevant factors that are known to contribute to the earning power of lawyers. In other words, I would have to show that a man and a woman who differed in no other way but their sex still differed in income. If I can do that, then I have made a case that discrimination is the cause. What this means in practice is that I must compare men and women who are matched for age, years of work in the profession, type of legal work, type of firm, hours worked, geographic location, quality of education, etc.

If I have done all that and a gap remains, then discrimination becomes a likely source of that gap. I have not, however, established proof for the discrimination hypothesis in any absolute sense, as I may have missed some important factors beside discrimination which could account for the difference. In any case, when one examines income differences between men and women or blacks and whites in this way, and one has controlled for fairly obvious factors, what at first seem very large income differences are usually narrowed and often disappear altogether. For instance, female lawyers earn less than male lawyers, but a large factor is age. In 1970, only 5 percent of law school graduates were women. By 1980, the figure rose to 30 percent, and by 1990, it was over 40 percent.[36] The great majority of women practicing law today are relatively recent graduates, and very few have the seniority that commands high salaries. It will be interesting to compare the future salaries of men and women currently graduating law school to see if an income gap remains. If it does, will it be due to discrimination, or to the operation of other factors such as different personal expectations as to the meaning of work, family commitments, or some combination of factors?

Is the requirement of *ceteris paribus,* of holding all else equal, met by those who claim that black-white income disparities are due to discrimination? In most cases those who support the discrimination model make no attempt to see that ''everything else is equal,'' and for that reason alone, their claim is suspect on scientific grounds. Thomas Sowell is one of the few who has actually performed the analysis which would determine the true effects of discrimination, and his results stand as a powerful, almost unassailable rebuttal to the civil rights vision. Without rehashing Sowell's extraordinarily thorough analysis, made in numerous books and articles throughout the 1980s, let me simply outline the main argument.[37] The first and most important issue is that the figures above refer to *household* or *family* income. If one ethnic group tends to have more family members employed than another, then even if the individual members of each group are paid identical salaries, the group with more family members employed will have higher income. For that reason female-headed families almost always have smaller incomes than married-couple families.

Perusal of recent census data confirms Sowell's analysis. Census data for 1991 indicates that only 47.8 percent of all black families are married-couple families, compared to 82.8 percent of white families.[38] Among families with children under eighteen the disparity is even greater. In 1991, only 37.4 percent of black families with children under eighteen were married-couple families, whereas among white families the figure was 77 percent.[39] This is a powerful reason why there are so many poor black families today. In an age in which most middle-class families are supported by two wage-earners, any group with large numbers of families supported by one wage-earner will have much lower family income, even if those who do work earn exactly the same amount. In fact, with median married-couple family income fast approaching forty thousand dollars per year, it is almost impossible for most American families, unless they are headed by professionals, to attain middle-class status with only one income.[40]

While there have always, in this century, been disparities in black and white family composition, recent trends have greatly exacerbated the problem. In

1960, for instance, 89.2 percent of white families (and 90 percent with children under eighteen) were married-couple families. Among black families in 1960, 77.7 percent were married-couple families and, of those with children under eighteen, 67 percent were.[41] The upshot is that in the ensuing thirty years, while the incomes of individual black men and women were moving closer to parity with white incomes, black *family* income stagnated. No matter how you read the figures, most of the disparity in black-white family income results from the higher proportion of black families with only one wage-earner.

Census figures indicate that in 1990, among all black families below the poverty line, 75 percent were headed by single women, while only 20 percent were married-couple families. Fifty-three percent of all black families with children under eighteen that were maintained by single women in 1990 were below the poverty line. By contrast, only 14.3 percent of black married-couple families with children were below the poverty line in that year.[42]

There is a direct and important relationship between family income and family composition. In 1991, of those black families with children under eighteen, only 12 percent with incomes of $15,000 or less were two-parent families. By contrast, among those families with incomes over $25,000, 69 percent were two-parent families. Among black families with incomes over $40,000, fully 79 percent were two-parent families.[43]

Between 1967 and 1990, the ratio of black to white median family income for all families hardly changed at all, and in fact declined slightly from the 59 percent figure in 1967. By way of contrast, the ratio of black to white median family income for married-couple families rose almost continuously during this period, from 68 percent in 1967 to 84 percent in 1990.[44] These figures include older families formed before the important social changes of the fifties and sixties took place. Among married couples in the 15 to 24 year age range, the black-white income ratio was 94 percent in 1991. Among married couples in the 25 to 34 year age range, the ratio was 86 percent, and among those in the 35 to 44 year age range, the ratio was 92 percent. In other words, the median family income for married-couple black families formed in recent years approximates 90 percent of the income of white married-couple families.[45]

The income figures for married couples are especially striking, because they include all sources of income, including investment income in the form of dividends, interest, and rent, as well as income from welfare payments, pensions, etc. A much larger percentage of whites have investment income than do blacks, not least of all because whites are much more likely, at present, to inherit wealth than are blacks. Investment income is very likely to be in addition to other income, while welfare rarely is. This factor in and of itself explains a large portion of the black-white income gap for married-couple families.

In addition, these figures do not take into account educational differences, unemployment differences, the employment status of spouses, geographic location, or a host of other factors affecting family income. As we will see, when we factor in some of these variables, the income gap almost disappears. For instance, 55.8 percent of black families, but only 33 percent of white families, are located in the South, a region where incomes tend to be lower than in the rest of the country. Outside the South, median income for all black married-couple families was $39,462 and for white married-couple families it was $41,781, for a black-white ratio of 94.4 percent. In fact, among married-couple families outside the South where both husbands and wives worked, black families had median income of $46,657 and white families had median income of $46,094, for a black-white ratio of 101.2 percent.[46]

This progress is illustrated by a recent analysis of the census data on Queens County of the City of New York by the *New York Times*. The *Times* reported that in 1989, the median income of black and white families in Queens was virtually identical. This data is especially impressive since it includes all families, single-parent as well as married-couple families. Median family income was $34,500 for blacks and $34,600 for whites. Queens has nearly two million residents, of whom about 20 percent are black. It is important to note that these figures are for family *income,* not merely wages, and therefore include interest, dividends, and other sorts of nonwage income. The black average in Queens was in excess of the state-wide average for all residents of $32,965.[47]

There is very little evidence, therefore, for the ''discrimination breeds poverty'' hypothesis in the census figures. Black married-couple households that fit the predominant white pattern are beginning to approximate similar white families in their earning power, and may in fact have achieved parity if one factors in such things as investment income and the region in which people live. All of this does not mean that there is no discrimination in the workplace, but only that such discrimination as exists does not appear to hurt intact black families very much, especially when other factors are taken into account.

A similar pattern emerges when one examines the income data on black women. The median income from all sources for all black women in 1989 was approximately 80 percent of the median income for white women.[48] If one looks only at women who work, however, the picture improves. The median earnings (mainly in salary and wages) of all black women workers were $11,524 in 1989, compared to working white women's earnings of $11,724, or 98 percent of the white women's earnings, which is hardly a meaningful difference. The gap for full-time women workers is greater, but still modest. If we look only at women who worked year-round full-time in 1989, black women earned $17,389, compared to the $18,922 that white women earned, which produced a black-white ratio of 92 percent for full-time workers.[49]

These black-white earnings ratios have remained virtually unchanged since

1974. In 1939, the wage and salary earnings for all black women were 36 percent of white women's earnings, but by 1974, the ratio had increased to 95 percent. For year-round full-time workers, the black-white ratio increased from 38 percent in 1939 to 92 percent in 1974.[50] These figures include women of all ages and all levels of educational attainment, and from all regions of the country, factors that surely account for part of the differences that still exist.

One reason black women earn less than white women is that black women are more likely to face periods of unemployment than are white women. The unemployment rate for black women stood at 10.8 percent in 1990, which was approximately twice as high as that of white women.[51] This tends to depress the overall earnings of black women.

On the other hand, black women are more likely to work full-time than are white women, which has the effect of elevating the overall earnings of black women relative to white women, since year-round full-time workers generally have higher earnings than other workers.[52] Fifty-five percent of black women, compared to 50 percent of white women, are year-round full-time workers.[53]

The higher rates of unemployment for black women might be evidence of discrimination, but that argument is hard to reconcile with the fact that black women are more likely to hold full-time jobs. An equally likely explanation for the differences in unemployment between white and black women is the educational differences between them. In 1990, 21 percent of white females over the age of twenty-five had less than four years of high school, compared to 33.5 percent for black females. In addition, only 10.8 percent of black women, compared to 19 percent of white women, had four or more years of college.[54] These differences reflect the fact that many individuals in the current workforce are older and grew up in earlier decades when educational disparities between blacks and whites were greater than they are today. Individuals with limited education have more limited job opportunities and are therefore more likely to face periods of unemployment than are those with more education.

In fact, when one holds education constant, the income disparities between black and white women are reduced almost to a nullity. At almost all levels of education, black women full-time workers earn 97 percent of what white women full-time workers earn in those same categories. This ratio is the same for those with and without high school diplomas or four-year college degrees. The only exception is among those with only one to three years of college, where black women earn 91 percent of what white women earn.[55] All of this suggests that if white Americans are discriminating against black women, then as in the case of intact families, that discrimination is not, in fact, having much of an impact on their wages. Perhaps it is more reasonable to conclude that white Americans do not discriminate against black women in the workplace?

While the earnings gap for intact families and for women has all but disappeared, the same, unfortunately, cannot be said for the earnings gap between black and white men. Black men who worked had median earnings of $15,320 in 1989, which was only 69 percent of the $22,158 that employed white men earned. Among full-time workers, black men earned $20,426, compared to white men's earnings of $28,543, producing a black-white ratio of 72 percent.[56] As in the case of women, these black-white earnings ratios have not changed much since 1974. In 1939, the wage and salary earnings of all black men were 41 percent of white men's earnings, but by 1974, the ratio had climbed to 69 percent, the same as it was in 1989. For year-round full-time workers, the black-white ratio increased from 45 percent in 1939 to 71 percent in 1974, again about the same as in 1989.[57] The gap in earnings, therefore, between black and white men has remained consistently at about 30 percent since the mid-1970s and is more than three times the gap for women.

Furthermore, black men are more than twice as likely as white men to be registered as unemployed. In 1989, the unemployment rate for black men was 11.5 percent, whereas it was only 4.5 percent for white men.[58] In addition, black men's labor participation rate is lower than that of white men. In 1989, the labor participation rate for black men was 71 percent, while for white men it was 77 percent.[59] Moreover, unlike the case with women, black men are less likely to work full-time. Only 63 percent of black men were year-round full-time workers, compared to 70 percent of white men.[60]

The fact that black men are less likely than white men to participate in the labor force, more frequently unemployed, and less likely to work full-time tends to depress the overall earnings of black men relative to their white counterparts. The greater employment difficulties of black men reflect, in large measure, the educational differences between the races. In 1990, 21 percent of white men over the age of twenty-five had less than four years of high school, whereas 34.2 percent of black men fell into that category, a gap in education between black and white men almost identical to the gap for women. When it comes to those with college educations, the gap for men is greater than that for women. Only 11.9 percent of black men over twenty-five had college degrees in 1990, compared with 25.3 percent of white men, a ratio of less than one to two.[61]

When one holds education constant, the earnings gap between black and white men (who work full-time) is reduced to approximately 81 percent in all but one educational category. The exception is for men with four or more years of college, among whom black men earn 85 percent of what comparable white men earn.[62]

Why does the earnings gap between black and white men still remain sizable even after controlling for education, while for women it is just about closed? Part of the reason is that men tend to enter higher-paying occupations than women. They also remain at work more consistently than women, since women often leave the workforce for purposes of childbearing and child care. Men therefore have longer employment histories and greater seniority than women, and greater earnings potential. All of these factors produce greater variation in the earnings among men than in those among women. For instance, in 1989 among white workers, only 3.4 percent of women earned over $50,000, and less than 1 percent earned over $75,000. Among white male workers, on the other hand, fully 17.2 percent earned over $50,000, and 6 percent earned over $75,000.[63]

Because of this greater variation in men's earnings compared to women's, occupational choice and educational quality usually have a greater impact on earnings for men than for women. Not only do black men have less formal schooling than white men, the quality of education that many blacks receive, especially in the inner cities, is likely to be less valuable than that obtained by middle-class whites in the suburbs. This educational disparity is reflected in the differences between blacks and whites in the scores they receive on tests of academic preparedness such as the SAT exam.[64] To the extent that educational weakness inhibits the acquisition of skills or success in advanced education, it inhibits earning power, and that effect is likely to be greater for men than for women.

Furthermore, as Sowell has stressed, it is not only the quality of education that influences earnings, but the type of education as well. Sowell points out that Asians, for instance, tend to concentrate in scientific and technical fields, fields which tend to provide high salaries and prestigious jobs, often in private industry. Whites are less likely to choose such fields, and blacks are even less likely to do so.[65] According to Anthony DePalma, writing in the *New York Times,* ''[o]f the 36,027 Ph.D.'s granted in 1990 only 320—less than 1 percent—were awarded to black men. And only 508, or just over 1 percent, were given to black women.'' In addition, very few blacks obtained degrees in the sciences. According to DePalma there were no Ph.D.'s awarded to blacks in applied mathematics, molecular biology, biophysics, ecology, geology, oceanography, or particle physics. There are very few black chemists, computer scientists, and engineers compared to whites and Asians, but relatively more blacks in social work and education, fields which generally pay less well.[66] Technical and scientific occupations pay well and are usually dominated by men. Since black men are underrepresented in these fields, the effect is to increase disparities between black men and men of other races.

There are other important factors which must be taken into account when looking at income disparities. Anything which tends to delay entry into the full-time workforce will necessarily inhibit a person's ability to gain the seniority and work experience that lead to higher earnings. Young blacks tend to have higher unemployment rates than young whites. During most of the 1980s, the unemployment rate for blacks in the 20 to 24 year age range was over 20 percent and in fact exceeded 30 percent in 1982 and 1983. For whites in this age range unemployment never rose above 10 percent, except when it reached 12 percent in 1982 and 1983.[67] The existence of such high unemployment rates among young blacks clearly delays their entry into full-time employment and has an inhibiting effect on their wages later in life.

Another major contributor to the economic problems of black men is their disproportionately high participation in criminal activity when compared to whites. This is especially true for young males; nationwide in 1989, one in four black males between the ages of twenty and thirty was either in prison, on probation, or on parole. The figure in New York State in 1990 was 23 percent. In comparison, only 3 percent of white males of that age in New York State were involved with the criminal justice system. In Washington, D.C., 42 percent of black males in their twenties were either under supervision or being sought by the police. The New York and nationwide figures are lower than Washington's since the Washington figure includes young men being sought by the police and those on bond awaiting trial.[68]

Census data indicates that in 1989, 13.9 percent of black men in the 30 to 34 year age group had four or more years of college.[69] A reasonable extrapolation from the above figures suggests that in the 30 to 34 year age group, almost twice as many black men nationwide have criminal records as have four-year college degrees. High levels of criminal involvement contribute heavily to educational failure. Young people involved in crime are almost always at a high risk of dropping out of school. And a criminal record is hardly an advantage when seeking employment.

High crime rates in black communities also have an indirect and often overlooked negative impact on black earnings. High crime areas tend to be shunned by businesses because of the added burdens of insurance, losses from thefts and fires, etc. For that reason, there are probably many fewer jobs in areas where blacks reside than there would be if crime rates were lower. This is an especially vexing problem for young and inexperienced workers whose incomes may not be adequate to enable them to purchase cars so that they can take advantage of employment opportunities in the suburbs, where many jobs are now found. How many young people delay entering the labor force or never enter it for this reason is difficult to estimate, but it is bound to have a negative impact on blacks' employment experience.

High participation in criminal activity may account for some of the black men who report that they are not in the labor force at all. Some of these men, in effect, obtain income, but they do so in an underground criminal economy where income goes unreported and untaxed. How much is earned through such criminal activity is almost impossible to determine, but the failure to include such earnings certainly means that most measures of black men's income are probably underestimations, since illegal income is never counted in official income measures.

Another factor affecting income, not often considered, is marital status, which seems to contribute to economic success. Married men who worked earned 20 percent more than unmarried men in 1989, presumably because of greater motivation or need. By contrast, during the same year, married women who worked earned about 10 percent less than single women, perhaps due to lower motivation or need.[70] In 1989, only 39 percent of black men were married and living with their wives, while the comparable figure for white men was 60 percent.[71] To the extent that marriage has a disciplining effect on men's work habits, as it appears to do, black men are at a disadvantage to white men in this regard.

There are other important reasons for disparities in income that can only be touched upon here, such as the relative age of a population. Blacks are a younger group than whites, owing to the fact that they have a higher birthrate than do whites.[72] As people age they usually earn higher salaries and generally work more regularly. Unemployment among blacks under the age of twenty-five is very high, but it declines dramatically for those over twenty-five. Older men are more likely to be married and to have family responsibilities which tend, as noted above, to create motivation for obtaining a reliable source of income. There are currently more blacks in the 15 to 25 year age group than in the 45 to 55 year age group, when compared to whites.[73] Since people reach their peak earnings in the latter age group, this certainly accounts for part of the income gap between blacks and whites. This trend is exaggerated by the fact that the older cohort had far fewer college graduates when compared to the younger cohort among blacks as well as whites, since fewer people went to college thirty years ago. If demographic patterns for whites and blacks grow more similar, as appears to be happening, then even if nothing else changes, income disparities should decline.

In summary, the income gap between blacks and whites is produced by a complex host of factors. Family income is most seriously influenced by family makeup. More than half of all black families are single-parent families. When one examines the incomes of married-couple families, especially those formed since the 1960s, the income gap narrows markedly. When one takes into account the fact that family income includes investment income, which is much more common in white families, and when one also examines regional differences, the income differences which remain seem unimportant.

When one examines the earning power of individuals, the disparities in income are likewise diminished. If one controls for education, they almost disappear in the case of women. Among men the gap is greater, but even here when education is factored in, the income gap is much reduced. The influence of other factors, such as high youth unemployment and high rates of criminal participation, helps to explain the existing income differences.

In short, the argument that blacks suffer economic discrimination at the hands of whites in American society is seriously undercut by the evidence. When the condition of *ceteris paribus* is met, and important factors held equal, the evidence suggests that income disparities are small, and rapidly disappearing. This may sound surprising when we hear so much about discrimination in the media and from government officials in arguments supporting even stronger government action to overcome discrimination. Generally, however, the full force of the sort of analysis undertaken here is rarely if ever refuted, and most often is merely ignored.

It is difficult to determine just how much of the steady economic advancement of blacks since mid-century is the result of antidiscrimination laws and changing social attitudes among whites and how much is the result of the affirmative action policies adopted in the seventies.

The evidence on education, for instance, suggests that black advances in education were greatest in the fifties and sixties before extensive affirmative action policies were implemented. In 1940, among people twenty-five to twenty-nine years old, the median number of years of school completed was 10.3 for all persons and 7.0 for blacks, a gap of 3.3 years in schooling. By 1970, the median education gap was reduced to 0.4 years, which is close to the 0.2 years it was in 1990.[74] Similarly, the statistical data reviewed earlier showed that most of the reduction in black-white disparities in the earnings of individuals took place between 1940 and 1974. Since then the improvement has been modest. The current evidence clearly suggests that those blacks who enter stable marriages and work full-time have begun to achieve economic parity with whites, although the case is clearer for women than for men. This is not meant to deny the very real economic difficulties that the black population in its totality faces. Indeed, the economic problems of single-parent families are devastating. The problems of the large numbers of children born out of wedlock are enormous. So too are the problems of the young men who have fallen into delinquency or drug addiction.

The primary source of the economic disparities between blacks and whites appears to be in the differential behavioral patterns of young blacks and young whites. Far too many young people in the black community engage in activities and make choices that cripple them economically. If we wish to see the black community as a whole achieve economic parity with the white majority, then we must find ways to encourage more young blacks in the inner cities to make the sort of constructive choices that produce economic and social well-being.

IV. The Urban Underclass

It is well to point out that when most Americans today think about the "problems" of blacks, it is almost always about the problems of young men and women in distressed urban enclaves. They are certainly not thinking of the middle-class black doctors, lawyers, managers, government bureaucrats, school teachers, firefighters, and police officers who make up a substantial portion of the black population.

In fact, the term "underclass" has come into common usage to describe the large numbers of people who give urban black enclaves their distinctively troubled cast. The underclass is characterized by high unemployment, low educational attainment, high rates of illegitimacy, and high rates of criminal activity. Underclass neighborhoods are commonly decaying, dangerous, and anarchic places where young people lack adequate supervision and, therefore, are free to involve themselves in crime, drug use, premarital sex, and school truancy.

Illegitimacy in the underclass is extremely high, almost universal. While 64 percent of all black children are born to unwed mothers, illegitimacy is even higher among women in the underclass. Sociologist William Julius Wilson reports that in the largest housing projects in Chicago, 90 percent of the families with children are single-parent families.[75] Crime among underclass adolescent males is common, and is devastating to the young men themselves and to the communities in which they live. The schools attended by underclass children are frequently chaotic places, and many students are chronically truant. Depictions of inner-city life (such as that provided by Ze'ev Chafets's picture of Detroit in his *Devil's Night,* to name a recent example), and most installments of the evening news, convey a distressing, almost nightmarish image of black underclass existence.[76] Today, the economic disparities between blacks and whites are accounted for largely by the economic failure of blacks in this underclass. As we saw, those who adopt middle-class patterns of marital behavior are doing well relative to whites. Any attempt to reduce current disparities in income which fails to address underclass problems is unlikely to prove fruitful. Those problems reflect patterns of behavior which make economic advancement almost impossible. A vicious circle has come into being where crime, inadequate schooling, drug abuse, and illegitimacy have reached unprecedented proportions and all contribute to the difficulties which so many blacks face in their attempt to achieve economic parity with whites.

It is extremely important to determine what factors contributed to the creation of the present state of the underclass. It is important to determine the factors which continue to foster the obviously destructive patterns of behavior common to children in underclass communities. Most social scientists continue to locate the source of these problems in white racial attitudes. It is argued, for instance, that blacks are demoralized about schooling and turn to drugs and crime because they know that, even if they obtain schooling, they are unlikely to reap its benefits in the workplace because of white discrimination. But such an explanation is contradicted by the fact that blacks who advance academically do not, in fact, suffer economic hardship, and are now finding employment at salaries close to those of similarly educated whites. If young blacks hold such an erroneous belief, then it is the belief in white discrimination which may be holding them back rather than any purported discrimination itself.

It is hard to see how continuing to blame white discrimination, in the face of dwindling evidence, helps blacks overcome what may be false beliefs about American society, and yet most social scientists continue to resist looking to other factors for the source of black problems.

V. A Note on Prejudice and Generalization

One clear impediment to a reevaluation of current policies is, as we have seen, a reluctance among social scientists to accept most comparisons among groups for fear of being labeled bigoted. In fact, arguing that there are commonalities of a cultural or a biological nature among members of various ethnic groups is now taken as evidence of bias. This was not always the case. Prior to World War II, the opinions held by white Americans about blacks and various European ethnic groups were seen as unfortunate overgeneralizations which nevertheless had some basis in fact. It was, for instance, seen as unfair to stereotype all Irishmen as drunks, even though the evidence was abundantly clear that drunkenness was more prevalent among the Irish than among other ethnic Americans. A common stereotype of Jews as ''mercenary'' may have been an unkind way of describing the equally common stereotype of Jews as ''industrious.'' But however put, most would have agreed that Jews as a group seemed willing to work hard for economic advancement. Over the years, however, there developed a general tendency to see the holding of almost any belief about groups, whether correct or incorrect, as prejudicial. Today it is commonly thought that to hold any sort of generalization about ethnic or racial group characteristics is basically irrational, and such generalizations are thought to be indicative of feelings of animosity toward the groups in question. Both these assumptions are of dubious merit.

Generalized beliefs need not be incorrect, nor need they imply any animosity. This is obvious in the case of favorable generalizations. Most Americans believe that Jewish children are, in general, capable students. They base this belief on the fact that Jews, on average, do well in school. Such a belief is neither incorrect nor evidence of anti-Semitism. Most Americans hold the opinion that Chinese Americans, as a group, perform well in math and science. This belief is correct and is hardly evidence of animosity toward Chinese Americans. If a Chinese American were aware of the same facts, he might be of the opinion that white students do less well in math and science than Chinese students. He would be correct, and we could not attribute to him any animosity toward whites because he holds that belief. Even if the belief were incorrect, it would say little about his feelings toward whites.

Likewise, since it is a statistical fact that blacks commit more crimes, proportionate to their numbers, than whites, the fact that someone believes that blacks are more likely to commit crimes indicates that he is well-informed and not necessarily that he has negative feelings about blacks in general. Of course, we sometimes make the mistake of judging individuals on the basis of group membership; that is, we hold the belief that because someone is black he is likely to be a criminal or that because someone is Chinese he is likely to be good in math and science. The error here lies in assuming that most or even every individual in a group or sample possesses the characteristic thought more common to the sample. Such simplistic generalizations have come to be called stereotypes.

During the thirties, social scientists became concerned with the potentially harmful effects of group prejudice and, in an attempt to counteract crude racial and ethnic generalizations, argued that all such generalizations were basically irrational—that all were, in other words, stereotypes. The term ''stereotype'' was borrowed from the printing trade, in which it described a process of producing inexpensive printed plates for newspapers. It therefore implied the creation of fixed and identical patterns. Social scientists argued that statements such as ''All Jews are . . .'' and ''All blacks are . . .'' were fundamentally irrational since people in all groups exhibit considerable variation. But as the highly respected social psychologist Roger Brown points out, ''[t]oday it seems clear that the original analysis was quite wrong,'' since by and large very few people ever really believed that all members of a group possessed identical characteristics as if created uniformly by cookie cutters or ''stereo-types.''[77] Most people seem aware that the generalizations they hold reflect statistical averages, and most understand quite well that individual members of groups differ from each other.

It is of course possible, if not usual, for an individual to simplistically accept a commonly held belief about a group, without much reflection and without much experience with individuals, and to think therefore that every individual member must possess the characteristic common to the group. For instance, most people believe that men are stronger than women, but it would be rather crude stereotyping to believe that every man is stronger than every woman and that there is no overlap between the two groups. Most would agree that such mistakes should be avoided, but it would be incorrect to think that most people hold such crude, unreflective stereotypes. People appear in general to be more perceptive than that.

All too often, however, one gets the impression from discussions about prejudice that it is the holding of generalizations themselves which is to blame and that doing so is a sort of moral failing. One is admonished that to hold any generalized belief about a group of people makes it impossible to judge individuals fairly.[78]

This is a fundamental error. Many stereotypes (such as that about Chinese students and math) are not irrational and imply no enmity. In addition, common experience and research indicates that people can and usually do judge others on the basis of their personal experience with them.[79] The expression "But some of my best friends are . . ." may not always be the denial of prejudice by a prejudiced person, but rather may merely reflect the natural tendency to hold generalized beliefs about what is common to groups *and* to judge individuals as individuals.

The *Oxford English Dictionary* defines prejudice as "a judgement formed before due examination or consideration; a premature or hasty judgement; a prejudgement."[80] It is extremely important to distinguish prejudice as so defined from opinions or generalizations which are based on knowledge of the facts. Beliefs or opinions about groups which are clearly wrong may, but need not, be indicative of prejudice. However, in the case of beliefs based on sound evidence, no matter how negative the content of those beliefs, no presumption of prejudice is warranted.

In any case, the attempt to banish generalized opinion about groups is unlikely to be successful, because, by and large, it cannot be done. The tendency to form generalizations is a fundamental operation of the human brain. In fact, it is a fundamental operation of the brains of almost all species. Without the capacity to generalize we would never be able to learn from experience. Every time we see a particular person, we see a slightly different variation of what we saw before—hair, clothes, complexion, posture—are all somewhat different on each occasion. Were we unable to recognize the similarities between what we see today and what we saw yesterday, we could never come to identify anybody. The tendency to group together like experiences, to generalize, is what enables us to adjust to our environment, to learn. Without it we would confront every experience *sui generis.* Without generalization nothing could be recognized and no appropriate action could be taken.

The human tendency to generalize about classes was of interest to the ancient Greeks, who discussed the phenomenon in terms of what they called "universals." How can a person know or say anything about "cats" when all he has experience with is this or that individual cat? Plato's idealism was based on the supposition that there must be, somewhere, an ideal cat of which all individual cats are mere imperfect copies. This led him to think that true knowledge could only come from knowledge of such "ideals" or "universals" and not by any mucking around with real cats in the real world. Needless to say, much of Western history was shaped by Plato's way of looking at this intriguing problem.

Today, though we have yet to understand how the human brain accomplishes the feat, we assume that our tendency to generalize reflects an ability to select out the common elements in a group of seemingly disparate phenomena. William James, the father of American psychology, argued in the late nineteenth century that this ability is dependent on the highly developed human ability to base associations on similarity. He thought that the refined development of this ability was the mark of true intelligence and occasionally the source of genius.[81] James recognized that the refined capacity to detect similarities in seemingly disparate phenomena is the source of most creative problem-solving in that it enables us to discover, in some new and confusing situation, elements the present problem has in common with an older problem we have already solved. This capacity is also at the base of our desire to build models and analogies and simulations, which are essential to advanced science. These allow us to simplify complex phenomena by extracting significant elements. We use these elements to build simplified models which we can more easily understand. Mathematical thinking is based on such simplification by analogy. And today much modeling is carried out by computer simulations.

The point is that one can no more banish the tendency to generalize than one could banish the desire to eat; it is simply too much a part of human nature, and too crucial to our functioning. We can and should educate people about the human proclivity to generalize and teach them how to overcome the errors that are common when they overgeneralize. We can admonish them not to base generalizations on biased or inadequate samples. But we cannot, practically, overcome the tendency for humans to hold generalized beliefs about things or about people.

To the extent that people have generalized beliefs, it is unlikely that they can avoid the tendency for their beliefs about groups to color their impressions of individuals. While there is considerable evidence that people can put aside stereotypes in judging individuals, it is just as clear that until they have specific information about individuals, they are likely to depend on generalizations.

If I come across two people, one of whom is Asian and the other Caucasian, and I know that Asians tend as a group to perform better in math than Caucasians, and if I know nothing else, it is perfectly logical for me to guess that the Asian is more likely to be better at math than the Caucasian. I would, of course, prefer to have information about the individuals, and in almost all cases I would be wiser and fairer to avoid making any judgment until I have such individual information. But while this is clearly true it does not obviate the need, sometimes, to make judgments in the absence of such individual information.

If, in an emergency, I need assistance in carrying an unconscious person out of a burning building, it would be reasonable for me to look to a male for help and not to a female, if both are about the same size and age. Should I later discover that the woman was a firefighter I may feel foolish and I may feel called upon to apologize to her, but my action would have been neither illogical nor indicative of animosity toward women, even though it was clearly based on a generalization about women. To have acted differently would have required me to ignore important information and take on an additional risk to myself and the person in need of assistance.

By the same reasoning, it is rational for me to be somewhat more cautious about young black men than about young white men, if I am informed about crime statistics. As already discussed, about 25 percent of young black males have been convicted for some sort of criminal activity, while the rate for white males is under 5 percent.[82] The added caution among whites in the presence of black youngsters may offend those without criminal records. But that caution is hardly irrational, since the costs of determining the facts about the individuals in every case may be quite high.

Blacks often complain about the difficulty they have when trying to get a cab in New York City. Cabdrivers claim that the incidence of robberies and murders of cabdrivers by blacks is so high that they, in self-defense, sometimes avoid picking up blacks. Black professionals argue that cabdrivers ought to be able to see that a well-dressed man in the financial district is hardly likely to be a thief. Cabdrivers respond that driving into black neighborhoods to take a professional home can be dangerous, even if the passenger is not. And so it goes.

Clearly the black professional has a case, since the cabdriver is discriminating out of a generalized belief. But the problem is not so one-sided, since the generalization about blacks and the murder of cabdrivers is based in reality.[83] Given the risks, the cabdriver's behavior is not irrational. Nor is it possible to determine what he thinks about blacks, other than that he believes, correctly, that they pose a greater risk to his life than do whites.

One might object to the cabdriver's behavior on the basis that even if it is true that blacks pose a higher probability of danger than whites, the actual danger in either case is rather limited. Even though many cabdrivers are killed each year, the actual danger to any individual driver is, probabilistically speaking, relatively low. From the viewpoint of decision theory, however, differences in probability, even quite small differences, can be terribly important if the *consequences* are large.[84]

For example, many people travel on airplanes, even though they hear about airplane crashes every couple of months. People reason that with millions of flights a year, a few accidents per year gives them pretty good odds; the probability of dying in an airline crash is in fact on the order of one in a million. How many of us, however, would fly airplanes if there were a major crash every month? Probably not many, even though the odds would have only been increased from one in a million to something like five in a million, neither of which is a high probability. Most of us intuitively understand that when the consequences are great, even relatively small changes in probability are likely to be seen as important. We are, after all, exquisitely sensitive about risk when it involves our own lives and the lives of family members. Nor is there anything irrational about such thinking. We are involved in numerous activities every day which involve some small risk. It is rational for us to try to keep all such risks at a minimum. Those who are not concerned about the additive effects of risk-taking drive recklessly, smoke and drink with abandon, walk in unsafe places, swim in dangerous waters, etc. Such people would probably not be concerned with increased risks in airplane travel. But it is hardly irrational for the rest of us, who are generally risk-averse, to be concerned.

For similar reasons, the cabdriver who discriminates against blacks in New York City, given the fairly large numbers of cabdrivers killed each year, is not acting irrationally. It should be added that the overwhelming number of cabdrivers in New York City are recent immigrants, many from Eastern Europe and the Indian subcontinent. Whatever determined the attitudes of these recent immigrants, it is unlikely that they were influenced by the purported racism of American schools or American culture.[85]

In short, generalizing is a wholly natural human propensity without which we could not function in the world. We should certainly attempt to correct false generalizations, if only on the grounds that people operate more effectively when possessed of the truth. But we are not likely to change perceptions by denying what everyone knows to be true. It would be impossible and somewhat comic to attempt to convince people that females are as strong on average as males. Likewise, so long as black men have much higher proportional involvement in criminal activity than white men, it will be difficult if not impossible to overcome the wariness exhibited by whites which many black males unfairly, but unavoidably, suffer. It is unreasonable to claim otherwise.

To summarize, group generalizations arise naturally from the tendency of human beings to classify people on the basis of group membership. Sometimes the generalizations are erroneous, and sometimes overly sweeping, in which case they are mere prejudices which may lead to needlessly unfair treatment of individuals. Often, however, such generalizations emerge from some basis in reality; often, attitudes about groups are accurate generalizations about statistical tendencies. In this view, therefore, changing opinions about groups involves educating those who hold such opinions if they are based in error. But if the opinions are based in fact, they can only be changed by changing the behavior of the people in the group in question.

VI. Conclusion

The evidence gathered by various polling organizations since World War II indicates that negative attitudes toward blacks have declined significantly in recent years. Furthermore, this data suggests that the negative attitudes which still remain among whites are generally not based in beliefs that there are biological differences between the races. Of course, the data may not reflect the true feelings of people, since polls can never get inside people's heads. On the other hand, the polls do not support the claim that large numbers of white Americans hold racist ideas about blacks.

The statistical evidence on income disparities between blacks and whites gives little support to the thesis that those disparities are due to discrimination. The evidence relating to the earnings of black married-couple families and of black women suggests that discrimination is of limited importance to the economic well-being of blacks in general. When one considers the fact that blacks as a group are generally younger than whites and much less likely to have income from inherited wealth, the case for discrimination is even weaker. The data on individual income indicates that only among men is there a serious disparity, and that is best explained by the gap in educational attainment between black and white men and the higher rates of criminal involvement among black men.

The statistical record on black *family* income is indeed disheartening, but is very difficult to explain in terms of discrimination. The gap between black and white family income is hardly different from what it was forty years ago. To explain that gap in terms of discrimination requires the assumption that all of the changes of the past forty years have failed to decrease discrimination in any significant way. That is an untenable assumption. As we have seen, the gap in family income is largely the result of the hugely different makeup of black and white families. Large numbers of black families, and far fewer white families, are single-parent families. Ironically, as the earning power of black individuals rose over the years, the concurrent rise in black family instability nullified the economic gains which would have accrued to black families had they remained stable.

This unfortunate result is clearly tied to the rise of what has come to be called the underclass. Indeed, discussion of black difficulties today almost always turns to the problems of the underclass. Historically unprecedented rates of illegitimacy among black women, along with educational deficits and unprecedented rates of criminal involvement on the part of black men, are the most serious of these problems. It is these behavioral problems which most clearly explain current black economic difficulties. Discrimination, such as it may be, pales beside these other factors as a major hindrance to black economic and social betterment.

The need to face these problems squarely is hobbled by the now common belief that any characterization of an ethnic or racial group is a form of prejudice. This is clearly incorrect. Some generalizations are correct and as such offer no evidence of prejudice. This simple understanding came under severe challenge in the aftermath of World War II, and the holding of generalized beliefs about people came to be seen as a sort of moral and intellectual defect. This made it difficult to study group differences in a satisfactory way.

Part II, to which we now turn, explores the evolution of social science thinking on race over the past half-century. It is important to understand how the social science interpretation of race relations took form, and why it may have gone astray. A clearer understanding here may help guide the formulation of new and more useful approaches and policies. This understanding will also give us insight into why social scientists, in general, are reluctant to reevaluate theories which are no longer consistent with empirical evidence and with everyday experience.

Part II

The Formation of Current Thought on Race Relations

The current social-science understanding of black difficulties took shape in the years before and after World War II and was most forcefully argued by Gunnar Myrdal in *An American Dilemma.*[1] Myrdal argued that the difficulties blacks faced were the result of the segregationist doctrine of the South and widespread discrimination in the North. In the early 1940s, at the time Myrdal wrote, about 80 percent of all black Americans were living in the South and suffering under the extreme restrictions of Southern segregationist doctrine. Blacks in the North represented a very small percentage of the population and congregated in a few large cities.[2]

Myrdal argued that white Americans had been able to ignore the plight of black Americans through a variety of psychological devices, the most important of which was to deny the extent of the discrimination against blacks and to see their problems as resulting in large measure from black inadequacies.

In Myrdal's formulation, which will be examined in Chapter 3, the then conventional wisdom was 180 degrees deviant from the truth, which was that discrimination produced black inadequacies and not, as many claimed, that those inadequacies explained and justified the discrimination. Myrdal's thesis struck a vital chord with thoughtful people in the aftermath of World War II. Americans had suffered greatly to defeat the regime of Nazi Germany and everything it stood for, including its repulsive racial doctrines, and their horrendous genocidal consequences. The moral contradiction between abhorring and fighting racism abroad while justifying it at home was simply too great to be ignored by most people.

Myrdal furthermore demonstrated how racist practices and beliefs were totally inconsistent with traditional American values, with modern economic realities, and with the emergence of the United States as the preeminent world power in the aftermath of World War II. Myrdal's book was enormously influential in shaping the course of the struggle for civil rights that unfolded in the 1950s and 1960s. It is still influential today. Almost half a century since he wrote *An American Dilemma,* any attempt to locate the source of black problems in the behaviors of blacks themselves is seen as a plain attempt to justify racism and discrimination.

Chapter 4 examines another extremely influential book that helped to shape the postwar social science view of race relations. That book, *The Authoritarian Personality,* reported on a large-scale research project designed to gain an understanding of the psychological roots of prejudice. The researchers were guided by the belief that racism was a necessary feature of fascism and that fascism, in turn, appealed to a particular personality type, the authoritarian personality. Authoritarians suffered a powerful neurotic sense of inadequacy, induced during their upbringing, that produced a worshipful stance toward the powerful, and narrow-minded disdain and bigotry against those seen as weak and inferior.[3]

The researchers also believed that authoritarianism was most common in people of conservative views, especially people who subscribed to a belief in the value of free-market economic systems. They saw free-market systems as precursors to fascism. People who subscribed to free-market economics were, therefore, predisposed to fascist thinking, including the bigotry that the researchers thought was an inherent feature of fascism.

The Authoritarian Personality, like Myrdal's book, struck a sympathetic chord among American social scientists, most of whom identified with the political left and found economic conservatism distasteful. As we will see, the book's theory and research suffered from so many serious flaws that in time it fell into oblivion. Nevertheless, the basic thesis that free-market conservatism is an orientation predisposed to bigotry still has many defenders. In fact, the thesis informs a large body of recent research on a new, more subtle form of racism known as "symbolic racism." According to this research, symbolic racism is the form that bigotry takes in America today, now that "old-fashioned" or "redneck" racism is no longer socially acceptable.[4]

According to the symbolic-racism research, which is examined in Chapter 5, a person imbued with this new type of racism does not attack blacks directly, but does so obliquely through opposition to affirmative action policies that are thought necessary for black social and economic advancement. Such a person justifies his objections to affirmative action policies, in turn, by claiming an attachment to the traditional American values of self-reliance and fair play.

The symbolic-racism argument, if true, clearly exacerbates the problems of racial harmony in America, since a majority of white Americans claim to have faith in traditional American values and a majority express disagreement with many of the affirmative action policies that took shape during the past two to three decades. If true, it would certainly justify the political divergence of the races evident in their voting behavior since the 1960s.[5] If the symbolic-racism thesis is wrong, however, it truncates the debate over civil rights by confusing policy differences with antagonism to black advancement.

Part II, in sum, is an attempt to assess the current social science understanding of race by tracing its evolution during the last half-century. It is important to understand whether current theories, still based on the ideas of *An American Dilemma* and *The Authoritarian Personality,* continue to serve as valid guides for social policy, or if the intervening decades have rendered them obsolete. If the latter is the case, it is crucial that we acknowledge their obsolescence so that we can formulate clearer and more useful guides to action.

3

Gunnar Myrdal and *An American Dilemma*

I. Introduction

Gunnar Myrdal's *An American Dilemma,* published in 1944, played a pivotal role in changing the way Americans thought about race relations. Myrdal gathered together a vast amount of information about race relations in America during the prewar years, and his book has understandably been used ever since as the benchmark by which progress in these matters can be gauged.[1]

Put briefly, Myrdal's thesis was that the many problems he found among American blacks were the direct result of the southern system of segregation and of widespread discrimination toward blacks throughout the United States. This view ran counter to the opinion held by many at the time that it was the attributes and behavior of blacks that led to prejudice against them. Myrdal acknowledged that there was a mutual interaction at work, with white discrimination causing black behavior problems which, in turn, served to reinforce white prejudices. But he was clear in his argument that it was the white discrimination that was at the heart of the problem.[2]

He thought that this "vicious circle," which was so harmful to blacks, had to be brought to an end. He believed that the dynamic forces of modernization were likely to bring it to an end in any case, but that the process could be hastened by a truly national effort to end discrimination against blacks. Such an effort would, he thought, be a first priority of the postwar domestic agenda for two reasons. The first was the prominent position America would inevitably play in the postwar world, a world increasingly repelled by racist dogma. Second, the steady northward migration of blacks meant that race

77

could no longer be treated as a regional problem peculiar to the South, as it had been previously.[3]

The book was a tour de force indicting America for its shabby treatment of its black citizens, and at the same time setting forth a program of change which would allow an optimistic prognosis for the future. There can be no doubt that *An American Dilemma* contributed heavily, as Myrdal hoped it would, to bringing about the very changes he predicted would be forced on America. Myrdal was characteristically correct when he said of race relations in this country that "an era of more than half a century during which there had been no fundamental change was approaching its close."[4]

II. The Prewar View of Race Relations

Myrdal's argument was, in the main, that the social pathologies blacks often exhibited were at base the result of white prejudices and fears. In addition, he argued that for a number of reasons the problems of black-white relations had taken on an important national scope and could no longer be viewed as a regional problem peculiar to the South. On both counts he was at variance with the views held by many white Americans earlier in the century.

Before World War II, the attitudes of whites and the discriminatory treatment of blacks were, in most cases, viewed as the natural consequences of the characteristics of blacks themselves. In addition, the problems of the South were seen as best resolved by southerners, and most northerners had no interest in imposing northern values and practices on the South. To suggest such an imposition was perhaps too reminiscent of the circumstances leading up to the Civil War, whose terrible consequences were still vivid to many of those living in the early 1900s.

The Civil War had been a national disaster. The United States, with a total population of approximately forty million, had lost six hundred thousand young men in four years of bitter fighting.[5] The South's infrastructure and economy had been shattered and its white population demoralized and embittered. President Lincoln recognized the need to begin the process of reconciliation, but was assassinated before he could put his plans in place.[6] His successor, Andrew Johnson, also followed a conciliatory policy and tried to bring the defeated confederate states back into the Union without the excessive punishment of its leaders or citizens. Unfortunately, he was unsympathetic to the needs of the freed slaves and came into conflict with Congress when he vetoed a civil rights bill that would have granted blacks full rights of citizenship. Congress managed to override the veto, and from that point on, Congress was effectively in control of Reconstruction policies.[7]

The subsequent Reconstruction era was short-lived and tumultuous. By a series of acts, Congress tried to impose fair treatment of blacks and assure them the right to vote. These efforts were bitterly and, in the end, successfully resisted by southern whites who used physical violence and other sorts of intimidation to limit black political participation. The Ku Klux Klan came into being and took revenge, often in the form of lynching, against blacks who attempted to exercise their rights. The upshot was that by the 1870s, whites were in firm political control in most southern states, and had drastically reduced black and northern influence. The interests of southern whites were supported by the Democratic party, which by then had won control of Congress.[8]

Things came to a head in the presidential election of 1876, in which the Democratic candidate, Samuel Tilden, seemed to have carried the election, but charges of fraud threw the election into doubt. The Compromise of 1877 resolved what had become a major crisis: the Democrats agreed to allow Republican Rutherford B. Hayes to assume the presidency in return for his pledge to remove the northern troops which had been stationed in the South to enforce the Reconstruction laws. In effect, Hayes promised that the North would cease interfering in southern affairs, especially in regard to its treatment of blacks. With the end of Reconstruction, the South was left to manage race relations as it saw fit.[9]

The South immediately began to set up the intricate set of rules and restrictions known as Jim Crow laws—laws that severely limited black economic and political opportunities. Blacks were blocked from voting by rigged literacy tests and a variety of other fraudulent devices. Laws were passed requiring segregation in public conveyances and accommodations. By the end of the century a host of rules and regulations had been enacted throughout the South that denied blacks equal treatment and segregated the races in virtually all areas of life. In addition, law and custom dictated a strict social etiquette demeaning to blacks and designed to assure the dominance of whites in every imaginable circumstance.[10]

For many blacks, life under these new conditions may have been, in many ways, even more difficult than it had been under slavery. In retrospect, it is difficult to excuse the northern acquiescence in these southern practices that, in effect, made a mockery of the sacrifices of the Civil War. Clearly, however, northerners had no stomach for reigniting hostilities, a step which might have been required to end southern segregationist practices.

The relative indifference of northerners to the ill-treatment of blacks in the South is further explained, though not excused, by the fact that few white Americans outside the South had much contact with black Americans. The overwhelming majority of blacks continued to reside in the South as they had before the Civil War. In 1910, for instance, only 11 percent of all blacks lived outside the old Confederacy, and blacks constituted less than 3 percent of the total population of the North and the West. In California, Michigan, and New York, blacks made up only 1 percent of the population in 1910.[11] In that year there were ninety thousand blacks living in New York City, but they constituted less than 2 percent of the population.[12]

It was not until World War I that substantial numbers of blacks migrated to the North. But even by 1940, on the eve of America's entry into World War II, only 22 percent of all blacks lived outside the South, mainly in large northern cities. Even then, blacks still constituted less than 4 percent of the total population of the North and an even smaller percentage of the population of the West.[13] In fact, about half of all blacks living outside the South in 1940 were living in six northern cities: New York, Chicago, Philadelphia, Detroit, Cleveland, and Pittsburgh.[14] In none of these cities did they constitute more than 10 percent of the population.[15] By way of contrast, in 1990, blacks represented almost 20 percent of the population of such metropolitan areas as New York and Chicago, and a much larger percentage of the population living within the actual borders of those cities. Blacks make up two-thirds of the population of Washington, D.C.; Detroit, Michigan; Gary, Indiana; and Atlanta, Georgia—to name only a few of the cities where blacks are now the dominant racial group.[16]

Not only were blacks a relatively small proportion of the population in the North, there was little about their circumstances, other than their color, to distinguish them from the other immigrant groups taking up residence in the same few northern cities to which blacks migrated. In fact, in 1925, fully one-quarter of the blacks living in New York City were themselves recent immigrants from the West Indies.[17] While it was obviously true, for instance, that blacks were easily distinguished from other native-born Americans and were restricted to segregated neighborhoods, it was equally true at the time that many immigrant groups were easily distinguished and tended to live in segregated ethnic enclaves, though often voluntarily.[18] While it was clear that native-born white Americans held negative views about blacks and engaged in open discrimination against them, it was just as clear that other immigrant groups were also held in low esteem and experienced discrimination. The point is that there was little reason for the average American to think that the problems blacks had were unique to them or that they constituted a major problem requiring a national effort to resolve.

Today, of course, the indifference of the national society to such gross abuses in a major region is unthinkable. In 1910 and 1920, however, the Civil War was recent history, and most northern whites seemed unwilling to commit any further resources to the race question. This would probably have been the case even if whites in greater numbers were concerned about the conditions of southern blacks, which seems not to have been the case.

This apparent callousness should be viewed in light of the fact that mass communications and rapid transportation had not yet broken down regional differences as they have since World War II. Most northerners had never ventured into the South, and there was no television to graphically tell the story of black suffering. In addition, the fact that blacks were free to move out of the South, as they did in steady numbers during and after World War I, accounted for part of this indifference. And of course, America in the teens, twenties, and thirties had much to occupy the front pages of newspapers other than the appalling condition of blacks in the South. World War I was followed by the boom of the twenties and the rise of communism and fascism in Europe, which in turn were followed by the Great Depression of the thirties and the events that would eventually culminate in World War II. And all the while, Americans were being inundated with a steady stream of new scientific and technological innovations, such as motion pictures and automobiles, which, then as now, served to preoccupy the consciousness of large numbers of people.

Northern whites, in short, had little awareness of the plight of black Americans in the South and showed little concern for those in the North. Blacks who lived in the North were simply not numerous enough, nor were their problems unique enough for many Americans to feel any special responsibility for them. Most native-born white Americans did not feel responsibility for the problems of the Irish, Italian, and Jewish immigrants who had taken up residence in major American cities. In fact, the popular mood took a turn against immigration in general during the 1920s, especially of people who were thought difficult to assimilate into mainstream society. This negative mood produced new immigration legislation in the twenties that drastically curtailed the influx of all but northern Europeans.[19] It is not surprising, therefore, that sympathy toward blacks during this time was limited.

Part of the indifference to immigrant and black difficulties can be traced to the view held by most people that immigrants ought to take care of their own problems, and indeed, self-help organizations were common among all ethnic groups. To have suggested, for instance, that the Jews of the Lower East Side of New York lived in poverty because of the stereotypes and discrimination against Jews by native-born Americans would have seemed unreasonable. So would have a similar explanation of the poverty of blacks living in Harlem.

Let me add that the attempt to put northern white indifference to black difficulties in perspective is not meant to condone that indifference. In retrospect, America's reaction to the problems of adjustment facing its various minorities was in many respects harsh and callous in the period under discussion. It is an open question, however, whether immigrants fare better and make more rapid progress toward assimilation under the more enlightened regime of today's welfare state than under the harsher regime of the past. That is a question which need not be addressed here.

The social science treatment of racial and ethnic differences, at the time, reflected and reinforced the more general climate of public opinion. Such things as ethnic stereotyping and racial hatred were seen as unfortunate but natural outcomes when groups with different values and different ways of living were brought into close proximity. Such conflict was common throughout the world and hardly unique to America. Furthermore, as already discussed, most people (and many influential social scientists until the twenties) thought of group differences as fundamental and based in biological as well as cultural differences.

William McDougall of Harvard—whom historian Carl Degler thought perhaps the "best-known psychologist" of the time—believed racial and ethnic differences were heavily influenced by heredity. He contended that the "races differ in intellectual stature just as they do in physical stature."[20] McDougall and many other influential psychologists were supporters of the eugenics movement, a movement arguing for improving the human race through the encouragement of selective breeding. Many followers of this movement favored sterilization of those found to be "feeble-minded."[21]

Eugenicists also tended to support highly selective immigration. Lewis Terman, a respected Stanford University psychologist prominent in the development of IQ testing, warned in 1922 of the dangers of unrestricted immigration, arguing that more recent immigrants "are distinctly inferior mentally" to those who had earlier arrived from northern Europe. Similar sentiments were expressed by the eminent sociologist Edward Ross.[22] Psychologist Robert Yerkes, who directed mental testing for the Army during World War I, also argued that those who supported unrestricted immigration must also desire "high taxes, full almshouses, a constantly increasing number of schools for defectives, of correctional institutions, penitentiaries. . . ."[23]

Those Americans, therefore, who thought that blacks were lacking in ability, and that the Irish were pugnacious, rarely thought themselves prejudiced. They held what at the time were conventional views, views reinforced by scientific writings in psychology and biology, especially writings influenced by Darwinian theory.

This is not to say that the conventional wisdom went unchallenged, but only that it was not successfully challenged. The anthropologist Franz Boas argued strenuously throughout his career for the view that culture and not genes determined differences between people of different races.[24] John Watson, the founder of behaviorist psychology, argued in the mid-twenties in his popular book *Behaviorism* that differential experience and learning could account for all differences between people and that heredity played at best a minor role.[25]

Cultural determinism, as expressed by Boas and Watson, eventually began to have an impact in the twenties among social scientists and among those with progressive social views. Margaret Mead's 1928 report on her research on sex and adolescence among the natives of Samoa in the widely acclaimed *Coming of Age in Samoa* contributed greatly to the popularity of cultural determinism.[26] There can be no doubt that by the mid-1930s biological determinism had been rejected by mainstream social scientists as well as by progressive elites, but as is clear from the polling data discussed in the previous chapter, this rejection did not affect the general public until somewhat later.[27] Most people continued to believe that their opinions about various ethnic groups and about blacks were sound and, at least to some extent, had a biological basis. Most people would therefore have found alien the idea that it was their discriminatory behavior toward blacks that created the very problems among blacks that had the effect of reinforcing their negative opinions. However, that was precisely the argument that Myrdal was to make and that, in time, came to dominate thinking in the social sciences and to form the basis of civil rights policy down to the present day.

III. World War II and the Impetus for Change

Perhaps the single most important factor leading to a change in northern attitudes toward the southern treatment of blacks was the revelation of the methodical killing of the Jews and other groups by Hitler's regime. Most people were stunned by the enormity of what had taken place, and intellectuals, in particular, struggled to understand it and to somehow come to grips with the unspeakable evil and brutality that Nazi racism had unleashed. Few who participated in that discussion could ignore their own prejudices and hatreds, nor could they easily reconcile the racist policies in their own societies that they had hitherto ignored or, however reluctantly, accepted and tolerated. Certainly America had much to answer for in regard to its treatment of black Americans.

The whole issue of American race relations was brought to the fore and crystallized by the publication of Myrdal's *An American Dilemma* in 1944. Myrdal, a prominent Swedish economist, was recruited by the Carnegie Corporation to undertake a study of black-white relations in America.[28] The book, written in conjunction with a host of collaborators, came to almost fifteen hundred pages and drew a devastating portrait of the pathetic condition of black Americans. The portrait included well-documented descriptions of the South's brutally discriminatory legal system. It also depicted the myriad ways in which mean-spirited whites forced blacks into subservience and made everyday living a painful and degrading experience for them. Myrdal's detailed depiction of life in the South was particularly disturbing to those northerners who, for the most part, had been willing to remain ignorant of the circumstances there. But he did not spare the North, which hardly could be held up as a model for the fair treatment of minorities. In writing on his early travels around the country in preparation for the project, he reported that he "was shocked and scared to the bones by all the evils I saw. . . ."[29]

There can be no doubt that the book's favorable reception was conditioned by the circumstances of World War II. As news of Nazi atrocities and genocidal policies spread, a general revulsion against all forms of racial and ethnic prejudice became common, at least among educated Americans. The officers of the Carnegie Corporation, who conceived the study in 1935, were undoubtedly concerned by the rise of racism in Europe and its likely impact on America when they originally planned the project, but they could hardly have anticipated the truly horrible nature of Hitler's program. The widespread and honorable participation of black Americans in the war also contributed to the favorable reception of Myrdal's analysis. The sight of blacks returning from service in World War II, where they had fought to defeat an evil and racist regime, underscored the hypocrisy of America's own racism.[30]

An additional factor predisposing a favorable reception of Myrdal's thesis was that the discriminatory treatment of blacks had come under heightened protests by blacks themselves during the war. Manpower needs, labor shortages, and production needs provided added impetus for greater government responsiveness to those protests, not to mention the concern with national unity in very trying times.[31]

Therefore, the publication of *An American Dilemma* in 1944 was auspicious. The Carnegie Corporation had recruited Myrdal on the ground that as a European and an outsider to America, he was likely to bring a more objective view to the task of describing the deplorable conditions imposed on American blacks. It is also the case that he was recruited because he was an outspoken and politically active social scientist who had taken an active role in shaping Swedish welfare policy.[32] The Carnegie project, it should be noted, was consistent with other projects of the corporation to improve the lot of black Americans. Frederick Keppel, the president of the Carnegie Corporation, explained that Andrew Carnegie had given "generously to Negro institutions, and was closely identified with both Hampton and Tuskegee Institutes."[33]

Myrdal was given considerable funding and much freedom in his oversight of the study and in soliciting contributions from other scholars. The list of contributors is extremely long and reads like a who's who of American social science, including the names of Franz Boas, Ruth Benedict, Otto Klineberg, Robert Park, Edward Shils, E. Franklin Frazier, and Ralph Linton, to name only a few of the luminaries included. Richard Sterner and Arnold Rose worked closely with Myrdal and were given title-page credit for their assistance. Myrdal also consulted with and gave credit to many figures in the civil rights movement, such as W. E. B. Du Bois and Ralph Bunche. By the time the book was published it had already generated considerable anticipation among American social scientists. Undoubtedly, Myrdal's inclusion of so many well-known social scientists contributed to the book's generally favorable reception.[34]

Myrdal assembled vast amounts of material, including many useful statistics and powerful anecdotal accounts illustrating and confirming his thorough and thoughtful analysis. His writing was accessible and his manner gracious. As critical as he was, for instance, of the South's treatment of blacks, he continually commented on the basic decency of most Americans and the fundamental virtues of American society. Though his topic forced him to focus on what he called "various forms of social pathology in America," he made it clear that he thought well of Americans, who on the whole "probably live a more 'righteous' life, measured by whatever standard one chooses, than any large group of people anywhere else in the Western world."[35] Such praise of Americans may seem merely politic in light of the role Americans were playing in the fight against fascism. As we will see, however, Myrdal did in fact have a true respect for the American system and the American people.

IV. Myrdal's Argument

Myrdal's argument had a number of important premises. The first was that the problems blacks faced in America were largely caused by white attitudes and treatment of blacks. According to Myrdal, "the Negro problem is predominantly a white man's problem."[36] Myrdal explained that he did not start his research with this view. In the beginning, he had focused on the characteristics of American blacks, for this focus seemed natural, considering that "most of the literature on the Negro problem dealt with the Negroes: their racial and cultural characteristics, their living standards and occupational pursuits . . . their religion, their illiteracy, delinquency and disease. . . ."[37]

As he proceeded with his studies, however, it became "increasingly evident that little, if anything, could be scientifically explained in terms of the peculiarities of the Negroes themselves." Further, as the work progressed, it became clear that, "[a]ll our attempts to reach scientific explanations of why the Negroes are what they are and why they live as they do have regularly led to determinants on the white side of the race line."[38] In short, Myrdal's main thesis reversed the common perception that white attitudes toward blacks were the logical result of black characteristics and black behaviors.

The second important element in Myrdal's argument was that America's treatment of its black citizens posed an irreconcilable moral dilemma for Americans which they had failed to confront at great social cost. The core American values of fairness and open opportunity were daily contradicted by the ubiquitous discrimination that blacks suffered, especially in the South.

Americans were able to live with this inconsistency in large part because so many remained ignorant of the terrible circumstances in which most blacks were forced to live. Others who were not ignorant resolved the dilemma, in Myrdal's view, by various neurotic responses that allowed them to rationalize their complicity in the mistreatment of black Americans.[39]

The third important element in Myrdal's argument was his belief that Americans were so attached to their basic core values that if confronted with the full force of the contradiction between their values and their behavior, they would opt to change their behavior. For Myrdal, Americans held to their traditional values with an almost religious zeal. The American creed was "the most explicitly expressed system of general ideals" to be found anywhere in the world and included the "essential dignity of the individual human being, the fundamental equality of all men, and of certain inalienable rights to freedom, justice, and a fair opportunity. . . ." Myrdal furthermore maintained that these values were shared by "Americans of all national origins, classes, religions, creeds, and colors," and were essential to the American experience.[40]

As Myrdal saw it, "[t]he average northerner does not understand the reality and the effects of such discriminations as those in which he himself is taking part in his routine of life." But such people "get shocked and shaken in their conscience when they learn the facts." Even southerners, in Myrdal's view, "would be prepared for much more justice to the Negro if they were really brought to know the situation."[41]

Myrdal thought that education about the conditions of blacks, the sort of education he presented in his book, was an indispensable precondition for change, and would by itself go a long way toward righting the injustices blacks faced. But more than education would be required. Strong governmental action would be needed to change the institutional structure of discrimination in the South. He believed that such an intervention in southern affairs would be supported by most Americans. In his view the South was out of step with the rest of the country, and recent improvements in communication and transportation made the differences glaring and obvious. Myrdal reasoned that the time had come for the country as a whole to force the South to reform and that the nation would be moved to do so by a plain and forthright recognition of the moral dilemma it faced.[42]

Americans, however, would be driven to deal with the problem not merely out of moral concern, but also because of fundamental national interests. Myrdal argued that in the postwar world America would undoubtedly be the world's leading nation and the foremost champion of democratic reform. America could hardly perform that role well if it did not rid itself of the taint of racism, especially in the eyes of the peoples of Africa and the Far East.[43] There can be no doubt that Hitler's atrocities furthered the general feeling that decent societies ought not impose second-class status on citizens by virtue of race or religion, and there can be little doubt that this feeling was widespread among the American populace, especially outside the South. World events had, in a sense, readied the country for a major reevaluation of race relations.

Myrdal called on social scientists, especially, to take a more active role in the reforming of America. He saw no inconsistency in pursuing a just political agenda and at the same time practicing honest social science. He urged social scientists to eschew the doctrine of value-free, disinterested science, which he thought disingenuous given the great injustices confronting America's black minority.[44]

Myrdal was confident that once blacks were given greater opportunity, they would rise to the occasion, and their lack of economic progress and associated problems would gradually evaporate. If blacks were given the opportunity to assimilate, they would do so and the American dilemma would finally be resolved. If blacks were accorded "the elemental civil and political rights of formal democracy, including a fair opportunity to earn [their] living," many problems would undoubtedly remain, but, as Myrdal put it, "there would no longer be a *Negro* problem" in America.[45]

V. The Vicious Circle

Myrdal was optimistic about the prospect for racial harmony in large measure because of his faith in the fundamental decency of the American people. Based on his impressions from interviews and the readings that he had undertaken in the course of the study, he came to the conclusion that white Americans were not fundamentally xenophobic. Myrdal saw Americans as generally open to immigrant groups and anxious for them to become integrated into American culture. Asians, for instance, seemed reasonably welcome from his impressions. The one glaring exception was whites' attitude toward blacks, which he attributed to a widespread belief among white Americans that blacks could not practically be assimilated into the American mainstream. He attributed this belief to the erroneous acceptance of the idea that the general backwardness of sub-Saharan Africa was the result of the racial inferiority of black Africans. This explained to Myrdal the greater acceptance of Asians; Asians were different to be sure, but since they came from societies that had created advanced cultures, they were not judged to be biologically inferior. Africa had not produced advanced civilizations on a par with Asia or Europe, and this seemed to suggest, to the majority of whites, that people from Africa were simply incapable of doing so for reasons of biological inferiority. Most whites, according to Myrdal, held this belief, and thought therefore that blacks could never effectively be assimilated.[46]

Of course, Myrdal recognized that the doctrine of racial inferiority served as a powerful mechanism to justify the otherwise (within the American ethos) unjustifiable practice of slavery in the years preceding the Civil War. In this justification, Africans were "natural slaves," to use Aristotle's unfortunate phrase, and were unlikely to lead productive or happy lives unless directed by others. Myrdal pointed out that this particular justification of black slavery was not prominent in earlier times and only came to the fore in the early nineteenth century as a defense against the rising moral indignation expressed by northerners toward the practice of slavery.[47]

Whatever may have been the true origins of the theory of African racial inferiority, Myrdal argued that out of it grew a fear of "amalgamation" or race mixing. Myrdal viewed this fear as illogical, since he felt that modern science had shown the error of hereditarian claims for racial differences. In this he relied heavily on the work of psychologist Otto Klineberg of Columbia University, whom historian Carl Degler identified as "in the forefront of the attack on racial explanations."[48] Degler reports that, in large measure due to Klineberg's work, by the 1930s cultural explanations for racial differences had displaced the hereditarian doctrines as the dominant view in the social sciences.[49] Since Myrdal thought that it was the fear of racial amalgamation that drove the program of racial segregation and discrimination, a key element in any program for progress would have to be the eradication of the erroneous belief in African inferiority.

Myrdal recognized that economic and other factors such as "sexual urges, inhibitions, and jealousies, and social fears and cravings for prestige and security" were important to the maintenance of segregationist doctrines.[50] Nevertheless, in Myrdal's view, it was the "anti-amalgamation maxim" that was the bedrock of the "racial caste system" and the "white man's theory of color caste." According to segregationist theory, racial purity was the overriding concern and whites were "determined to utilize every means" to protect it.[51]

From Myrdal's perspective the rejection of equal rights and social equality were best understood as a means to prevent miscegenation and intermarriage. So great was the fear of miscegenation that the races had to be kept apart in all walks of life. "There must be segregation and discrimination in recreation, in religious service, in education, before the law, in politics, in housing, in stores and in breadwinning."[52]

Given this analysis, Myrdal's prognosis was surprisingly optimistic. Since he believed that the whole system was based on an enormous factual error about African inferiority, he thought the error could be overcome by education and by experience. If the doctrine of racial inferiority were overturned and blacks were afforded greater opportunities, he believed they would make economic and social progress. Such progress would, in turn, give the lie to the idea of African inferiority, and in time the fear of racial amalgamation would abate.

Education was important, and experience was the best educator in Myrdal's view. Only when whites saw blacks rise in social and economic terms would they finally be convinced of black equality. For that reason governmental coercion would be necessary to dismantle the entrenched, institutionalized structures of segregation in the South. Too many whites benefited from these arrangements, and these practices had been the bedrock of the South's ethos and way of life for too many years for them to be given up easily or voluntarily.

These southern practices made it impossible for blacks to demonstrate their worth. Only when blacks had the opportunities would they be in a position to demonstrate their equal capacities. Myrdal posited a "principle of cumulation" which he related to the notion of "the vicious circle" to explain the relationship between white beliefs and black problems.[53] The assumption of black inferiority led to segregation and discrimination that kept blacks in degraded circumstances. The degraded condition of blacks, in turn, was given as evidence that blacks were inferior and served to justify the segregation and discrimination that created the degraded condition in the first place. As Myrdal put it: "White prejudice and discrimination keep the Negro low in standards of living, health, education, manners and morals. This, in turn, gives support to white prejudice." The condition of blacks and the prejudice of whites were, in this view, mutually reinforcing and in a sense caused each other.[54]

But Myrdal thought the principle of cumulation could work in the opposite way as well. He thought that if "white prejudice could be decreased and discrimination mitigated, this is likely to cause a rise in Negro standards, which may decrease white prejudice still a little more, which would again allow Negro standards to rise, and so on through mutual interaction."[55]

In order for the principle of cumulation to bring about a positive effect, the vicious circle had to be broken. Since southern blacks were in no position to improve their degraded condition so long as discrimination persisted, and southern whites had little incentive to do so, the only way the process could begin would be through intervention by Washington in southern affairs. In effect, Myrdal was calling for the end of the compromise reached between North and South in 1877 that had brought the Reconstruction era to an end, a compromise that had lasted for over half a century. Myrdal knew, of course, that Washington would be reluctant to take such a course, but he believed that this reluctance would be overcome by the new moral temper of the time that was fostered by the changing needs of an industrializing America, by the central position of the United States in the postwar world, and not least by the greater willingness of blacks to demand justice. In his view Washington would have little choice but to spearhead a national movement toward racial equality.[56]

Myrdal thought that the government's task would not be as formidable as it first appeared. His optimism was based in part on the fact that whites exhibited a "rank order of discrimination" in their concerns about racial integration. Top on the list of white concerns was a desire to prevent sexual mingling. Second in importance were concerns about other, less intimate social relations, such as dancing, bathing, dining, etc. Lower on the list were concerns about allowing blacks political rights and fair treatment in the courts. Of least concern to whites, according to Myrdal, was whether blacks were allowed economic opportunities in such matters as "securing land, credit, jobs, or other means of earning a living."[57]

Myrdal took hope from the fact that when blacks ranked their concerns, these seemed to be an almost mirror or reverse image of white concerns. Blacks were most concerned with economic fairness, somewhat less concerned with political rights, only slightly interested in greater social relations with whites. They were hardly concerned at all with marrying or having sexual relations with whites.[58]

The result of these rankings was that since the values that whites and blacks assigned to these various forms of discrimination were so different, it would not be difficult to arrange social changes that would be mutually satisfying, since the things blacks cared about most seemed relatively unimportant to whites. In other words, whites could grant blacks greater economic opportunities, which were very important to blacks, at very little cost to themselves. This was so, according to Myrdal, because whites' desire to limit black economic opportunities was not desired for its own sake but merely as a means to prevent race mixing.[59] Furthermore, by giving up relatively little of importance to themselves, whites could reap considerable psychic gain by moving closer to realizing the basic American values to which they subscribed.[60]

Myrdal differentiated his own approach from the approach of those who insisted on the primacy of economic matters. He recognized, of course, that discrimination against blacks served to protect whites against competition in the workplace. But he explicitly rejected the sort of extreme economic determinism which argued that economics was at the heart of everything. He argued instead that the race problem was part of an "interdependent system of dynamic causation" where there is "no 'primary cause' but everything is cause to everything else."[61]

Despite his general optimism, Myrdal recognized that old ways and beliefs would not fall easily and expected a prolonged, difficult struggle, especially in the South. In this struggle he thought that social scientists would play an important role. He chastised them, however, for their earlier failure to take an active role in the race issue and their failure to challenge with sufficient vigor the myth of black inferiority. In Myrdal's view the social sciences had "been associated in America, as in the rest of the world, with conservative and even reactionary ideologies." He maintained that their support for theories of biological causation "for a century and more" had a profound influence on public understanding and, in particular, on "people's attitudes toward the racial traits of the Negro."[62]

Of course, by the time Myrdal wrote those lines, the social sciences had, during the previous decade, undergone profound changes and had become increasingly opposed to Darwinian thought. Myrdal acknowledged that a "handful of social and biological scientists over the last fifty years [had] gradually forced informed people to give up some of the more blatant of [their] biological errors." And he also acknowledged that by the late thirties, social scientists had become "militantly critical" of biological doctrines of racial inferiority.[63]

This newly reformed social science, in Myrdal's view, was "constantly disproving inherent differences and explaining apparent ones in cultural and social terms," so that the "popular race dogma" was "effectively exposed as fallacious or at least unsubstantiated."[64]

In the final analysis, it was Myrdal's faith in the essential fairness at the core of American democracy and his belief in the rationality of the American people that made him optimistic about the eventual resolution of the American dilemma. That optimism also reflected a faith in the value of activist social science and the possibilities of social engineering. The tone of Myrdal's book is captured in the following lines of the closing chapter:

> The rationalism and moralism which is the driving force behind social study, whether we admit it or not, is the faith that institutions can be improved and strengthened and that people are good enough to live a happier life. With all we know today, there should be the possibility to build a nation and a world where people's great propensities for sympathy and cooperation would not be so thwarted.[65]

Myrdal's book was a watershed in the history of social science. It was warmly received and applauded in the North and by most fair-minded people everywhere. In addition, it served as a rallying cry for a new, more engaged social science, one that would not simply analyze social problems but attempt to solve them. The book seemed to undercut the premises, as Myrdal had intended, of the claims for a neutral or "value-free" social science. That certainly was the inference drawn, but it was a false inference since Myrdal's work was carried out fairly and honestly. I do not think that his ideological bias, which is clear throughout the book, seriously affected his depiction of the problem, although it clearly affected his prescriptions for large-scale governmental intervention. Nevertheless, in part as a consequence of his identification of value-free social science with the support and justification of racial discrimination, many came to associate a disinterested or value-free social science with an indifference to social justice.

VI. An Assessment

In the twentieth-anniversary edition of *An American Dilemma*, Arnold Rose, who had contributed heavily to the initial volume, wrote: "We believe that the prognosis of twenty years ago has proved to be quite accurate." He went on to say that even though changes came about more rapidly than anticipated, "the changes have occurred without revolution, in harmony with the traditions of the American Creed. . . ."[66]

The events of the years immediately following World War II do indeed seem to have confirmed Myrdal's analysis of the American dilemma. His book helped in no small way to hasten the changes he prescribed. In many of the legal arguments over segregation in the South in the 1950s, Myrdal was regularly cited by integrationists as an authoritative source.[67] There can be no doubt that Myrdal's formulation of the problem as a white problem had in the popular mind replaced the older formulation locating the source of the problem in black behavior and black characteristics.

Writing in 1962, Rose mirrored the optimism among social scientists of the time when he noted that "[t]here could be no doubt that the races were moving rapidly toward equality and desegregation. . . ." He went on to note that racism and caste have been so "debilitated, that I venture to predict the end of all formal segregation and discrimination within a decade. . . ." He even predicted a decline of informal segregation and discrimination to the point where it would "be a mere shadow in two decades."[68]

Of course, three decades have passed since Rose wrote those words and no doubt they seem naively optimistic today. I think, however, that it would be a mistake to dismiss Rose's optimism, which was shared by many people at the time. Rose was, after all, quite accurate in his assessment of the changes that had taken place in the twenty years following World War II. Progress had been rapid and it had been real and substantial. In addition, it appeared that Myrdal's analysis had been basically sound. Segregation and discrimination *were* at variance with fundamental American values, and when confronted by the contradiction, Americans *did* respond positively. It should be recalled from Chapter 2 that blacks had made major economic and educational advances during these two decades.

In 1964, only two years after Rose wrote so optimistically, Congress passed the Civil Rights Act, which barred discrimination from wide areas of life. The act barred discrimination by schools and colleges, by employers and unions in their hiring practices, and barred segregation in public accommodations.

Furthermore, it put the full force of the federal government behind these strictures by depriving institutions, such as universities or hospitals, of federal funds if found in violation of the act. Moreover, the public generally supported this act and gave a landslide majority in the 1964 presidential election to Lyndon Johnson, who strongly supported the act, and ran against Barry Goldwater, who opposed it.[69] Goldwater was a maverick on this issue. The members of his own party, the Republicans, supported the bill by greater proportions in the House and Senate than did the Democrats. Eighty percent of the Republicans and 62 percent of the Democrats voted for the act in the House. In the Senate, 94 percent of the Republicans and 73 percent of the Democrats supported the act.[70]

In 1965, Congress passed the Voting Rights Act, which was designed to assure political equality for blacks. It made literacy tests illegal, required approval for any changes in voting laws, and made violations of the act criminal actions punishable by imprisonment.[71] The success of both of these acts has been undeniable. America appeared determined, one century after the Civil War, to rid itself completely of the taint of racial injustice.

Perhaps as instructive of the public mood of the time as these two acts was the passage of the Immigration Act of 1965, which eliminated the offensive racial bias which had guided immigration policy for decades.[72] In his important 1975 book *Affirmative Discrimination,* Harvard scholar Nathan Glazer noted that in the mid-sixties a new American consensus on ethnicity and race had been forged and cemented by these historical congressional actions. He stressed however that this consensus did not represent a break with the American past as some would have it, but was rather "the culmination of the development of a distinctive American orientation to ethnic difference and diversity with a history of almost 200 years."[73] By the mid-sixties what Myrdal had called the American creed seemed finally to have gained ascendance, at least for most Americans, over the human tendency of intolerance.

Of course, as Myrdal had expected, the changes he predicted and the policies he recommended did not come about without resistance. The decade and a half following the 1954 *Brown* decision barring segregated schooling was among the most tumultuous and divisive in American history.[74] There was tremendous resistance in the South to what many saw as the imposition of radical views designed to undermine "the southern way of life"—views which called to mind for many the hated Reconstruction era following the Civil War. Racial fears were easily inflamed in the South, and numerous white demagogues arose to take advantage of those fears.

Television demonstrated its power to shape public opinion, perhaps for the first time, with images of white southern policemen taking nightsticks to, and setting dogs upon, black and white protesters demanding simple equality of treatment for blacks. Ugly segregationists brandishing clubs stood in front of schools denying black children entry. Beatings and murders of protesters were not uncommon. Such images seared themselves into the conscience of a generation.

The net result was that by the mid-sixties few thoughtful people in America were prepared to attempt a serious justification for racial separation. Pockets of resistance remained, of course, but these seemed only to require what amounted to mopping-up operations. Skirmishes would continue, but the intellectual and legal war for racial justice seemed to have been won, and Myrdal's analysis seemed clearly to have been confirmed, at least by the mid-sixties.

Such is not, of course, the current social-science assessment, which is that the war against racism and intolerance is an ongoing struggle requiring ever-greater expenditures of effort. The continuing difficulties confronting blacks are offered as evidence for this view. And it is true that many of the problems facing blacks have gotten worse in the last three decades. Nevertheless, I think that Rose was right in his optimism and correct in his understanding and that the current orthodoxy is incorrect. There is no paradox here. What Myrdal and early civil rights advocates wanted had in fact been largely achieved by 1965, but civil rights advocates changed the goals, and these new goals had not, in fact could not have, been achieved by that time.

Myrdal had thought that government intervention in the economic and legal spheres would be necessary to provide blacks with the opportunities that would lead in time to greater equality among blacks and whites in the social sphere. Any fair reading of Myrdal, however, and especially his theory of cumulation and the vicious circle, makes clear that he thought of the process as a dynamic one involving considerable amounts of time.

What Myrdal had advocated toward the end of World War II had in most regards been achieved by 1965. Blacks could no longer be lawfully treated in a discriminatory fashion by the government, and anyone who denied blacks economic and educational opportunities had to face the threat of criminal and civil action. Discrimination in public conveyances and in restaurants and hotels had been made illegal. Thus, while many barriers to black advancement remained, the preconditions had been put in place that Myrdal thought would allow blacks to *begin* the process of demonstrating their true capacities and thus break the vicious circle.

In his analysis, prejudice would not disappear overnight, but would remain until blacks had begun to make the progress that the changed legal climate allowed. Myrdal did not refrain from making clear that there were many improvements in black life that would be required before a majority of whites saw them as social equals. Just as discrimination kept blacks in straitened circumstances, so did the "plane of living" of blacks reinforce the prejudices of whites: "The Negroes' poverty, ignorance, superstition, slum dwellings, health deficiencies, dirty appearance, disorderly conduct, bad odor and criminality stimulate and feed the antipathy of the whites for them." No one can read that sentence and imagine that Myrdal thought that changed social relations would occur quickly.[75]

Myrdal hoped that government action would break the stability of the vicious circle, a stability that had been maintained by "just enough prejudice on the part of whites to keep down the Negro plane of living to that level which maintains the specific degree of prejudice."[76] It had taken twenty years after the publication of *An American Dilemma* to dismantle the legal edifice which was the bulwark of southern segregation and discrimination. It was not until that task was done that blacks could begin the work of improving their lot, a task that in time would sunder the vicious circle.

What happened in the late 1960s was, in fact, that civil rights activists and their supporters in the social sciences abandoned Myrdal's analysis. They looked about them and saw that many blacks were still living in degraded circumstances and decided that not enough had been done. They misunderstood the fact that Myrdal's analysis required time for blacks to begin to acquire the skills and attitudes that would allow them to compete on an equal footing with whites. It might take blacks a generation or more to compete effectively with whites, much as it had taken pre–World War I immigrant groups a generation or more to begin to compete effectively with native-born Americans.

These critics of then current policies argued that black Americans had suffered long enough and demanded equality, *now.* They also tended to overlook or downplay the undeniable and truly substantial progress blacks had made, and were continuing to make, in the period after World War II.

It should also be pointed out that the late 1960s was an extremely turbulent time both politically and socially. The Vietnam War called more and more young men into battle as the decade wore on. Opposition to the war was bitter and furious. To many, especially students on university campuses, the war called into question many of the nation's institutions and values. Radical students demonstrated and rioted against almost any imposition of traditional authority.

In addition, new, more militant civil rights advocates appeared who demanded immediate racial justice and implied that failure to obtain such justice would result in violent reaction. These threats were not taken lightly in the wake of the urban riots that had broken out in numerous cities all over the country in the late sixties. Only days after the passage of the Voting Rights Act in 1965, a huge violent riot erupted in the predominantly black Watts section of Los Angeles. Between 1964 and 1968, there were an estimated "329 significant outbreaks in 257 cities."[77]

Martin Luther King was assassinated in the spring of 1968, and Robert Kennedy, closely identified with the civil rights movement, was killed later in that same year. Furthermore, in the late 1960s, court-ordered busing to integrate schools become a divisive issue bitterly opposed by many whites.[78]

Myrdal's original analysis assumed equality would come eventually with the equalization of opportunity, not concurrently; this point was explicit in his discussion of the vicious circle. By demanding that the two occur simultaneously, civil rights advocates were demanding what had before seemed an impossibility, and what was in fact an impossibility. The civil rights movement redefined social justice in terms of an immediate equality of outcome, whereas previously it had been defined in terms of equality of opportunity.

Under this new formulation, any existing inequalities between blacks and whites were characterized as evidence of a failure to achieve civil rights and as evidence of racial discrimination. In addition, as political commentators Thomas and Mary Edsall put it in their 1991 book *Chain Reaction*, "[t]he substantive content of racially significant legislation began . . . to change from a focus on civil rights to a focus on government-led efforts in behalf of blacks. . . ."[79] It is a main thesis of the present book that the change in goals of the civil rights advocates and their allies in the social sciences was a serious blow against black economic and social advancement. As I will outline in later chapters, it was this change that led to social policies which served to foster the social pathologies of crime, illegitimacy, and inadequate education that so seriously impede black economic betterment today.

The difficulty, in part, was that Myrdal had made the argument that the race problem was at its heart a white problem perhaps too well. Too many analysts misinterpreted any discussion of deficiencies in the black community as disagreement with Myrdal's overall thesis. In the next two chapters I will examine the origin of this faulty understanding and analyze the harm it has done. For now, it is enough to stress how erroneous it is to equate an examination of black weaknesses with a rejection of Myrdal's basic thesis.

Myrdal talked quite freely of the "degraded condition" of blacks and of their low "plane of living"—that is, their educational deficits, their failure to take entrepreneurial initiatives, their higher rates of crime and of illegitimacy, etc. True, he saw these problems as resulting from discrimination, but there is nothing in his book to suggest that he thought these problems would disappear immediately following an end of discrimination. Rather, his argument suggested that these problems would continue to plague blacks even given equal opportunities, though with time they would begin to decline as opportunity increased. Myrdal was too astute a social analyst to argue that the habits of mind and behavior that had existed for many generations, whatever the reasons they were taken on, could be discarded in an instant.

Let me close this chapter by saying that Gunnar Myrdal made a lasting and positive contribution to American society. He was right to argue that the race problem in America lay in the mistreatment of blacks by white Americans rather than in any peculiarities of black Americans themselves. Furthermore, the evidence to date supports his argument that black Americans will in time achieve economic and social parity if provided a level playing field. That there is still some distance to travel does not deny the fundamental validity of his position.

4

The Authoritarian Personality

I. Introduction

There can be no doubt as to the influence *An American Dilemma* had in shaping the way social scientists thought, and continue to think, about race relations. Another book that had a great influence on the way social scientists thought about race relations, especially in the fifties and sixties, was *The Authoritarian Personality*.[1] The book, commissioned by the American Jewish Committee at the end of World War II, was devoted to an examination of the origins of anti-Semitism and of prejudice in general. The Nazi genocide, waged by Germany, which had been among the most advanced nations of the world, shook Jews to their roots. The committee understandably hoped to gain a clearer understanding of anti-Semitism and, if possible, to discover how and why such irrational prejudices as existed against Jews and other minority groups originated and came to flourish.

The committee sponsored a collaborative research effort by T. W. Adorno, Else Frenkel-Brunswik, Daniel J. Levinson, and R. Nevitt Sanford that resulted in the publication of *The Authoritarian Personality* in 1950. Adorno was a philosopher who had been chairman of his department at the University of Frankfurt in pre-Nazi Germany; the other three were psychologists. Their massive research effort became the focus for much of the discussion about prejudice among psychologists and sociologists for the following two decades. The book generated enormous controversy and numerous critiques, some of which were devastating. Nevertheless, the authors of *The Authoritarian Personality* established a way of thinking about prejudice that is still influential today. Even Herbert Hyman and Paul Sheatsley, who in 1954 published the most thorough critique of the book, acknowledged that in "the recent annals of the social sciences," the book was rivaled by few other works "in scope, prestige and influence." They added that in the few years since its publication, it had "achieved the status of a classic in its field."[2]

II. The Validity of Questionnaires

Since much of the research to be reviewed in this and the following chapter is based on data obtained through the use of questionnaires, it is worthwhile to discuss some of the problems that can arise in this area. Questionnaires, broadly speaking, are used by social scientists for two different purposes. Most people are familiar with questionnaires used to obtain an estimate of public opinion on this or that matter. Election polling is the most well-known example of this sort, but the method is widely used for other purposes, such as in marketing research and to aid in the formulation of public policy. This type of data was reviewed in Chapter 2 in the discussion of white Americans' attitudes toward black Americans.

Questionnaires are also used by social scientists as a way of verifying hypotheses and finding correlations. Suppose, for example, one suspects that people who think there is much evidence for global warming are also likely to think that women should serve in combat roles in the military. There is no obvious logical reason why these beliefs should be correlated, but based on anecdotal evidence suppose one suspects that they are, and believes that the reason has to do with, let us say, a desire to conform to views popularly associated with television and movie celebrities. In order to test such a hypothesis, one would have to devise a questionnaire which would sample beliefs about global warming, about women in the military, and about what a person believes celebrities think on these issues. In addition, one would have to try to find a valid way of determining a person's motives, i.e., that he believes as he does out of a desire to conform. Such a questionnaire and its interpretation are likely to prove far more difficult than a simple questionnaire about a person's likely voting behavior.

The most obvious concern in the use of questionnaires is the need to assure a representative sample of the group whose attitude one wishes to assess. One can hardly make valid statements about *Americans*' attitudes toward some issue by asking the opinion of a hundred or so Harvard students, for reasons that I think are obvious. Samples must be fair and unbiased, which usually means they must be *random*. A random sample is defined technically as one in which all members of the group about which one seeks information have an equal likelihood to be polled, regardless of where they live or how easy or difficult it is to solicit their opinions. The U.S. Census bureau does an admirable job of gaining highly accurate information about Americans by strenuously assuring sample fairness. Census data are so accurate because the samples taken are very large. Smaller samples are of necessity less representative, but even relatively small samples, if fair, can give highly accurate information about large numbers of people. When political pollsters report their polling data, they usually also report a "margin of error" of two to five percentage points, which is determined by the size of the sample taken; smaller samples have larger margins of error.

A second problem that arises with the use of questionnaires is the need to assure that what one is trying to measure is in fact measured by the questions asked, i.e., that the questions are valid. Validity is rarely a problem when the question asked is, for instance, "At this moment in time, are you more inclined to vote for candidate A or candidate B?" However, when a question has social or psychological implications, many factors can have a biasing effect on the validity of a person's response. This is obvious if a researcher asks about a person's marital fidelity in the presence of the person's spouse. Likewise, the question "Do you think blacks have an unfair advantage because of affirmative action?" may receive different responses depending on whether the person doing the interview is black or white. Furthermore, many opinions may be widely known to be out of fashion or known to be considered socially offensive. Asking males on today's politically sensitive campuses whether they think females are as capable as males in all areas of endeavor may not elicit responses that reflect the respondents' true beliefs on the issue. Many other things, such as the order of questions, or information provided before a question is asked, can also bias responses to questionnaires.

In trying to overcome these problems, social scientists sometimes go to great lengths to gauge people's real beliefs, especially on sensitive issues. Sometimes they are quite successful in this attempt, sometimes, as we will see, they are widely off the mark. Errors along these lines can lead one to conclude that a hypothesis was confirmed when in fact no such confirmation was produced. In some of the cases we will examine in the following pages, the errors are so apparent and so serious that one suspects the researchers were led astray by an overzealous attachment to their theoretical beliefs.

III. The Primary Hypotheses of *The Authoritarian Personality*

The study whose findings were reported in *The Authoritarian Personality* was informed by psychoanalytic (Freudian) and Marxist theory, and reflected the professional and political backgrounds of the authors.[3] A primary assumption of the researchers was based in the Freudian belief that adult attitudes and prejudices are merely symptoms of larger personality dynamics.

In the Freudian model all adult thoughts and behaviors are, at base, expressions of unconscious impulses shaped by childhood experience. In the Freudian view a trait, such as excessive talkativeness, is always part of a larger syndrome, part of an integrated group of personality characteristics. Excessive talkativeness, for instance, was to be expected in those people known as "oral personality types," since their primary orientation toward life had been shaped or "fixated" during the oral stage of infancy.

Using this psychoanalytic theory, the authors of *The Authoritarian Personality* hypothesized that prejudice was never, or only rarely, merely an attitude, but was rather a personality trait that would almost always be correlated with other personality traits. These traits would, in turn, be correlated with a particular set of childhood experiences. The authors also hypothesized that the personality dynamics of the authoritarian personality would tend to drive him to the political right, toward politically conservative ideologies. In other words, the authors tried to demonstrate by their research that a conservative political orientation was correlated with ethnic and racial prejudice and that both had their origins in a particular type of upbringing.

It should be noted parenthetically that psychoanalytic theory was very much respected at the time, especially among intellectuals, though it certainly had its critics. It was, for instance, the dominant model in psychiatric training and practice, and in addition, was a powerful influence in the creative arts. Today, by contrast, psychoanalytic thinking is in decline and is far less influential than it was in the immediate aftermath of World War II.[4] The linkage of prejudice with conservatism was consistent with Marxist theory that at the time was not unpopular with American academics, the majority of whom took positions on the political left.[5] It should be recalled that Gunnar Myrdal was outspokenly on the left of the political spectrum, though not avowedly socialist or Marxist. The Marxist view on the political divisions of the time, a view shared by many academics, was that fascism, including Nazism, was an extreme form of capitalism and of free-market conservatism. Since Nazism was so obviously racist, it seemed reasonable to many that racism had its seeds in free-market conservatism, or so the authors of *The Authoritarian Personality* hypothesized.

According to Marxist theory, the capitalist ruling class would always tend to foster ethnic and nationalistic antagonisms in order to thwart the formation of a universal union of workers. The working classes, in this view, would have to shed their consciousness of national identity in order to see that their true adversaries were not the citizens of other nations, but were in fact the members of ruling economic elites within their own societies. If the workers of the world were to unite to forward their true class interests, they would first have to overcome the narrow confines of nationality in order to attack their real enemies in the ruling classes.[6] This universalism, according to Marxist theory, would be opposed by capitalists in their efforts to preserve their own class interest. In this way of thinking, the racism and anti-Semitism of the Nazi regime were not merely coincidental, but were essential to any fascist, i.e., extreme capitalist or conservative, movement.

There can be no doubt that the authors of *The Authoritarian Personality* saw things this way and believed that conservatism was inherently ethnocentric and racist. Many American social scientists agreed with them at the time, and many continue to do so. According to Adorno and his coauthors, "[t]here is good reason to believe that the 'right-left' dimension politically is correlated with ethnocentrism." They argued that fascism, which represented "the most extreme right-wing political and economic structure and ideology, is also the most virulent antidemocratic form of ethnocentrism." They went on to assert that "[t]here is considerable evidence suggesting a psychological affinity between conservatism and ethnocentrism. . . ."[7]

In contrast to their view of conservatism, the authors depicted "left-wing, socialistic ideology" as leading away from racism and ethnocentrism. They argued that the socialist program to eliminate economic class was a precondition for the "complete removal of stratification and outgroup exploitation."[8]

There can be no doubt, moreover, that the authors of *The Authoritarian Personality* believed that the essence of conservatism was a commitment to free-market economics. "Conservatism," the authors explained, "is taken to mean traditional economic laissez-faire individualism," in which economic competition is left unregulated by the state. The authors also noted that "[c]onservative ideology has traditionally urged that the economic functions of government be minimized . . . and great concern is expressed for the freedom of the individual, particularly the individual businessman."[9]

The authors made no attempt to hide their own ideological bias. They claimed, for instance, that the conservative attachment to economic freedom was at best naive, since the doctrine served to forward the interests of business "monopoly power." Elaborating on their view of free-market conservatism, they added: "This way of thinking assumes that the individual has 'freedom' economically to the extent that there are no government restrictions on him; it overlooks the fact that economic freedom for most people today is limited to the greatest degree by economic forces originating in business monopoly."[10]

In brief, it is clear that the authors of *The Authoritarian Personality* thought that racism was an essential element of fascism and that fascism, in turn, was rooted in free-market economics. From this analysis they concluded that those who support free-market capitalism were likely also to be prejudiced and racist, while those who adopted left-liberal ideas were likely to be free of prejudice.

The authors' position was seriously contradicted by the fact that at the time they wrote, poor southern whites were without question the most hostile of all

Americans to blacks, but generally quite liberal on economic matters. Political analysts Thomas and Mary Edsall wrote in their 1991 book on politics and race, *Chain Reaction,* that poor southern whites before the 1960s were "supportive of government intervention in behalf of full employment, improved education, and low-cost medical care. On these non-racial issues, the liberalism of poor white southerners in the 1950s was exceeded only by the nation's two most left-leaning constituencies, blacks and Jews. . . ."[11] It should also be pointed out that the white segregationist South had supported the Democratic party of Franklin Roosevelt and its left-of-center economic program.

The supposed linkage of economic conservatism with prejudice is so common in intellectual circles that it is easy to overlook many of the glaring weaknesses in the formulation. Ethnic prejudice and anti-Semitism have been around for a long time. To suggest that they arose as a byproduct of modern economic practices is to ignore the historical record. As I will attempt to demonstrate in later chapters, out-group hostility may in fact be a fundamental aspect of human nature, having its origins in human evolution.

Another clear problem is that the authors of *The Authoritarian Personality* made no serious attempt to differentiate economic free-market conservatism from, say, religious conservatism or social conservatism, even though these represent very different points of view. To suggest, as the authors do, that belief in the virtues of the free-market theories of Adam Smith is somehow related to racism seems to be stretching things somewhat.

The hallmark of fascism was its economic interventionism—evident, for instance, in the banning of independent labor unions and in government control of major industries—which renders its economic thinking much closer to communist ideology, and antithetical to the idea behind free-market capitalism.

It is well to recall that what we call free-market conservatism today was until recently referred to as "liberalism" and continues to be called "classical liberalism" by many. Classical liberalism was the philosophy that informed the American founding fathers and directed in large measure the construction of the American Constitution.[12] To lump together the classical liberalism of Washington and Jefferson with the Nazism of Hitler is hardly possible from any but a left-wing perspective that views all enemies of socialism as somehow friends and relatives of each other. It is difficult to escape the conclusion that in lumping together such antithetical forms of government as liberal democracy and fascist totalitarianism, Adorno and his coauthors adopted that narrow perspective.

The linkage of free-market conservatism with fascism and in turn with racism, common even today, is particularly unfortunate not only because it is unsubstantiated, as soon will become clear, but also because it wrongly imputes a racist taint to beliefs that are at the heart of American democracy. It is important to note that the view of fascism as an extreme form of free-market thinking was not universally accepted at the time. The contrary view, put forward most persuasively by Friedrich von Hayek in his 1944 book *The Road to Serfdom,* was that fascism was a form of statist absolutism, and therefore far more similar to communism. Both types of government went to great lengths to gain control over economic matters; both nationalized important industries and abolished free labor unions. Hayek emphasized that totalitarian regimes of both the left and the right abhor democracy and all its forms, not least of which is the freedom to exchange one's goods and services in an open market at a price freely negotiated. Free-market capitalism was therefore, according to Hayek, the natural enemy of communism *and* of fascism.[13]

The failure to see the similarity in all totalitarian movements and their common rejection of democracy was also the topic of philosopher Karl Popper's justly famous *The Open Society and Its Enemies,* first published in 1945. Popper traced the roots and philosophic legitimation of twentieth-century absolutist and antidemocratic thinking to G. W. F. Hegel, whose ideas Popper in turn traced to the utopian vision of the state put forward in Plato's *Republic.* Popper said of both Plato and Hegel that "[t]heir doctrine is that the state is everything, and the individual nothing; for [the individual] owes everything to the state, his physical as well as his spiritual existence."[14] Hegel spurned the idea of simple representative democracy. Instead, he thought that the true interests of any people could only be grasped by heroic "world historical men" who alone had "insight into the requirements of the time," and of those things "ripe for development." Only truly heroic figures could fathom what was true and important for "their age, for their world," or as Hegel put it, for "the species next in order, so to speak."[15] Marx and his communist followers never denied their debt to Hegel's antidemocratic, statist thinking. But Hegel is equally important to the ideas of Nazism and fascism. Who can seriously doubt that Hitler and Mussolini, along with Stalin, reckoned themselves truly "world historical men"? Nor is it possible to doubt that they could justify their brutal methods on the basis of Hegel's defense of heroic types, who, in acting out the great impulses of their age and people, need not be restrained by moral and legal niceties. According to Hegel, it will be necessary for "such men to treat other greater, even sacred interests, inconsiderately," and to engage in "conduct which is indeed obnoxious to moral reprehension [*sic*]" and crush "to pieces many an object in [their] path."[16]

The authors of *The Authoritarian Personality* also failed to acknowledge that it was Winston Churchill, a British conservative, who most ardently opposed Nazism. Indeed, without Churchill's leadership and his passionate hatred for the Nazi regime, it is not unreasonable to suppose that the continent of Europe would be, to this day, ruled by the followers of Hitler. There was never any hint that Churchill would arrive at an accommodation with Hitler as Stalin arranged to do, an arrangement that led directly to the outbreak of World War II.

Perhaps as questionable as *The Authoritarian Personality*'s linkage of fascism with free-market economics was the book's assertion of a necessary association between fascism and racism. This linkage is so generally held, especially by academics, that it is common for those who champion capitalism to be labeled fascists by their opponents and, as a result, to be branded as racists almost by definition. As we will see, this charge continues to be made and forms the underpinning for more-recent assertions linking racism with traditional American values, assertions that will be explored in Chapter 5. For that reason, it is, I think, worth a digression to explore more fully the soundness of this association.

The linkage of anti-Semitism with fascism was seriously contradicted by the historical facts of the Italian, Spanish, and Portuguese fascist regimes. Spain and Portugal never elevated anti-Semitism to state policy, and Spain remained a refuge for Jews throughout the war.[17]

Don Vittorio Segre describes in his *Memoirs of a Fortunate Jew* (1987) his experience as an upper-class Italian Jew growing up in fascist Italy. He was born in 1922, a month after Mussolini's ascension to power. He explains that he grew up in an assimilated Jewish family surrounded by Jewish friends who approved of the fascist regime "without reservation." In reflecting on those years, he explains:

> I do not remember, either in school or outside, one single occasion when I felt uneasy because I was a Jew. I was convinced that being Jewish was a treat no different from Cirio brand marmalade, the more so because I was the constant object of jealousy among my school friends for being allowed "for religious reasons" to be absent from the boring lessons of the Gymnasium priest.[18]

I doubt that many American Jews born in the United States in 1922 could have made such a statement. Fascism was indeed an unpleasant and antidemocratic movement, but in three of the four countries where it came to power before World War II, anti-Semitism was in no sense crucial to its ideology.

The point of the above is not to defend fascism or to deny the xenophobic and ethnocentric elements it contained, but to emphasize the point that as a movement it was not, except among the German Nazis, uniquely vicious or genocidal in its ethnocentrism. The use of mass ethnic deportation and mass slaughter for political ends is a commonplace of the twentieth century. Stalin's death camps were filled with ethnic as well as political opponents, and anti-Semitism played a prominent role in his many bloody purges. Genocidal slaughter neither originated nor ended with World War II, and it is taking place with particular virulence in Eastern Europe as I write.

Demagogues everywhere and in all periods of history have resorted to xenophobia and ethnic animosity in their attempts to gain power. Right-wing demagogues almost always appeal to national chauvinism and often appeal to racial and ethnic chauvinism as well. Left-wing demagogues appeal to class antagonism, and sometimes religious intolerance. The twentieth century could aptly be called a golden age of demagoguery. But demagoguery is the enemy of liberal democracy and bears no relation whatsoever to the principles of free-market capitalism—principles which, on theoretical and practical grounds, tend to break down national and ethnic barriers and favor the free flow of labor across national borders.

IV. Research Methods and Main Results

The research undertaken by the authors of *The Authoritarian Personality* involved the use of questionnaires and, to a more limited extent, intensive personal interviews. The results of the study appeared to confirm the authors' thesis. Prejudice did appear to be part of a personality pattern. Prejudice toward one out-group was generally associated with prejudice toward all out-groups. In the authors' samples, if someone was anti-Semitic, for instance, he was also likely to be anti-black, anti-Asian, etc.[19] In addition, the results suggested that prejudiced people, at least in the samples surveyed, were likely to hold conventional beliefs and to take conservative stands on political, economic, and social issues.[20] In their famous F-scale (Fascism scale), the researchers discovered that prejudiced people were generally intolerant of differences and seemed to admire toughness and power, especially in leaders. Adorno and his coauthors saw such feelings as "anti-democratic" and "proto-Fascist."[21] An important additional finding was a negative correlation of authoritarianism with IQ and educational attainment. In other words, less intelligent and less well-educated people tended to score higher on measures of authoritarianism.[22]

The authors concluded that the correlation of such traits was not accidental and that there was in fact a personality type, which they labeled the "authoritarian personality," whose characteristics included a generalized prejudice toward out-groups, a general tendency to eschew tolerant values, and a tendency to take politically conservative and socially conventional positions. This conclusion was of course perfectly consistent with their original hypotheses.

In their attempt to explain the psychological formation of this personality type, the researchers utilized the psychoanalytic method of the intensive (depth) interview and also such things as projective tests like the Thematic Apperception Test (a test in which the subject must explain the meaning of an intentionally ambiguous drawing). Their main conclusion from this aspect of their work was that authoritarianism resulted from a particularly repressive upbringing not uncommon in the homes of lower-middle-class people. The parents in such homes, having achieved only modest economic success, were extremely status conscious and insecure in their social position. This insecurity, the researchers reasoned, led them to be overly concerned that they and their children make an acceptable presentation of themselves to their social betters, and turn a cold eye on their lessers. Such parents were likely to place a premium on conventional behavior and to be anxious to keep a safe distance from those beneath them, lest they draw attention to the precarious nature of their own economic and social position. For children to make friends from the ''wrong side of the tracks'' was threatening and unacceptable. Discipline in such homes was likely to be harsh and often unreasonable.[23]

Such upbringing, according to the authors, creates a good deal of hostility in children that cannot be expressed toward the parents. The child therefore represses and effectively denies the hostility and displaces it onto those he has learned are deserving of contempt. Typically these are members of groups whose behavior, or ethnicity or religion, differs from his own. The child will also attempt to placate his parents by adopting their, typically conventional, social and political values. In general, the authoritarian will feel uncomfortable with openness to differences and somewhat hostile toward democratic pluralism. Furthermore, in idealizing his parents, the authoritarian will come to admire the value of stern discipline—an attitude that translates into admiration for political leaders and political programs that stress the virtues of discipline and power.[24] By the time such a person reaches adulthood, he will have become a prime candidate for recruitment into fascist political parties or similarly motivated enterprises such as the Ku Klux Klan.

In sum, the researchers had discovered the ''redneck'' type and saw in him the prototypical racist. He was uneducated, was conservative in his politics, and hated all those who differed from himself. Using the Freudian model and Freudian research techniques, the researchers developed a model of an individual (the authoritarian) whose upbringing has created powerful, but unconscious, hostilities that he projects onto scapegoated groups who are weaker than himself. The authoritarian racist, in turn, rationalizes his anger by finding good reasons for his hostility in the flaws of the other—blaming the victim, as it were.

To give an indication of the way the authors' political views tended to color their interpretations, consider the way they treated the anti-labor sentiment they found among their subjects. It should be pointed out that there were a number of serious union strikes during World War II that led to congressional acts limiting the rights of unions.[25] Many people with sons and husbands in the military could easily have become antagonistic toward unions which appeared to be taking advantage of the labor shortages brought on by the war. When unions engaged in work stoppages in industries important for the war effort, it was easy for many to see such actions as unpatriotic. It should also be stressed that there was concern at the time, which subsequently proved well-founded, with the infiltration of unions by organized crime.

The authors thought such concerns misguided and pointed out rather condescendingly that people who expressed concern with unions seemed untroubled by "industrial monopolies and their pricing agreements," though they failed to cite examples of such industrial practices. They equated a concern with "labor racketeering" with beliefs in "Jewish clannishness." Both are, in the authors' view, traceable to "the lack of an adequately internalized identification with paternal authority during the Oedipus situation." They argue that such people "fear the father and try to side with him in order to participate in his power." In this view the "racketeers" (always enclosed in scare quotes, by the way) demand too much and may therefore arouse the father's anger "and hence the subject's castration anxiety." According to Adorno and his coauthors, in the mind of such a neurotic personality, "workers become 'racketeers,' [i.e.,] criminals . . . as soon as they organize."[26]

In other words, a perfectly legitimate concern about the influence of organized crime was viewed as siding with the father (big business) against the underdog (the workers) out of neurotic fear (the fear of castration). The subjects were then said to rationalize their craven attack on the underdog by defining him as a criminal worthy of attack. Perhaps without realizing it, the authors had demeaned (in classic *ad hominem* fashion) the motives of people who held political attitudes with which they disagreed. Similar lapses, as we will see, occur regularly in the literature on racial attitudes. William Ryan's theory of victim-blaming, discussed earlier in Chapter 1, is merely a more recent example of this tendency.[27]

V. Problems with the Theory

While there are undoubtedly such "redneck" or authoritarian types in the world, as a general theory of racism there is much to criticize in the analysis of *The Authoritarian Personality*. First, it relies very heavily upon the Freudian model, whose validity has in recent years come under heavy criticism, especially in studies on the healing powers of psychoanalysis.[28] Second, it is hard to see how the authors' depiction was more valuable than the everyday explanation of lower-class prejudice. In the common-sense view, lower-class, poorly educated individuals adopt the values and attitudes common among their peers, among which is often a general animosity toward out-groups, an acceptance of physical violence, and rather conventional views of morality. This was true of poor, uneducated people in the thirties and forties and is just as true today. Furthermore, as the respected psychologist Thomas Pettigrew has pointed out, the theory is not particularly useful in explaining prejudice when it is nearly universal, as it was in the South.[29] It was simply unreasonable to assume that most people in the South, no matter what their social background, would have been of the same neurotic personality type, a type thought to derive from growing up in marginal economic circumstances.

Within a few years of its publication, *The Authoritarian Personality* came in for rather pointed criticism, some of which I will review shortly. However, for many years its basic thesis was considered sound. For example, Harvard psychologist Roger Brown, in the highly regarded 1965 edition of his text *Social Psychology,* devoted a seventy-page chapter to a discussion of authoritarianism, a chapter which, though critical, suggested that the linkage of conservatism with prejudice had been reasonably well demonstrated. In that text, which was widely used in the sixties and seventies in the education of both graduate and undergraduate students, Brown was able to say about *The Authoritarian Personality* that "the theory of prejudice it propounded has become part of popular culture and a force against discrimination."[30] A measure of the extent to which the thesis has fallen into disfavor is the fact that in the revised 1986 second edition of the text, Brown devotes not one word of explanation to the topic of authoritarianism. (He mentions it only once, suggests that it might explain some "extreme" cases of prejudice, and refers the reader to the earlier edition for a full discussion.)[31] Similarly, the highly respected and much honored psychologist Ernest R. Hilgard, a past president of the American Psychological Association, did not even cite *The Authoritarian Personality* in his authoritative 1987 text *Psychology in America: A Historical Survey.* This is surprising, since Hilgard covers the field of social psychology during the 1940s and 1950s in the book and was at one time chairman of the Society for the Psychological Study of Social Issues, a group that over the years has been particularly concerned with issues relating to racial prejudice.[32]

While it would be impossible to give the full flavor of the various critiques that over time have consigned the theory of authoritarianism to near oblivion, I think it is important to examine some of the evidence regarding the hypothesized relationship between prejudice and free-market conservatism, insofar as that association has continued to influence thinking in the social sciences. It is also important to examine the kinds of errors that can creep into questionnaire studies, as these same problems will crop up in Chapter 5, where I examine more-recent questionnaire research.

In the main, the researchers of *The Authoritarian Personality* depended on the use of an extended questionnaire that included four parts or "subscales" designed to measure ethnocentrism, anti-Semitism, authoritarian or fascistic tendencies (the F-scale), and political-economic conservatism.

One problem noted in the oft-cited critique by Herbert Hyman and Paul Sheatsley was the lack of representativeness in the sample of people who were surveyed.[33] In order to facilitate the collection of data, the researchers did not take random samples, but utilized existing groups of people who belonged to organizations (such as unions and the Kiwanis and Rotary clubs), or who were in prison, were patients in a psychiatric clinic, or were attending classes of one sort or another. Almost all the subjects were from the San Francisco area, most were middle class, and most were young, "the bulk falling between twenty and thirty-five."[34] This sampling bias means that it is just about impossible to meaningfully generalize the research findings to Americans at large.

There were serious problems with the subscales used in the questionnaire. In the final version they were quite short, consisting of five to ten questions. In many cases the items included in the questionnaire were ambiguous or seem unrelated to what was supposed to have been measured.

For example, the questionnaire designed to measure ethnocentrism asked for agreement or disagreement with the following statement: "The worst dangers to real Americanism during the last fifty years came from foreign ideas and agitators." Another item included was: "If and when a new world organization is set up, America must be sure that she loses none of her independence and complete powers in matters that affect this country."[35] Both of these questions tap political orientation far more than they do anti-Semitic or anti-black feelings. At the time, conservatives and liberals differed significantly on how much authority they felt should be delegated to world tribunals such as the League of Nations or the new United Nations. Likewise, to characterize as ethnocentric those people who, in the late 1940s, thought that foreign ideas and agitators threatened American values seems odd, especially in light of the havoc wrought in Europe by the European ideologies of fascism and communism. It seems more reasonable to think of such people, at least many of them, as having been level-headed realists who were committed to traditional American pluralism and recognized the dangers posed by extreme ideologies to America's political culture. Of course, given the widespread revulsion toward fascism at the time, the only foreign ideology competing with traditional American values was socialism, which was far more likely to have been perceived as a threat by conservatives than by liberals.

A person's political orientation was more likely to determine his response to these questions than his attitudes toward Jews or blacks. Since people scored higher on the scale of ethnocentrism for agreeing with these statements, people would likely be scored as ''ethnocentric,'' especially on the shorter five-item version, for merely expressing conservative views. In other words, the ethnocentrism scale confounded political views with intolerant views.

This might not have been so severe a problem had the other questions been more robust in distinguishing ethnocentric types from more tolerant people. However, the responses people made to these questions suggest that the questions were not robust in that sense, perhaps because they were so transparent.[36] This is reflected in the fact that the range of responses from people in widely different groups was very limited, with most groups coming out as mildly tolerant. Given the very narrow range of the responses, the political items could have had the effect of determining the overall outcome, even though these items were not reflective of anti-black and anti-Semitic attitudes.[37]

Another major problem in the study which was highlighted in the critique by Hyman and Sheatsley is the failure to control for education and intelligence, both of which were found to be related to ethnocentric feelings. People with greater education seem to be less hostile to minority groups than are people with less education, or, and this caveat must be entered, they may be less willing to express such hostile attitudes. Hyman and Sheatsley criticize the authors, and rightly, for failing to control for this factor. Without such control, all Adorno and his colleagues may have measured in the ethnocentrism scale was a lack of social sophistication.[38] This interpretation is given added weight by the fact that the most ethnocentric score among all groups was found for the 110 San Quentin prison inmates. Perhaps such types are unaware that it is not nice to express anti-Semitic and racist sentiments. Perhaps they know, but don't care, i.e., are antisocial.

The scale designed to measure conservatism was equally troublesome. Conservatives were characterized as people who supported the American values of individualism and free-market capitalism, who admired economic success, who disliked socialism, and who were not enamored of Roosevelt's New Deal policies. This is not an unfair representation of conservative views in the late 1940s. The problem was in the way the researchers assessed these views. The scale was heavily weighted with items dealing with attitudes toward labor unions and business. The scale seems to have been designed to discriminate between those of a rather extreme pro-union, anti-business orientation and those who held the more moderate attitudes shared by most people at the time.

Some of the items were ambiguous, which was a serious problem given that the scale contained only five items in most cases. One item on the questionnaire asked for agreement or disagreement with the following statement: ''America may not be perfect, but the American way has brought us about as close as human beings can get to a perfect society.'' Another asked for agreement or disagreement with this statement: "Men like Henry Ford or J. P. Morgan, who overcame all competition on the road to success, are models for all young people to admire and imitate."[39] What does agreement or disagreement with these items imply? Marxists obviously would disagree with them, but would the typical moderate or liberal person do so in the immediate postwar period? Does moderate agreement with the first item indicate that the respondent thinks America is perfect or merely better than the existing alternatives? Is admiring successful people something only conservatives do?

The results for the various groups who were given the questionnaire seemed to reflect the ambiguity of the items. Contrary to expectation, samples of middle-class men and women, and samples taken from universities (where one would expect to find liberal views), were all classified as moderately conservative by the scale. Working class men and women, by contrast, turned out to be the least conservative, contrary to the researchers' hypothesis that lower-class backgrounds were likely to produce conservatives. The authors explained this anomaly by pointing out that half the subjects in these groups were from "the United Electrical Workers (C.I.O.), a militant union, or from the California Labor School, a strongly left-wing institution."[40] The second most conservative group turned out to be inmates serving time at San Quentin Penitentiary, not exactly your better-business-bureau types. The authors explained: "The criminal does not oppose the principles of rugged individualism; he simply carries them *ad absurdum.*"[41]

Some of these problems become acute when one tries to interpret the correlations between scales. Since the ethnocentrism scale included items with clear political content, it was almost guaranteed that this measure of ethnocentrism would, in part, reflect political beliefs, and therefore would correlate with any scale of political belief, including the authors' own scale of political conservatism. If two questionnaires contain overlapping content in the items used, they will of necessity tend to correlate with each other.

This problem of overlapping scales becomes especially serious when one attempts to interpret the correlations that were reported. For instance, a number of the groups polled were generally conservative, while others were decidedly on the left of the political spectrum. If people from both groups responded identically to all questions except for those with political content, the result would have been to cast the liberal groups as tolerant and the conservative groups as ethnocentric.

Hyman and Sheatsley criticize Adorno et al. severely on these grounds. They argue that "the actual content of the scales is given little regard, while many pages of text and tables are devoted to statistical means, rank order correlations . . . etc." Hyman and Sheatsley make the obvious point that one can develop "a hundred different questionnaires" and one can "give them the same name . . . but an inspection of the contents is really the only way to know just what it is that one is measuring."[42]

An additional factor forcing a correlation between the scales was the fact that the authors began the study using much longer scales and then reduced their size in order to keep the overall questionnaire at a reasonable length. Good science would have required that the abbreviated scales be highly correlated with the longer original versions. Furthermore, care would have had to be taken to assure that in eliminating items, one did not retain only those that showed high correlations with other scales, for that would have in effect forced even higher correlations.

In most cases the shortening process proceeded in a manner exactly the opposite of that required by good science. Hyman and Sheatsley point out that in the construction of the F-scale of authoritarianism, there were three items that were "very good measures of personality on the F scale" which were dropped because they did not correlate with anti-Semitism. Likewise, "[f]our other items which were found to correlate highly with anti-semitism were retained in the scale, even though they were poor measures of the larger personality dimension which was being tapped." Hyman and Sheatsley charge that the F-scale that emerged contained items that "are employed to provide evidence of the theory in spite of the fact that they are among the least appropriate as measures of authoritarianism."[43]

One could go on into the other serious problems with the study, but it is enough to point out that over the years most of the research on authoritarianism has discredited the thesis or shown it to be irrelevant to most instances of racial animosity. Just about all the main tenets of the study were critiqued and effectively rebutted over the decades following its publication. Nevertheless, as is often the case in such matters, the general public, and many social scientists, were never exposed to these devastating critiques, many of which involved fairly technical concerns with sampling, questionnaire construction, interviewing techniques, etc. The upshot was that *The Authoritarian Personality* continued to influence popular opinion long after it had been discarded as irrelevant by those professional social scientists most familiar with the research. In addition, the characterization of free-market thinking as a sort of mental defect continued to remain popular among social scientists. In the 1962 edition of the popular social psychology text *The Individual in Society,* by David Krech, Richard Crutchfield, and Egerton Ballachey, the authors devoted considerable space to a study of political conservatism published by Herbert McCloskey in 1958 during the Republican administration of Dwight Eisenhower.[44] They reported that "[o]ne of the clearest findings is that conservatism is not the political doctrine of the intellectual elite. On the contrary . . . conservative attitudes tend to characterize the uninformed, the poorly educated, and the unintelligent."[45] The authors go on to quote McCloskey, whose views mirror those expressed in *The Authoritarian Personality.* Some of the flavor of those quotations follows:

> Conservatism, in our society at least, appears to be far more characteristic of social isolates, of people who think poorly of themselves, who suffer personal disgruntlement and frustration, who are submissive, timid and wanting in confidence, who lack a clear sense of direction and purpose, who are uncertain about their values, and who are generally bewildered by the alarming task of having to thread their way through a society which seems to them too complex to fathom.[46]

In case their college readers have failed to understand the true nature of people with conservative views, the authors go on to quote McCloskey further:

> The extreme conservatives are easily the most hostile and suspicious, the most rigid and compulsive, the quickest to condemn others for their imperfections or weaknesses, the most intolerant, the most easily moved to scorn and disappointment in others, the most inflexible and unyielding in their perceptions and judgments. . . . Poorly integrated psychologically, anxious, often perceiving themselves as inadequate, and subject to excessive feelings of guilt, they seem inclined to project onto others the traits they most dislike or fear in themselves.[47]

In this attack on conservative beliefs, beliefs that many Americans would have at the time readily endorsed, the authors evidenced not a hint of irony in the fact that this almost comically stereotyped view of conservatism is surrounded by chapters discussing the dangers of stereotypes. That such a text was widely used in the 1960s in classrooms goes a long way in explaining the lack of balance in the views of many students educated then, and to some extent, of many educated since. How could a self-respecting college student admit to holding conservative beliefs in light of this devastating portrait? Who would possibly come to his defense? For those who think ''political correctness'' is a new phenomenon on campus, the passages quoted above are instructive. Within the social sciences, at least, political correctness has been with us for quite a while. In addition, the view of free-market conservatives as moral cretins continues to influence opinion among social scientists and academics even today.

The ideological bias of social scientists was not merely displayed by their tendency to disparage those with conservative beliefs, but also influenced their characterization of those with liberal orientations. Throughout the sixties and seventies, liberal student activists were seen as representing the very highest levels of moral and psychological development. In their 1982 book *Roots of Radicalism,* political scientists Stanley Rothman and S. Robert Lichter reviewed a host of studies done in the 1960s and early 1970s which purported to demonstrate the moral and psychological health of those holding left-wing views. Rothman and Lichter demonstrate that the bulk of these studies exhibited the same sort of biases and flaws which marred the research upon which *The Authoritarian Personality* was based. In explaining the bias in this body of research, Rothman and Lichter make a convincing case that it was

> far less a matter of conscious distortion than of adherence to a shared sociopolitical paradigm that has influenced both research on radical students and the reception accorded research findings. The instruments and research methods that produced the mass of data were "contaminated" by the sociopolitical perspective of liberal social science. Moreover, findings were often accepted somewhat uncritically, because they conformed to expectations generated by this same perspective.[48]

Unfortunately, the bias that Rothman and Lichter outline continues to influence almost all attempts to study political attitudes in America; this will become very clear in the chapter which follows.

VI. Conclusion

Prior to World War II, what I have called the traditional view of prejudice prevailed. Beliefs about groups were often seen as erroneous or as overgeneralizations, but such beliefs were also thought to have some basis in fact. Even Myrdal suggested that many of the beliefs whites held about blacks were, at least in part, true. Myrdal's principle of the "vicious circle" clearly suggested that prejudicial attitudes were both causes and effects of problematic black behavior. Nevertheless, while Myrdal did not deny that some of the stereotypes held about blacks were based in reality, his efforts were almost completely directed toward demonstrating how that reality was shaped by white attitudes. By the 1950s and 1960s, however, largely as a result of the views put forward in *The Authoritarian Personality,* beliefs about minority groups had come to be seen as almost singularly irrational and without any basis in facts or real circumstances. The argument that one held a negative opinion about a group because of some real characteristic common to many people in the group was dismissed as mere neurotic denial. At the time, it appeared obvious, for instance, that pointing to deficiencies in black social behavior was merely an attempt to justify continued prejudice and discrimination. In other words, any analysis of black problems which might locate the source of those problems in black attitudes or cultural practices was seen as an attempt to absolve white racists.

As a consequence, no serious attempt to understand the dynamics of black poverty and high rates of crime, to take obvious examples, which did not attribute such problems to white discrimination, was ever taken seriously. A case in point was the reception given to the famous "Moynihan Report" published in 1965. Daniel P. Moynihan, currently the Democratic senator representing New York, was at the time a Harvard sociologist on leave and working in the Johnson Administration. He wrote a policy paper in which he addressed the issue of the growing instability among black families, arguing that this trend would likely undercut the attempts being made to promote the economic advancement of blacks, and suggesting that the government undertake efforts to strengthen black families. Moynihan was immediately and almost unanimously condemned for unfairly blaming blacks for the problems brought on by American racism. The Moynihan Report, as it came to be known, was characterized as a slanderous and racist attempt to blame the black victims of racism for their difficulties. Moynihan was merely "blaming the victim" to use William Ryan's oft-quoted phrase, and in so doing exposed his own racist frame of mind.[49]

The bitter attacks on Moynihan that followed the release of the report stifled almost any further attempts to address the troublesome behavioral patterns common among blacks. It was not until the late 1980s that blacks and those who were thought sympathetic to their cause felt free to once again examine the issue of family instability.[50] The pity, of course, is that during that twenty-year hiatus, the problem had grown far more severe than it had been when first addressed by Moynihan. As reported in Chapter 2, black illegitimacy, which stood at about 25 percent in the late sixties, had risen to over 60 percent by the late eighties.

The new way of thinking about prejudice popularized by the authors of *The Authoritarian Personality* had other unfortunate consequences for political and scientific discourse. Conservative political ideas, especially those associated with a commitment to free-market economics, became suspect as indicative of unkind and potentially racist tendencies. This association of free-market economics with racism is without foundation, but has nevertheless had an important influence on subsequent social science thinking and the public policies derived from that thinking. In the next chapter, I will explore this association further and see how it still serves as a basis for social-psychological research claiming that fundamental American values, especially those related to free-market thinking, are really a cloak for anti-black sentiments.

5

Racism and Traditional American Values

I. Introduction

Gunnar Myrdal's thesis that the racial prejudices of white Americans are the primary cause of the problems confronting black Americans continues to dominate debate on race relations. If this understanding, certainly correct at the time when it was formulated by Myrdal, is no longer sound, its continued endorsement only serves to block the development of alternative and more realistic explanations upon which to base social policy. A good deal of research effort, for instance, is devoted to finding the causes of white prejudice, a task that may not be very useful if whatever prejudice remains among whites is relatively unimportant for an understanding of black difficulties.

This is well illustrated by recent research in social psychology that follows the logic of *The Authoritarian Personality* in attempting to link prejudice with adherence to free-market and other traditional American values. This research tries to show that the traditional values of individualism and self-reliance, for example, are mainly a cloak for prejudice and are used to justify opposition to policies designed to promote racial equality.

People who express disagreement with affirmative action policies favoring minorities in university admissions, for instance, and who justify their objections on the basis of a commitment to the American values of self-reliance and equal treatment, are said to use those traditional values as a disguise for opposition to equality. This new understanding, ironically, turns Myrdal's thesis on its head. Myrdal argued that a true commitment to America's traditional values was the best antidote to discrimination against blacks. Today those selfsame traditional values are said to be the primary hindrance to racial equality.

As I argued earlier, the original agenda of the civil rights movement, at least those aspects which could be effected in the legal and legislative spheres, had been achieved by the late 1960s. At that point, civil rights activists and their social science allies drastically redefined their goals, calling for an immediate equality of outcome for blacks in all areas of life, and they attributed the failure to achieve immediate equality to a continuing racism on the part of whites. It was this new definition of civil rights which justified almost all the affirmative action policies that have been adopted in the name of civil rights since the early 1970s.

II. Affirmative Action: Equal Opportunity versus Preferential Treatment

Since the research to be reviewed in the following pages relies so heavily on the attitudes of whites toward affirmative action policies, it is important to review briefly the evolution of those policies in recent years. Affirmative action as originally propounded in the 1960s involved attempting to assure that blacks received, in practice, the equal opportunities that the various civil rights acts required by law. To take "affirmative action" meant, therefore, that colleges and employers would have to show that they were actively recruiting blacks who might not otherwise be aware of opportunities or who might think that they would be excluded because of their race. It was not until the early seventies that affirmative action become associated with the idea of specific goals and timetables for achieving fair representation of blacks in major American institutions.[1]

An immediate problem arose, however, in the question of how to define a "fair" representation of blacks and other minorities. Most white Americans assumed that as long as the procedures in college admissions, hiring, and job promotion were fair and free of bias, the resulting representation of blacks was fair, almost by definition, whatever the actual proportion of blacks that resulted. Others, including civil rights activists, many social scientists, and many government bureaucrats, thought differently. They argued that since blacks and whites are inherently equal in abilities and motivation, blacks ought to be, if the process were truly fair and free of bias, represented in all institutions in the same or nearly the same proportion as they are represented in the population at large. From this reasoning, it followed that any major deviation from proportional representation was evidence, on its face, of discrimination. This became the official policy of the federal agencies that monitored and enforced the civil rights laws. The United States Supreme Court endorsed this view in its 1971 decision in *Griggs v. Duke Power Company*. The Court ruled that any procedure or test that had a "disparate impact" (meaning a substantial deviation from proportional representation) on minority groups was, on its face, evidence of discrimination. The Court put the burden of proving otherwise on the employer in such "disparate impact" cases.[2]

Throughout the 1970s and 1980s, the logic of proportional representation began to shape a host of practices in numerous institutions. School busing programs were required by courts in many cities to attempt to assure proportional representation in public schools. Universities heavily recruited black students and faculty in an attempt to increase their numbers, and in many cases lower standards were set for black and minority students than were set for white students. Government and private employers altered their hiring practices for similar reasons. Municipal governments initiated set-aside programs to increase the percentage of government contracts going to minority-owned businesses. Tests in which blacks and other minorities did not perform as well as whites were revised or eliminated.[3]

The justification for many of these policies was challenged for a variety of reasons, not least of which was that, given the history of discrimination against blacks, it was unreasonable to expect them to achieve parity with whites as quickly as advocates of proportional representation thought proper. In addition, differences in schooling, motivation, and cultural practices might easily produce major deviations from proportional representation. The fact that blacks are less likely to study advanced mathematics than are whites, for instance, means that they are unlikely to be well represented in scientific and technical fields requiring expertise in math. The same is true whenever average black academic interests or performance differs from the average for whites.

Many opposed these affirmative action programs because they seemed unfair. Why, they asked, should a young white male born in Boston, for instance, be asked to step aside in favor of a black person born in that same city in order to rectify wrongs committed in the South by whites decades ago? Others objected to these policies because they believed that they undercut critical values like the work ethic which they thought were crucial to America's economic well-being. Still others objected on the grounds that these policies involved very heavy federal involvement in what many viewed as local affairs.

In 1989, under the urgings of the Reagan Administration, the issue of disparate impact came before the Supreme Court in *Wards Cove Packing Company, Inc. v. Atonio*. The Court ruled in favor, broadly, of those who opposed proportional representation or the use of quotas in hiring and admissions.[4] The Court's decision shifted the burden of proof so that those who claimed discrimination, were required thereafter to show which procedures or practices were discriminatory and caused them harm. Prior practice, following the 1971 *Griggs* decision, had placed the burden of proof on the defendant; employers, for instance, had to prove that deviation from proportionality was not caused by their procedures and practices. In *Wards Cove* the burden was placed on those who claimed the disparate impact resulted from discrimination. The Court had also, in *City of Richmond v. J. A. Croson Company* (1989), placed restrictions on the use of minority set-asides, and had made other decisions to limit the scope of affirmative action policies.[5]

In the Civil Rights Act of 1991, Congress wrote legislation that returned things to their earlier state, at least in disparate-impact cases, by placing the burden of proof once again on employers, universities, etc., who must, under the provisions of the act, prove the absence of discrimination when disputes arise. The opponents of this bill argued that it was in effect a quota bill, since employers would be tempted to hire minority group members simply to avoid civil rights litigation. They pointed out—correctly, I think—that it is almost impossible to prove the absence of something and that forcing employers to prove an absence of discrimination is an almost impossibly difficult task in many circumstances. Employers, they said, would simply fill whatever quota of minority workers federal civil rights compliance officers indicated was acceptable.[6]

These concerns were not merely speculative. As an example, Liberty National Bank and Trust Company of Louisville, Kentucky, paid $270,000 in 1991 to avoid going to trial over a discrimination claim. According to *Business Week,* the bank "enjoyed a local reputation as a model equal-opportunity employer." Of the two hundred tellers and clerical workers the bank hired, 16 percent were black, a percentage greater than the percentage of blacks in the local workforce. Still, the compliance officers of the Department of Labor charged them with discrimination, since 32 percent of job applicants were black. The bank argued that it had so many black applicants because it had taken strong measures to reach out to the black community. Nevertheless, it was threatened with a lawsuit by the federal government. Similar cases are common, and many businesses simply settle out of court to avoid the expense and negative publicity attendant upon civil rights cases.[7]

Affirmative action in its current form is, needless to say, a matter of great contention among Americans. Although most Americans support efforts to aid black advancement, most whites oppose preferential treatment of blacks over whites. In 1978, well-known sociologist Seymour Martin Lipset and his coauthor William Schneider reviewed much of the polling data on this issue that had been gathered in the 1970s. While there were important differences among the various polls, a clear pattern did emerge. Lipset and Schneider argued that people make a distinction between compensatory policies designed to help minorities compete more effectively and policies that give outright preferences to minorities: "Relatively few object to compensation for past deprivations in the form of special training programs, Head Start efforts, financial aid, community development funds, and the like." On the other hand, most whites "draw the line at predetermining the results," and in particular object to policies that require "fixed racial and sexual proportions."[8]

According to Lipset and Schneider, "policies favoring quotas and goals" are rejected because they "violate traditional conceptions of equality of opportunity." The authors argued that the data indicate that white Americans are anxious for the playing field to be leveled so that the "initial terms of competition are fair," but most whites, and a substantial minority of blacks, object to any attempt to guarantee the outcome of competition.[9]

In a 1977 poll, 68 percent of whites agreed that "[t]he government should see to it that people who have been discriminated against in the past, get a better break in the future."[10] In that same year, a Gallup poll found that only 9 percent of whites favored preferential treatment of minorities in college admissions or hiring, whereas 84 percent thought selection should be based on ability (the remaining respondents were undecided). Among blacks, who in most cases have been more sympathetic to preferential treatment, 30 percent favored preferential treatment, but fully 55 percent favored selection based on ability and 15 percent were undecided.[11] In a more recent 1985 nationwide poll of black Americans, Linda Lichter found that only 23 percent of blacks favored outright preferential treatment.[12]

The wording of these questions can make a major difference in the answers they produce. Those that seem to suggest special efforts to help blacks help themselves, produce widespread agreement, while those that suggest giving blacks an advantage produce the opposite reaction. Sixty-three percent of whites (and 88 percent of blacks) approved of requiring large companies to set up special training programs for members of minority groups. On the other hand, only 35 percent of whites (and 64 percent of blacks) favored "requiring business to hire a certain number of minority workers"; and only 32 percent of whites (and 46 percent of blacks) agreed with the proposition that universities should set aside a certain number of places for qualified minority applicants.[13]

There appears to be a certain ambivalence in the minds of both blacks and whites on these issues. On the one hand, many seem to accept the idea that companies and universities should be required to see that blacks are fairly represented. On the other hand, most whites and a minority of blacks seem to reject the idea that fairness requires fixed proportions in hiring and admissions. Perhaps some whites, and many blacks, believe that the presence of very few blacks in a company or university is reasonable evidence of discrimination given the obvious fact that a sizable pool of qualified blacks exists. They therefore seem to believe that companies and universities should be required to hire or admit at least some minimal number of qualified blacks. Yet most whites clearly object to policies which imply that qualifications will be ignored and that less-qualified blacks will be hired or admitted over more-qualified whites.

Attitudes on the issue of preferential treatment seem to have grown more racially polarized in recent years, with more blacks now approving of racial preferences than did so earlier. In a 1991 ABC News and *Washington Post* poll, only 10 percent of whites, but 64 percent of blacks, thought that "blacks and other minorities should receive preference in hiring to make up for past inequalities." In the area of college admissions, 16 percent of whites and 58 percent of blacks thought minorities should be given preference to make up for past inequalities.[14]

Many social scientists interpret whites' rejection of policies of preferential treatment for minorities as evidence of continued widespread racism. This general view is expressed in numerous books and articles which in recent years have lamented the fact that although whites increasingly seem to support the general principles of racial equality, they seem to resist strategies, such as employment guidelines, which many social scientists claim are necessary to implement those principles.

The view of University of Michigan political scientist Donald Kinder is representative of many. He acknowledges that few white Americans today express support for discrimination. According to Kinder, "[d]enial of equal rights and opportunities to blacks no longer enjoys majority support. On voting rights, public accommodations, housing, and employment practices, racist sentiment has drastically diminished; in some cases it has virtually disappeared. . . . This is a striking change and a momentous achievement." However, Kinder continues, conflict over racial matters still troubles American society:

> Indeed, affirmative action, racial quotas, "forced busing," and the "welfare mess" are among the most contentious public issues of our time. Forty years after Myrdal, in the wake of dramatic changes in public opinion and social custom, *why do so many white Americans continue to resist efforts designed to bring about racial equality?* (Emphasis added)[15]

Instead of interpreting opposition to affirmative action policies, current welfare policies, quotas, and school busing as reflecting honest disagreements over how best to achieve racial equality, many social scientists agree with Kinder in seeing such opposition as an attempt to resist racial equality.

It is important to note that the policies and programs being discussed were in large measure conceived and supported by social scientists. But that hardly justifies an *ad hominem* attack on people who disagree—an attack which portrays that disagreement as a disingenuous attempt to forestall racial progress. So firmly rooted is the belief that it is improper to look to blacks themselves for some of the causes of their difficulties that even in the face of very strong evidence of declining racism, many researchers continue to insist that there *must* be some sort of racism at work if blacks fail to achieve full equality as quickly as some thought they would.

For instance, in *Racial Attitudes in America* (discussed in Chapter 2), Howard Schuman, Charlotte Steeh, and Lawrence Bobo report that 90 percent of whites support integrated education.[16] Yet 90 percent oppose school busing and almost that many oppose federal intervention to achieve racial balance in the schools.[17] In the area of equal employment, almost 100 percent support equal job opportunities.[18] At the same time, approximately 65 percent oppose federal intervention to assure fair employment practices.[19] And as we saw, white Americans generally oppose quotas in employment and university admissions, whereas academic social scientists tend to support these policies.

Schuman, Steeh, and Bobo summarize their analysis as showing that insofar as the principles of equal opportunity are concerned, white Americans exhibit "a much lower level of support for government intervention to promote principles than for the principles themselves." Furthermore, they point out that "the level of support for intervention is almost always low in absolute terms." They report that the only case where a majority of white Americans support government intervention is to assure equal access to hotels and restaurants.[20]

III. Racism and Traditional American Values

The majority of social scientists who express unhappiness with these findings seem unwilling to allow for the possibility that most white Americans support equal opportunity, but oppose various implementation policies out of a sincere belief that those policies *do not* forward the principles of racial equality, that such policies are in fact unfair and violate important values. What's more, white Americans are not alone in holding these beliefs. Black Americans, as we saw earlier, are not uniform in their support of preferential policies. Depending on the question asked, a sizable minority of blacks, and sometimes a majority, oppose such policies.[21]

Many researchers seem unwilling to entertain the possibility that Americans who hold these beliefs may be right about the shortcomings of government intervention. After all, much has happened since the passage of the Civil Rights Act of 1964 and the Voting Rights Act of 1965. Americans have been witness to various efforts undertaken by the federal government since the

1960s, many coercive and unpopular, in the name of racial justice. Many of these efforts went beyond attempting to equalize opportunities for blacks and whites and instead, as discussed earlier, seemed to require the imposition of statistically equal outcomes in ways that many thought violated the work ethic. Perhaps the majority who express opposition to federal intervention do so because they have come to believe that many of those efforts were ill advised. Social scientists, on the other hand, seem reluctant to acknowledge that some of their original policy prescriptions may be counterproductive today.

Part of the reluctance of social scientists to grant simple rationality to those who oppose their positions on civil rights is undoubtedly rooted in the Freudian and behaviorist beliefs to which many social scientists subscribe. Rationality assumes conscious awareness of needs and desires, an awareness which Freudian theory denies. Rationality also assumes that behavior is purposive and directed toward ends that have been planned and thought through. In classic behaviorist theory, such as that of B. F. Skinner, behavior is the product of reinforcement and is largely a matter of habit. Planned, thoughtful action is therefore of little significance in explaining behavior in the behaviorist model.[22]

Whatever the reason, there has been a pervasive resistance among social scientists to accepting the possibility that many people might oppose various government policies that affect blacks because their logic or experience leads them in good conscience to question the value of those policies. Too often such objections are dismissed as crude Freudian rationalizations for simple selfishness or racial prejudice. The overwhelmingly liberal political orientation of social scientists also helps explain their frustration with those who reject liberal remedies for racial problems. The left-leaning orientation of social scientists is no recent development. In their important 1958 book *The Academic Mind,* sociologists Paul Lazarsfeld and Wagner Thielens, Jr. (then at Columbia University) reported on a large-scale survey of American academic and social scientists undertaken in 1955.[23] They reported that 58 percent of social scientists voted for the liberal Democratic candidate Adlai Stevenson in the 1952 presidential election, while only 30 percent voted for Eisenhower.[24] Interestingly, as their productivity rose (measured by number of publications), so did their tendency to vote Democratic. Sixty-nine percent of those social scientists classified as productive voted for Stevenson.[25] Furthermore, the trend toward liberal voting was greatest for younger social scientists (those under forty), among whom almost 80 percent (rated moderate to high on productivity) voted for Stevenson.[26] Democratic voting was also related to the quality and size of the colleges and universities where the social scientists taught. At the largest universities, 75 percent of the professors reported voting for Stevenson.[27] These data indicate that the most influential social scientists, that is, those who taught at influential universities and who published a great deal, were in the 1950s overwhelmingly liberal in their political orientation. This was a decade, it should be recalled, in which the general public gave Republican Dwight Eisenhower two terms in office.

The liberal bias of social scientists continued into the seventies and is documented in *The Divided Academy* by political scientist Everett Carll Ladd, Jr. and sociologist Seymour Martin Lipset.[28] Their work relies on a survey sponsored by the Carnegie Commission on Higher Education and is based on over sixty thousand completed questionnaires. When respondents were asked to indicate their own political orientation, 82 percent of social psychologists, for instance, characterized themselves as "Left" or "Liberal" as opposed to "Middle of the road," "Moderately conservative," or "Strongly conservative." Similarly, 77 percent of sociologists, 72 percent of political scientists, 71 percent of anthropologists, and 64 percent of economists characterized themselves as "Left" or "Liberal."[29]

These views were confirmed by the voting patterns of respondents. Approximately 90 percent of the social scientists reported having voted for Democratic candidate Lyndon Johnson in the 1964 presidential race. The support for Democrat Hubert Humphrey was lower (in the 75 percent range) in the presidential race in 1968.[30] Ladd and Lipset argue that this was largely the result of the fact that many liberals defected from the Democrats over opposition to the Vietnam War. For instance, many of the academics who voted for Republican Richard Nixon identified themselves as left or liberal. The researchers argue that many liberals voted for Nixon "as a protest against the Democratic Party establishment, or identified Nixon as more likely to end the war" than his Democratic opponent.[31] Even so, Nixon received only 25 percent of the social scientists' votes, while the general public voted him into the presidency in 1968. Furthermore, as in the Lazarsfeld/Thielens survey made during the 1950s, Ladd and Lipset reported that social scientists at the elite research universities were considerably more liberal than their colleagues at less prestigious institutions.[32]

Recent data collected for the Carnegie Commission on Higher Education by the Survey Research Center at Berkeley University reveals little change in the political attitudes of social scientists. In 1989, 72 percent of social scientists at all types of colleges and universities characterized themselves as liberal and only 14 percent as conservative. The most liberal faculties were those specializing in public affairs, with fully 88 percent describing themselves as liberal and none as even moderately conservative. Sixty-eight percent of psychology faculty described themselves as liberal, as did 63 percent in economics. By way of contrast, only 54 percent of physical scientists, 47 percent of those in mathematics, 40 percent of those in engineering, and 31 percent of those in business and management characterized themselves as liberal.[33]

As in the earlier studies, faculties in the most distinguished colleges and universities were more liberal than their colleagues in less prestigious institutions. Seventy percent of all faculty in highly selective liberal arts colleges described themselves as liberal, while only 15 percent called themselves moderately conservative and only 4 percent admitted to being conservative. Similarly, in the most prestigious research universities 70 percent called themselves liberal and only 12 percent called themselves moderately conservative. A mere 3 percent chose to characterize themselves as conservative. It should be noted that these figures are for all faculty, including those in engineering and business. Clearly the faculties at those universities where most research is done and from which most publications emanate are lopsidedly to the left in their political orientation.[34]

Not only are social scientists overwhelmingly left and liberal in their politics, but in addition they tend to take a condescending view of members of the general public, who often disagree with them and who are much less likely to be characterized as liberal. For instance, many social scientists accept left-wing economic thinking and reject free-market economics as a mere rationalization for injustice and inequality, and think Americans who accept market principles are at best naive and lacking in social sophistication. Adherence to conventional middle-class values and middle-class concerns is seen as evidence of intellectual shallowness. The "Protestant work ethic," by which is meant a belief that effort and hard work will in time be rewarded by material and spiritual well-being, is held as evidence of an endemic simple-mindedness. Social scientists, by and large, favor large-scale government programs to correct what they see as the inadequacies of the market. The misgivings that many white Americans express about the virtues and efficiency of government programs are usually dismissed as reflecting ignorance of the way things *really* work in America. Many of those in the social sciences seem unwilling to accept the possibility that the majority of white Americans hold the beliefs they do out of good and sound reasons, and social scientists are quick to attribute the anti-statism of most whites to naiveté or, when it relates to government policies on race, to thinly veiled racial animosity.

This view has been common for quite some time among social scientists. The authors of *The Authoritarian Personality* made no effort to hide their own ideological bias and expressed disdain for those Americans who rejected statist solutions to social problems. For instance, Adorno et al. explained Americans' rejection of "socialized medicine, and various other programs designed to help the 'common man'," in terms of the fact that "most Americans are, politically, relatively uneducated and uninformed." Americans are confused by the "technicality and abstractness of the basic issues involved." Rejection of such programs is rooted in the "antipolitical, anti-intellectual tradition" of American life.[35]

In addition to naiveté, Adorno and his coauthors thought that many Americans opposed federal programs for reasons of callousness. For instance, these authors argued that Americans believe that "ability will find its socioeconomic rewards." Americans think that "those who end up on the low end of the social ladder—since they did not have what it takes—are hardly to be pitied."[36] The authors acknowledge that Americans' callousness toward the poor is tempered by the fact that "our religious tradition is one of charity and tolerance." But the average American's understanding of the role of charity is also misguided, since "charity is mainly a soothing of conscience and a means of maintaining an unjust state of affairs." According to the authors, the cause of poverty is the "concentration of economic power, [which] creates poverty as a symptom." The answer to poverty is therefore not charity but the "modification of [poverty's] societal causes."[37]

These views are mirrored in similar treatments today. Paul Sniderman of Stanford and Michael Hagen of Berkeley, in their 1985 book *Race and Inequality,* feel that white Americans do not really understand the American class system of stratification and do not really understand the difficulties that blacks and other minorities face in their efforts to achieve equality. To the dismay of Sniderman and Hagen, Americans really *do* believe in what the authors characterize as the "folk ideology" of the Protestant work ethic and are beset by a naive faith in individualism. According to Sniderman and Hagen, individualism involves "a bedrock belief in the ethic of self-reliance." In this ethic "[i]ndividuals must take care of themselves. They must not pretend to be victims of circumstance, or ask for special favors, in an effort to get others to do for them what they should do for themselves. . . ."[38]

The authors argue that individualism is, in their words, an "ungenerous idea," since "it refuses to acknowledge that some are in fact handicapped and must overcome obstacles that are not of their making and that others do not face. In this sense the individualist lacks empathy for those disadvantaged by race or by poverty or by gender. . . ."[39]

According to the authors, "there is something extraordinary . . . about the individualists' understanding of equality of opportunity."[40] They express surprise that people really believe in the Protestant work ethic and claim that this must be because they do not understand the difficulties some people face. Sniderman and Hagen comment that "so far as the individualist can make out . . . everyone can get ahead, regardless of whether he or she is black, female, or poor."[41] Their condescension toward the average American's understanding clearly influences the way Sniderman and Hagen interpret the questionnaires they designed to assess public opinion. For instance, people were asked the extent of their agreement with the following two statements:

> It's a lack of skill and abilities that keeps *many* black people from getting a job. It's not *just* because they are black. When a black person is trained to do something, he is able to get a job. (Emphasis added)

> Black people *may not have the same opportunities* as whites, but *many* blacks haven't prepared themselves enough to make use of the opportunities that come their way. (Emphasis added)[42]

Those who agreed with the above statements were, according to Sniderman and Hagen, betraying an "ungenerous individualism." On the other hand, those who agreed with the following statement exhibited, in the view of the authors, a more sophisticated and generous understanding:

> Even with the new programs, minorities still face the same old job discrimination once the program is over.[43]

In other words, those who disagreed with the view that discrimination is widespread were, by definition, characterized as ungenerous and resistant to racial equality. The authors do not acknowledge the possibility that the "wrong" answers to the above questions may be closer to reality than the alternatives which they think correct. Given the widespread application of affirmative action rules and guidelines, it is hardly unreasonable for people to reject the assertion that "minorities still face the same old discrimination."

Furthermore, given well-known problems among blacks in the inner cities, it seems hardly irrational to conclude that many blacks suffer "a lack of skill and abilities" that "keeps many black people from getting a job." Similarly, is it not true that "[w]hen a black person is trained to do something, he is able to get a job"? The statistics reviewed in Chapter 2 clearly suggest that blacks who are trained for employment find employment. The belief that blacks with job training can find jobs does not suggest antipathy toward blacks, but rather, simple familiarity with the facts.

It is instructive to note that a 1989 survey by ABC News and the *Washington Post* found very little difference between blacks and whites who were asked questions similar to those given above. Sixty percent of whites and 60 percent of blacks agreed with the statement: "If blacks would try harder, they could be just as well off as whites." Fifty-six percent of whites and 52 percent of blacks agreed with the statement: "Discrimination has unfairly held down blacks, but many of the problems which blacks have today are brought on by blacks themselves."[44]

Other researchers also explain opposition to quotas and set-asides in terms of Americans' naiveté. In a 1983 paper on attitudes toward affirmative action, James Kluegel and Eliot Smith argue that while whites recognize that blacks suffered from discrimination in the past, and therefore support programs "offering to help blacks acquire skills," they nevertheless oppose preferential hiring quotas "because they are thought to violate dominant equity norms." The authors continue:

> The premise that affirmative action programs are necessary to equalize opportunity requires that whites believe that the stratification system currently does not provide equal opportunity for all persons and groups. In this regard the seeming insensitivity of whites to the socioeconomic disadvantage of blacks may stem more from racial segregation, and the resulting limited and naive perspective whites have on blacks' circumstances, than from prejudice and racism.[45]

To assert that people who disagree with you are naive or callous is, of course, to engage in fairly obvious *ad hominem* rhetoric, a tactic that has become all too common among social scientists working in this area. It is grossly unfair to attack people on such grounds without any independent evidence of naiveté or callousness, and yet researchers such as Sniderman and Hagen, and Kluegel and Smith, offer no such independent evidence. They merely assume that those who do not agree with their views *must* be naive. The evidence reviewed in Chapter 2 indicates, however, that it is more reasonable to charge these researchers with a lack of understanding, rather than to so charge the "unsophisticated" people who disagree with them. Perhaps the public has viewed the events of the last twenty-five years and has drawn different conclusions than social scientists have about the effectiveness of government programs? Unfortunately, the obvious ideological bias evidenced by these social scientists makes it difficult for them to accept the possibility that such disagreement may, in fact, be well reasoned.

This bias, of course, makes it even harder for social scientists to consider the possibility that blacks themselves might be ill served by the various policies designed to help them. Those policies that encourage reliance upon government support may, if anything, make their situation worse. Furthermore, social scientists rarely deal with the possibility that incorrect social science theories might cause harm. How can we expect young black Americans to struggle to succeed when we keep telling them that the system is so stacked against them that they are bound to fail? Even if the social scientists are right and American society is stacked against blacks, defeatist attitudes are not likely to be helpful and may be self-confirming. Very few social scientists seem to entertain the possibility that the "naive" credo which urges people to "stand on their own two feet" might, even in the face of serious discrimination, be the best advice for young people to follow.

IV. Symbolic Racism

The most striking example of the continuing influence of the association between traditional values and bigotry is contained in recent work that attributes the continuing opposition to many civil rights policies to a subtle new form of racism. David Sears, Donald Kinder, and John McConahay, along with various colleagues and independent researchers, have generated a sizable and influential research literature which purports to confirm the existence of this new type of racism.[46]

The main difficulty for this group is showing how racism is the problem when all objective measures on white American attitudes reveal, as illustrated in Chapter 2, a steady decline in racist attitudes. They have developed an elusive theory, clearly reminiscent of the thesis of *The Authoritarian Personality,* that people develop prejudiced attitudes in childhood and thereafter carry a "racial affect" with them into adult life. When confronted with programs designed to help blacks, they oppose those programs because of this new form of racism. The opposition is in turn rationalized in terms of a commitment to traditional American values.

Donald Kinder, a political scientist whom I quoted earlier, and social psychologist David Sears have written widely on the problem of symbolic racism among whites. They agree that in wide areas of American life, white opposition to equal opportunity for blacks has declined sharply: "On voting rights, schools, public accommodations, housing, and employment practices, segregationist sentiment has all but disappeared. White America has become, in principle at least, racially egalitarian—a momentous and undeniably significant change." Kinder and Sears argue, however, that opposition to equality still remains, but can no longer be based on the discredited "explicitly segregationist, white supremacist view." In its place, they suggest,

> is a new variant that might be called symbolic racism. This we define as a blend of antiblack affect and the kind of traditional American moral values embedded in the Protestant ethic. [It is] . . . a form of resistance to change in the racial status quo based on moral feelings that blacks violate such traditional American values as individualism and self-reliance, the work ethic, obedience, and discipline.[47]

The authors go on to argue that white Americans feel that "individuals should be rewarded on their merits, which in turn should be based on hard work and diligent service." This is of course the view of things embodied in the Protestant ethic. Kinder and Sears argue that since opposition to equality is now based on the Protestant ethic, "symbolic racism should find its most vociferous expression on political issues that involve 'unfair' government assistance to blacks . . . ," including welfare, reverse discrimination and racial quotas, forced busing, and government-funded abortions for the poor.[48]

In other words, agreement with traditional American values is, on the view of these authors, actually an expression of deeply felt prejudice and is therefore evidence of racial hostility. But how is this startling assertion validated—that is, how do Kinder and Sears know whether people who hold traditional views do so out of racism, rather than simply because they believe traditional values are important and worthwhile?

In order to distinguish opposition based on racial animosity from opposition based on political belief, one would need separate and independently validated measures of each. For instance, one would have to show, first, that there is a correlation between a belief in something like self-reliance and an expressed hatred toward blacks. Second, one would have to demonstrate that the belief in self-reliance is adopted *because* it is a way of criticizing blacks, who are thought to be lacking in self-reliance. This Kinder and Sears did not do. Rather, they used a questionnaire which, in effect, confused rationally motivated and racially motivated opposition to affirmative action policies. The questionnaire was originally administered in 1969 and 1973, during a period of considerable turmoil produced by Vietnam War protests and the rash of riots in black inner-city neighborhoods. The following questions were asked (items with an asterisk were not used in the 1969 study):

1. Do you think that most Negroes/blacks who receive money from welfare programs could get along without it if they tried, or do they really need the help?
2. Negroes/blacks shouldn't push where they're not wanted.
*3. Because of past discrimination, it is sometimes necessary to set up quotas for admission to college of minority group students.
4. Do you think Los Angeles city officials pay more, less or the same attention to a request or complaint from a black person?
5. Of the groups on the card are there any which you think have gained more than they are entitled to?
*6. It is wrong to set up quotas to admit black students to college who don't meet the usual requirements.
7. Over the past two years blacks have got more than they deserve.
8. In Los Angeles, would you say many, some, or only a few blacks miss out on jobs or promotions because of racial discrimination?
9. Busing elementary school children to schools in other parts of the city only harms their education.
10. In some cases it is best for children to attend elementary schools outside their neighborhood.
*11. Are you in favor or opposed to the busing of children to achieve racial desegregation?
*12. If the supreme court ordered busing to achieve racial desegregation of public schools would you be opposed to it?
*13. If necessary, children should be bused to achieve racial desegregation.[49]

A person's "score" on this symbolic-racism scale is determined by how many questions he answers in the "wrong" way. Those who oppose busing and quotas are therefore guaranteed to score high on symbolic racism, even if they disagreed with all the other items, since seven of the thirteen questions deal with busing and quotas. If, on top of that, respondents did not like welfare policies (item 1) and objected to special treatment for blacks in general (items 4, 5, and 7), they would be scored hopelessly racist in the "symbolic" sense. Item 2, "[B]lacks shouldn't push . . . ," does seem to suggest agreement with segregationist attitudes. But this is not clear, for while 64 percent of respondents agreed with that statement, 70 percent said they would not mind if a black moved next door to them, in response to a question on another questionnaire whose results were reported in the same article.[50] On the other hand, the item "[B]lacks shouldn't push" may have tapped the strong feelings generated by the Watts riot of 1965. It is interesting in this regard that there were no questions about riots in the questionnaire, even though the riots were much discussed and created divisions even among liberal civil rights activists. In any case, just about anyone who disagreed with the liberal policy agenda of the time would have been classified as a symbolic racist by this questionnaire, and it is hardly surprising that so many of the respondents were so labeled. How could it be otherwise when popular opinion was, and still is, against coercive, as opposed to opportunity-enhancing, affirmative action policies?

It is well to keep in mind how disturbing the riot in the predominantly black Watts section of Los Angeles in the summer of 1965 was, coming so shortly after the signing of the Voting Rights Act of that year. The riot lasted for five days and was one of many riots around the country that produced enormous property losses and considerable loss of life. Political journalist Thomas Edsall and his coauthor Mary Edsall discuss the impact of those riots in their book *Chain Reaction.* They point out that the riots created grave doubts in the minds of most people about the course of civil rights policy: "Liberalism had unleashed forces that its leaders could neither control nor keep within the confines of traditional political negotiations, and the once dominant, left-center coalition began to crack."[51]

Most liberals at the time saw the riots as understandable (some thought legitimate) reactions to American racism, and urged even more government action to aid blacks so as to prevent a racial conflagration. Conservatives argued that the property damage and loss of life (mainly the lives of blacks) required an immediate restoration of order. "Law and order" became the rallying cry of many Republican candidates and were labeled code words for racism by liberal Democrats. It was at this time that black Americans came to identify their interests most closely with the Democratic party. Prior to this period, blacks were about equally divided in terms of which party they thought could best serve their interests.[52] Most Americans, whatever their interpretation of the riots, were seriously troubled by them and their implications for racial harmony.

When Kinder and Sears polled people in Los Angeles in 1969 and 1973 about their attitude toward government programs, the Watts riot was still fresh in most people's memories. The continued rioting throughout the late sixties in other cities merely reinforced people's doubts about any easy resolution of black grievances. In any case, it is unfortunate that Kinder and Sears failed to explore the possibility that some people's rejection of liberal policies may have been based on the belief that those policies were in part responsible for the riots—and the consequent undermining of white sympathy for blacks—rather than based on any desire to limit black opportunity.

Furthermore, during the period in which the research was undertaken, affirmative action meant taking actions to assure blacks received equal opportunity. It did not mean that they should be guaranteed jobs or admission to universities on the basis of quotas. The 1973 respondents were scored as giving evidence of racism if they agreed that ''[i]t is wrong to set up quotas to admit black students to college who don't meet the usual standards.'' Seventy-three percent of the respondents agreed with that statement.[53] This is hardly surprising, since in 1973 the Supreme Court had yet to rule on whether such quotas were, in fact, legal. The Supreme Court subsequently ruled in the famous *Bakke* case that race could be taken into account to the advantage of blacks to assure diversity much as geographic location could give advantages to people from certain regions of the country, but that explicit quotas on admission were not legal.[54] By the logic of symbolic racism, the judges who agreed with the majority in *Bakke* were symbolically expressing their hostility toward blacks in their ruling.

Eighty-six percent of the respondents to Kinder and Sears's questionnaire opposed the busing of school children out of neighborhoods, and such opposition was also counted as evidence of racism. Those who opposed busing because they thought that busing interferes with the education of school children were likewise counted as racist, even though 62 percent of the respondents thought that way.[55] Many mainstream leaders, at the time, also expressed strong opposition to busing, especially for young children. Such opposition was not limited to whites. In most years throughout the sixties and seventies, about 50 percent of black Americans (depending on the poll) expressed opposition to school busing.[56]

How did Kinder and Sears determine that the people who expressed a concern about the educational impact of busing were merely dissembling? How did the authors verify the assertion that these attitudes were racist—that is, how did they measure the validity of the questionnaire? They did so by showing that there was a correlation between respondents' answers and their votes in the 1969 and 1973 Los Angeles mayoral elections, elections that happened to pit a black Democrat against a white Republican. In other words, the assertion that people who opposed busing and hiring quotas were racist was proven by the fact that they voted for a white conservative candidate who also opposed these policies, and against a black liberal who was thought more likely to support them.[57]

It is important to stress that the only independent validation of Kinder and Sears's symbolic-racism scale was the voting behavior of the respondents. Those who scored high on symbolic racism (i.e., expressed prevailing moderate to conservative views) were found to be more likely to vote for the white Republican, Sam Yorty, in the mayoral elections of 1969 and 1973 than for the black Democrat, Tom Bradley. This perfectly rational voting pattern was characterized by Kinder and Sears as ''antiblack voting behavior.''[58] From the authors' data it is impossible to determine whether the voters chose the white conservative because he was white or because he was conservative. Kinder and Sears did not attempt to empirically answer that question but merely asserted that it must have been a vote based on race.

No evidence was produced to show that this new ''symbolic'' racism (which seemed to mirror the attitudes held by many reputable public figures at the time) was related to the real kind. In fact, Sears's colleague John McConahay, a psychologist at Duke University, had stressed in an earlier research paper that there was no relation between the two. McConahay and his coauthor Joseph Hough found that symbolic racism was most highly correlated with such things as believing that children should be taught patriotism in schools and identifying with the Republican party.[59] This is hardly surprising, since the questionnaire used to measure symbolic racism is really a truncated measure of political conservatism and therefore would have had to have been correlated with conservative values.

Consider the following explanation of opposition to coercive government policies offered by Kinder and Sears:

> Our samples resemble the rest of the white public in this respect. Despite Jensenism, few thought blacks less intelligent than whites (15% in 1969; 16% in 1973); despite controversy over ''forced busing'' for school integration, almost no one supported separate schools for blacks (8% and 10%, respectively). *Consequently,* the major political impact of racism must be carried by other forms of prejudice. (Emphasis added)[60]

In other words, even if Americans believe in the equal capacities of the races and favor school integration, and thereby demonstrate an absence of racism, their opposition to elementary school busing and to hiring quotas must be expressions of racism. But, of course, without the hidden premise that Americans must be racist, the above explanation is no explanation at all, and what follows the ''consequently'' in the passage quoted above is a non sequitur.

So ingrained is the assumption of an association between conservative beliefs and racism, that it was taken as more or less obvious by these authors that conservatives and even those who take moderate positions are, by definition, racists. What else could explain how it would be possible to confuse opposition to such things as admissions quotas and welfare policies, an attitude so clearly associated with a commitment to the American values of fair play and self-reliance, with racism? Let me add that while it may be true that *some* people oppose quotas because they are racist, it is a terrible confusion to translate that into the suggestion that all those who oppose quotas do so because *all of them* are, *in part,* racists.

Kinder and Sears are not alone in this way of thinking. The research on symbolic racism has been favorably reported in most social psychology texts and has received important institutional support; the Kinder and Sears study (on which their 1981 article was based) received the 1978 Gordon Allport Intergroup Relations Prize from the Society for the Psychological Study of Social Issues.[61]

The political bias of this research was pointed out in a review by scholars Paul Sniderman and Philip Tetlock, who at the time were at the University of California at Berkeley. Their critique lays to rest any further claim to the scientific legitimacy of symbolic racism. They maintain that symbolic-racism scales scandalously confuse racism with political belief. They argue that symbolic racism could be construed as an example of what sociologist C. Wright Mills called ''motive-mongering,'' which the authors explain is, ''in this case, the use of social science research methods to cast aspersions on political viewpoints with which the researchers disagree.'' While Sniderman and Tetlock allow that the symbolic-racism researchers may not have intended such motive-mongering, they do contend that ''their approach lends itself to such abuse,'' and they find especially objectionable the ''labeling of particular policy positions as racist by definition.''[62]

Sniderman and Tetlock, I should add, also see a link between traditional American values and racial inequality; however, they posit such a link, not because traditional values are racist, but because they stress self-reliance. Sniderman and Tetlock argue that ''values such as individualism may undercut support for efforts to achieve racial equality, even when those values have nothing whatever to do with racism.'' They suggest that many Americans ''may oppose government assistance for blacks, not out of aversion to blacks, but rather out of a set of normative beliefs defining the propriety both of asking for, and providing, public assistance.'' They go on to suggest that

> even supposing prejudice were to disappear completely, there would in all probability remain substantial popular opposition to government efforts to achieve racial equality. From this perspective, the American dilemma may

involve a deep paradox; resistance to efforts to achieve racial equality may be rooted in a commitment to a distinctly American conception of equality.[63]

The authors appear to argue that what makes the American conception of equality distinct is that it is rooted in self-reliance and the work ethic. Presumably they mean to distinguish that sort of equality, i.e., equality of opportunity, from a conception based on government-engineered equality, i.e., equality of result. But why should the American conception of equality of opportunity be incompatible with racial equality, especially if "prejudice were to disappear completely"?

The above passage only makes sense if one introduces the hidden assumption that blacks cannot achieve equality with whites without government assistance. Why blacks should be incapable of advancement through self-reliance, absent prejudice and discrimination, is a point the authors fail to address. Are we to suppose that the past victimization of blacks by whites has been so severe that they cannot rise above it? Perhaps the authors believe that black cultural values are incompatible with the work ethic? Or perhaps they are suggesting that blacks lack the inherent capacity to achieve equality on their own? It is not clear what views the authors hold on these issues.

Perhaps the average American who thinks blacks can advance by virtue of their own efforts, and who objects to many affirmative action policies on the grounds that they are both unfair and unnecessary, has a clearer understanding of these matters than do these authors.

V. Ignoring the Underclass

One of the glaring weaknesses in the social science research literature assessing racial attitudes is its failure to come to grips with the growing pattern of pathology within underclass black communities. Most researchers ignore the possibility that the attitudes of many white Americans toward civil rights policies may have been affected by the trends so evident over the past thirty years in the inner cities. Maybe those trends explain why many white Americans have become reluctant to support a continuation of the policies which many interpret as causing those problems. Consider three important books on racial attitudes written in the 1980s by respected scholars: *Race and Inequality* by Paul Sniderman and Michael Hagen; *Racial Attitudes in America* by Howard Schuman, Charlotte Steeh, and Lawrence Bobo; and *Beliefs about Inequality* by James Kluegel and Eliot Smith.[64] In all three the topics of crime and illegitimacy are completely ignored, and neither term appears in any of the indexes. It is a serious weakness of these books about white attitudes toward blacks that they fail to address some of the most obvious reasons why whites might be having second thoughts about present policies.

The "American Public" whose responses to various questionnaires are analyzed in social science research, is generally a middle-class population, whose attachment to the Protestant ethic is well known. Also well known is the fact that middle-class Americans of all races place great value on home ownership, safe neighborhoods, and good schools as vehicles for the upward mobility of their children. In the questionnaires used to assess their attitudes, such people are asked to take positions on "blacks." But to which blacks are they supposed to refer? All the questionnaires are surprisingly vague on this point, especially in light of the widely acknowledged chasm that has developed between middle-class and underclass blacks. The former, in income, education, and lifestyle, are increasingly indistinguishable from their white counterparts. The latter, however, are marked by a degree of social pathology—in illegitimacy, crime, school failure, drug abuse, unemployment, etc.—that is highly disturbing to those, both black and white, in the middle class. This dichotomy within the black population goes completely without comment in the debates about the meaning of white attitudes toward busing, integration, and hiring and admissions quotas.

One obvious reason why so many whites reject the need for quotas and do not see black problems in terms of discrimination, may be the *fact* that blacks, even *very poor* blacks, who have adopted middle-class behavior patterns—who postpone parenthood, finish school, avoid drugs and crime, etc.—are doing quite well, while those in the underclass, who by their behavior appear to reject those values, are not. How, given this undeniable reality, is one supposed to respond to a request to choose between the following statements from Sniderman and Hagen's questionnaire?

    A. Many blacks have only themselves to blame for not doing better in life. If they tried harder, they'd do better.
    B. When two qualified people, one black and one white, are considered for the same job, the black won't get the job no matter how hard he tries.[65]

To choose "A" is to find yourself labeled "ungenerous" toward the plight of blacks, even though on its face it is a true statement. On the other hand, to agree with the second statement is to endorse what, at the present time, flies in the face of most people's experience. Affirmative action policies have meant that in recent years if a black and a white who are equally qualified apply for admission to an elite college or seek employment as police officers or firefighters, it is almost always the case that the black gets the admission notice or the job. The fact that people appear to give contradictory responses on such questionnaires does not imply that they are ambivalent about racial equality. But it does suggest that the usefulness of such questionnaires is limited indeed.

The failure to acknowledge the reality of the black underclass also makes problematic any easy assertions about the extent of real or "old-fashioned redneck racism." All researchers agree that support for segregation is a mark of real racism. It is typically measured by responses to such questions as the following in Gallup polls taken in 1978 and 1980:

1. Would you, yourself, have any objection to sending your children to school where a few of the children were black. [95 percent of respondents said no]
2. Would you, yourself, have any objection to sending your children to school where half the children were black. [76 percent said no]
3. Would you, yourself, have any objection to sending your children to school where more than half the children were black. [42 percent said no]
4. If a black person came to live next door would you move? [86 percent said no, 10 percent said they might, and 4 percent said yes]
5. Would you move if black people came to live in great numbers in your neighborhood? [46 percent said no, 33 percent said they might, and 21 percent said yes][66]

Is the fact that a majority of white parents object to their children attending a largely black school indicative of a lingering racial hostility? Or is it a response to the fact (and not merely the perception) that many such schools are dangerous places and have seriously compromised educational standards? Does the fact that 33 percent of respondents said they might move, and 21 percent said they would move, if large numbers of blacks came to live in their neighborhoods support the contention that a majority of whites reject integration "in practice"? Or does it reflect a concern that the "large numbers of blacks" may contain many members of the underclass? Very few people from the middle class, whether white or black, see such people as desirable neighbors. In fact, in a poll of residential preferences in the Detroit area in 1976, only 11 percent of *blacks* responded that they would prefer to live in a neighborhood where the residents were "all black" or "mostly black."[67] In truth, the hard data that forms the foundation for the current argument about racial attitudes is so fraught with difficulties that just about any interpretation can be gotten from it. And yet it is on these grounds that many social scientists charge white Americans with resisting racial equality.

VI. Conclusion

What the symbolic-racism literature clearly demonstrates is that the main thesis of *The Authoritarian Personality,* while it has been discredited by a host of research, continues to have a powerful influence among social scientists.

Conservative ideology is still taken as evidence of racism, and racism is still seen as a sort of neurosis developed in childhood which is bound to be denied, but which will, nevertheless, express itself in a variety of disguised or symbolic forms. The symbolic-racism literature reinforces this conception and in addition promotes the idea that criticizing current civil rights policies is merely a disguised form of anti-black bigotry.

So entrenched is this idea, especially on university campuses, that it has become almost impossible to question this or that civil rights policy without immediately drawing the charge of bigotry. The normal give and take that should inform discussion on government policy has been rejected in favor of a self-righteous claim that only those who abide by the current liberal policy agenda are interested in racial fairness.

The tendency to see disagreement with the white-racism hypothesis as racism itself, leads to ever more coercive methods on the part of those who maintain it. As an example, consider the widespread introduction on college campuses of programs to increase racial sensitivity and of speech codes limiting "racially and sexually offensive speech." Such a speech code at the prestigious University of Michigan was struck down in 1989 in federal court on First Amendment grounds. The code had made it a violation to verbally create "an intimidating, hostile or demeaning environment for educational pursuits, employment or participation in University sponsored extra-curricular activities. . . ."[68] The university guide on discriminatory behavior included as an example of improper conduct a case where "[a] male student makes remarks in a class like 'Women just aren't as good in this field as men,' thus creating a hostile learning atmosphere for female classmates." A psychology graduate student and teaching assistant, named John Doe in the court papers, argued that the code threatened his freedom and ability to conduct classes, since topics relating to racial and sexual differences often arose in the course he taught on Comparative Animal Behavior.[69]

John Doe argued that it was common to discuss biological differences between men and women when attempting to understand differences such as the fact that there are fewer female engineers than there are male engineers. Doe argued that since some students and teachers thought these ideas sexist, he might be brought before university authorities on charges of creating an intimidating environment for students. The court found Doe's argument persuasive and ruled the speech code in violation of the First Amendment right to freedom of expression.[70]

These codes do not only ban racial epithets, which were always unacceptable in the classroom, but rather prohibit any sort of statement that could give offense to a member of a minority group or to women. An unstated assumption seems to be that blacks and women are so thin-skinned that they cannot handle such arguments or the sort of sophomoric insults and slurs so common among undergraduates. Likewise, these codes reinforce the notion that blacks and women have been so victimized by American society that they are incapable of defending themselves and rebutting ideas they find offensive.

The point here is not merely that such codes are offensive to mature people or that they undermine free debate in a university setting. The point is that they also reinforce the notion that black efforts will be undermined by whites. This not only generates resentment against whites, but also promotes the sort of demoralization and fatalism that is born of a sense that nothing one can do can improve one's lot. It should be pointed out that the students who attend major universities have been influenced by strenuous civil rights advocacy during all of their formative years. Is it reasonable to believe that these students, the best and the brightest America has to offer, have failed to learn the lesson of tolerance and are so racist that they actually hinder black performance? If that is the case, what does it suggest about future attempts to eliminate racism by rational appeals? More likely, the truth is that few of these students are racist.

The failure to expose and repudiate the false claims of the ''symbolic-racism'' researchers is a serious failure on the part of social scientists. Symbolic-racism research falsely gives additional credence to the view that the problems blacks face can only be solved by further efforts at reducing white racism. The danger in continuing to support that view is that if it is wrong, as seems to be the case, it leads to a waste of intellectual and material resources and results in counterproductive policies and actions.

Furthermore, the false linkage of free-market conservatism with racism tends to drive out many good and useful ideas from the debate on civil rights. For instance, Thomas Sowell has argued effectively that many market regulations, such as licensing laws, tend to keep blacks from many entrepreneurial activities. Sowell uses the taxi industry in New York City as a prime example: because taxi licenses are limited, they cost huge sums of money, making it difficult for people to get a foot into the industry. Many other examples could be cited.[71] Sowell objects to many of these restrictions not merely because he is a free-market conservative, but also because they harm blacks and other minorities. Unfortunately, the specious linkage of such thinking with racism makes it difficult for many in the civil rights establishment to take to heart what Sowell says. Similarly, concerns with crime and illegitimacy are seen as conservative concerns, and therefore as unworthy of serious consideration in the civil rights debate.

It seems odd to say it in the 1990s, but America is an economically vibrant society whose institutions are in large measure dependent on free markets. Most of our leaders accept the market model and few people today support the sort of radical egalitarianism implicit in the symbolic-racism literature. I make this point in order to illustrate the utter pessimism inherent in the thrust of this literature. According to the symbolic-racism researchers, racism is tied to the traditional American values of individualism and self-reliance, values intimately connected with the workings of the American economy. It follows from this view that an end to white American racism is dependent on white Americans' repudiation of the free market and the values it engenders, and their adoption, in its place, of a radical egalitarianism in which equality of outcome is guaranteed by the government. In America today, such a message is a message of despair in as much as it makes the attainment of racial harmony dependent upon changed social conditions very unlikely to be realized.

There are other problems with the claim that traditional American values are merely code words for white racism. The values of self-reliance, postponement of gratification, fair dealings, and hard work are not white values or black values, but rather the values essential for success in any free and politically uncorrupted society. Gunnar Myrdal, writing in the 1940s, and anticipating greater opportunities for blacks, urged them to develop a clear understanding of their predicament. He saw the need for black individuals to attribute most of their problems to white mistreatment, if only to preserve black self-respect and counter the denigrating charge of black inferiority. But he also saw that blacks could go too far in this direction and thereby undermine their cause. Successful blacks, according to Myrdal, were able to "measure their failures and accomplishments in realistic terms." They took into account "their own abilities . . . caste deprivations, and . . . the factor of pure chance. . . ."[72]

Myrdal talked about the dangers of defeatism among blacks, and argued that they would have to resist the temptation to "exaggerate the accusation against the whites and so use the caste disabilities to cover all personal failures." He went on to argue that such thinking can "provide a ready excuse for sub-standard performance and for beliefs which are just as effective as the old inferiority doctrine" in hindering black advancement. He added that even more demoralizing is the temptation to succumb to "complacency," a "comforting self-pity," or a "cynical disregard for 'the rules of the game'."[73]

Rather than help young blacks gain a balanced view of the place of discrimination *and* of their own efforts in determining their future, as Myrdal had urged, current civil rights policies seem designed to prevent such a balanced assessment. Those who support these policies seem oblivious to the dangers of defeatism, cynicism, and hostility that such an unbalanced view can create. I will have much to say about this in future chapters where I discuss the problems of underclass communities, but I do not think it is unreasonable to attribute many of those problems to an ever more evident sense of defeatism, cynicism, and hostility among young people in the inner cities.

The association of traditional values with racism is particularly dangerous if it causes blacks to reject those values and thereby put themselves at odds with the majority of white Americans. The politicization of race has already created dangerous schisms between blacks and whites, and hopes for racial harmony

are not aided if blacks and whites adopt radically different political orientations. The tendency of many blacks and their supporters to equate market
capitalism and traditional ''middle-class'' values with bigotry is therefore not
helpful. It is unfortunate that social scientists, who ought to enlighten us on
these issues, have in fact contributed to the false idea that American values and
free-market economics are inimical to black interests. It is also unfortunate that
they have done so on the basis of very questionable theories and research.

Part III

Evolution and Human Nature

During the past two decades there has been an explosive growth in the study of the evolutionary origins of social behavior. Whether that research goes under the name of "sociobiology," coined by Edward O. Wilson, or "selfish gene theory," following the title of Richard Dawkins's important book, it has developed into a sophisticated and convincing body of theory and research for the explanation of social behavior among animals.[1] These same theories and explanations have been increasingly applied to human behavior: Pierre van den Berghe's *Human Family Systems* is a notable example from the field of anthropology.[2] As yet, however, this approach has made only limited inroads into general social science.

The evolutionary approach is particularly suited for providing insights into the nature of human development. It allows us to gain insight into why the transformation of the human child into the human adult follows nearly universal patterns, patterns that transcend racial and ethnic identity. Evolutionary theory helps us gain an understanding of the extent to which cultural practices can modify biologically conditioned human tendencies, and the extent to which culture must accommodate itself to those biological tendencies. For that reason, evolutionary explanations are particularly helpful in clarifying the reasons why development, especially adolescent development, sometimes goes awry.

When we survey the social scene in America today, it is difficult to avoid the conclusion that many of our society's failings, in education, law enforcement, single parenthood, and ethnic conflict, to name the most obvious, are problems that emerge during adolescence. This is true whether we look at the problems

145

of the inner cities or those in the affluent suburbs. If there are differences in the magnitude of the difficulties faced by adolescents in the inner cities and those in the suburbs, they are differences of degree and not of kind. The evolutionary perspective provides a powerful framework for analyzing the sources of these problems and may provide guidelines as to how they may be alleviated. The chapters in this section are designed as a broad introduction to this way of thinking.

Let me respond immediately to the reasonable, if unwarranted, concern that differential patterns of adolescent development, especially differences associated with race, will be attributed to genetic differences. While there may well be genetic differences, the overwhelming thrust of modern evolutionary thinking deals with the fundamental universality of human biological nature, not with the differences that accidents of ancestry may create. If black children in inner cities confront problems in adjustment that their suburban counterparts do not, modern evolutionary theory focuses on the ecological conditions which create these different patterns of adjustment. If children, whatever their ancestry, confront universal dilemmas in their transition to adulthood, we can hardly hope to ease that transition by ignoring those universal dilemmas, or by asserting that such universal dilemmas do not exist. As we will see, such an assertion is, in light of scientific evidence, untenable.

Human biology has been shaped by millions of years of evolution. Although our early hominid ancestors appeared on the scene some twenty million years ago, it was only within the last fifty to one hundred thousand years that human beings began to take their present form. There is little reason to believe that human biology has changed markedly since then.[3] Millions of years of evolution have produced in man a remarkable creature capable of complex planning and sophisticated communication. For the first time in the realm of living things, a creature evolved that could store up knowledge and skill and pass it across the barrier of generational and individual survival. The ability to communicate and store complicated information, to create a sophisticated *culture,* was a cataclysmic biological revolution that set in motion a remarkable series of events that continue to unfold to this day.

In the geologic or evolutionary time frame, the biological success of Homo sapiens, especially over the past five thousand years, has been a meteoric and rapidly accelerating phenomenon. The success of these five thousand years can only be understood as resulting from the cultural and technological advances gained through experience. Human biological evolution could not possibly have proceeded rapidly enough to account for the cultural changes during this period. The upshot is that modern truck drivers and nuclear physicists must go about their respective tasks with virtually the same sorts of bodies and the same sorts of brains as those possessed by their stone-age antecedents. To the extent, furthermore, that human emotional responses are shaped by neural structure and hormonal chemistry, modern human beings bring the same sort of emotional predispositions to their encounters as did the people who lived thousands of years ago.

Human beings can be taught in any generation to do things in ways unimagined by their parents' generation, but there are also limits to human adaptability. For instance, human beings adjusted rather easily to the automobile and the airplane. The basic physiology and mental acuity that served our ancestors at walking speeds seems more than adequate to accommodate the much greater speeds at which we propel ourselves today. But clearly there are limits even in such circumstances. It would be unreasonable to think that the average human being, with normal reflexes, could navigate a crowded modern highway at three hundred miles per hour; to do that, we would need different highways or automobiles with special electronic guidance systems.

In dealing with questions of public policy, it is important to have a clear understanding as to just how fixed or flexible human nature is. If there are important human characteristics or traits that are biologically fixed, then any attempt to foster social institutions that ignore those fixed traits are bound, at the least, to run into difficulties. No one could imagine a successful social organization that, for instance, ignored the need of people to eat and drink and sleep on a regular basis. Not all inherited human traits are so inflexible, but ignoring those that are almost always creates problems or requires special and often costly measures.

The answers to many public policy questions hang on the extent to which human beings can successfully adjust to new social arrangements. Should the military sanction a combat role for women, or would such a policy be counterproductive? Should men be expected to play a larger role in nurturing children, or would such an expectation lead to unwanted consequences? The likely success of various social programs is very much dependent on the extent to which human proclivities and traits are readily amenable to cultural modification. What sorts of human needs and propensities must, like hunger and thirst, be viewed as relatively fixed, and which are highly malleable?

Are the desires for sexual fulfillment and parenthood of the sort that it would be foolish to ignore them in shaping public policy? Is the current tendency for people to favor their own children relatively invariant, or could a human nature be fostered which made people equally concerned with all children, including those unrelated to them? Is the widespread human proclivity to identify with groups and be suspicious of outsiders an example of an invariant trait? What of the tendency of human males to engage in hostile conflict? What sorts of things can we expect children to learn easily and naturally, and what sorts of things will require diligent lessons to instill?

What, in brief, are those characteristics of human nature which we would be foolish to ignore in attempting to find social responses to the opportunities and difficulties of the modern age? What are the likely costs of ignoring those characteristics in terms of social harmony and human happiness? These are the sorts of questions to be addressed in the following two chapters.

6

Evolution and Adolescent Behavior

I. Introduction

A trait or proclivity can be attributed to human nature if it can be shown that it is a characteristic that all humans, or the overwhelming majority of humans, possess by virtue of the genetic material they share. Our genes direct the construction of our bodies. Those same genes direct the building of our brains, and the brain is the mechanism upon which are built all those things we associate with the mind. The human brain is inordinately well suited to being programmed by the environment, but that does not mean that it comes into the world without any important pre-wiring.

Those of us alive today are here because our ancestors possessed characteristics that enabled them to survive and reproduce in the environments in which they found themselves. Had they lacked some of these characteristics, or had the environment been different, they might very well have perished or failed to reproduce and we, needless to say, wouldn't exist. Darwin's theory of evolution demonstrated that in any particular environment some organisms, some combinations of characteristics, if you will, will be more likely to survive and reproduce than will others.[1]

Those that are successful are said to exhibit "Darwinian fitness." Such fitness means simply that an organism has been successful in having offspring and passing on characteristics to the next generation. Since Darwin's time, we have come to understand that such characteristics are shaped by genes, and we can now say that fitness involves the passing on of genes. Those who pass on their genes through many offspring are fit in this sense, those who pass on their genes through fewer offspring are less so.

149

It was Darwin's genius to recognize that since the environment is highly variable, the combinations of genes likely to be successful in different environments would likewise be highly variable. Species are groups of creatures whose members share a broad combination of characteristics and have found an "ecological niche" or place in the environment that they come, in time, to exploit. Such a species, if it is successful or "fit," will tend to fill up that niche. New species originate or evolve out of existing species, in chance fashion, by slight variations in the existing combinations of characteristics that allow for the further exploitation of the old niche, or by the capacity to exploit a new or changed niche. Not the least of such new "adaptations" may be changes that allow members of the new species to feed on members of the older one. Sometimes a new combination will be so much more effective in making use of the existing niche that it will, in time, come to displace the old combination.

Life, in this view, is extraordinarily opportunistic. Once a species comes to dominate an environment, new variants evolve to exploit some slightly different component of that environment and so carve out a new niche. The new variant may live side by side with the old. Sometimes the new displaces the old in some locations, but not in others. Sometimes the replacement is complete and the older species becomes extinct.

Such evolutionary change is continual and generally quite slow. The reason for this is straightforward. Totally new combinations of genes, formed randomly, are unlikely to be successful—no more likely to be successful, for instance, than a pile of bricks is likely to be a habitable structure. Only a few such combinations are likely to "work," meaning to survive for any appreciable period of time. A random deviation from that workable combination is very unlikely to be an improvement and, if it produces a significant change, is very likely to prove lethal. Most mutations, or random changes in genetic material, are in fact either unimportant or dangerous.[2]

Occasionally a small change can be very significant. The evolution of human beings from their primate ancestors can be seen to be the result of a series of small but significant changes. As different as men and chimpanzees are, for instance, they share, according to Oxford University zoologist Richard Dawkins, "about 99.5 percent of their evolutionary history."[3] Recent developments, which allow for the precise measurement of genetic similarity between species, suggest that Dawkins's estimate was not far off. These newer procedures indicate that 98.4 percent of the genetic material (DNA) of humans and chimps is the same. In discussing this data, anthropologist Derek Freeman points out that humans "are more closely related genetically to chimpanzees than are chiff-chaffs and willow warblers," birds belonging to the same genus.[4]

Because evolutionary change is so painfully slow, it is very unlikely that modern humans differ in any fundamental way from their hunter-gatherer human forebears, who appeared on the earth some fifty thousand years ago. For this reason, most anthropologists and psychologists look to the hunting and gathering way of life—the way of life common to all humans prior to the development of large-scale agriculture—for insights into what is most fundamentally, biologically human. The earliest humans, living before the advent of agriculture, lacked the tools to preserve all but the most rudimentary knowledge, and had to cope with the environment without the benefit that accrues to us after thousands of years of human learning and experimentation. Since early humans managed to survive and flourish, it had to be because they were equipped, genetically, with the tools to do so. Likewise, if most humans originally inhabited relatively mild climates, it is because their bodies were suited to survive in such climates. It took hundreds of years, perhaps thousands, for humans to acquire the knowledge that wrapping themselves in the skins of animals could enable them to survive in more harsh environments, and certainly as long to master the skills necessary to make such garments a mainstay of their existence. The same is true for all the other early innovations that allowed humans to voyage to every continent and, in time, to dominate most of the environments which they encountered. In the beginning, however, they had nothing but their own genetic endowment upon which to rely. Given the slow pace of evolutionary change, whatever they did, instinctively or intuitively, by virtue of their genetic endowment, is still part of our own nature, however overlaid by civilization.

Anyone who would contend that there is no such human nature would have to argue that early hominid types, with the advent of cultural practices such as language, lost the instinctual capacities which had enabled them to thrive without culture. In addition, one would have to argue that the earliest humans were able to acquire almost instantaneously, through learning, the rudimentary survival techniques that their nearest primate relatives possessed by inheritance. It is highly implausible that the combination of mutations that produced early hominid types and made them different from their primate ancestors was simultaneously accompanied by a host of other mutations that wiped out all of the earlier inherited survival skills enabling those primate ancestors to survive and flourish. On what grounds could one argue that inherited behavior patterns that aided the survival of earlier primates would have been selectively removed from the human gene pool at the very same time that the changes producing human types were unfolding?

One might argue, alternatively, that early men had important instinctual capacities but that over thousands of years they lost their fitness-conferring advantage because people could acquire such capacities through learning. This would require very rapid evolutionary change and would also imply that those who only possessed learned capacities were somehow more capable of surviving than those who possessed a combination of learned and instinctive tendencies. That would imply, for instance, that a human female who possessed only learned tendencies to care for her offspring would be better able to care for and protect her offspring than one whose learning reinforced her instinctive tendencies. As will become clear in the next chapter, this is a highly unlikely circumstance.

An example might lend support to the idea that inherited behavior patterns are still with us today. We now know, from thousands of years of experience, what sorts of substances in our environment are dangerous to ingest, and why. We know, for example, that it is dangerous to eat decomposing flesh, because it is infested with microbes. Dead organisms cannot fend off such microbes as can living organisms possessed of protective antibodies. If we were to ingest large quantities of such microbes, they might well overwhelm our own protective mechanisms, which, while they work quite well under limited attack, may fail under massive assault. But early humans had no knowledge of microbes and antibodies, nor of course do our primate relatives today. Nevertheless, most primates avoid eating the flesh of decaying carcasses, and the reason is plain: such carcasses smell bad and many primates are repelled by them. Fortunately for us, humans come equipped with a sense of smell very similar to the other primates, and with the genetic predisposition to avoid eating objects that emit chemical gases characteristic of decaying flesh. In human terms, such chemicals smell bad. We avoid them because they repel us instinctively and not because we come to learn they are bad for us. Of course, we now know that the gases emitted are the result of the work of microbes, but such knowledge was unavailable even two centuries ago, when humans knew nothing about microbes and little about gases.[5]

This point cannot be overemphasized. Since we possess so much in common with the apes, it is reasonable to assume that many of the characteristics that enabled apes to survive continue to exist in us. Clearly this does not imply that we have all of those traits, but merely that we did not emerge as a species, *de novo* as it were, with none of those characteristics. Hunters and gatherers, since they represent humans with relatively little advanced cultural experience, offer important insights into what sort of characteristics come naturally to us. If the earliest humans did not possess, by nature, certain physical and psychological characteristics, they could not possibly have survived long enough to exploit their advantages in planning and communication, advantages that, we can now see, enabled them to transcend the other primates. Among the critical skills that members of any species must possess are those that enable them, first, to survive long enough to reach sexual maturity; second, to successfully reproduce; and third, to protect their offspring long enough so that they in turn can reproduce. Any organism and, by extension, any human that lacked such skills would leave no progeny.

II. Sexual Reproduction

The simplest mode of reproduction is asexual. Some asexual organisms send off spores that are genetically identical to the parent and that develop by simple cell division. Others grow long runners or appendages that bud off and then develop independently. Some merely clone themselves. Bacteria, sponges, and many algae and fungi are examples of such asexual organisms, as is the pesky weed crabgrass.[6]

For such organisms, fitness involves living long enough to generate clones or otherwise generate copies of themselves. Asexual reproduction has the obvious advantage of being simple. It is also an advantage in that all clones or buds, with the exception of those containing the occasional mutation, are identical and are uniform copies of the original. Since the original worked well in its niche, so will the identical copies or clones. This advantage holds, however, only so long as the environment remains unchanged. In new or different environments, things may not work out as well. Furthermore, such organisms are unlikely to survive an invasion of new predators, which, given the opportunistic aspect of living things, are likely to arise. Asexual organisms can adapt only because, in general, they reproduce at a prodigious rate. As we will see, they can only do so because they are small and lacking in complexity.[7]

Somewhere fairly early in evolutionary history, sexual reproduction arose, and it has persisted despite the complications it entails because it produces greater diversity and greater opportunities to fully exploit the environment than cloning does. By mixing together the genes of two slightly different organisms, sexual reproduction regularly produces new and slightly different offspring in each generation.[8] The important point here is that the differences produced are regular and slight. If the changes were not slight, the chances that the offspring would survive in their parents' environment would be severely reduced. Slight variations, however, allow for survival in the original habitat and may allow for the exploitation of new or changed environments in which parents might not survive or flourish. For instance, fur-bearing animals can survive in climates that would be inhospitable without such protective insulation. The offspring of fur-bearing animals may have slightly more or less protective insulation, or fur of a different color, or fur with characteristics that differ slightly from the fur of their parents and siblings. A modest change in climate that might seriously undermine the parents or some of their offspring may allow others to flourish.

Sexual reproduction, in allowing for limited variation, has been the driving force for complexity in evolution. It is no accident that all large, complicated creatures reproduce sexually. The kind of change that results from mutations in the course of asexual reproduction could conceivably have, over a far greater span of time, produced such complexity, but once sexual reproduction entered the scene, asexual reproduction was no longer in the complexity-generating contest.

Whatever the advantages of sexual reproduction, however, it introduces considerable costs. In the case of plants, sometimes extraordinary physical structures evolve to allow the efficient and timely distribution of gametes (sex cells). The development of gametes must be timed appropriately, and coloration and chemical attractants must evolve to foster the spread of gametes by insects and other organisms.

Among animals, sexual reproduction is even more complex. It requires, almost always, that two independent organisms coordinate their activities. They must identify appropriate mates, and appropriate times to mate, and must somehow engage in mating activity to assure the mixing of genetic material.

Animals are, in addition, sometimes capable of protecting their genetic material while their offspring develop over what is sometimes an extended period of cell division. Animals that evolve mechanisms to protect their offspring, therefore, are likely to be more successful than animals that fail to evolve such mechanisms. In some species, especially complex ones like mammals and many birds, there is the need to protect the newly emerging offspring for an extended period after birth until it reaches the point where it can fend for itself.

All of the above activities require a degree of coordination and locomotion in the world totally unnecessary for asexual reproduction. Without sophisticated sensory and motor systems to guide organisms to each other, without complicated systems to coordinate their behavior as mates and parents, the process could not succeed. As organisms become more complex, these coordinating activities become increasingly complicated and sophisticated. The reason this is so follows directly from the dynamics of cell division and growth. All life is constructed on the basis of plans coded in DNA, and all growth involves the division of cells following the pattern specified in the DNA. Small, simple creatures require small plans and not much time to build. As creatures get more complicated, so must the plan encoded in the DNA, and the length of time required must increase. It is no accident that insects reproduce rapidly and prolifically, while humans and similar large, complex animals reproduce at a much slower and considerably more limited rate.

Simpler organisms thrive, in general, because they are enormously fecund and reproduce profusely. They cast their seed to the wind, as it were, and some of their offspring are willy-nilly likely to end up in favorable environments. This sort of prolific, incautious reproduction is called, by evolutionary biologists, the "r reproductive strategy."[9] It is a common strategy among asexual organisms and simple sexually reproducing organisms such as seed plants, insects, and many fish.

Building a large, complicated animal like a rat or a dog or a human being takes so much time and energy that relatively few can be produced. In many complex organisms, development cannot practically be completed within the protective body of the parent, but must continue outside the parent's body, and this in turn often requires considerable parental care and protection for the growing offspring, even after birth. Sexually reproducing complex animals like birds and mammals are said to follow a "K reproductive strategy."[10] The K strategy involves limited reproduction of fairly complex offspring and requires a considerable *parental investment* of time and energy on the part of one or both parents until the offspring reaches the point of self-sufficiency.[11] Human beings and elephants are, in this sense, extreme K strategists.

Since successful reproduction is the absolutely essential condition for fitness, it follows that organisms whose nervous systems lacked a guidance system resulting in reproduction would long since have become extinct. Since no organisms besides humans possess any comprehension of what reproduction is about, all sexually reproducing complex organisms, with the possible exception of humans, come equipped with pre-wired guidance systems, typically called reproductive instincts, that assure mating, reproduction, and, where necessary, parental care. The sexual reproduction of a complex organism requires, at the minimum, mechanisms for the location and selection of mates, for the physical act of copulation, and, where necessary, for the care of the young. No one seriously doubts that all three phases of reproduction are basically pre-wired and instinctive in rats and cats and birds and monkeys. In the case of human beings, however, we generally tend to imagine that only the physical act of copulation, and a few simple behaviors preceding it, are instinctive. Most sociologists, anthropologists, and psychologists would argue that mate selection and parental behavior are, in humans, essentially learned and socially programmed. But are they?

III. Mate Choice

Is it really reasonable to suppose that among all the genes we share with apes, we share none to direct us to appropriate mates and none to aid us in critically important parental activities? I think it is not.

The onset of mature sexual behavior is no accident and follows directly on reproductive readiness. Freudians are alone in asserting that sexual desire in humans arises before humans are capable of reproduction. Most observers will grant that sexual motivation in humans, as in all other organisms, is nicely synchronized with reproductive biology. When the human body has developed the capacity to reproduce, human sexual desire follows, sometimes a little late or a little prematurely, but not by much in most people. Furthermore, once sexual desire arrives on the scene, human beings seem remarkably clear on what it means and how that desire should be satisfied. Some instruction may be necessary, but not very much. In fact, given the sexual proclivities of human beings, it would require an extraordinary stretch of the imagination to suggest that we, alone among sexual reproducers, require detailed instruction.

After all, it is not obvious why children are born. Small children haven't a clue, which is why we need to explain it to them in biology classes. It is doubtful if early men understood the details, but they nevertheless managed to produce offspring easily enough. I don't think that it is reasonable to suppose that a group of children stranded on an island would become extinct for lack of proper sex education. It seems clear that humans, like all other sexually reproducing animals, are genetically programmed to engage in reproductive behavior.

According to psychologist and zoologist David Barash, sex is naturally ''sweet'' and asking a person why he likes sex is like asking a child why he likes sweet things.[12] In both cases the only appropriate response is that one just does; that is, it is part of the way we are built. By the same token, why should we need to teach ourselves to like sex with appropriate others and to like to care for our offspring? While most would agree with Barash on the genetic basis for sexual desire, many balk at the idea that mate selection and parental care may also be under neurological control directed in important ways by evolution. Let us examine if that objection can be sustained.

The seeming counterexample of homosexuality is a good place to start. In all societies a small percentage of the population is homosexual, and it is sometimes asserted that the fact of homosexuality in and of itself proves that mate choice must be learned. But the case of homosexuality proves no such thing. Empirical investigation involving interviews with homosexuals suggests that homosexual choice is as much innate as is heterosexual choice. Most homosexuals report that they came to their orientation naturally, much as do heterosexuals, without much instruction.[13] In fact, given the many difficulties that homosexuality poses for people in the societies that proscribe it, it is difficult to imagine why it would be learned in those societies.

It is true that certain societies, such as ancient Sparta, are said to have encouraged homosexuality, and in Rome it seems to have been tolerated as an approved form of sexual expression. It is also the case that in special circumstances, such as that of men confined to prison, some heterosexuals will resort to homosexuality and may learn to enjoy homosexual relations. Homosexuality as discussed here, however, refers to the tendency of individuals to prefer same-sex partners from the first stirrings of sexual desire in puberty and to find heterosexual relations either distasteful or clearly less desirable than homosexual relations.

Few social scientists any longer take seriously the psychoanalytic theory that this type of homosexuality is learned in infancy and is the product of an unresolved oedipal conflict. Psychiatrists were singularly ineffective in retraining homosexuals through psychoanalysis. Perhaps as a result, they no longer classify homosexuality as a behavior disorder. No one has demonstrated that homosexuality can be learned—or unlearned, for that matter. The attempts in the fifties and sixties to reorient homosexuals through training and various behavior-modification techniques were largely unsuccessful.[14]

Can genetic theories succeed in accounting for homosexuality where these others fail? A common objection to genetic theories is the fact that homosexuality seems to be fitness-reducing. How could homosexuality, if innate, have survived over time, since in interfering with reproductive success, it should long since have disappeared? This objection overlooks the fact that historically, many, if not most, homosexuals have reproduced. Many homosexuals clearly wish to have offspring and can arrange to do so. Furthermore, in those societies in which homosexuality is severely proscribed, most homosexuals will marry and bear offspring, if somewhat reluctantly and unhappily. How many of the women in ages past whose marriages were arranged were in fact lesbians? How many homosexual men in patriarchal and Christian Europe chose wives so as to have heirs and to avoid the suspicion and rejection that open homosexuality would have brought? It is somewhat ironic that societies that drive homosexuality underground may, if it is an inherited trait, inadvertently increase the number of homosexuals in those societies by forcing homosexuals to marry in order to hide their orientation.

Lee Ellis and M. Ashley Ames undertook an extensive and comprehensive review of the recent research literature in this area and concluded that the evidence for the learning of sexual orientation is very weak and "only appears to alter how, when and where the orientation is expressed."[15] They also examined a large number of animal studies that demonstrate that sexual inversions (what we call homosexuality in humans) can be experimentally induced in animals. In most animals the determination of sex is largely dependent upon the presence or absence of male hormones or androgens during fetal development. If androgens and related hormones are present during various critical phases of development, the organism will be physically and behaviorally male. If they are absent, the organism will be female. Under normal circumstances the presence of androgens is determined by the genetic makeup of the organism in question, but under certain conditions the uterine hormonal environment can influence the exposure of the fetus to androgens. Ellis and Ames report that this can result from the experimental manipulation of androgens, from stress on the mother during pregnancy, and from exposure to certain pharmacological agents that can block or augment androgen function.[16]

Depending on when during development the normal androgen level is altered, different effects will be produced. The effects of early androgen-level alterations tend to show up in physical inversions, while later alterations are more likely to affect brain development and tend to show up as behavioral inversions. In experimental studies on rodents, depriving a male fetus of testosterone late in its development produces a male who looks like a male but who, at puberty, exhibits female patterns of behavior. Ellis and Ames report that such males, "instead of mounting receptive females and behaving combatively toward other males" as do normal males, "show little or no interest in females and often display feminine-like presenting postures when in the proximity of other males."[17]

Female rodents who are exposed to androgens late in fetal development tend to mount other females and resist mounting by males to a degree, according to Ellis and Ames, "that is quite uncommon among most other females." In addition, the researchers report that "[t]he predominant response these females make to an approaching male is dominating and aggressive, especially if the interactants are strangers."[18]

Ellis and Ames argue that while there is no experimental evidence to relate the animal studies to humans, a number of findings suggest that similar mechanisms are at work in determining human sexual orientation. Genetic defects, drug exposure, and stress during development can all affect the fetus's exposure to hormones, and studies of such effects are suggestive, though hardly conclusive, regarding a biological mechanism for homosexuality. Ellis and Ames theorize that sexual orientation is "determined in humans in essentially the same way as in all other mammals . . . by the degree to which the nervous system is exposed to testosterone, its metabolite estradiol, and to certain other sex hormones while neural organization is taking place." They argue that fetal hormone exposure not only determines sexual orientation but also "[s]ex-typical behavior patterns" that are "more common or intense in one sex than in the other. . . ."[19]

Recent studies of male twins seem to support this interpretation of homosexuality. In 52 percent of identical twins, if one member of the pair was homosexual so was the other member. On the other hand, only 22 percent of fraternal twins were both homosexual, which is similar to the rate for brothers who were not fraternal twins.[20] This suggests that both genetic and intrauterine effects may be important. Also suggestive is the recent finding by neurobiologist Simon Levay of significant differences between heterosexual and homosexual men in the hypothalamic region of the brain, a region known to regulate sexual behavior.[21]

If the theory put forth by Ellis and Ames is confirmed, and as yet the evidence is merely suggestive, it would mean that sexual orientation is determined by neurological factors over which the individual has little control. It would also mean, as Ellis and Ames argue, that many of the behavioral predispositions normally thought of as masculine and feminine may also be determined in similar fashion.

Whatever the final resolution to such questions, the attention to the anomaly of homosexuality sometimes obscures the more fundamental point that the overwhelming majority of people, including homosexuals, seem to come by their sexual preferences instinctively. But how does one inherit the knowledge of what is and what is not an appropriate mate?

In the case of animals the answer is fairly clear. Animal sexual behavior is, in almost all cases, an innately programmed response to fairly specific stimuli. The male dog reacts automatically to the chemicals put out by the receptive female. In fact, chemical signals are the triggering mechanism in most, if not all, animals. Primates are very often aided by visual signals, such as the coloration of the genital region of many females when they are ovulating. In addition, receptive females in many species present themselves to the male, and this presentation is an additional visual stimulus for sexual behavior in males. Do humans inherit predispositions to visual stimuli that produce sexual arousal? If sexual preference is under genetic control, then it would appear that they must.

Many studies have been performed with infants to determine if they can react to certain visual patterns intuitively. Perhaps the best known of these are the "visual cliff" studies that demonstrate clearly that infants intuitively detect and retreat from the drops that occur at the edges of a surface. This is demonstrated by setting two tables at a distance from each other and bridging them with a glass top. Infants trying to reach their mothers by crawling from one end of the glass to the other will usually refuse to cross over the section of glass bridging the gap between the tables.[22] Furthermore, other studies have shown that infants, even those only a few days old, will mimic the emotional expressions of adults, indicating that they recognize different facial expressions, and suggesting that the ability to do so is inherited.[23] It does appear, therefore, that infant brains come pre-wired to react instinctively to a limited range of visual patterns or stimuli.

Is the human brain built so as to begin to react instinctively during puberty to certain visual patterns with sexual emotions, as is the case in other primates? At present there is no definitive answer to this question, but it is not unreasonable to suggest an affirmative answer. In any case, the attempts currently under way to map the human genome may give us a definitive answer within the lifetimes of many living today.

IV. Courtship and Sexual Selection

In many species, fairly complex rituals precede copulation. Receptive females attract males, who then engage in a variety of "courtship" behaviors that may or may not result in mating. What are these courtship rituals all about? Why has evolution produced so many complicated and seemingly wasteful ways to bring sperm and egg together? Wouldn't males and females who, when ready, merely accepted the first mate to come along, save a lot of time and energy, and wouldn't they therefore leave more offspring than their finicky neighbors? The answer is that sometimes they might and sometimes they might not. They might not fare very well if their promiscuous couplings produced defective offspring that failed to survive to maturity. Clearly, therefore, among the things that make sexually reproducing animals fit is the capacity to select mates with whom they are likely to produce healthy offspring. This is particularly obvious if one considers what would happen if animals from different species were so obtuse as to attempt to engage in copulation. This rarely occurs, since animals clearly prefer mating with members of their own species.

In addition, among the animals in those species where extensive parental care is required, we would expect successful animals to be able to detect in prospective mates the potential for providing such care. For example, the rearing of young sparrow hawks is a time- and energy-consuming business requiring the full-time efforts of both parents. Since sparrow hawks are predators relying on small game, it is critical that they be good at hunting if their offspring are to be reared successfully. I quote from David Barash's *The Whisperings Within,* from which this example is taken:

> I once spent almost an hour watching a spectacular aerial display: two sparrow hawks were courting, flying in elaborate loops alternating with power dives. They had a small mouse which one of them had caught, and at different points in the exhibition, one of the birds would drop its prize and the other would gracefully swoop down and snatch it in mid-air. It was an impressive demonstration, and it occurred to me only afterward that I was probably not the only one who was impressed. Certainly I was not the one for whom it was intended.

For Barash, the display is an opportunity for potential mates to size up each other's competence as hunters. As Barash puts it, would you, if a sparrow hawk, "wish to make a reproductive commitment" to a partner who was physically or otherwise incompetent?[24]

It is important to note that in their acrobatic exercise the sparrow hawks are not merely transmitting information about their ability as hunters but also information about their general health and physical robustness. It is not stretching things to suggest that in performing this courtship ritual they are attempting to convince each other, without conscious awareness of course, that together they can produce robust offspring. A sparrow hawk who could not perform the ritual well, or who could not judge whether another performed it well, would be less likely to have viable offspring.

There is an interesting sidelight here. Once a species has evolved a way of judging the merits of prospective mates, the characteristics associated with desirable mates become in and of themselves desirable, whether or not they continue to have any real survival or reproductive value, at least until new criteria for judging have evolved. The reason is that reproductive success depends on having successful offspring. Those who possess desirable traits are likely to pass on those traits to offspring who will themselves, by virtue of possessing those traits, be more desirable. In human terms, finding a spouse generally considered attractive, for whatever reason, makes it more likely that your children will be attractive and therefore more likely that you will have grandchildren, without which, of course, all your mating would have been for naught.

V. Sexual Competition and Human Aggression

Birds such as sparrow hawks are relatively unusual in the animal kingdom in that both parents are critical to the successful rearing of the young. In most species, little care is required. Courtship among insects and fish, for example, seems to serve primarily to provide clues to genetic well-being. If all that two creatures need to do in order to produce offspring is mix sperm and egg together, then the only important information about prospective mates is whether they carry genes likely to produce robust offspring.

Such cases raise the issue of differential behavior on the part of mothers and fathers, and more fundamentally, of sexual differences in general. In the case of many fish, for example, where the female deposits eggs on the ocean floor and males deposit sperm over them, and nothing else is required, it is hard to discern identifiable patterns of behavior to distinguish between paternal and maternal behavior. We would expect sexual differentiation in such cases to be rather limited. The meaning of maleness and femaleness comes down to the rudimentary question of who carries eggs and who carries sperm, and little else.

In terms of the need to provide care for their young, most mammals are intermediate between insects and sparrow hawks. Mammalian offspring require care, but not necessarily the extensive care of both parents. In mammals it is always the case that the egg-carrying female bears the brunt of the parental work, since she alone bears the burden of gestation and nursing. This difference in parental investment produces clearly identifiable physical and behavioral differences between males and females. Why should this be so? There is no obvious reason why mammals are divided into two sexes, male and female, in which the female is stuck with the greater burden of carrying the fetus. There is no simple reason why creatures similar to mammals might not have evolved as hermaphroditic types who carried both sperm and eggs, and who, when they mated, impregnated each other. In such a species there would be no identifiable division between males and females. Such a reproductive system, known as "isogamy," does in fact exist among some fungi and some other simple organisms.[25]

Richard Dawkins has suggested that the division of the sexes may have to do with the fact that in isogamous reproduction there is an advantage to cheating. If one partner can somehow secretively block the reception of sperm, it might trick the other into accepting its sperm without reciprocation. In this way, one partner's body is tied up with gestating an egg and the other is free to go on to try to deceive another partner, since it has not tied up its own body with gestation. Cheaters in this sort of game can have far more offspring than can the trusting souls which become impregnated. Under this scenario, the cheaters should spread rapidly in the population, but they could not become too common or they would find no one to cheat on. In time, the honest souls would come to be highly desirable, and they could in turn be fairly discriminating and cautious about their choice of mates. Eventually an equilibrium between cheaters and trusting souls should arise.[26] In such a way, maleness (cheating) and femaleness (being cautious) would arise as "evolutionary stable strategies," to borrow British zoologist J. Maynard Smith's important concept.[27]

Whatever the origin of sexual differences, the fundamental distinction is that males provide sperm and females eggs, and from that fact follows a host of interesting and important differences. The eggs of the female carry nutrients critical for the early growth of the fetus. They are therefore larger than the sperm, which are really little more than vehicles for the carrying of chromosomal material to the eggs. The female egg therefore requires more biological work and more time to produce than do sperm. As a consequence, eggs are considerably more scarce than sperm. The female's energies go to producing a small number of large eggs, the male's energies to producing a large number of small sperm.

The law of supply and demand—which dictates that if something is desirable or necessary, it will be in greater demand to the extent that it is scarce—produces the expected result. Eggs, being scarcer than sperm, are in greater demand than sperm, or to put it another way, females possess something over which we would expect males to compete, and that they most assuredly do.

In species in which parental care on the part of the female is sufficient and males contribute only sperm, some males can impregnate many females and others will, necessarily, impregnate few. It follows that those males who are successful in gaining access to many females will leave many sons who possess characteristics similar to their own. In other words, we should expect males to evolve in the direction of becoming specialized competitors for eggs. Two options are available to males. They can attempt to drive off their competitors through aggressive actions or displays, or they can compete with other males to become more attractive to females. These options are not necessarily mutually exclusive.

Edward O. Wilson refers to the first of these options as "intrasexual" and the second as "epigamic." Intrasexual competition involves the competition between the males for access to females. With rare exceptions, the more aggressive the male, the greater his success in obtaining mates. Epigamic competitive behaviors, on the other hand, are displays, such as the aerial display of the sparrow hawk, designed to win the favor of the female. In general, these behaviors allow for the demonstration of physical health and competence in the male. By demonstrating such health, the male advertises the likelihood that his sperm will produce healthy and competent offspring.[28]

Often intrasexual and epigamic competition overlap. In species in which males must fight with each other for access to females, the fact of success in such fighting is evidence of genetic worth. A male who wins in such struggles is more likely to have sons who will also triumph. The female who chooses successful combatants is therefore likely to have sons who are in turn successful.

Of course, I am being figurative in these descriptions of animal mating strategies. Except in humans, these behaviors are genetically programmed and involve no intentionality on the part of the participants. Animals merely act "as if" they were trying to maximize fitness and pass on their genes successfully. Those animals which possess genes which program them to act in specific ways got those genes from parents similarly programmed. If that programming had not produced viable offspring, the programming would have died along with the parents carrying it, or with the incompetent offspring they produced. To take a familiar example, a female horse which allows a donkey to impregnate her will give birth to a sterile mule. Genes which program mares to reject the advances of donkeys in favor of male horses are therefore more likely to be passed on than genes which program mares to be undiscriminating in this regard.

Consider the case of male bowerbirds (studied in Australia by Gerald Borgia), who are unusual but hardly extraordinary in their efforts to attract females. They build elaborate and colorful structures (bowers) that the female examines with great care; the female will only allow the male to mate with her if she approves of his workmanship. The bower is used solely for courtship; nesting structures are created separately. Competent bower builders are therefore more likely to mate and leave offspring. Since the females are making comparative judgments, males attempt to dismantle or damage the bowers of their competitors by attacking them and stealing colorful or otherwise attractive objects from them. The more-aggressive birds destroy their neighbors' work and protect their own. Since the bower is a sort of bowerbird billboard, advertising the competence and aggressiveness of its builder, the more colorful and undamaged a bower, the better it conveys the desired message.[29]

In many mammals and birds, the assistance of the male in caring for the young is important but not absolutely critical. Humans are surely a case in point. Depending on the environment in which humans find themselves, the male's assistance in parental care may be critical or largely superfluous. Obviously it is to the advantage of the female to secure the male's assistance, if only as a sort of insurance policy. The male, however, may be inclined to desert a female after impregnating her and to go off in search of another female. We would expect that in species where desertion may be profitable to the male and harmful to the female, the females would evolve means of detecting loyalty in males. We would expect in such cases for courtship rituals to advertise the male's loyalty as well as his aggressiveness, genetic well-being, and ability to provide resources. Obviously it might pay for the male to devise strategies of deception, especially if he could be relatively assured that his offspring would receive adequate care from the female if he deserts her. Of course, the female may be induced to abandon a newborn in such cases if she can be assured of a quick replacement by a more reliable mate. In that case, a wily male can hang around long enough to induce sufficient maternal investment so as to make maternal desertion of the offspring too costly.

Among human hunters and gatherers, physical strength and prowess are prerequisites for successful competition for mates *and* for providing resources for offspring *and* for providing evidence of physical health. The extended period of human gestation and nursing puts a high priority on the male's capacity as resource provider, especially if it is necessary to forage widely for food.

Where polygamy is practiced among humans, physical strength and competence at aggressive contests are common features of successful males. In polygamous societies, weaker males often find themselves permanent bachelors. From a raw, calculating Darwinian perspective, a female in such a society might prefer to share with other females the favors of a powerful polygamous male who may give her sons with equal propensities, rather than accepting a monogamous union with a weaker, less desirable male whose sons might, like their father, lack the qualities to provide many grandchildren.

In many species, and especially among humans, large harems are the exception, since it is rarely possible for one male to provide for more than a few mates.[30] Therefore, not all females can expect to win the most successful males, but it will be a rare female who will have to go without any mate. This is not so for males. Evolutionary biologists would argue that this difference explains why female competition, though it may be intense in some species, rarely reaches the level found in the males. It also explains why female competition, if it exists at all, generally takes the form of epigamic displays of fitness rather than the aggressive combat of intrasexual competition. Females do not have to compete for partners per se as do many males, though they do compete for the more desirable partners. While displays of physical beauty and grace are important in the human male and female alike, they seem more important for the human female.

Interestingly, studies of attractiveness in humans done by psychologists indicate that facial features and bodily physique are considered pleasing if they are relatively close to the group average and do not deviate too much from the norm.[31] This suggests that physical appearance may be used by both sexes as a sort of proxy for general well-being. In other words, if there is nothing peculiar in the way one's body or face is shaped, there is little reason to expect that less visible aspects of the body suffer peculiarities and potential defects. The universal custom of dancing may be a simple way for humans to demonstrate physical fitness and agility, especially for the human female, who need not, in most cases, demonstrate strength or fierceness.

VI. Human Adolescent Behavior

It seems reasonable to argue that the courtship activities of human adolescents, such as dancing, are cultural elaborations built upon fundamental biological predispositions, rather than purely cultural inventions. The competitive activities of adolescent males, especially those activities that demonstrate physical fitness, athletic prowess, and aggressive potential, are nearly universal. Such competition is common, in one form or another, in almost all societies and is almost invariably looked upon with admiration and approval by young females. In fact, the tastes of young females for males who demonstrate evidence of physical well-being and aggressive potential seem remarkably intractable, to the chagrin of parents who often favor very different qualities in their daughters' suitors (such as a suitor's promise as a resource provider). The tastes of young females surely vary greatly within cultures and across cultures, but that variation is not so great as to completely obscure their underlying basis in biology.

As a sidelight, it is interesting that among many species, including humans, fully mature males are more likely than neophytes to be successful in competition for females. A young male's ability to challenge and overcome a mature male is therefore a sign of readiness for mating, and if the male is especially young, a sign of unusual fitness. It hardly requires a major leap to see the rebelliousness of precocious adolescent human males, and their tendency to bridle at authority, as a fairly straightforward advertisement of their suitability for mating.

The appeal of the flamboyant rock star advertising his masculinity and his rebellion, is now near-universal, and seems to illustrate the points made above. But this type is a wildly exaggerated and relatively recent phenomenon. Most societies are controlled by older men, who recognize the adolescent male as the threat to them he is. Considerable energies are devoted to keeping youthful passions under control. In hunter-gatherer societies, and in fact in most societies until recently, there was little in the way of material possessions which people could devote time to acquiring and with which they could advertise their status and worth. It is hardly surprising that the possession of wives and children was, until very recently, a universally recognized sign of well-being and status. Wives and children are in some cases the only "wealth" available in society. For that reason, older men are not at all happy to allow younger men to take women away from them if they can prevent it, which they usually can by virtue of superior strength and experience.

Many societies have elaborate initiation rituals through which young men must go before they are entitled to take a wife. In some societies they must perform heroically in battle or bring home a sufficient number of scalps, to prove their readiness for marriage. Among the Yanomamo of South America, for example, wives are often taken in raids on neighboring villages and are usually taken by older, more powerful males, who often have more than one wife. Young men must sometimes forgo marriage until middle age and in the interim engage in a great deal of warfare. Needless to say, many young men never survive to enjoy the benefits of matrimony.[32]

These practices can often be understood as ways to keep young men out of the market for women, and to make good use of their aggressive potential in the bargain. The Christian ban against polygamy seems designed to create greater marital democracy among men of different material conditions, and perhaps inadvertently allows young men greater opportunities. Even in Europe, however, before this century young men were not allowed to take wives until they had satisfied the parents of a young woman that they were capable of providing for her, and that often meant obtaining land or ownership of a business, or some other visible means of support. Most people were simply not in a position to assume the burdens of providing for the children of their daughters, nor did they look kindly on those who might impose that burden on them.

The consequence was that in Europe, until fairly recently, most men did not marry until their late twenties.[33] It was only among the wealthy that younger people entered into marriages. Customs all over the world are clearly designed as safeguards to protect communities against premature sexual encounters. Almost all societies, until very recently, had mechanisms to prevent young men and women from producing offspring before they were prepared to provide for them.

It was not simple prudery that kept young women constantly under surveillance in most societies, but simple prudence. Determining readiness for marriage and the choice of a partner were often too important to leave in the hands of the young. Arranged marriages were, as Jean-Louis Flandrin explains, rarely merely marriages of convenience:

> In our own century, when we believe only in marriages of love, we laugh at, or are indignant at, ''marriages of reason'' arranged by families, in which there is the tendency to see only ''marriages of money.'' However in a society in which the vast majority of families owed their subsistence to a small or large capital, which they made, or failed to make, bear fruit by their own efforts or others, it was *criminally thoughtless* to marry without having the capital needed to maintain the future children. (Emphasis added)[34]

The most common mechanism for keeping young people under control in Europe and early America was the apprenticeship system, where youngsters were put out to work in households, in shops, and on farms. Those who took in such children and benefited by their labor were required to provide proper preparation for a trade as well as moral supervision until a youngster was prepared to enter his or her own household through marriage. The Puritans who settled the Massachusetts Colony were so suspicious of single people that the colony's government forbade them from establishing households on their own, and in fact made single living a criminal offense.[35] New arrivals from England had to find lodging in an existing household and, if they refused, could be fined, imprisoned, or sent back to England. The Puritans of Plymouth Colony did not go so far as to make single living criminal, but required young men to obtain permission to do so from town authorities.[36]

The point of this is straightforward: Should the normal constraints that were everywhere placed on young men and women break down, we should expect young men to tend to engage in competitive contests of physical prowess to attempt to please women. We should expect young women to tend to admire men who are successful in those contests. And if no restraints are imposed, we should expect a good number of pregnancies among relatively young women.

Of course, young women who are attractive to males are likely to have high expectations in their selection of mates. They can wait for an attractive male who possesses the traits essential for economic success, or one with inherited wealth. Desirable women with high expectations are therefore likely to display prudence in their mating behavior even if not constrained by parents. Today, birth control and abortion allow women to enjoy the sexual favors of men without committing themselves too early to motherhood.

It is well to point out that prior to the modern period, engaging in sexual behavior was, for women, tantamount to deciding in favor of motherhood. In most cases the roles available to women were so limited that few alternatives were open to the average woman besides marriage and motherhood, and to choose to forgo motherhood in favor of those few alternatives often meant denying oneself sexual gratification as well. Today, of course, contraception allows women to make conscious choices about sexual behavior and motherhood—and to make those choices independently of one another. This should not blind us to the fact that, with few exceptions, the biological drives which predispose men and women to engage in sexual behavior, had in the past the concurrent effect of predisposing them to parenthood.

As will become clear in the discussion of single parenthood in Chapter 10, many poor women are fairly cavalier about birth control, so that in a great many cases the choice of sexual gratification for them implies, albeit perhaps without full conscious recognition, a choice of motherhood. This somewhat perplexing behavior on the part of a good number of poor women can be partially explained by the fact that such women often have very low expectations of entering into a favorable marriage or obtaining a desirable vocation. Such women may, therefore, have little reason to postpone motherhood, especially if they can reasonably expect to support the child on their own with government support. If a woman believes herself undesirable or if she finds the men available to her lacking the skills to provide support or lacking in reliability and loyalty, she may decide to get on with the business of child-rearing without the help of a male. If she, for various reasons, believes that her occupational options are limited and unpromising, motherhood may appear to be one of the few desirable roles available. The evidence marshaled in Chapter 10, dealing with illegitimacy among the poor, suggests that this interpretation is not far off the mark. Putting off motherhood in such circumstances would only make sense if it allowed a female to eventually attract a loyal, resourceful male who also possessed the sorts of characteristics (genes) she desires in her offspring. If loyal and resourceful men are unavailable, she may find that her only recourse is to look for an attractive male who will father attractive children. If, in addition, she need not worry about the support of her child, such a choice is eminently sensible, especially if the only likely alternative is to go through life childless.

VII. Cultural Constraints on Mate Choice

In most societies human beings are not allowed to simply follow their natural inclinations when it comes to reproduction. Often reproduction is tied in with other cultural ends thought sufficiently important to severely constrain the choices that individuals make. Nevertheless, few of these constraints run directly counter to evolutionary programming. Most often they are cultural variations that serve evolutionary as well as cultural ends. It is important to understand how culture interacts with genes in such matters, for such an understanding sheds light on the particular patterns of courtship and reproduction that have taken root among the men and women in the American underclass. In particular, it may help us to understand the truly extraordinary and highly debilitating rates of illegitimacy found in the inner cities.

The simplest social organizations involve nuclear families tied together by kinship and reciprocity in small hunting and gathering bands living in small villages. Larger social organizations require the coordination of activity between individuals who live in separate villages. The most common such organization to emerge is that of the kinship-based clan or lineage group. The most common form of lineage or clan is the patrilineage, which traces descent through the male line.

In a patrilineal descent group, males form social and political bonds based on their sharing of a common ancestor. The sons of a man, and their sons in turn, belong to the same clan or lineage. When in need of assistance, they can look to others in the clan for help, and they are in turn obliged to provide help when called upon. The chain of authority in such an organization is relatively simple: it runs from father to son to son's son. Typically, daughters are married out and they and their offspring are lost to the clan, joining the clan of their husbands. In turn, men within the clan marry women from outside, women whose male offspring contribute to the size and therefore the political and military power of the lineage. The more women brought into the clan by marriage, the greater the clan's prestige and power.

In southern China before the twentieth century, for instance, such lineages spanned many generations, and the stronger ones held sway over considerable territory—in most cases constituting not only kinship groups but governance structures as well, defining their own laws and enforcing them. The political structure of early feudal Europe was somewhat different but nonetheless reflected a similar pattern.

The patrilineal system is simple in that its line of command is straightforward and its membership well-defined. Contrast this to the modern American kinship system, which is bilateral; we belong to both our mother's and father's families, and there is no prescriptive preference should a conflict arise between these families. Bilateral descent blurs the lines of mutual obligation. If one's paternal grandfather and maternal grandfather are at odds and demand one's allegiance, to whom is one obligated? If a man's brother-in-law should ask for assistance, how can he provide it if the brother-in-law is at odds with the man's own biological brothers? No such problems arise in a patrilineal descent system, where one always owes obligations to, and can seek help from, a single set of relatives united by common ancestry through one ancestral male. There are no overlapping obligations that could create confused or dual loyalties.[37] This may be the reason that this social structure is so widespread and stable. In many cases, such as in southern China until this century, it continued as the prime form of social organization until it was replaced by the modern state.[38]

A somewhat different social organization is also found in various societies, far less often than the patrilineage, but common enough to require explanation. These societies are also organizations of men linked by common ancestors, but in this case they are linked through their mothers and grandmothers in a system known as matrilineal descent. All the brothers of a particular mother form a descent group. This has the unusual effect that a man's children belong to the descent group of his wife and not his own. The only way the descent group can add members, therefore, is through the childbearing of sisters. A woman's children are born into her brothers' descent group and share mutual benefits and obligations with them. They in turn share obligations with their maternal uncles and aunts, but not with the brothers and sisters of their father. In these societies, therefore, men usually take a greater interest in their sisters' children than in the children of their wives.[39] It would be as if, in our own society, men normally left their inheritance to their sisters' children rather than to those born to their wives.

Matrilineal systems are fairly complicated, and the bonds between matrilineal kin are often not as strong as in patrilineages, especially when marriages occur between men and women whose families live in widely separated areas. How does one arrange for the care of a sister's children when they are spread over the countryside? The Navajo of the southwestern United States are an important example of a matrilineal society of this sort.[40] Things are less complicated if women and men live in close proximity and the bonds between uncle and sister's children can be strengthened. The most extreme example of this type is found among the Nayar of southwest India.[41] Another example are the Ashanti people of the west coast of Africa, who played a prominent role in the slave trade. The Ashanti live in cities and can therefore maintain close ties with their brothers and their sisters' children, as well as with their own wives.[42]

However, in cases where men live side by side with their brothers, their bonds to their wives tend to be relatively weak. Among the Nayar, a husband is little more than a temporary lover (and there may be more than one) with ''visiting rights.''[43] Likewise, the visiting husband is common among the Ashanti, but the Ashanti husband has the advantage of being fed by his wife. Anthropologist Robin Fox writes:

> Any evening in an Ashanti town, we are told, we will see children running between the houses carrying dishes and bowls of food. They are taking it from

the mother's house to the father's house. The father will be at home with his mother, and his sisters and their children.[44]

How could a pattern arise in which men take more interest in their sisters' children than in their wives' children? How can a man invest more in his uterine nieces and nephews, than in his sons and daughters, when he is so much more closely related to the latter? It seems to run contrary to the fundamental principles of evolution, and is indeed a troubling paradox for sociobiological theory.

Canadian anthropologist Pierre van den Berghe has suggested that such a pattern would make biological sense in societies where men are so unsure of their wives' faithfulness that they seriously doubt that they themselves are the fathers of their wives' children. Should that probability fall sufficiently low, it would make good biological sense for them to use their energies to help their sisters' children, since they are sure to share at least some of their own genes with them, whereas they may share none with their wives' children. One is always certain of maternity, whereas paternity is far more problematical, and therefore kin relationships running through females are always more certain than kin relationships running through males.[45]

It is hard to know how such an arrangement could originate, but van den Berghe suggests that it might be the result of conditions where men are required to go off for extended periods of time to hunt, sail, or make war. This certainly seems to explain the case of the Nayar, who were a caste of warriors in which the men lived in barracks much of the time or were off fighting wars. Robin Fox explains that it was the custom for the young women to go as servants into upper-class Brahmin families and that they were "often taken as concubines by the Brahmin men." Such servant women, at puberty, were frequently already married to a Nayar man, but for largely ceremonial or political purposes. When a girl became pregnant during her service in a wealthy home, she would return to her mother's home, at which time the ceremonial marriage was "dissolved and the woman was free to take as many as twelve 'lovers' or temporary husbands."[46]

Since these lovers were Nayar men and were frequently away on military service, their opportunities to avail themselves of visiting rights were generally quite limited. In the Nayar arrangement, it was almost impossible to determine paternity with any accuracy and it was not thought very important. Children, whoever fathered them, belonged to their maternal uncles' lineage. The Nayar's lack of interest in paternity represents an extreme and in Fox's terms a "notorious" example of matrilineality.[47]

Among the Ashanti, as we saw, children do have recognized fathers, though their biological paternity may be uncertain, since the men do not actually live with their wives. Other matrilineal arrangements exist where men do live with their wives and may contribute substantially to the support and well-being of their wives' children. Nevertheless, in all such societies, the children belong to the lineage or clan controlled by their mothers' brothers.

One would expect very different attitudes toward the role of women in these divergent types of lineage. In patrilineal societies, men should be, and generally are, greatly concerned with their wives' sexual behavior, since a wife's infidelity might burden a man with the support of another man's children, and would confuse the line of paternal descent. In such societies, men are the sole supporters of their wives' children. In contrast, according to van den Berghe, "[i]n matrilineal societies, where men invest principally in their uterine nephews, men want their sisters to marry and to reproduce, but they care relatively little about their nephew's paternity (and hence their sister's marital fidelity)."[48] Likewise, husbands in matrilineal societies are less interested in their wives' fidelity, since a wife's children "belong" to the clan of their mother's brothers and receive substantial assistance from their maternal uncles. As I said earlier, matrilineal arrangements are complicated, which is why they are not nearly as common as patrilineages.

When it comes to the sexual behavior of women before marriage, as opposed to that of women already married, men in both types of societies have reason to be concerned, although the reasons are different (as are the degrees of concern). In patrilineages, men seek to have their daughters marry into other patrilineages, and a daughter who is promiscuous may be difficult to marry off if she becomes pregnant, especially where virginity is highly valued. On the other hand, an illegitimate child is evidence of fertility, and the child can be adopted by the patrilineage and can add to its strength, albeit at the cost of providing for the child. Alternatively, the biological father may adopt the child if a marriage can be arranged. Premarital sex among women is approved or tolerated in 57 percent of a large sample of patrilineal societies.[49]

In matrilineal societies, on the other hand, where new members can only be gotten through men's sisters, men are somewhat more anxious to police their sisters' premarital activity for economic and social reasons. Husbands are usually expected to make at least some contribution to the support of wives and children. For that reason, women are urged to marry their lovers in order to obtain that support. As van den Berghe puts it, "matrilineally related men have an interest in parasitizing their brothers-in-law for the benefit of their uterine nephews and thus of themselves." As a consequence, matrilineal societies are more likely to frown upon women engaging in premarital sex than are patrilineal societies. Premarital sex is approved or tolerated in only 36 percent of matrilineal societies.[50] Another reason for this, perhaps, is that men in matrilineal societies have reason to be concerned with the quality of their sisters' lovers. If they take as lovers men who produce incompetent children, the matrilineage will acquire members who, instead of becoming helpmates, prove to be burdens. Maybe this is why the Nayar accept the concubinage of their sisters to Brahmin men: perhaps they believe that the higher status of such men will be converted into able offspring and valuable members of the matrilineal clan. The quality of men whom daughters and sisters marry in patrilineal society is of only modest concern to the patrilineage, since the offspring of those unions do not become part of the patrilineage.

The net result is that unmarried women are guarded more closely in matrilineal societies, while married women are guarded more closely in patrilineal societies. In addition, women have much greater freedom of choice and divorce is easier in matrilineal societies. If a woman is unhappy with a husband, her brothers do not care much if she takes another, so long as he seems reasonably competent. Likewise, an unhappy husband can usually be replaced by another.

In patrilineal organizations, on the other hand, wives' fidelity is essential, since men are extremely anxious that the children they invest in should be their own. Moreover, divorce is rarely tolerated, since men are reluctant to give up a woman's reproductive value. If they do so, it is usually at the man's pleasure and not the woman's.

In summary, the most important point is that males—who have in the past, by virtue of their greater aggressive potential, dominated all societies—have been most concerned about, and therefore have regulated most closely, the reproductive behavior of women to serve their own interests and the interests of their lineage.

VIII. Courtship Patterns in the Underclass

The considerations discussed above shed light on the courtship and reproductive patterns that are prevalent in underclass communities. Few underclass men can provide resources much superior to those provided by government welfare programs, and therefore these men are, in a sense, economically superfluous to the well-being of the children they father. For that reason, brothers and fathers need not be too concerned with their sisters' and daughters' premarital sexual behavior, since in most cases the children resulting from premarital relations are provided for by the government. The resulting promiscuity among underclass women makes paternity very uncertain. Men in underclass communities are often unsure whether the children of their lovers are their own. This of course is the condition which is thought to give rise to matrilineal arrangements, and with them a reduced interest of men in their putative offspring.

However, no clear lineage system has arisen among underclass males, and therefore many underclass men, unlike men in matrilineages, seem indifferent to the quality of the men their sisters or daughters take as consorts. In essence, underclass men have neither an economic nor a social reason to police their female family members' sexual behavior either before or after marriage and, not surprisingly, do not do so.

As a consequence, men in the American underclass, unlike men in almost all other societies, have little to fear from the male relatives of the women they court and make pregnant. In addition, since they are relatively confident that their children will survive even should they desert them, they have little genetically influenced incentive to remain loyal, and perhaps little or no incentive of any kind, except for whatever attachment they feel toward a particular woman. Needless to say, male attachment to a particular woman has in few societies been sufficient to prevent all cases of male abandonment. The upshot is that the males who are likely to take the most interest in children, if there is any male interest at all, are likely to be the children's maternal uncles, if only because sibling relationships tend to be more stable than relationships between lovers. In addition, if women are promiscuous, the only sure kinship men have, like men in matrilineal societies, is with their sisters' children. Of course, if brothers and sisters are half-siblings, as is often the case, even that interest is likely to be diluted if genetics plays a role in sibling affection.

Since most men in the underclass contribute very little to the support of their offspring, and show only limited interest in children whose paternity is uncertain, most underclass families take on a matriarchal or female-controlled cast. When men are unimportant or absent, they have little power.

It is important to note that there has been no society in the historical or anthropological literature that can be characterized as truly matriarchal—that is, none in which women play the dominant political and economic role. It is of course possible that matriarchal societies have existed, but none have survived long enough to have entered into the historical record. Most underclass men have at best questionable biological ties to children of their consorts or their sisters, and they seem reluctant to contribute to the support of those children. To the extent that they fail to contribute to the support of families, they lack power or influence over them. It is difficult to imagine that the way of life common in underclass communities could long be sustained were it not for the support of the federal government. The underclass way of life seems to be an artificial creation of the modern state that could not have come into existence naturally, and could not be sustained, without government support. From the perspective of evolution, it is a highly artificial and unstable state of affairs.

In other words, should the government cease to support the underclass in its current patterns, those patterns would probably disappear and, in all likelihood, be replaced by more conventional ones. Parents would have a much more powerful economic incentive to monitor the sexual behavior of their adolescent daughters, who in turn would become far more likely to demand support from the men who father their children.[51] Women would be far less likely to succumb to the blandishments of masculine bravado if not backed up by the likelihood of meaningful economic support. People would have a powerful interest in policing the sexual behavior of their daughters and sisters, lest they find themselves burdened with the support of children whose fathers have deserted them. In addition, when men are responsible for their wives' children, the question of infidelity takes on added significance.

The underclass way of life in the United States today is common among poor blacks in disordered urban environments and seems less common in rural areas. One clear-cut reason for this is that it is only in urban contexts that population densities allow a critical mass of troubled people to gain an important influence over everyday patterns of life. Part IV attempts a thorough analysis of why urban areas, and black urban areas in particular, currently contain so many troubled people as to allow their behaviors to become dominant. The development of an underclass does not appear to be a "black" phenomenon per se, though in America today there are few areas where a critical mass of troubled whites is sufficient to constitute an underclass. Charles Murray of the American Enterprise Institute reports, however, that an urban white underclass has begun to develop in English cities which resembles the American black underclass and appears to have similar causes. In Britain the illegitimacy rate jumped from 5 percent in the early sixties to 25 percent by the late eighties. As in America, illegitimacy is most common, as high as 40 percent, in poor neighborhoods where large numbers of people are "economically inactive"; and the problem appears to be getting worse. Crime, another characteristic of underclass life, has been rising dramatically as well, along with welfare dependency.[52]

The evidence strongly suggests that men, whatever their race or ethnicity, who are made economically superfluous for the support of their children because of government welfare programs, have little to offer women but their loyalty and their attractiveness as sexual partners. Loyalty, however, is often not much valued if it does not imply the provision of resources. As a consequence, men are reduced to the role of relatively temporary sexual consorts, and such things as physical attractiveness and personal flamboyance on the part of men come to play a powerful role. Women, in effect, cease looking for resource providers and look instead, or so it seems, for providers of good and desirable genes for their children. Men, in turn, become "night visitors," who may be fed and housed on a temporary basis, but otherwise have little authority.

If a woman has decided to forgo marriage, then her selection of a father for her children will be powerfully affected by what she finds sexually attractive. Sexual attractiveness, in turn, according to sociobiology, is influenced in a fundamental way by the sorts of characteristics most women are genetically programmed to want in their children. The sociobiological model would predict further that young men in these circumstances would be prompted by their genetic programming to engage in intense intrasexual rivalries over women and would tend toward flamboyant epigamic displays of masculinity to gain the favor of women.

Among women in the middle class, on the other hand, where women can reasonably expect to find men who can appreciably better their lives economically, their tastes will likely reflect that fact, and so will the behavior of the young men who court them. Of course, women look to men for a wide variety of reasons, and rarely look to men merely as a means of support. However, today, when a middle-class standard of living very often requires the wages of both partners in a marriage, a man's economic prospects cannot be readily dismissed from the collection of criteria women assess in choosing mates. The fact that most middle-class women socialize with middle-class men of similar abilities (in college or on the job), and rarely find themselves in social circumstances with men of much inferior means or abilities, serves to obscure the importance of this factor.

It follows, therefore, that masculine displays among middle-class men are likely to be less flamboyant and to emphasize demonstration of skills for the acquisition of resources. There is also likely to be a premium placed on male loyalty. Both virtues are likely to be of much greater concern to middle-class women since they, unlike underclass women, are likely to suffer a much greater decline in living standards if they give birth to children out of wedlock, or if their husbands lack earning power or inherited wealth.

The sexual and reproductive choices made by members of the underclass only become explicable if one assumes that underclass women and their guardians really do not think that the men available can make an important difference in their standard of living. Perhaps the defining characteristic of the underclass is its fatalistic acceptance of poverty and government support. Children born into the underclass who reject that fatalism have a very good chance of rising out of it through education, military training, etc. The problem is that too many young men and women succumb to that fatalism. Once a young man comes to doubt his capacity to become an adequate resource provider, he may have few alternatives other than personal flamboyance with which to attract women. Women, in turn, who come to believe that no men with good prospects are available, may find the flamboyant male's enticements hard to resist.

Unfortunately, the personal flamboyance of young underclass males often takes the form of open defiance of adult authorities. It often requires participation in individual and gang combat, and all too often involves risky criminal conduct. Much of the mayhem of inner-city streets becomes understandable from this perspective. The streets are the tournament grounds where daring young men demonstrate their worth to admiring young women.

Of course, these young men and women are wrong in believing that the men cannot become adequate providers. The overwhelming majority of men do, in time, obtain employment. Most women could expect to find adequate providers if they waited until the men gained maturity and experience in the world of work. Unfortunately, by bearing children at an early age, they undercut that possibility, since men generally prefer not to take on the support of other men's children.

While this interpretation of underclass adolescent behavior is open to challenge, it cannot be readily dismissed. No other theory currently available so easily and parsimoniously explains the spontaneous emergence of a set of behavior patterns that appear on their face to be so totally inexplicable because they are so self-defeating, especially when compared to the sort of behavior common to adolescents in the middle classes, who, beset with the same biological imperatives, nevertheless choose, in overwhelming numbers, to postpone childbearing.[53] I will explore these ideas further in Chapters 8, 9, and 10, which address more fully and directly the sources of the problems that beset the urban poor in America today.

7

The Evolutionary Roots of Ethnocentrism

I. Introduction

Human beings are undeniably prone to group conflict and violence. Humans readily and naturally divide the social world into an "us" and a "them," and are endlessly inventive in finding criteria upon which to base that dichotomy. There have been few human differences that have not at one time or another been the source of division, strife, and violence.

So commonplace is group conflict that we often fail to see the utter incompatibility between the norms that govern behavior among in-group members and those that govern relations with members of out-groups. Compassion and concern are the required emotions when an in-group member is in pain or suffering, whereas the suffering of out-group members is often met with indifference, or in cases of violent conflict, is the occasion for gloating and rejoicing. The killing of an in-group member is everywhere condemned as murder, whereas the killing of out-group members is often forgiven and sometimes the occasion for admiration, applause, and reward.

It is ironic and almost paradoxical that the human proclivity for violence and indifference to the suffering of others seems to have its roots in the contrary tendency to be altruistically concerned with the happiness and welfare of those closest to ourselves.

II. The Roots of Altruism and Group Conflict

In all animals, with the possible exception of human beings, the behaviors associated with parental care are regulated by biological mechanisms, much as are the courtship behaviors discussed in the last chapter. Like all instinctive behavior, parental care involves programmed sequential responses to specific stimuli which are monitored and regulated by brain structures that have been shaped during the course of evolution. Little if any learning seems to be required for appropriate parental responses in most species. The obsessive devotion to the young so visible among many birds has its counterpart in other species. Is it possible that human beings are alone in lacking programmed impulses to provide nurturance and protection for their helpless infants? How else are we to explain the fact that human beings, almost universally, exert selfless effort to secure the well-being of their offspring, when in most cases they are admitted egoists concerned with their own personal interests? Indeed, we are so normally egoistic that it is grounds for effusive praise when we act so as to benefit another without obvious personal gain. To say that we act altruistically toward our children because we love them begs the question of why we love our children, and why so selflessly.

In species in which parental care is essential, parental behavior is generally conditioned upon the establishment of a parent-offspring bond. Such a bond is usually established shortly after birth, and is often based on odor. The mother seems to learn almost immediately to identify the odor of her own offspring and thereafter recognizes them by that odor. Such rapid learning for purposes of identification is often called "imprinting." The odor of offspring can be said to be imprinted upon the mother and thereafter serves as the basis for the mother-infant bond. Mothers sometimes reject newborns, even their own, if for some reason the bond was prevented from forming immediately after birth by, for example, an experimenter removing the infant.[1]

However animals come to recognize their own offspring, they are singularly disposed to care for them once they have done so. They also demonstrate a clear aversion to devoting resources to the offspring of others. Such behavior clearly confers fitness and in all likelihood is regulated by specific genes. The offspring of an organism carrying genes that did not encourage kin favoritism, but induced parents to provide care indiscriminately, would find themselves at a severe disadvantage to offspring whose parents were more discriminating. Such genes for indiscriminate nurturing would, over time, become extinct.

How then are we to explain the practice of adoption that is common among humans, and that sometimes occurs in other species?[2] In animals, adoption is sometimes the result of mistaken identity. Animal breeders have long known that animals can sometimes be induced to bond with, or imprint on, strange infants during the critical bonding period. The reason is fairly straightforward. In most cases the bonding mechanism takes the form of the rule "Treat the little creature you see or smell immediately after birth as your own; reject those you see or smell at other times as strangers." Such a rule is simple and doesn't require much complicated neural engineering, and it is almost always foolproof. But not quite. If we can slip a strange infant in at the right time, we can fool the mother into adopting it as her own.

Cuckoo birds have in fact evolved the capacity to take advantage of this weakness in some of the species with which they coexist. They lay their eggs in other birds' nests (i.e., they *cuckold* them), and they have prospered in those cases where the host species have failed to develop the means to detect the deception.[3]

Humans, however, consciously adopt strangers' offspring, and usually become attached to their adopted children with as much passion as to their own. Why should human beings do so? They are clearly not fooled like the hapless victims of the cuckoo bird. What is the evolutionary payoff? Why has such altruistic behavior not long since disappeared in humans? Those who adopt a child say that it satisfies a deeply felt need to be a parent; but why should people have such a need? (The existence of such a need, by the way, if it exists, suggests that the desire to have offspring may be quite independent of the desire for sexual gratification.)

Human beings seem favorably disposed toward infants in general. Baby-like features, which are used to good effect in various cartoon characters, elicit in most adults the sort of affectionate emotional responses upon which parental care depends. Immature animals and their awkward efforts have a similar effect on us. But if these things suggest that we may be predisposed to adopt, this merely begs the question of why we are so predisposed. How could such a tendency survive the pruning of natural selection, which ought to favor offspring whose parents devote all their energies to their welfare rather than the welfare of strangers?

Adoption is only one example of many cases of apparent altruism in animals and humans that evolutionary theory, as conventionally formulated, has had difficulty explaining. Natural selection should favor animals who are ruthlessly devoted to their own survival and the survival of their offspring. In fact, evolution suggests that animals ought to be ruthless in eliminating the offspring of others, especially if those offspring are in competition with their own. Truly altruistic behavior, in evolutionary terms, would be behavior that increases the fitness of another individual at the expense of the altruist's fitness, and such behavior is fitness-decreasing. Altruism is, on its face, paradoxical: how can a fitness-decreasing characteristic survive in a population over many generations?

There are other instances of altruistic behavior that seem equally paradoxical. Consider the "pant-hoots" of chimpanzees. Chimpanzees forage for food, usually fruit, either singly or in small groups. Primatologist Michael P. Ghiglieri reports that if an individual happens upon a tree that has a large supply of fruit, the chimp will signal its presence by loudly uttering "pant-hoots" that can be detected at quite a distance and often bring a large number of chimps to the site. Ghiglieri reports that such hooting ''sometimes produced an impressive din that lasted for at least 10 minutes.''[4] Why should a chimpanzee create such a ruckus in order to share food when in so doing he exposes himself to the considerable danger of predators, who no doubt hear the impressive din created by his calls as easily as other chimps do? He gets no obvious benefit himself and clearly exposes himself to danger. By the logic of evolution (as conventionally understood), those predisposed to such altruistic hooting should, over many generations, begin to suffer from their generosity and leave fewer offspring like themselves, while their more selfish compatriots should live and reproduce and become an increasing proportion of the population. Similarly, gregarious animals who signal the presence of predators by warning calls expose themselves to greater risk than those who silently scurry at the first sight of danger, leaving others to satisfy the appetite of the predator.[5]

Such altruism, if inherited, as it almost always is in animals, seems truly paradoxical. Altruistic behavior can only be inherited if it somehow confers an evolutionary benefit on the altruist, and if it does, it is not really altruistic in the purest evolutionary sense. To understand how paradoxical altruism is in conventional evolutionary thinking, it is important to review what we know about Darwinian fitness as usually defined. An animal is said to be fit in the Darwinian sense if it leaves offspring. One animal is said to be more fit, in this sense, if it leaves more offspring than another. The key to evolutionary success in this view is reproduction. Individual survival is obviously a prerequisite for success, but is not a sufficient condition. The use of the term ''fitness'' in this biological sense has caused untold confusion. Fitness implies no moral or physical superiority, only reproductive success. It may seem odd, but in this sense an uneducated woman in poverty with five children is more fit than a woman who practices medicine but has only two children.

The characteristics carried by an individual who survived to old age but failed to reproduce would not be passed to ensuing generations. Survival of the fittest, in other words, refers to the survival of characteristics in a gene pool and not, as is commonly thought, to the survival of the individual. Even though one individual can be said to be more fit than another, at a more fundamental genetic level fitness does not really inhere in individuals per se, but rather in the characteristics those individuals carry. Characteristics confer fitness on individuals, who in gaining fitness from those characteristics, pass them into future bodies. In that sense, characteristics confer fitness on themselves.[6]

No individual organism survives for very long; what survive are the genes that shape the physiology and nervous system, and by extension the behavior, of organisms. As Richard Dawkins put it in his brilliant book *The Selfish Gene,* genes are the ''immortal coils'' that we carry and pass on during our brief sojourn on earth. From Dawkins's perspective we are merely the somewhat awkward vehicles by which genetic material is preserved. Chickens are the medium through which eggs assure more eggs. Dawkins's "genocentric" view of things may be disconcerting, but it has proved enormously enlightening.[7]

The traditional Chinese view of the relationship between individual and family is a clear-cut cultural elaboration of the above view of human existence. In *Chinese Family and Kinship,* Oxford scholar Hugh D. R. Baker explains that in traditional China the individual is thought to live for the sake of the family and it is not the case, as in modern Europe, that the family exists to support the individual. Baker argues that the Chinese view of the family or the lineage is premised upon the idea of a "Continuum of Descent" that Baker likens to "a rope which began somewhere back in the remote past, and which stretches on to the infinite future." The individuals alive at any one time owe their existence to past ancestors and owe an obligation to descendants to maintain the integrity of the rope by prudent concern with self-preservation and a proper concern for reproduction. As Baker puts it:

> [T]he individual alive is the personification of all his forebears and of all his descendants yet unborn. He exists by virtue of his ancestors, and his descendants exist only through him. . . . If the rope is cut, both ends fall away from the middle and the rope is no more. If the man alive now dies without heir, the whole continuum of ancestors and unborn descendants dies with him. In short the individual alive now is the manifestation of his whole Continuum of Descent. His existence as an individual is necessary but insignificant beside his existence as a representative of the whole.[8]

Dawkins's view of genes explains why animals are so single-mindedly determined to mate and to care for their offspring. It also explains why animals, including humans, will go to extraordinary lengths to assure the safety of their young, including risking their own lives. Moreover, it also explains the peculiar pleasure we receive from being grandparents, since grandchildren are in a sense proof of our evolutionary success. Not only did we bring offspring into the world, but we nurtured our young and aided them in their own evolutionary success. For indeed, if our children fail to reproduce our evolutionary work has gone for naught. Such thinking leads to the suggestion that Darwinian success ought not to be measured in how many offspring, relative to others, a particular animal has, but rather in how many grandoffspring he has, and by extension, by how many great-grandoffspring, etc. In fact, any characteristic or gene that enables an animal to leave more progeny than his competitors would be said to be fit in this extended Darwinian sense.

There is, however, an incompatibility between this sort of fitness and our everyday, common-sense anthropocentric way of thinking about evolution. We tend to think that we reproduce in order to make things like ourselves. When people are asked why they want children, they often say that it gives them a certain sense of immortality. But if we wanted to make copies of ourselves, to preserve ourselves, we should clone ourselves, not engage in sexual reproduction with unrelated others. Offspring of sexual unions carry in them only half the characteristics of either partner. Each of our children carries only half of those genes that make us distinct from other humans. If we take pride in grandchildren, as we surely do, it can hardly be because they are copies of us, since they carry only one-quarter of "us" in them. Our great-grandchildren carry only one-eighth. In fact, after only a few generations our progeny, as individuals, carry very little of the unique *us* in them, though we can take some satisfaction in knowing there are a lot of our characteristics or genes spread around in a variety of them—which is the point Dawkins was making. In reproducing and seeing that our children reproduce, we are not so much acting to preserve ourselves as we are seeing that our genes are widely represented in future populations. We are acting to assure our genes' immortality, but not the particular *combination* of genes which we identify as "us." That particular combination is truly unique (with the exception of identical twins) and in all likelihood will never appear on earth again.

Once we take the point of view that animals are programmed to preserve characteristics of themselves, to preserve genes, we have arrived at a possible explanation for biological altruism. An explanation that seems to resolve the paradox was outlined by William D. Hamilton in his concept of "inclusive fitness."[9] Prior to Hamilton's work, most treatments of evolution relied on the concept of Darwinian fitness, which emphasized the role of reproduction. An animal's fitness was measured by how many offspring it produced. Hamilton's insight was that if animals are programmed to care for offspring, it must be because they carry a gene to do so. When a parent organism produces offspring, it has a fair chance of passing on a copy of the "care-giving" gene to those offspring. By inducing the parent to care for and protect its offspring, the parent's gene, in effect, helps preserve the copies of itself contained in the offspring.

But by this reasoning, shouldn't an organism's genes program it to show care and concern for siblings and parents, with whom it shares, on average, half of its genes, just as many as it shares with its own offspring? By similar logic, a gene inducing a person to show concern for the well-being of, let us say, nieces and nephews, preserves itself to the extent that nieces and nephews also carry copies of that same gene, that is, the gene inducing people to show concern for nieces and nephews. An individual is as closely related to nieces and nephews as he is to his grandchildren. In both cases, he shares approximately one-quarter of those genes which make him a unique individual. For that reason, any particular gene in a person has a 25 percent chance of also being carried by a niece or nephew or a grandchild. A gene which induces a person to care for and protect these close relatives helps to preserve copies of itself in them. Shouldn't an organism, following Hamilton's insight, be programmed to show concern about the welfare of any organism with whom it shares many genes?

Hamilton's answer, in short, is yes. From his perspective, measuring the fitness of an animal only through its own offspring is unsatisfactory. Rather, fitness should be measured *inclusively* to include all organisms who share substantial numbers of genes in common above and beyond those they share as members of the same species.[10] Remember, from this perspective it is genes that are preserved and that can be characterized as fit, and not the individuals who carry them. A gene that predisposes you to look after your children, who are also probably carrying that gene, is fit because it preserves copies of itself in your children. Likewise, a gene that predisposes you to care for sisters and brothers, who probably carry the same gene, is fit if in so predisposing you, it assures the preservation of copies of itself in your sisters and brothers and, in turn, in their children. Such genes are using you, figuratively speaking, for their own ends; you are, in Dawkins's terms, acting as an agent for your selfish genes.

Since most gregarious species live in inbred groups, altruistic behavior directed toward close kin can be understood as conferring inclusive fitness on animals. The chimpanzee who signals the presence of food is saving the gene for hooting in his siblings and cousins. Ghiglieri reports that the males in chimpanzee groups are in fact closely related, and therefore when they hoot are calling out to close kin. He also reports that they often share access to females for similar reasons. Their altruism, however, does not extend to unrelated chimpanzees. Ghiglieri reports that the chimps patrol the borders of their territory and will kill other chimps, often mothers with infants, if they are found infringing on their normal feeding territory.[11]

Most human life, until fairly recently, has been lived in highly inbred hunter-gatherer groups of limited size. To adopt the child of a deceased neighbor was almost always to adopt the child of a sister or a cousin. A gene that induces individuals to adopt close relatives is likely to be preserving copies of itself in those relatives.

One can speculate a bit further and suggest that human females may be predisposed to nurture children in general, and if this is true, such a predisposition would greatly aid their own children. Such a predisposition would be more likely to survive if, in addition, it encouraged childless women to aid in the nurturance of their sisters' and cousins' children. In other words, perhaps women (and perhaps men) are inclined by evolution to *like* caring for children. Many lesbians who reject the idea of marriage, nevertheless express a longing for motherhood. The common play activities of little girls may, in this view, be more the product of evolutionary shaping than the product of socialization.

Adoption today, which most often involves the transnational or transracial adoption of strangers, is from this perspective not so paradoxical. Adoption will continue as a practice so long as the desire to nurture children remains a fitness-conferring characteristic.

Inclusive fitness or kin selection may also explain the fact that most contests within groups, such as the competition between males for access to females, generally stop short of lethal action, and are generally broken off when one party gains the upper hand. If reproduction is the all-important element for evolutionary success, how can a tendency to give up in sexual competition continue to exist in a population? The paradox is partially resolved by recognizing the fact that the males competing in small groups are often close kin, and are likely to be brothers and first cousins. The genes that predispose male animals to compete over mates are partially offset and kept in check by genes that predispose animals to protect close relatives.

Another reason, having nothing to do with kinship, helps explain the relative lack of deadly fights between group members: members of the same species are usually equally matched for aggressive combat. As J. Maynard Smith and G. R. Price have suggested, animals in equally matched contests may resist mortal battle simply out of prudence.[12] Pressing a battle to its bitter end will undoubtedly cost both participants, even the winner, dearly. Often it is better to back off from a losing battle and wait for another contest that may be more easily won. This is especially prudent in the case of younger contestants who can surely wait for their older, more experienced competitors to pass from the scene.

Animals who are born, live, and die in the same closely related group have little need to develop mechanisms to detect kin. In these groups we may mistake behaviors driven by kin selection as a generalized desire to spare members of the same species, that is, as a sort of taboo on murder within species. What we may be witnessing, in fact, are contests between animals of the same species who avoid mortal combat out of prudence, and in addition avoid killing members of the same species because they have not developed the capacity to distinguish near kin from other members of the species.

This interpretation is supported by the fact that while killing within species is not common, neither is it altogether absent. Infanticide among lions is an interesting case in point. Brian C. R. Bertram of Cambridge University reports witnessing this behavior among lions in the Serengeti Park in Africa. Lion prides are made up of two or three adult males, a similar number of adult females, and their offspring. When the males approach maturity, they are driven out of the pride by the older males. Female offspring remain within the pride. This may appear to create dangerous incestuous conditions, but it usually does not, since the adult males are often not related to the younger females. The reason lies in the pattern of conflict between adult males and younger males. When driven from a pride, the young males, who are probably closely related, remain together as a troop and roam the savanna until they are in a position to overpower and drive out the adult males from another existing pride, and take it over for themselves. Thus, there is a relatively constant turnover of males, with females remaining fairly constant.[13]

The adult females seem indifferent as to which males come to reside with them. Perhaps their indifference lies in the fact that the males are largely parasitic; females do the bulk of the hunting. Another possibility is related to the fact that lions are incredibly inefficient reproducers. Bertram estimated that it takes three thousand copulations to produce one offspring likely to survive into adulthood.[14] Perhaps the younger males are desired for their more youthful and active libidos.

The price such females pay for their younger and more vigorous consorts is, however, high. Bertram reports instances where newly installed males systematically kill off the nursing infants found in the pride. In doing so they bring the females into heat more quickly, owing to the cessation of nursing, which often interferes with sexual receptivity. By killing the nursing offspring of the now-departed males, these murderous lion stepfathers eliminate the competition for their own sons and daughters, who are likely to follow quickly after the infanticide. Presumably in most cases the females are able to thwart such villainy, though there is as yet no field evidence to sustain this suspicion. The females would be able to protect more mature offspring, perhaps, since it is more difficult for the older males to kill them. Once male offspring reach sexual maturity and can fend for themselves, their mothers seem content to allow them to be driven off. It should be pointed out that by allowing their sons to be driven from the pride at sexual maturity, they benefit from the avoidance of incestuous pairings (involving either themselves or their daughters).

People who breed cats are well aware that even the domesticated tabby is capable of similar behavior. Nurslings left unprotected by their mothers are unlikely to survive very long, since males quite commonly kill them for reasons quite similar to those of their lion counterparts.

Harvard anthropologist Sarah Hrdy reported on similar infanticide among the langur monkeys she studied in India. In the case of langurs, one dominant male controls a harem of many females and their offspring. A harem of females is valuable and often contested, and not surprisingly harems often change hands. When they do, bloody mayhem ensues. David Barash, in discussing Hrdy's research, explains that the newly ascendant male cannot take full advantage of his harem if many females are nursing offspring, since nursing interferes with ovulation in primates. Rather than wait for nursing to take its natural course, the new male, in Barash's words,

> embarks on a bloody and ruthless course of fitness maximization. Methodically, remorselessly, he pursues the suckling infants and kills them. Sometimes the slaughter is quick, sometimes it takes days or even weeks as the helpless infant monkeys gradually succumb to a combination of trauma, blood loss and infection from their repeated wounding. The whole grisly process has been described and photographed in great detail by Harvard anthropologist Sarah Hrdy.[15]

Inclusive fitness, therefore, has its limits. If it did not, then of course all creatures, and especially those in the same species, would be equally concerned for each other, since they share many genes in common. Altruism would be the rule rather than the exception, which is clearly not the case. The reason is that organisms, and by extension the genes that build them, are in constant competition with each other for scarce resources. This is especially true of organisms who share many genes in common, as do members of the same species, since they tend to occupy the same ecological niche and require similar resources. From an evolutionary standpoint, then, when should an animal act altruistically and when competitively? When are other animals from the same species to be treated as kin and when as competitors?

The example of the lions is a case where a troop of closely related young males cooperate with each other and mute their own competition in order to take over a group of females. These same cooperative males are, on the other hand, violently aggressive toward the unrelated males whom they must conquer in order to take over sexual control of the females. And they are ruthless killers of the nursing offspring of the males they have vanquished.

III. The Roots of Ethnic Conflict

The line between kin and non-kin is likely to be differently drawn in different species and in differing circumstances. Hamilton has suggested that the line is best understood as maximizing fitness in cost/benefit terms.[16] Our own offspring, for instance, are twice as closely related to us as are our nieces and nephews, and therefore we should be twice as concerned with sons and daughters as with nieces and nephews. But aiding nieces and nephews hurts our own sons and daughters, since to some extent, cousins are often in competition with each other. At some point, aiding a relative who is sufficiently far removed from us will incur a potential loss greater than the potential gain. Any aid I give to the children of third cousins benefits my genes in only a small fashion, since those children carry very few of my genes and the aid I give them must be taken from my own children. In addition, the children of third cousins will undoubtedly be in competition for the same resources and mates as my own children, especially if we all live in the same geographic area. In general, we would expect an animal's altruistic behavior to decline fairly sharply as relatedness and the associated benefit-to-cost ratio of altruistic behavior declines.

Kin identification appears even in relatively simple organisms. Tadpoles have been shown to identify siblings by olfactory means. If given the choice, tadpoles swim in the presence of siblings rather than others. It is not at all clear what advantage such kin identification confers upon an organism like a tadpole.[17] In some cases kin identification may be advantageous in the selection of mates. Dawkins has suggested that there may be an intermediate degree of relatedness for sexual reproduction which confers the highest fitness on characteristics or gene assemblages that underlie those characteristics.[18] Each individual receives two sets of chromosomes which determine his characteristics, one set from his mother and one set from his father. Thus, in most cases there are two genes or ''alleles'' for each characteristic. In some cases one allele will dominate another, as in the case of eye color, while in others both alleles may play a role in determining a characteristic. Close incestuous matings are dangerous because both individuals may have inherited a mutated and potentially damaging gene that was passed on by a common recent ancestor, and their offspring, if it gets the mutated gene from both mother and father, will be unable to overcome a harmful trait by suppressing the damaged allele in favor of an unmutated healthy one. On the other hand, two very distantly related individuals may not carry the same gene pattern, or if they do, may carry it in such a way that it will not be expressed in their offspring. When animals are sufficiently different, the organization of genes and chromosomes may be so incompatible as to make reproduction impossible. Different species, for instance, may be quite similar and have much in common, but there may be sufficient incompatibilities between their chromosomes that, even if they could mate, such mating would be unlikely to result in viable offspring.

In general, animals cannot benefit from the advantages made possible by inclusive fitness if they cannot identify close kin. Among members of species living in groups, the problem of kin identification is much simplified. All members of the group are probably relatively close kin. If the young remain in close proximity to their parents, identification of kin is a relatively simple matter. Those animals with whom one has day-to-day contact are in all likelihood close kin.

Among primates, group living is common, with the size of the group very often determined by ecological factors such as the availability of food, etc.[19] Hamadryas baboons sort themselves into groups dominated by individual males who control a harem of females and their attendant offspring. Dominant males come together in slightly larger bands for purposes of foraging, and sometimes these foraging bands gather in even larger troops.[20]

It is not always clear what advantage group living confers on animals. In the case of a ''family'' made up of a single dominant male and his female consorts, the advantage is fairly obvious. Each male has an interest in guarding his own females and protecting their offspring. The reasons for the larger groupings are less clear, and such groupings are often based on differing needs and circumstances. In some cases large groups can more readily defend feeding and nesting territories than can small groups or single individuals.

In addition, if important food sources, such as large game, are rarely encountered, a large foraging group is more likely to find such game, and to benefit from finds, than are smaller foraging groups. Some animals, such as wolves and wild dogs, are pack hunters and as a group can prey on animals that singly they could not hope to subdue. Furthermore, a large group is more likely to detect dangerous predators in time to take defensive action, and groups can sometimes intimidate potential predators who would pose a mortal danger to single animals.

For these and other reasons, many species, including many primates, live in groups. An important point here is that such groups will almost always be relatively inbred, if only because they will contain the offspring of a limited number of mothers and fathers. In addition, individuals tend to mate with others in limited geographic areas, and within those areas inbreeding is likely to be relatively high. The upshot is that once animals start to live in groups for whatever reasons, they are likely to continue to do so for reasons of inclusive fitness, even should the original factors become unimportant. Put another way, brothers motivated by inclusive fitness to aid each other will find it easier to do so if they remain in close proximity. Only if the advantages of solitary living outweighed the advantages conferred by such aid would we expect individuals to avoid group living.

Human beings are clearly animals that prefer living in groups. Hunters and gatherers, for example, live in small groups, separated from each other in clearly defined territories. The reason for this arrangement among hunters and gatherers is based on fundamental ecological constraints. The areas of human habitation are rarely sufficiently rich in food to support great numbers, especially since humans are usually in competition with other species for those same food resources. If humans are able to do so, they will drive out their competitors. Of course, they are not always able to do so. Insects and small rodents are often too reproductively efficient, and larger predators are often too dangerous, to be eliminated.

Hunter-gatherer groups cannot expand beyond limited numbers that are fixed fairly rigidly by the density of food available. When food is dense, the numbers who can forage from it will be greater than when food is more sparsely distributed, but in no case can the energy expended in obtaining food be greater than that which the food supplies. If the daily trek from home or sleeping site to the group's food sources consumes more energy than the food can provide, some members will necessarily be undernourished, and in time some will starve. These Malthusian considerations produce equilibrium populations for most hunter-gatherer groups of between fifty and two hundred people.

These human groups are usually made up of a relatively small number of families dominated by a small number of adult males. Hunters and gatherers usually tolerate polygamy, but by and large it is uncommon, since it is rarely possible for one male to provide sufficient resources for more than one female and her children. In addition, slavery is rare among such groups for similar reasons. The amount of food each adult can provide must first feed him- or herself, and there is rarely much left over to provide for others. Even young children are expected to contribute to their own food supply. A slave would hardly provide much of a benefit and would, in addition, have to be policed. How would one go about policing a slave in such circumstances? It was not until agricultural innovations made it possible for a person to produce much more food than he consumed himself that slavery became commonplace.

Hunter-gatherer groups are based in kinship and exhibit little in the way of coercive control by some individuals over others. Groups usually maintain friendly relations with other nearby groups, since they rarely have much to gain from fighting. Conquering a neighboring tribe's territory makes no sense if it cannot be used. Fighting over territory is uncommon, since it is rare for one particular piece of ground to be sufficiently more valuable than another to risk life and limb to obtain it.[21] In addition, since all hunter-gatherer groups in the same geographic area are constrained by the same ecological conditions, they are likely to be of similar size and fighting capacity. Strategic prudence will counsel against unnecessary and potentially deadly fighting.

Conflict may arise over an important resource such as a water source, especially during a drought, but such fighting is likely to cease once the crisis has passed. Fighting in order to capture slaves is uncommon and would likewise be unproductive, for the reasons given above. Fighting sometimes takes place with the aim of capturing young women, as among the Yanomamo of South America. The Yanomamo, however, have developed a primitive form of agriculture, and individual men can support the offspring of more than one wife. Such is rarely the case in true hunter-gatherer groups, who must rely solely on the natural resources in their area. In most cases, especially among those lacking agriculture, fighting for women is rare and usually unnecessary, since neighboring bands almost always exchange women for marriage purposes.[22] The common practice of wife exchange has been much discussed in the anthropological literature, where it is often explained as serving economic ends. Those explanations, however, often overlook the biological roots of this practice that seem plain, namely the prevention of incest and excessive inbreeding. Since hunter-gatherer bands are small, they are invariably composed of close kin; the adults are usually siblings and close cousins. To prevent excessive inbreeding, the easiest solution is to marry outside the group, and such exogamy is widely practiced among hunters and gatherers. This exchange of wives tends to create bonds of kinship between neighboring groups. Men from any group will undoubtedly have sisters and daughters, nieces and nephews, and grandchildren in the others.

It is hardly surprising, therefore, that people in geographic proximity come to regard themselves as one *people* and to assemble frequently for ceremonial purposes. The size of an association of neighboring groups is likely to grow so long as the groups are biologically successful. Especially successful groups will produce more offspring than can be supported on the original territory, and colony groups will tend to bud off to occupy territories at the margin of the currently occupied region. Such budding-off and colonizing could theoretically go on forever, but practically is limited by the nature of the environment. The earth is not uniform, nor is it uniformly hospitable to human habitation. Early groups will naturally gravitate to the most promising regions and new colonies will invariably find that the territories at the margin will be less fruitful. Rivers, oceans, deserts, and mountain ranges all act as natural boundaries tending to keep associated populations of hunter-gatherer groups relatively small and relatively isolated.

In most cases, therefore, successful human populations (in fact any successful animal population) will over time tend to fully exploit a particular, often isolated region. Such a population will consist of groups which, even if dispersed over a fairly large geographic region, will nevertheless still tend to be fairly inbred. Not only will kinship be high among them, but they will share language and customs, mystical beliefs and practices, etc. People in geographically isolated populations tend to look alike, not only because they are biologically related, but also because they have similar styles of dress and ornamentation.

Because neighboring groups are in fact groups of extended kin, we would expect their relations with each other to be reasonably cordial and would expect aggressive competition to be muted and ritualized, as it usually is. It is hardly surprising that people in a regional population should come to regard themselves and their ways of doing things as normal and particularly "human," and to be somewhat amused and taken aback when confronting people who are different from them—indeed, to view such people as strange and abnormal and somehow not quite human. What is attractive to us in others is often what is familiar, what we have grown up with.

How should we expect the members of a hunter-gatherer group to look upon the appearance of outsiders, easily identified as such by appearance and language? In most cases a small group of strangers is greeted with curiosity and amusement. But that amusement is usually tempered by the possibility that the strangers may be a vanguard for a much larger group on the move—scouts for a wandering band of potential invaders. Such a wandering group is probably making an appearance because their own home territory can no longer support them, or because they have been driven from it, or because they are a colonizing group that has budded-off in search of additional homelands.

A wandering group represents a clear and present threat to a stationary group and must be encouraged to look elsewhere for sustenance. For a population of people that successfully dominates its region, an invasion by outsiders cannot possibly be tolerated and no compromise arrangement is possible. It is, in fact, a true zero-sum situation, that is, one in which the gain for one group can only be had at the expense of the other. Any territory ceded to an invading band is territory no longer available to feed one's own people, one's own kin. If the invading band manages to secure a foothold, it can only grow and prosper at the expense of those already there. Strangers therefore, especially if they represent a vanguard of potential invaders, pose an unmitigated threat. Rarely is a population of hunters and gatherers so powerful that it cannot be displaced, and rarely, therefore, can it look upon strangers with equanimity.

If the aboriginal people occupy only a small portion of a vast territory and the wandering band seems content to move on, it may be more prudent to let them pass unmolested than to get into a deadly confrontation. This was of course the circumstance surrounding the original meetings of the North American Indian tribes and the European explorers. In most cases the meetings were friendly, if cautious. Of course, the superior firepower that the Europeans carried undoubtedly tempered the Indian's willingness to confront them in open conflict. However, once it became clear to the Indian groups that the Europeans were coming to stay, and were in fact threatening to usurp their territory, the confrontation became bloody and often genocidal.

The point is that hunting and gathering peoples have good grounds to fear the appearance of strangers. Xenophobia is clearly a fitness-conferring disposition, and it is hardly surprising that it is an almost universal trait of human groups. An important question is whether this trait or disposition is the result of rational calculation passed on in cultural practice or whether it is more deeply rooted in our genetic programming. The case for the latter interpretation is fairly strong.

IV. The Ubiquity of Group Conflict

The above discussion leads to the straightforward suggestion that human beings may be predisposed biologically to be wary of strangers and predisposed to engage in hostile actions toward them if given even moderate provocation. We would expect this readiness to attack to be tempered by prudence. If a band is confronted by an obviously superior group, then hostile actions are likely to be muted. If, on the other hand, the group that seems to threaten is weak, then the reaction may well be quick and violent.

A stranger is, by definition, anyone who looks or acts in ways different from what is common in the local neighborhood. Physical appearance, dress, language, and religious belief are all clear indicators of group membership. From this point of view, tension between different racial, ethnic, or religious groups is to be expected; in the absence of countervailing influences, conflict may break out between groups as a result of what often appear to be rather modest provocations, and when conflict does occur it is likely to be constrained only by strategic prudence.

The evolution of human societies and the development of empires and nation-states has therefore, not surprisingly, required the subjugation of ethnic rivalries by strong central authorities willing to coerce peaceful relations among otherwise hostile groups. The rapid decline into ethnic and racial enmity and tribal warfare that follows upon the demise of strong central authorities gives evidence for this view. Numerous regions in the former Soviet Union have been the scenes of ethnic conflagrations as the forces of the central power retreated from the periphery of the collapsing state. These events and those in Eastern Europe, in particular the "ethnic cleansing" in the former Yugoslavia in the wake of the Soviet collapse, are only the most recent examples of the tragic tendency toward ethnic conflict.

The readiness with which humans are prone to divide the world between an "us" and a "them" does not rely on ethnic difference alone. Religious differences among people who are ethnically quite similar have taken untold millions of lives over the centuries. Similarly, class differences, especially in the wake of Marxist theorizing, have claimed millions of lives in the former Soviet Union and in China. The mass slaughter in Cambodia is a particularly odious example, but is not unlike many others. And tribal Africa, since the retreat of the European colonial powers, has seen an almost unending series of tribal wars, a nasty feature of which has been the blocking of food relief efforts for genocidal ends.

For generations, sometimes centuries, empires and nation-states are able to keep ethnic rivalries within manageable bounds. They do so in large measure by pure force of arms, but they also admonish their populations to live at peace with one another. For fifteen centuries the Christian Church exercised a powerful monopoly on moral teachings in all of Europe and yet was never successful in educating out the ethnic and religious rivalries that were forever breaking out in bloody conflict and mayhem. In large agricultural societies, kinship-based social organization is often the rule. In China in earlier centuries, the central government had difficulty gaining hegemony over territories in the south that were ruled by large extended families of clans and lineages. Clans occupied groups of villages and controlled the surrounding territory.[23] The clans or lineages were able to grow, but since they needed increased food and income to do so, they tended to seek to expand their territory, which led to clan rivalries. According to Hugh D. R. Baker:

> It is hardly an exaggeration to say that in areas where lineages were common and strong the whole society was in a constant state of war, though actual battles were infrequent. It was through this system that the lineages, which we have seen to be virtually self-governing internally, conducted their ''foreign affairs'' to determine their position in society.[24]

In Europe before the emergence of large nation-states, a similar pattern prevailed, with kinship-based alliances of feudal lords continually engaged in battle with each other for land and resources. In both feudal Europe and the lineage areas of China, the continual state of war led to an endless making and breaking of opportunistic and usually short-lived alliances. Similar patterns exist today in the Middle East and wherever central authorities lack the power to maintain the peace.

Modern pluralistic democracies such as the United States and Canada make strenuous efforts to restrain ethnic strife. Both have been relatively successful in the past, but Canada is now almost at the point of fissure on the basis of language differences, and the United States faces severe problems in its attempt at reconciling black and white differences, which of late have become increasingly troubled. Yet, with important exceptions, few in either society are teaching hate in any significant way. On the contrary, in both countries hate-mongering has for years been viewed as a sign of moral degeneracy and, in Canada, has been made a criminal offense, following the example of France. The truth is that the teaching of ethnic and racial hatred is very limited in comparison with teachings admonishing citizens to be tolerant and accepting of differences. If ethnic and racial enmity continues to exist, it suggests that it is all too natural and not that it is taught. Put another way, if group animosity were the result of teaching, then preventing such teaching, or teaching against intolerance, should be sufficient to eliminate it. The fact that hate is such an easily learned lesson and tolerance a difficult one suggests that the propensity for enmity to arise between groups is there to start with.

Who is it who teaches young men in urban areas, where central authorities tend to be weak, to divide themselves into territorial groups and to engage in sometimes murderous tribal warfare to protect their "turf"? True, when the turf in question happens to be a valuable resource, such as a drug market, the warfare becomes even deadlier, but hardly different in character. The point is that turf warfare is endemic to inner cities and always was, even before drugs become a lucrative enterprise. (The popular Broadway musical *West Side Story* depicts the sort of gang warfare common in New York City earlier in the century.) It is worth remembering that all the important institutions in the inner cities, including the family, the church, and the schools, inveigh against gang formation and decry gang warfare. Yet it spontaneously develops if not prevented by energetic police action.

When central authority disintegrated in Beirut, Lebanon, in the 1970s, previously peaceful neighborhoods degenerated into warring battlegrounds of ethnic and familial armies whose brutality toward each other was unmitigated by pity or reason. The same is true in other conflicts in the Middle East, on the Indian subcontinent, and in Northern Ireland. I have already mentioned the problems in the former Soviet Union and the odious "ethnic cleansing" in Yugoslavia. The examples are endless.

Furthermore, the genocidal character of these conflicts is plain. The wanton slaughter of innocents, of women and children, makes no sense in the modern world, but it does make sense if viewed as the natural reaction of a people whose genetic programming inclines them to see other groups as potential usurpers who will in time, if given the chance, drive them to extinction.

The common genocidal aspect of tribal conflict sets it apart from modern conventional warfare, in which nations fight over interests that can be resolved, and in which gratuitous killing is seen as unproductive or even counterproductive. But from the perspective of human evolution, conflict that pits one population, one gene pool as it were, against another in a mortal zero-sum struggle for survival is by its very nature genocidal. In such wars the killing of innocents is neither gratuitous nor accidental, but the very essence of the thing.

In fact, in the world today it is very rarely the case that two groups are confronted with zero-sum conflicts over territory or some other resource. Because of the enormous productivity of modern agriculture, human groups today only rarely fully exploit the survival potential of any territory, as did many of their hunter-gatherer forebears. This only confirms the essentially irrational nature of tribal warfare in the modern age.

Social scientists have had a hard time explaining the sheer violence and unforgiving brutality of much ethnic and tribal conflict in the modern age. They have denied evolutionary explanations and must therefore assume that the hate that breeds such violence is taught. But why should it be taught? To say that it is taught for no reason is to beg the question and to confirm unwittingly the evolutionary explanation. The problem is usually resolved by arguing that hate is taught in pursuance of some real or perceived conflict of interest. From this point of view, people are said to believe that they must fight each other in order to obtain some important good and must teach their children to hate those with whom they are in competition for that good. In this view, if people can be shown that their conflicts are all a misunderstanding and are not really irreconcilable, then they will gladly settle matters peacefully.

The problem with this environmental or nurturist point of view is that it is disconfirmed in too many cases. Perhaps the nurturists have the causation backwards. This is certainly not to deny that many, perhaps all, conflicts involve some real conflict of interest over resources or political claims. But all too often it appears that groups fight with each other not so much because they have a rational conflict of interest, but rather because they are driven to fight with each other and then they justify their hostilities, after the fact, with the most readily available rationale. In other words, maybe it is natural (though unfortunate) for people of different genetic makeup to view each other as biological adversaries and to take the existence of real or imagined grievances as the justification for violent confrontation. Perhaps the grievances are merely the occasion for the expression of hostility and are, in and of themselves, relatively unimportant in causing it.

When one examines many recent examples of ethnic warfare, this latter interpretation is far more compelling than the alternative. This is especially clear when what the groups are ostensibly warring about can usually be resolved in a relatively fair manner if a solution is imposed by a stronger third party. In most cases, formerly adamant opponents find they can live amicably together with relative ease, especially if a third party installs a powerful central authority to assure the peace. Often what was seen as a raging and unquenchable thirst for revenge, for example, becomes muted when it is no longer feasible to give vent to the desire for revenge. Certainly that proved to be the case in Yugoslavia in the aftermath of World War II, once Tito, with the support of the Soviet Union, was able to consolidate his power and impose restraints on ethnic strife. Once the central authorities in Yugoslavia collapsed in the early 1990s, neighbors of different ethnicity who had lived side by side in relative harmony for four decades found themselves in a genocidal conflict, spurred by ethnic leaders who easily rekindled the old hatreds.

The fact that demagogues are often rewarded for hate-mongering suggests to some that they are unusual in their powers of persuasion. Some, like Hitler, are thought to have possessed the capacity for overwhelmingly hypnotic oratory. More likely, the success of demagogues reflects the fact that they grasp the readiness with which people jump on the idea that outsiders are threatening. It may reflect, as well, their ability to exploit the fact that people can be easily hypnotized by the fear and loathing appropriate to mortal biological competitors. Demagogues everywhere tap into a ubiquitous source of glory and power, and are often richly rewarded by the many who flock to their banner, even when they bring about untold tragedies for their followers. That the followers of demagogues are often the most uneducated, the most provincial, and the weakest economically in any society is hardly surprising. It is also not surprising that ignorant people are prepared to accept the most flagrant, demeaning, and irrational characterizations of the group that is said to be a threat.

Rather strong support for the evolutionary view that humans are predisposed to group conflict is provided by the nearly universal popularity of team sports, especially among men. Young men everywhere engage in team activities, and almost as common is the pleasure such activities give to spectators. The phenomenon of team sports is difficult to understand in purely instrumental terms, as there seem to be so many more productive things for people to do with their time. Why should humans, and young males in particular, take almost spontaneously to intense activity in the collective rivalries that team sports involve? It is difficult to understand the benefit derived from such activities, especially if one considers the expenditure of time and energy involved. To argue that we engage in team activities because we enjoy them is to beg the question of why in fact we enjoy team play. Perhaps we enjoy team efforts for the same reason we enjoy sex, namely because we are programmed to do so. The tendency for humans to engage in team sports is so natural that we often fail to see it as the remarkable phenomenon it is. The historian Johan Huizinga argued that play is so characteristically human that we might reasonably call ourselves ''Homo Ludens,'' man the player.[25]

Virtually all zoologists, according to Edward O. Wilson, see play as serving ''an important role in the socialization of mammals.'' Wilson reports that ''the more intelligent and social the species, the more elaborate the play.'' In general, play is viewed as a means for complex animals to develop and perfect behavioral routines that will be crucial to later survival. Wilson points out that the play activities of kittens ''are forerunners of the . . . basic hunting maneuvers of the adult cat.''[26]

From the evolutionary perspective, play can only be fitness-enhancing if the expenditure of time and energy it requires is paid back in increased competence in those skills that contribute to survival and reproduction. Team play among humans, from this perspective, is something that we take to naturally and take seriously because it prepares us for engaging in the coordinated group efforts that are fundamental to human success—among which, surely, are efforts aimed at collective defense against predators and against human interlopers—as well as preparing us for successful hunting and other activities.

Team play and group activities in general also reflect what Harvard zoologist Robert Trivers has called ''reciprocal altruism.'' Social animals with advanced memory capacity, Trivers argues, can obtain a fitness benefit by aiding each other in things like grooming, food sharing, and hunting, so long as their aid is reciprocated. Trivers shows how such apparently altruistic helping behavior can survive in a population; all that is required is that animals remember and refuse to help those who have failed to reciprocate.[27]

Among humans, where so much activity involves group activity, reciprocity is practically ubiquitous. Economic exchange allows reciprocity to be arranged with extraordinary refinement. Humans are exquisitely sensitive about such matters and usually frame questions of reciprocity in terms of fairness and equity. Failure to return a favor or repay a debt is, of course, one of the most powerful reasons for social estrangement and ostracism. In team efforts, failure to make an all-out effort is a failure of reciprocity. Betrayal of the team by aiding the opponent (being disloyal or traitorous) is the most egregious failure of reciprocity and is looked upon with the utmost scorn and contempt, and punished commensurately in all societies.

In this interpretation, human beings are so naturally predisposed to divide the world into an ''us'' and a ''them,'' that we do it even in the absence of any instrumental reason. If there is no real occasion for group conflict, we invent an occasion and play at it. It is true that such play has instrumental value for the young, especially males, in developing their physical skills. But if there were no anticipated conflicts, then there would be no need for males to play at competitive activities. The play of girls very often lacks this competitive element and seems no less valuable for the developing of adult skills. In other words, boys seem to be learning those skills in play that will make them more effective warriors as adults.

It is difficult to deny the fact that people are drawn to group competition and seem to have an almost impulsive desire to identify with one side or the other on what are often arbitrary bases. It is hard, in short, to resist the conclusion that this impulse is a feature of human nature because, over the course of our evolution, it contributed in a significant way to our fitness. Put another way, humans who did not readily take to group competition would not likely have survived in competition with those who did.

V. Minimal Group Effects

Recent social-psychological research, though not widely publicized outside the field, seems to confirm the above conclusion. While many social psychologists, such as the symbolic-racism researchers, continue to seek the sources of prejudice in the particular learning experiences of individuals, this newer approach looks more to cognitive predispositions and situational factors in trying to understand prejudice and ethnocentrism. Unfortunately, this research has not as yet had much impact on social policy, which continues to rely on the more popular treatments that emphasize the role of learning and enculturation. Perhaps this is so because the more recent work contradicts in fundamental ways the theoretical underpinnings of many current policies.

Psychologist Henri Tajfel and his colleagues provided the main impetus for this new orientation. Tajfel was interested in how competition produces in-group/out-group stereotyping and discrimination. In order to study the phenomenon, he and his colleagues set about to find the "minimal conditions" that would create intergroup discrimination. What they found was surprising.[28]

Their research demonstrated that people spontaneously exhibit in-group favoritism on almost ludicrously arbitrary grounds. In one of their experiments, teenage English schoolboys were told that some of their classmates were found to be "underestimators" and others "overestimators" in a task of guessing the number of dots projected on a screen. In fact, the boys were assigned to one or the other category on a purely random basis. Once the boys were informed of which type they were, they showed clear favoritism toward members of their own category when given the opportunity to assign points to classmates in both groups. Subjects assigned more points to in-group members than to out-group members. Similar results were obtained after arbitrarily identifying some students as preferring the works of the painter Paul Klee and others as preferring those of the painter Wassily Kandinsky.[29]

In fact, the "minimal group phenomenon," as it is called, has been demonstrated numerous times in various countries. In an important review of the literature, Tajfel claimed that he was able to catalogue over thirty studies demonstrating the effect and testifying to its ubiquity.[30] Once laboratory subjects are categorized into two groups, no matter how trivial the categorization, they tend to show favoritism to members of their own category. It appears as though mere categorization creates the conditions for in-group favoritism, especially when there is no other objective basis for assigning rewards.[31] Even when subjects knew the assignment was purely random, they nevertheless showed intergroup discrimination. An experiment by Anne Locksley, Vilma Ortiz, and Christine Hepburn of New York University is illustrative. These researchers worked with groups of six subjects who were "told that they would be classified as a Phi or a Gamma by pulling a lottery ticket out of a can containing three Phi tickets and three Gamma tickets." Subjects were assigned the tasks of describing the personalities of the other subjects and awarding prizes in the form of tokens among them; each subject could award each other subject up to one hundred tokens. Even though it was clear that the assignment to groups was random and purely arbitrary, the subjects awarded more tokens to in-group members than to out-group members. The difference in allocation was sizable: in-group members received an average of eighty-five tokens out of a possible one hundred, whereas out-group members received only sixty-five tokens on average. Furthermore, Locksley and her associates found in a separate study that subjects rated in-group members as having more socially-desirable characteristics than out-group members. This effect was small but statistically significant.[32]

While the minimal group phenomenon has been well established in numerous studies, it has yet to be adequately explained. Perhaps the most influential explanation is Tajfel's own, which explains the discrimination in terms of a desire to enhance self-esteem. Tajfel thinks that people seek to improve their own self-esteem by associating with highly regarded groups. They can enhance their self-esteem, in Tajfel's view, by assuming that whatever category they are in is the better one. By treating their own group better, they are asserting that it *is* better, and by extension so are they. In other words, by showing favoritism to the in-group, subjects confirm, as it were, that their group must be the better group.[33] Tajfel's explanation assumes, among other things, that an individual's self-esteem is related to the worth he ascribes to the group with which he identifies. This is an important question that will be taken up in Chapter 9. It is enough, for now, to point out that the evidence for this assertion is relatively weak.

In a lengthy overview of this literature, the highly respected social psychologist David Messick and his coauthor Diane Mackie suggest that Tajfel's self-esteem explanation is inadequate. They argue that "[a] direct test of such a causal relation is, in fact, hard to imagine."[34] Messick and Mackie praise Tajfel's work for "almost single-handedly reviving intergroup research," but conclude that "invoking the concept of self-esteem has not provided a definitive understanding of in-group discrimination. . . ."[35] In fact, there appears to be no adequate explanation for the phenomenon in the psychological literature. Messick and Mackie conclude that "nearly 20 years after the discovery that mere categorization produced intergroup bias, an adequate theory of the phenomenon has yet to be developed."[36]

Perhaps part of the reason that an explanation is lacking is that the researchers in this area seem completely uninterested or uninformed about the work of sociobiologists, especially Hamilton's work on inclusive fitness (discussed earlier, in Section II of this chapter). In the Messick and Mackie review, which included over 250 citations, there is not one from the sociobiological literature. It is interesting that the authors decry the insularity of the field, but they do so in relation to general decision theory. They themselves ignore sociobiology.

This is unfortunate, since evolutionary theory can easily accommodate the minimal group phenomenon. The theory of inclusive fitness suggests that humans are prone to divide the world into an "us" and a "them"; and the early ecology of hunters and gatherers suggests that humans are equally prone to engage in cooperative group or team efforts.

If human beings are predisposed to engage in team play, then the minimal group phenomenon hardly requires explanation at all. We all engage in team efforts at work and at play on a regular basis, and the assignment to one or another team or work-group is often quite arbitrary. We would therefore expect laboratory subjects who are assigned to arbitrary groups to anticipate that those groups have been formed for some purpose. It must be emphasized that subjects come to laboratory experiments with clear expectations that they will be asked to *do* something, not merely to be placed in arbitrary categories for no reason at all. In these laboratory exercises, it would be difficult for a subject not to imagine that he is being assigned to a team or work-group. Once a person is assigned to what he believes is a team, the normal obligations of team membership should then guide his behavior, as it clearly did in these studies. An essential ingredient of team spirit is in-group solidarity; individuals are expected to subordinate personal goals to forward the team effort. If what is at stake is the assignment of points or tokens, then proper team spirit requires that people assign more to their own team members. To fail to do so is to betray the team effort. One could argue that subjects were not specifically instructed to treat their category in terms of team membership, but how else were they to interpret the procedure?

The "choose-up" teams so common on school grounds are almost always transitory associations of players; that is, the five members of a basketball team today will almost certainly be distributed differently in tomorrow's game. Nevertheless, for the duration of the game, players are expected to devote the maximum effort for their own team. They must interpret close calls to their team's advantage, show proper anger at the abuse of teammates by the other side, etc.

The same is true for temporary work details or special assignments in most walks of life. People engaged in some common effort that sets them apart from others usually exhibit in-group solidarity. In his book *The Presentation of Self in Everyday Life,* social psychologist Erving Goffman has described in intriguing detail the ways in which all manner of social groups maintain solidarity. He describes how a "front" is erected and maintained to enable team players to carry out their often difficult and sometimes demeaning tasks and still preserve their "face," and their sense of personal worth and integrity. It is important and everywhere understood that team members, whether hotel kitchen staff, salespeople, teachers, or simply good country folk, should support each other and be ready to defend their "own" against unfair treatment by others.[37]

This interpretation of the minimal group phenomenon is given considerable support by additional findings reported by Locksley, Ortiz, and Hepburn in the experiment discussed above in which subjects were arbitrarily categorized as Phis or Gammas. It was found that out-group discrimination disappeared if subjects came to believe that their favoritism was not reciprocated by group-mates. The experimenters provided information during the experiment which indicated to subjects how many tokens they had been assigned by the other subjects in the study. Subjects who were led to believe their generosity to group-mates was reciprocated continued to show in-group favoritism, but when they thought it was not, they ceased to exhibit out-group discrimination. Similar findings were obtained with the ratings of others' social characteristics. When subjects were led to believe that there were no differences in the way in-group members and out-group members rated them, they stopped rating in-group members higher than out-group members.[38]

These results strongly suggest that a norm of reciprocity, or group loyalty, is at work in the minimal group effect. Subjects seemed to think that being a member of a group or team, even one arbitrarily arrived at, should imply some reciprocated favoritism. When such favoritism was not forthcoming, the subjects quickly adjusted and the intergroup discrimination was eliminated. In the other minimal group studies, subjects received no information about group-mate behavior; in all likelihood, subjects presumed others were reciprocating.

This suggests that mere categorization is not enough to create the minimal social group. Being assigned to a category is a precondition to group membership, but a social group is not merely a collection of people with something in common. The minimal condition above and beyond categorization seems to be a belief in some kind of internal reciprocity. Without such reciprocity the very existence and meaning of a group is put into doubt.

This understanding conforms to everyday experience. We all belong to dozens of recognizable categories. Some of us are Catholic, some Jewish; some are tall, some short. There are men and women, old people and young people, lawyers and truck drivers. Some people's ancestors are African, some Asian, some European; we are Philadelphians and New Yorkers. Some of the categories are socially meaningful to us and some are not. Some are meaningful only in special circumstances.

In order for a category to be meaningful socially, it must first be salient. If you do not know your blood type, or even that blood types differ, you can hardly feel any solidarity with others of similar type. But mere salience is not enough, there must in addition be some ostensible reason why members of the category should treat each other differently from others. People with a particular blood type are unlikely to show in-group solidarity unless, for instance, a shortage of that blood type should develop, in which case mutual concern might be appropriate.

An important finding in the minimal group literature, which adds support to the above interpretation, is that competing categorizations completely eliminate intergroup discrimination. Norbert Vanbeselaere, a research associate with the Belgian National Fund for Scientific Research, categorized schoolboys between twelve and fifteen years old into Reds and Greens. He then used a procedure, like the one used by Tajfel in the Klee-Kandinsky study, to independently classify the boys into those who preferred scenes of forests and those who preferred scenes of the seashore. He told the boys that he was able to detect their preferences from short, written samples he had them write about both scenes at an earlier time. This created four possible categories: Red-Seashore, Red-Forest, Green-Seashore, and Green-Forest. For control purposes some groups were merely split into Reds and Greens, and others only into Seashore and Forest.[39]

The results were clear and unequivocal. When only one categorization was used, as in the control conditions, in-group favoritism was clearly exhibited. When two categories were used, the effect disappeared. Even in the case where the boys differed on both categories, there was no discrimination. For instance, Green-Forest boys did not discriminate against Red-Seashore boys.[40]

Vanbeselaere offers no explanation for his findings, and is content to point out that the result is inconsistent with Tajfel's self-esteem hypothesis. I think the result is consistent with the team-expectation explanation offered here. When schoolboys are dichotomized, they naturally imagine they are supposed to act as teams or work-groups. However, in the double-categorization procedure they are broken into four categories. Vanbeselaere reports that he went to some effort to be sure they understood this.[41] In this circumstance it is much less clear what the social expectation is. It is unclear who may be asked to compete with or cooperate with whom. I suggest that in this situation, it is well to sit and wait for further instructions, in which case there is no point in taking a competitive team posture until you find out what is going on. Without a team posture, there are no teammates, and therefore the norms of loyalty and in-group favoritism that are based (hypothetically) in our genetic programming would have no effect.

In attempting to draw some implications for social policy from the wide-ranging literature on intergroup discrimination, Messick and Mackie argue that "to the extent that intergroup boundaries are blurred or weakened, intergroup interaction will be more likely to occur in terms of personal characteristics than category labels, and intergroup bias will be reduced." They suggest that increasing the saliency of competing categories is one way to blur intergroup boundaries. In addition, they argue that such boundaries "are likely to be more salient when one's membership in the ingroup serves important personal goals." The authors conclude that reducing the "instrumental importance of group membership, perhaps by providing alternative routes to goal achievement, may decrease the tendency to perceive and to interact with others in categorical terms.''[42]

That, of course, is the position taken throughout this book. I would add to their conclusion the observation that increasing the saliency and significance of group membership is also likely to increase intergroup hostility. Unfortunately, as Messick and Mackie correctly point out, there has not been much research on this point. Perhaps little research is undertaken to explore this fairly obvious conclusion, which also reflects common sense, because it is so much at variance with current policies designed to heighten group identity and to make group membership an important basis of entitlement.

VI. Conclusion

The implication of the conclusion drawn above is straightforward. If we wish to promote harmony among people from diverse ethnic and racial groups, we should attempt to create alternative categories of group membership that reduce the saliency and importance of ethnicity and race. People should be encouraged to think of themselves as aligned with others who have similar philosophies, occupations, and leisure interests, to mention only a few bases of group identification. People do this naturally, of course, and they should be encouraged in this tendency, since such identifications tend to break down the significance of the more volatile associations based on ethnicity and race.

In addition, we must encourage people, and children in particular, to see themselves primarily as, for instance, Americans, rather than as Italians or blacks or Hispanics. In an ideal world, they might be taught to see themselves as simply human. We cannot, and should not, deny people's identification with and loyalty to their own group, but we should encourage them to subordinate such identifications and loyalties to as great an extent as is feasible. This is, of course, the doctrine of ethnic assimilation that guided educational policy earlier in the century. It was also the guiding force of the early civil rights movement. In recent years the principle of assimilation has been de-emphasized in favor of the doctrine of multiculturalism. The scientific literature and common experience suggest that this is a development unlikely to have positive consequences for racial or ethnic harmony.

It is important to keep in mind that assimilation is not an all-or-nothing thing; assimilation admits of degrees. In particular, we should be reminded of Gunnar Myrdal's ''rank order of discrimination'' in black-white relations (discussed above in Section V of Chapter 3). In some areas of life whites had little resistance to integration, while in other areas they resisted it greatly.

This is an example of the tendency for people to adjust their expectations and behaviors to the differing requirements of different areas of life, in differing "social domains." Language that is acceptable in the domain of the locker room is not acceptable in the domain of the dinner table. We know this and adjust our language accordingly.

Similarly, discrimination on the basis of race or ethnicity or religion may be seen as acceptable and even desirable in one social domain but not another. Some may find it offensive to discriminate on the basis of religion, for instance, on the job, but not in choosing schools for their children. Others may find discrimination in selecting schools offensive, but not in selecting close friends or marriage partners. Some may find even this latter discrimination offensive.

One measure of the extent to which a group has been assimilated into American society is the number of social domains in which discrimination is practiced against its members. Most Americans of European ancestry whose ancestors arrived here before World War II can be said to have been almost completely assimilated in this regard, since there is no domain in which separation from and discrimination against them is common. American Jews, for instance, experienced considerable discrimination in earlier years, and even now experience occasional social discrimination. Today, however, the most common concern of Jewish religious leaders is not discrimination against Jews, but rather the high rate of out-marriage of assimilated Jews, which threatens the survival of Jews as an identifiable group. In this regard, blacks and other nonwhite minorities have been considerably less assimilated than are the European ethnics.

Some groups, such as Hasidic Jews, consciously resist assimilation in order to preserve group identity. First-generation immigrants, whose attachment to their ethnic identity is great, often frown upon the out-marriage of their children. Public policy, quite correctly, is primarily directed at reducing intergroup discrimination in the public domains of school and work, and much less concerned with discrimination in the personal spheres of friendship and marriage. Such a policy proscribes discrimination in those public domains where important values and civil order require it, but avoids intrusion into domains where the general good is not much affected. People of different backgrounds can work together and learn together amicably without necessarily wishing to form close personal friendships or to marry each other.

This became very clear in Vietnam, where black and white soldiers fought side by side with little difficulty and with much reported mutual respect, and yet during leisure periods tended to segregate into same-race groups. The point is that on a military assignment the instrumental requirements of the task mightily overwhelm distinctions of class or race or religion. The categories important on the battlefield are those of skill, of courage, and perhaps most important, of loyalty and reliability. The categories of race, religion, and ethnicity are simply not significant.

On the other hand, during leisure time, when one wishes to relax and share conversation, the categories of race, religion, and ethnicity might be very important indeed. It is easier and more comfortable for people to communicate with people whose backgrounds are similar to their own. Much less needs to be explained and so much more can be communicated by the cultural shorthand common to all ethnic groups.

The history of ethnic assimilation suggests that as integration in the public domain is secured, it tends to follow more or less naturally in the more private domains. Such, of course, was the hope of the original civil rights movement. For such a development to take place, however, real differences between people need to diminish and people have to want those differences to diminish.

Some groups, such as Hasidic Jews and the Amish, desire only a limited assimilation and resist integration in the personal domain. Hasidic Jews quite obviously wish to maintain a separate identity and thus, so long as they set themselves apart, cannot be fully assimilated. There is nothing wrong with this as long as people acknowledge the price they pay for such separate status. One particularly harsh and unjust price is that their members are more likely to suffer the physical and verbal assaults that are commonly directed at minorities by uneducated and boorish young men in all societies. Distinct sects like the Hasidic Jews must go to great lengths to avoid offending or threatening the majority. There is the danger, however remote, that the majority will reject pluralism and demand conformity, and attack those who refuse to conform on the basis of a presumed disloyalty to the larger group. Jewish history is too full of such examples to need repeating here. Jews have, over the centuries, maintained their distinct social identity, but no one could deny that the cost to many of their individual members was enormous.

The case of blacks in America is of course quite different from the case of Hasidic Jews. Hasidic Jews could replace their distinctive clothes with more nondescript garb, remove their distinguishing facial hair, and mingle unnoticed among the majority; their lack of assimilation is freely chosen. Black Americans, quite obviously, have no such freedom to become undetectable as a distinct group.

On the other hand, ineradicable physical features make Asian Americans readily distinguishable from the majority. The general harmony that prevails in Hawaii between Asians and Caucasians suggests that racial distinctiveness need not be as great a barrier as at first appears to be the case. Clearly assimilation is not complete, but interracial marriage is on the increase. *Time* magazine reports that ''[a]mong Japanese Americans, 65% marry people who have no Japanese heritage.''[43] It is by no means clear that complete assimilation is impossible.

America is now at an important crossroads in its history. It can embark on a new and untested course of the kind promoted in the educational doctrine of multiculturalism and increasingly emphasize the diversity among ethnic and racial groups. Or it can return to its earlier commitment to assimilation. If it chooses a return to assimilation, American children will have to be instructed to look to and emphasize those nonracial categories that unite people independently of race and ethnicity. Children will have to be encouraged to look to people's values and personal capacities—and not to their racial background—in all domains of life, but most crucially in the public domains where alternative, nonracial categories are most easily applied. The significance of blackness or whiteness is much reduced when other factors are salient. On the job and in the school, the importance of skin color is much reduced by the instrumental needs of the tasks at hand. Likewise, political and ethical beliefs are often more important to people than race or ethnicity.

If the goal of most Americans is to move in the direction of greater assimilation, and I think it is, then many current policies are extremely counterproductive, and are in fact quite perverse. Multiculturalism in education is one such misguided policy. Others include current affirmative action policies that have the unfortunate effect of heightening the significance of race by making it an important criterion for advancement in the public domains of school and work, while playing down the significance of other personal qualities for advancement. If affirmative action policies are seen as providing unfair and unwarranted advantages to blacks, then white resentment is thereby increased. If those policies reinforce the belief that whites will not treat blacks fairly without coercive measures, then black resentment toward whites is increased in turn.

Affirmative action is not, however, the most problematic of the current policies affecting race relations. Perhaps far more serious are those policies relating to education, crime control, and welfare that were developed in an attempt to reduce discrimination against blacks, and that will be discussed in great detail in Part IV. While these policies have no doubt reduced discrimination, they seem to have exacerbated the problems of the black underclass. As I have stressed in other chapters, the behavior patterns and the values so common in the underclass are alien to most middle-class people, and assimilation of underclass blacks will be resisted so long as those behavioral problems remain.

Middle-class Americans, both white and black, see nothing wrong in discriminating against people whose behavior and values they find abhorrent, whatever their color. It is difficult to provide reasons why they should not discriminate on such grounds. Of course, most white Americans can and do distinguish between middle-class blacks and underclass blacks, but in so doing they must ignore those who would deny such distinctions. Among those who do so are black leaders and their white supporters who argue that there is nothing problematic about the behavior of the black underclass and who claim that whites are incapable of making distinctions among blacks due to endemic racism. The point is that denying the distinction between middle-class blacks and those in the underclass does not eliminate that distinction and, even more importantly, does nothing to improve the conditions in the inner cities.

The position taken throughout this book is that the most serious danger for racial harmony in America lies in the counterproductive behavior among many members of the black underclass. In the three chapters that follow, I attempt to determine the sources of crime, illegitimacy, and school failure—problems which contribute most to the crisis of the inner cities, and which represent almost unbreachable impediments to social and economic mobility for those who live in them.

So long as those problems continue to fester, there can be little hope for improved race relations. Societies are dynamic systems, and things rarely remain the same for very long, even when it appears that a stable equilibrium has been achieved. Forces engendering racial harmony are self-reinforcing, but so are forces fostering racial enmity. If race relations turn sour, they are not likely to get better on their own. The widespread rioting in numerous cities in the spring and summer of 1992 in the wake of the Rodney King verdict suggests that what appeared to be a stable social equilibrium may have already become unglued. What the new equilibrium will look like is of course impossible at this moment to divine, but it is none too soon to begin rethinking the policies that have allowed us to drift into the current circumstance. It is clear from this chapter that many policies that were supposed to increase racial harmony are not based in any sound social science. To the contrary, the social science literature on intergroup relations strongly suggests that many of those policies are likely to undermine intergroup harmony.

Part IV

The Debilitating Triad: Crime, Illegitimacy, and Inadequate Education

In the early nineteenth century, London experienced problems similar to what we see in our own inner cities today. According to British historian and criminologist J. J. Tobias, London's population underwent a period of rapid growth as a result of industrialization. Since public sanitation had not yet resulted in significant health improvement, death rates remained high; but birth rates also went up, because the population contained large numbers of young people starting families. The net result of these trends was that many children lost one or both parents to disease. In addition, the glut of employees flooding into the cities created a difficult labor market that often made long hours of work a necessity for subsistence. Since there were no free schools, young parents had little choice but to allow their children to roam the streets while they worked. Some parents, often unmarried women, found themselves so destitute as to be hardly able to care for themselves, and these parents sometimes abandoned their children altogether. The streets of London's working quarters were, therefore, overrun by unsupervised or abandoned children prone to criminal behavior.[1] The situation of these children is sympathetically portrayed in Charles Dickens's *Oliver Twist.*

J. J. Tobias says the following about the conditions which gave rise to juvenile criminality:

> In London and other large towns, children saw others living a life of apparent ease and idleness on the proceeds of crime, free from the restraints which hemmed in honest youngsters. They lived in a community whose values were such as to make crime seem normal—a child who chose to remain honest and

starve, or even merely to beg, was looked down upon. Everything was there to assist the entry into criminal life.[2]

Tobias explains that the rampant criminality in lower-class London did not abate until authorities recognized their responsibility to see to the regulation and education of abandoned children, and acted on that responsibility. When they did so, the children, not surprisingly, reaped the benefit. Children were placed in "industrial schools" to obtain occupational training. In addition, law enforcement was dramatically improved and reform schools for delinquent children were established. Young criminals were sent for extended stays at these reform schools and no longer enjoyed "the glory of frequent appearances in court and a succession of short sentences and triumphant releases." As recalcitrant youngsters were removed from the streets, the children "were prevented from committing crime themselves and were no longer able to draw others into a criminal life by example or by direct encouragement." The resulting "more settled social environment," according to Tobias, explains the reduction in youth crime after the 1850s. In addition, when these improvements came, "they were self reinforcing, for the vicious cycle turned to a benign one."[3] Not surprisingly, as juvenile crime decreased, attitudes toward the young became more sympathetic: "[T]he fact that people no longer automatically regarded them as potential criminals may have helped some to remain honest."[4]

Tobias is surely correct that London's problems were the direct result of the Industrial Revolution in England, which swelled the cities with large numbers of people fresh from the English countryside. Such people were ill equipped for the rigors of factory work, ill equipped to fight off the biological ravages of urban diseases, and equally ill equipped to regulate their offspring amid the anonymity and social diversity of the growing city. In the small towns and rural hamlets from which they came, children were constantly under the gaze of adults whether at work or play, and there was sufficient unanimity of belief that neighbors felt free to discipline their neighbor's children, and felt sufficiently concerned to take them in or find relatives to do so when they were orphaned.

None of those conditions were evident in the slums of London where rural folk found themselves. With parents at work, there was no one to supervise their children, and when parents died, no one to take them in. If children ran away from home or were abandoned by parents, there was no one with sufficient sympathy or means to adopt them. The Dickensian "Artful Dodgers" were therefore almost bound to find themselves taken under the wing of the wily Fagins who saw great opportunities in the human flotsam and jetsam the rapidly growing city produced.

The correlation of nineteenth-century London's problems with those of today is strong but not perfect. Today much urban mayhem is the result of undirected and often not very remunerative criminality on the part of young people. There may be Fagins and Artful Dodgers in the drug trade, but the business of theft and brigandage is often carried out by groups of young people without any adult leadership. Furthermore, the young children who roam the streets in today's cities have not really been abandoned by parents, but are often the illegitimate children of young women who lack the moral or physical capacity to supervise them. Yet the result is much the same. Claude Brown, author of *Manchild in the Promised Land,* described the conditions of life for these children in the inner cities of America:

> Yet the unimaginably difficult struggle to arrive at a productive manhood in urban America is more devastatingly monstrous than ever before. All street kids are at least semi-abandoned, out on those mean streets for the major portion of the day and night, they are at the mercy of a ruthless and cold-blooded environment; survival is a matter of fortuity, instinct, ingenuity and unavoidable conditioning. Consequently, the man-child who survives is usually more cunning, more devious and often more vicious than his middle-class counter-part.[5]

A fundamental argument of this book is that blacks as a group have failed to gain economic parity with whites primarily because of the poor economic performance of underclass blacks and not because of the racism and discrimination of whites. The thesis further argues that underclass poverty is in large measure the result of the crime and disorder in underclass neighborhoods. This disorder is a prime agent in educational failure, which impedes economic advancement and, in turn, has the effect of producing high rates of illegitimacy. The order of causation, however, is not unidirectional. It is also the case that illegitimacy, in turn, contributes to crime and to educational difficulties.

It is important to stress that the problems of the underclass are different from those of people who are working-class or are simply poor. There are many poor people—the aged, the handicapped, the temporarily unemployed—who suffer few of the behavioral problems which in combination serve to define what is meant by the term ''underclass.'' People who work on a steady basis, even if very poor, are by definition not part of the underclass. The term ''underclass'' refers to that group of blacks and other minorities who have come to dominate poor urban neighborhoods since the mid-1960s and who are enmeshed in a web of behavioral problems that have, since the 1960s, taken on a pathological cast. It should be understood that middle-class and upper-class blacks and minorities also inhabit the same cities as do members of the underclass, though often in different neighborhoods. It should also be clear that many of the problems common among underclass people are not unique to them. Whites, for instance, engage in crime, rely on welfare assistance, and have illegitimate babies. In the case of whites, however, there are few settings where the number and density of people who exhibit such behavior patterns are sufficient to determine the dominant norms for their communities. The term "underclass" implies a set of special ecological conditions which rarely arises outside of urban areas. When crime, educational failure, dependence on government support, illegitimacy, and father absence reach a critical mass, as they do in many of the nation's black neighborhoods, they can overwhelm a community and come to dominate its mores. One can, when such a condition develops, talk about an underclass "way of life."

Immigrant groups often experience problems similar to those plaguing the underclass, but the poorer, more troubled members of immigrant groups are often, for a host of reasons, living side by side with middle-class and upwardly mobile people from that same ethnic group. When the poor and troubled members of immigrant groups are separated from the more stable members of their own ethnic background in large housing complexes or other similar settings, underclass patterns often come into being.

In what follows, when I refer to underclass behaviors and problems I am almost always referring to the behaviors and problems associated with the urban black underclass. This should not be taken to mean that I do not recognize the emergence of these patterns in other racial or ethnic groups, but only that in treating questions of race relations, the emergence of the black underclass is especially important. This is because racial differences, which are often the source of tension in the best of circumstances, are made radically more so if they are perceived to be aligned with behavioral and value differences.

The problems of the poorer members of an ethnic group whose members are not, in general, racially distinct, are not likely to harm the prospects of more-prosperous members of that group, who are likely to become assimilated and indistinguishable from the majority population.

It is of course grossly unfair that middle-class blacks cannot so easily escape the effects of the negative impressions generated by the behavior of the black underclass. That is why it is so vitally important to address the problems of underclass blacks in order to maintain harmonious relations between blacks and whites.

In the following pages I argue that a vicious circle has come into effect in black underclass neighborhoods. It is impossible to understand this vicious circle without examining how the factors of crime, educational failure, and illegitimacy all contribute to a high degree of social disorder which, in turn, fosters these problems and often compounds their independent effects. For instance, the lack of social order allows criminal activity to be sufficiently rewarding so as to discourage serious engagement with school work on the part of many inner-city children. It is important to keep in mind that for most young people (including young people of all social classes) school is a difficult and often unrewarding activity, and some young people everywhere look for alternatives to it. In most places there are no reasonable alternatives, and therefore young people stick with school long enough to acquire the skills and the frame of mind that make them employable. The chaotic inner cities, however, provide an exciting and often socially and economically rewarding alternative to school. Trying to improve black educational performance by attending only to the problems of the schools themselves will not be very effective so long as the urban streets remain an inviting and easily accessible alternative to the drudgery and boredom that schools must inevitably represent to many students.

High crime rates and high rates of school failure contribute heavily to the illegitimacy problem since they interfere with the ability of men to attain the skills and attitudes essential for successful family life. In black underclass communities there are simply not enough men in a position to act as responsible husbands for all the women seeking partners. About one-quarter of black men in their twenties are in jail, on probation, or on parole.[6] A fair number are murdered every year. Of those who finish high school, many take much longer than usual and are often grossly deficient in basic skills. In the inner cities a youthful underclass subculture has come into being which glorifies violence and mocks diligent effort in school and work. This subculture also spawns an extremely misogynist attitude among young men. Women are viewed in a demeaning light as sexual trophies who are to be used rather than cherished. Likewise, young men are thought foolish if they take responsibility for the children they father.[7]

Under these circumstances, many young women may come to the conclusion, not unrealistically, that the odds of finding an acceptable husband are not very promising. Among these are many who believe they have very poor prospects for rewarding careers or advanced education, and who look upon marriage and motherhood as eminently desirable options. As will become clear in Chapter 10, many women in these circumstances allow themselves to become pregnant by their boyfriends in the mistaken belief, sometimes encouraged by their boyfriends, that this will lead to marriage. Others become pregnant by accident, but carry their babies to term in the same, usually misguided, hope. Still others, especially those whose prospects for marriage seem especially unpromising, may decide to get on with the important business of starting a family without a husband. Parenthood, as we saw in previous chapters, is universally recognized as a potent good in and of itself. Under the circumstances, the decision to bear a child out of wedlock is not, strictly speaking, quite as irrational as it appears at first sight. This is even more the case if welfare dependency is very common, as it is in underclass neighborhoods, and has no social stigma attached to it.

Once illegitimacy becomes the norm, as it has in underclass communities, the problems of crime and education are compounded. Young women attempting to raise children on their own are bound to have more difficulties than those who have the assistance of husbands. Children of single mothers are therefore more likely to exhibit the high rates of school failure that are common in underclass neighborhoods. High rates of delinquency are also closely associated with communities suffering high rates of illegitimacy and single parenthood, for complex reasons that are taken up in the pages which follow.

Most criminal behavior, and especially violent crime, is committed by young men who start their criminal careers in early adolescence. By the time they reach their late twenties many are removed from the criminal scene by incarceration, injury, and death. Many men simply lose the impulsiveness and bravado of youth as they grow older and some, of course, grow wiser. In addition, the criminal justice system deals much more harshly with older men. In any case, since the most disruptive criminal activities are the product of young men, crime cannot be reduced until ways are found to reduce the number of young men who are seduced into self-destructive criminal behaviors.

Until greater adult authority over adolescents is established, the various problems of inner-city neighborhoods will continue to grow more troublesome. While this prescription is straightforward, it is unlikely, for a host of reasons, to be easy to implement. Not the least of the reasons for that difficulty is the continuing tendency of black leaders and their supporters to see the imposition of social control in terms of racial oppression.

As I have argued in earlier chapters, the attitudes of whites toward blacks today are more often the product of correct public perception of black underclass pathologies than of ignorance or malevolent intent. From this perspective, race relations in America cannot improve, and in fact will deteriorate, so long as the inner cities remain the chaotic and unwholesome places they have become during the last thirty years. Now as in nineteenth-century London, those problems are clearly the result of young people being allowed to follow their natural inclinations unchecked by any meaningful adult authority.

The debilitating triad of educational failure, criminal behavior, and illegitimacy are mutually reinforcing and tend to have additive effects on economic performance and, in addition, to place severe strains on relations between blacks and whites. They form the vicious circle which black communities confront today, and they are as debilitating, in some ways more debilitating, than the vicious circle Myrdal discussed fifty years ago. If any one of these problems grows worse, it is likely that the others will be exacerbated. Likewise, improvement in any one of these three problem areas is likely to have salutary effects on the other two. The problem for social policy is to determine where to intervene so as to produce the maximal benefit at minimal economic and social cost. It is important to come to grips with the factors that produced the spiral of pathology in the inner cities in the first place. It is important to know why this spiral of pathology took the particular form that it did, and why it did so at a particular historical moment. Since each element of the triad had causes, some of which were similar and others different, it seems best to examine each element in turn. This is what I do in the chapters that follow.

8

Crime

I. Introduction

It is my contention that criminal behavior in black neighborhoods is today the single most serious impediment to black economic advancement. It is also the most serious impediment to improved race relations and increased racial integration. There can be no doubt that crime is a major concern of all Americans. The fear of crime has motivated large numbers of middle-class people, whites in particular, to flee urban areas where crime is rampant. It is unreasonable to expect greater racial integration so long as whites fear the sort of crime that has become increasingly associated with black youth in underclass neighborhoods.

It is not only race relations, however, that suffer from mayhem and disorder. Criminal activity among young males, who are the most common perpetrators of crime, serves to undercut their educational advancement, and seriously impedes their economic progress. Young men involved in criminal activities are diverted from the tasks of acquiring the skills and knowledge that make them employable, and that coincidentally make them good marriage prospects for young women. For that reason, crime contributes to the problem of illegitimacy, since it deprives young women of men able or willing to undertake the responsibilities of marriage. In addition, criminal disorder interferes with normal economic activity and reduces investment in black communities, thereby reducing employment and entrepreneurial opportunities.

Perhaps most importantly, crime deprives people of the freedom to carry on their routine activities free from the fear of predatory attack. The simple pleasures of taking a walk during the evening are denied to people who live in high crime areas. They are deprived of the peace of mind about their safety from violent assault that most people take for granted and that is the most important right of civil society. No matter what other factors contribute to black difficulties, there can be no doubt that until underclass black communities are made orderly and safe, blacks as a group cannot reasonably expect to make the sort of progress in American society that people of good will hope for all Americans.

The conventional wisdom holds that crime among blacks is the direct result of poverty and discrimination. In this chapter I demonstrate that this conventional view is supported neither by the evidence nor by prominent criminological theories. The prominent theories of crime do indeed stress the importance of blocked opportunities in producing criminality. But they also stress, in widely different ways, the importance of social norms in curtailing criminal responses in the face of deprivation. In this view blocked opportunities are the occasion for crime, not the cause of it. Crime results rather from a flawed socialization that fails to inculcate norms proscribing criminal activity as a means to attain desired ends. Young people who have developed appropriate internal norms are unlikely to become delinquent no matter how much they are frustrated by a lack of economic opportunities. Nevertheless, these prominent criminological theories have been interpreted by government officials and most media spokespeople to mean that providing greater opportunities to young blacks would almost automatically eliminate delinquency in black communities. Put another way, these people have argued that crime could not effectively be curtailed until its root causes in poverty and discrimination had been greatly reduced.

Though the criminological theories rarely stress the point, it follows from most of these theories that if there is an absence of internal norms to inhibit criminal behavior, communities must, if they are to limit crime, exert greater than usual external restraints. In other words, if substantial numbers of people fail to voluntarily abide by the law, police forces must be dramatically enlarged to see that the law is not widely violated. Failure to take adequate policing measures, in areas where socialization is weak, guarantees an increase in crime.

In the 1960s, the federal government, following the conventional wisdom that poverty and racism cause crime, attempted to reduce crime by liberalizing welfare provisions and by employing other means designed to raise black living standards. The government also adopted policies designed to reduce discrimination against blacks, especially the widely reported discrimination on the part of police. Among the measures adopted were some that drastically reduced police discretion in dealing with black adolescents. Since poverty and discrimination were not the primary causes of crime, these measures were ineffective. In fact, crime has increased dramatically since the 1960s.

This foreseeable but largely unexpected outcome resulted from the fact that many of these changes served in complex ways to make it more difficult to socialize young people and that, as a consequence, fewer young people were motivated to voluntarily abstain from criminal conduct. At the same time, new constraints on police behavior seriously undermined communities' ability to impose external deterrents to crime. The combined effect of these developments was an explosive growth of criminal behavior among young men in black neighborhoods. Crime rates, furthermore, are currently on the rise and promise to reach even more intolerable levels than those common today.

It bears repeating that reducing crime in black communities is the single most effective thing government can do to dramatically improve the lives and economic prospects of black Americans. Illegitimacy and school failure are also potent enemies of black progress, but little can be done to correct those problems until order is restored to underclass neighborhoods. The maintenance of public safety is the most basic of all governmental functions and one that most governments perform with relative success. A government that cannot maintain public order is, in a fundamental sense, bankrupt.

Unfortunately, any policy maker who argues for the importance of crime reduction risks being charged with racism and ignorance regarding the root causes of crime in poverty and discrimination. These latter problems, it is said, must be attacked first, and when they are resolved, crime itself will whither away for lack of causes. This position, as the following discussion will demonstrate, is wrongheaded in the extreme and gains little support from the scholarly literature on crime. For twenty-five years crime in black communities has not been seriously addressed, and as a consequence blacks, and race relations, have suffered greatly. It seems long past the time for policy makers to cease equivocating on the issue of crime, to recognize it for the devastating problem it is, and to start addressing means of reducing it.

II. The Prevalence of Crime

Crime is more prevalent in America than in most other places in the modern world, and far more common than in other industrialized societies. In most parts of the industrialized world the homicide rate hovers around 1 to 2 homicides per 100,000 people each year. This rate has remained fairly constant throughout this century. Even during the tumultuous period of industrialization and rapid urbanization in the nineteenth century, the homicide rate in northern France, for instance, remained constant at about 1 per 100,000.[1]

Recent murder rates (for the period 1980–1984) were 1.4 per 100,000 in France (the highest in Western Europe); 1.2 per 100,000 in Great Britain; 1 per 100,000 in Japan; and .7 per 100,000 in Greece and West Germany. The

United States murder rate, by contrast, was almost 10 per 100,000, a figure seven to ten times the rate of most other modern societies.[2]

In large cities, crime statistics are even more disturbing. New York City in 1990, for instance, experienced over 2,000 murders—a rate of 31 murders per 100,000 population. The nation's second most populous city, Los Angeles, had a similar rate of 28 per 100,000. In fact, these sorts of rates are common in most of the largest cities in the United States. Washington, D.C., had the highest rate in the country with 78 murders per 100,000. New Orleans had a rate of 61 per 100,000. Other cities with higher than average rates were Detroit and Atlanta, with 57 and 59 murders per 100,000 people, respectively.[3]

Homicide rates are important measures of crime because they are usually quite reliable and mirror the rates of other crimes. Reported rapes, for instance, are usually about twice as high as murder rates. New York City and Los Angeles, with homicide rates near 30 per 100,000, reported 43 and 58 rapes per 100,000 inhabitants, respectively. Detroit reported 161 rapes per 100,000 inhabitants in 1990, and Atlanta, 176 per 100,000. Interestingly, Washington, with the highest rate for homicide, was somewhat of an anomaly with 50 reported rapes per 100,000 people, a rate lower than its murder rate.[4]

Robbery, which involves the taking of property with the threat of bodily harm, generally has rates about forty or fifty times that of homicide. In New York City in 1990, for instance, there were 1,370 reported robberies per 100,000 people, or forty-four times the homicide rate. Chicago, which also had a murder rate of approximately 31 per 100,000, had a robbery rate of 1,335 per 100,000, or forty-three times the rate for murder.[5]

Reported property crimes such as burglary and theft are about two hundred times more numerous than murders. The five largest U.S. cities—New York, Los Angeles, Chicago, Houston, and Philadelphia—all with similar murder rates, had property crime rates of 7,316, 6,821, 8,220, 9,950, and 5,843, respectively, per 100,000 people in 1990.[6]

The Census bureau reports on the overall incidence of serious crime in a "total crime index." For most large cities the crime index is about 10,000 per 100,000 inhabitants. For New York and Los Angeles in 1990, the index was 9,699 and 9,225 per 100,000, respectively. Some large cities, however, have rates higher than that. Atlanta reported the highest index of 19,236 crimes per 100,000 population. Dallas, Texas, the eighth largest U.S. city, had an index of 15,520 per 100,000. San Antonio and Detroit both had rates of over 12,000 per 100,000 people.[7]

These statistics indicate that approximately one out of every ten people living in large American cities reported to police that they were the victim of a serious crime in any recent year (assuming few are victimized more than one time per year). However, even this underestimates the magnitude of the problem, since not all crimes are reported to the police. Government surveys of crime victimization provide an estimate of crime independent of those crimes reported to police departments. These surveys suggest that overall crime is probably more than twice as high as that indicated above, since fewer than half of all crimes are reported to the police. Some crimes like murder and car theft are usually well reported, but only about half of all rapes, and fewer than 30 percent of all thefts, are reported to the police.[8] If we correct for this widespread underreporting, it is safe to say that about one-fifth of all city-dwellers have been the victims of serious crimes in any recent year.

The above figures reflect overall averages for people of all races and classes. When one examines individual cities, it becomes clear that most of the crime that is committed is committed in the poorer enclaves, especially underclass areas, within cities. In New York City's poorer neighborhoods the murder rate averages about 100 per 100,000; in one district in the South Bronx it reached 125 per 100,000 in 1991.[9] By comparison, the homicide rate in middle-class neighborhoods of New York City in the same year was in the range of 4 to 6 per 100,000, which is below the national rate.[10] In the United States as a whole, black men had rates as homicide victims of 61.1 per 100,000 in 1989, which is seven times more than the white male victimization rate of 8.2 per 100,000.[11]

Other crime rates reflect the same pattern. Reporter Jonathan Greenberg, writing in *New York Magazine,* reports that in 1989, robbery rates in the largely black areas of Harlem and Bedford-Stuyvesant were 3,268 and 3,775 per 100,000 residents, respectively. In the white, largely working-class area of Bensonhurst the rate was 520 per 100,000, or approximately one-seventh the rate in the black neighborhoods.[12] In New York City robbery represents only about 13 percent of all crimes reported.[13] If one extrapolates this figure for the robbery rate in the black communities of Harlem and Bedford-Stuyvesant, then the overall crime index in those areas is probably in the range of 25,000 per 100,000. If one corrects for the nationwide underreporting of crime, the victimization rate is more like 50,000 per 100,000. Thus, one out of two residents of inner-city black neighborhoods is very likely to have been a victim of serious crime in any one year. This is probably a low estimate, since underreporting of crime is higher in New York City than in most places because the police openly admit that minor thefts and assaults are given a low priority. The fact that inner-city residents often lack insurance coverage further reduces incentives to report crimes to the police.

While blacks are more likely, proportionately, than whites to be the victims of crime, they are also more likely, proportionately, to be the perpetrators. Even though whites make up 80 percent of the population and blacks about 12 percent (meaning whites outnumber blacks by almost seven to one), there are approximately equal numbers of blacks and whites housed in state and federal prisons, with whites accounting for 51 percent and blacks 47.5 percent of all inmates.[14]

Furthermore, blacks are more likely to be violent repeat criminals. Among repeat offenders, blacks represented 56.2 and whites 40.2 percent of those convicted of a violent crime.[15] Greenberg reports that although blacks made up only about a quarter of the population of New York City, they accounted in 1989 for 67 percent (in terms of arrests) of the robberies, 53 percent of the burglaries, and 57 percent of the murders. Hispanics, who also make up about a quarter of the population, show arrest rates closer to parity with their proportion of the population. Greenberg reports that they accounted for 24 percent of the robberies, 30 percent of the burglaries, and 32 percent of the murders. By contrast, Asians, who make up 7 percent of the population, were arrested for 1.7 percent of the robberies, less than 1 percent of the burglaries, and about 2 percent of the murders. Whites, who make up approximately 45 percent of the population, accounted for 7.5 percent of robbery arrests, 15.6 percent of burglary arrests, and 8.8 percent of murder arrests.[16]

These figures help explain why whites have come to view black men with apprehension, since whites are very often victims of black criminal assaults. Black criminals prey upon whites even more than they do upon blacks, mainly because there are so many more whites to prey upon. According to U.S. Department of Justice statistics for 1990, about 57 percent of all violent crimes committed by blacks were perpetrated against white victims. In the case of white criminals, only 2 percent of their victims were black.[17] This does not mean that most crimes committed against whites are committed by blacks. Since there are so many fewer blacks than whites in the general population, only about 18 percent of white victims of violent crimes reported black assailants. In the case of crimes like robbery, however, which are more likely to involve strangers, interracial crime is more common. Approximately 43 percent of white robbery victims reported that their assailants were black. On the other hand, only 8 percent of black robbery victims reported they were robbed by white criminals, who overwhelmingly prey on the larger white population.[18]

When trying to understand these very high rates of crime, it is important to understand that crime, especially the predatory crime that debilitates communities, is largely an urban phenomenon committed, on the whole, by young men. Large metropolitan areas in 1990 had roughly twice the rate of violent crime (856 per 100,000 people) than smaller cities (458 per 100,000) and four times the rate of rural areas (207 per 100,000).[19] In addition, the overwhelming majority of criminals are men, and most of them are young. Only in the case of larceny, which includes shoplifting, do women represent a substantial proportion (32 percent) of those arrested. On the other hand, over 90 percent of all robberies and burglaries are committed by men. Moreover, 56 percent of those arrested for serious crimes are under the age of twenty-five, and 28 percent are under the age of eighteen.[20]

These statistics help explain the fact that nationwide about 25 percent of black men between the ages of twenty and twenty-nine were either in prison, on parole, or on probation. By contrast, only 3 percent of white men in their twenties in New York State were in prison, on parole, or on probation. In New York State the figure for young black men is 23 percent. In Washington, D.C., fully 42 percent of black men in their twenties were caught up in the criminal justice system. The Washington figure is higher, in large part, because it included men on bail and those being sought for arrest. If these categories were included, no doubt the figures nationwide and in New York State would also be higher, though perhaps not as high as in Washington. The overwhelming proportion of the inmates in large city jails are black men. While blacks make up 66 percent of the population of Washington, D.C., 98 percent of the inmates of the main Washington prison are black men.[21]

These extremely high crime rates have been with us for approximately twenty years. In fact, there was somewhat of a decline in the 1980s. Unfortunately, that trend appears to be reversing, and violent crime rates are now near their all-time highs. The most dramatic increases in crime began in the mid-1960s. Crime rates had been fairly stable or in some cases declining in the fifties and early sixties. The murder rate, which had hovered between 4.5 and 5 per 100,000 until 1965, almost doubled to 9.6 per 100,000 in 1975, and since then has remained fairly stable. It reached 10.2 in 1980, declined appreciably in the mid-1980s to a low of 7.9, and has since climbed back to 9.4 per 100,000.[22]

Robbery rates, which are more reflective of everyday concerns about crime, showed similar dramatic increases in the 1960s. The robbery rate, which was approximately 60 per 100,000 in the early 1960s, jumped more than threefold to 218 per 100,000 by 1975. In 1981, the robbery rate peaked at 259 per 100,000; it declined to the range of 200 per 100,000 in the mid-1980s, and climbed back to 257 per 100,000 in 1990. Robbery is therefore over four times as common today as it was in the early 1960s. Forcible rapes also increased dramatically during the ten-year period between 1965 and 1975; in the early 1960s, rates for rape were in the range of 9 per 100,000, but the rate rose to 26.3 per 100,000 in 1975. Unfortunately, the rates for rape have not stabilized but have been increasing regularly since 1975; the rate climbed to 36.4 per 100,000 in 1980 and stood at 41.2 per 100,000 in 1990, a rate four times what it had been in the early 1960s. Aggravated assault climbed sharply during the 1980s, so that the overall rate for all violent crimes (murder, rape, robbery, and assault) reached an all-time high of 732 per 100,000 in 1990—well over four times the rate of violent crime in the early 1960s, which was approximately 160 per 100,000.[23]

The image that black neighborhoods are torn by crime and the image of underclass young black men as potentially violent predators are not media creations. For both whites and blacks in the nation's cities, young black men can represent a palpable threat to personal safety. There can be no denying that crime is a serious problem for blacks. They are proportionately much more likely to be the victims of crime and much more likely to be its perpetrators. Blacks lose their lives and property, not to mention their peace of mind, as victims. Young black men, in terrible numbers, forfeit their futures as the perpetrators.

III. Sociobiology and Crime

Evolutionary theory has no difficulty accounting for the spontaneous emergence of antisocial behavior among adolescent males. The genetic programming that produces the secondary sex characteristics in adolescents and gives them an adult appearance is also at work in their glandular systems. Those glandular changes, as we saw in the previous chapters, also produce the behaviors that, in our evolutionary ancestors, enhanced their Darwinian fitness. Among the more obvious behavioral effects of these changes are an intense interest in the opposite sex and a desire to demonstrate maturity and worth among one's peers. As I have already discussed, the willingness to successfully challenge existing adult male authority is a simple way of demonstrating one's own maturity and readiness for mating.

Adolescence is therefore a critical period in the life of the individual. Prior to adolescence a child is usually content to be under the control of the adults around him. He lacks the intellectual resources and the physical strength to rebel and generally has no wish to do so. In adolescence, however, the child begins to attain adult stature and cognitive abilities. As such, it is a time crucial for the formation of self-image, for the foundation of fundamental moral values, and for preparation for participation in adult life. If adolescence is successfully negotiated, the individual is prepared to take his place among adults and to acquire adult commitments and responsibilities.

All societies recognize the crucial nature of this period of development and take steps to assure that the adolescent remains firmly within the bounds set by adult society. Before the rise of the industrial city, the task was not particularly difficult. Adolescents were constantly under the supervision of adults. Before this century, for instance, it was common in Europe and America for young people at the age of ten or twelve to be put out to work in the homes and shops of others. Schools as we know them were reserved for a small minority. But whether at school or at work, adolescent children were rarely left unsupervised.[24]

Furthermore, the small size of most communities, and the significant distances between them, made it rare for large numbers of adolescents to come together on a regular basis. When they did so it was always under the eyes of adults who took a dim view of any behavior that deviated from acceptable standards. In these small communities there was nearly universal agreement on what was acceptable behavior, and adults had the power and resources and the desire to punish those who stepped out of bounds.[25]

It is for this reason that many social historians, such as Edward Shorter and Philippe Aries, have argued that what we today refer to as an adolescent subculture, distinct from the larger society, is a product of modernity.[26] Today it is easy to recognize the distinctive patterns associated with the adolescent subculture. The dress, the language, and the musical tastes of young people make them easily distinguishable from their elders. Within this subculture, as in the larger society, there is an intense interest in status and its symbols, but with adolescents the available status markers are more limited. Adolescents must, to a much greater degree than adults, rely on natural propensities such as physical beauty, athletic prowess, and native wit to demonstrate their worth.

Modern American adolescent subcultures usually sort themselves into recognizable subgroups, which can be surveyed by a visit to almost any American high school. There is the subgroup of those concerned with school and grades, for whom gaining admission to good colleges is uppermost in mind. Another subgroup consists of those concerned with success in officially sanctioned social, athletic, and service activities. These are the students prominent in school politics, prom committees, athletic teams, etc. There are still others who, because of parental wealth, concern themselves with conspicuous displays of dress and other material and symbolic signs of material status. Adolescents, like people everywhere, tend to congregate with others of like mind, with people of similar tastes and abilities.

For our purposes, an especially important subgroup consists of those who, for one reason or another, cannot or do not wish to master the officially sanctioned activities in schools and other organizations. Many of these young people have given up hope of entering college or obtaining desirable adult employment. For these individuals, it is often the case that the only avenue they may have for demonstrating personal worth is through daring and bravado, and they often demonstrate those qualities by defying adult authorities and adult conventions. Since they have very limited aspirations for the future, they are much less concerned with official reprimands handed down by school officials or judicial authorities.

In the vacuum created by their rejection of the prevailing values within the larger community, this subgroup sets up its own system of values and mores. What is interesting is that the values and patterns that spontaneously develop are remarkably similar wherever they arise and remarkably similar to patterns predictable from the principles of sociobiology. Young men demonstrate physical prowess by engaging in predatory attacks on outsiders, and they compete with each other in physical contests for status and resources, and for access to the favors of women. The young women in this subclass, in turn, find much to admire in the daring and machismo of young men, for the reasons discussed in the previous chapters. Given the lack of penalties for prematurely fathering children and the near certainty that their children will survive without them, there is little incentive for young men in such circles to demonstrate loyalty to women or the ability to provide resources for future children. Young women who find themselves limited to the company of such men come, in time, to expect neither.[27]

In most communities this antisocial subculture is correctly viewed as a threat to civil order, and most communities are successful in keeping such young people under reasonable control. In suburban and rural communities, where the numbers of these types are few, and densities low, this is not an especially difficult problem. In large urban areas, however, the density of population and the anonymity it provides makes keeping young people in line much more difficult. This is especially true if there are large numbers of young people disaffected with school and with their prospects for adult success. The problem is compounded if the adults, especially men, are themselves incapable or unwilling to take the problem seriously and to discipline wayward youngsters. The problem is exacerbated if the police are ineffectual.

In many large cities this delinquent adolescent subculture has grown so large and deviates so much from the larger society, that it is in fact at war with the larger society. Young predators can roam with relative impunity and can practice hit-and-run tactics with little risk of recognition or arrest. A snatched purse, a necklace ripped off, provide easy sources of income for young men, income with which to buy gifts and impress girlfriends and engage in various sorts of conspicuous consumption that would be otherwise unattainable.

It would be a mistake, however, to imagine that the urban street is only a source of income to disaffected young men. It is also a tournament ground where they can play out their manly roles. It is the place where a young man can demonstrate those virtues of machismo, wit, and daring that gain the respect of his fellows and the admiration of the opposite sex. It is, as social psychologist Erving Goffman put it, where the action is.[28]

The peculiar pathologies of the urban underclass, particularly the black underclass, are in large measure a product of a delinquent subculture created by disaffected adolescents. This is not a new problem in large cities in America, but in the past it was generally kept in bounds by effective police methods and by a variety of community controls. The problem today has become unmanageable because these traditional controls have been seriously undermined by changes in government policies.

Evolutionary theory and a study of history suggest that violent and aggressive behavior is likely to appear spontaneously among young men whenever their behavior is not restrained by civil order. Why such adolescent behavior was allowed to take on a life of its own in America's inner cities is of course a complicated question. A large part of the responsibility rests, however, on changes in government policies initiated during the 1960s. Most of those changes were based on serious misinterpretations of the criminological theories that were prominent at the time.

IV. The Dominant Social Science Explanations of Crime

It is important to understand what the prominent criminological theories in fact say, rather than what most popular understandings incorrectly assume they say. All the theories, for instance, agree that poverty is an important precondition for crime, but they are almost unanimous in denying that poverty in itself is a sufficient explanation. Almost all agree, however, that crime results when the social norms proscribing law-breaking are weak. In other words, poverty may tempt people to engage in criminal behavior, but only those who are weakly socialized will actually become criminals.

Most of the influential criminological theories of the past half-century have their theoretical roots in the thinking of Emile Durkheim, the French founder of sociology. Durkheim argued that sociological explanations must be based on *social facts* and not individual choice. In his classic study of suicide, Durkheim demonstrated that suicide rates varied with economic and social conditions. While he acknowledged that suicide was an individual choice, he nevertheless argued that sociologists could contribute unique insights by examining the social factors influencing suicide rates in different cultural contexts.[29]

In effect, Durkheim was arguing for the independent status of sociological modes of explanation. There is nothing incorrect in what Durkheim urged, and in fact sociologists have added unique insight to our understanding. However, when sociologists ignore other factors, as many have done in the study of crime, they needlessly limit the explanatory power of their theories.

For instance, most criminological theories play down the role of individual psychological factors in explaining crime. Most textbooks on criminology cite various "constitutional" theories popular in the late nineteenth century, as examples of the failure of the psychological approach. Some of these earlier theories had argued rather crudely that crime was the product of a constitutional "criminal type" who could be identified by physical features. By the 1930s, however, most social scientists had rejected the idea that individual biological differences might be important to behavior. Owing to the influence of Durkheim, most sociologists rejected the idea that individual traits, even learned traits, were of much significance in explaining crime.

Unfortunately, this means that modern criminology (a field dominated by sociologists) is weak when it comes to accounting for the fact that among people in very similar social circumstances, some are law-abiding while others are not. People differ in their abilities and aptitudes, in their emotional responses, and in their personal experiences, and these differences may explain why some individuals are disposed to crime while others seem inoculated against it.[30] On such questions most criminological theories have little to say.

For this reason, the major theories have difficulty explaining the results of one of the most important studies of youth crime ever undertaken. In *Delinquency in a Birth Cohort,* published in 1972, Marvin Wolfgang, Robert Figlio, and Thorsten Sellin analyzed the criminal careers of a cohort of Philadelphia boys born in 1945.[31] They found that while many teenagers have trouble with the police, a relative few are responsible for most serious crimes. Approximately 6 percent of the boys were classified as chronic delinquents, and these 6 percent accounted for about 52 percent of all the offenses committed by youngsters in the cohort.[32]

Wolfgang, Figlio, and Sellin found that socioeconomic status, education, and race were all related to chronic delinquency. Nevertheless, there were far more socially disadvantaged children who did not become chronic offenders than those who did. Though the researchers' data did not allow them to perform any detailed analysis of possible psychological co-factors that would explain this finding, it is hard to ignore the possibility that individual differences were important here.[33]

The resistance to taking into account factors other than those of a social nature has also lead criminologists to reject utilitarian theories of crime which assume that criminals act out of individual self-interest and that they weigh the costs and benefits of crime. Such utilitarian thinking often supports doctrines of punishment or deterrence, since anything that raises the costs of crime ought to reduce its incidence. In the postwar period, however, criminologists came to question the value of deterrence. According to Rodney Stark, writing in his respected text on sociology, "by the 1950s the accepted view among social scientists, presented in most introductory textbooks, was that the threat of punishment does not prevent deviant behavior. . . ." Stark points out that deterrence was "dismissed as an obsolete notion," even though "very little research had ever been done" to demonstrate its lack of effectiveness.[34]

Most of the theories I will discuss were heavily influenced not only by Durkheim's insistence on an independent sociological perspective but also by his theory of "anomie," which he defined as a condition where an individual lacks appropriate norms to use as guides to behavior. According to Durkheim, anomie arises in social circumstances where the moral norms that usually restrain people's appetites and ambitions have been seriously eroded, often during periods of economic turmoil. In this view anomie is a condition very common in industrial society. Before industrialization most societies and their social hierarchies were relatively static and stable. People in such societies came to believe that existing hierarchies were "natural," and children were socialized to accept their place with good humor and to attempt to gain respect by carrying out their allotted tasks well. To aspire beyond the rank to which one was born was not merely antisocial, but an offense to the natural order of things. Durkheim, of course, had feudal Europe in mind, as well as the stabilizing influence of the Catholic Church in maintaining the great "chain of being" in which everything had its proper place.[35]

Industrial capitalism everywhere destroys the stability of traditional orders. There are many reasons for this, of course, but perhaps most important is the social and geographic mobility which industrialization fosters. Firms compete on the basis of their productivity, and they seek out and bid up the price of talented and hardworking individuals who can contribute to productivity. The capitalist entrepreneur is unlikely, for long, to limit his search for talent to selected classes or geographic regions. One result is that birth is a much less powerful predictor of adult status than it is in more stable societies. People can and do move out of humble beginnings to achieve great wealth and prestige. They also tend to leave the smaller, stable communities in which their ancestors toiled in obscurity.

In the course of industrialization people begin to acquire aspirations, often encouraged by education—aspirations that may, but need not, be consonant with their abilities or opportunities. For Durkheim this implied that many individuals would be frustrated and would begin to question the norms and values that had created those frustrations. Anomie would rise, and with it the sort of social pathologies, such as crime and suicide, which are far less common in static societies where people's aspirations are much more limited.[36]

One of the earliest and most influential sociological theories of crime is the "structural-strain" theory developed by the highly respected sociologist Robert K. Merton. In a now classic paper, "Social Structure and Anomie," Merton argued, relying heavily on Durkheim's notion of anomie, that crime and delinquency arise when there is a mismatch between generally accepted social goals and socially accepted means to achieve those goals. "Aberrant conduct," Merton wrote, ". . . may be viewed as a symptom of [a] dissociation between culturally defined aspirations and socially structured means."[37] This dissociation, and the criminal behavior that attends it, are most likely to arise when the "channels of vertical mobility are closed or narrowed *in a society which places a high premium on economic affluence and social ascent for its members*" (emphasis in original).[38]

Merton made it clear that he did not mean to suggest that poverty itself produces criminality: "Poverty as such, and consequent limitations of opportunity, are not sufficient to induce a conspicuously high rate of criminal behaviors.'' He went on to point out that in societies where lower-class values do not induce people to aspire to higher status or wealth, as was the case in the more rigid class systems of Europe, there was less likely to be frustration, and therefore there was less crime. In America, however, where everyone is led to believe that they can achieve success, lower-class individuals who lack the means to obtain success will be frustrated and may well turn to crime.[39]

Writing in 1938, Merton made it clear that he was talking about crime among lower-class whites and not blacks. In the case of blacks, ''social ascent is at present restricted to their own caste almost exclusively.''[40] This made their condition more analogous to the lower-class Europeans in more stratified class structures.

Merton also argued that there is usually a tension between a society's emphasis upon goals and its emphasis upon means. In societies that place great stress upon playing by the rules, individuals are less likely to engage in criminal conduct even if poor and lacking in opportunities. It is the combination of poverty and a weaker societal emphasis upon appropriate means that produces high crime rates. While in no society ''is there an absence of regulatory codes governing conduct,'' in some there is a ''disproportionate accent on goals.''[41]

In Merton's view, in other words, crime is a product of a lack of opportunity and an absence of strong norms proscribing criminality. This is, of course, fairly close to what might be called the common-sense view of crime. However, Merton's theory does not make it clear why some people in impoverished circumstances are socialized to be rule-abiding and others never obtain that socialization.

A sociological perspective complementary to Merton's and also very influential is known as the ''differential association theory,'' outlined in *Criminology* by Edwin Sutherland and Donald Cressey. In their view, people learn criminal behavior from others with whom they have intimate contact: ''In some societies an individual is surrounded by persons who invariably define the legal codes as rules to be observed, while in others he is surrounded by persons whose definitions are favorable to the violation of the legal codes.'' Since these messages are usually mixed, a person becomes delinquent due to ''an excess of definitions favorable to violation of law over definitions unfavorable to violation of law.''[42] This is very similar to what Merton meant when he argued that crime is likely where the social structure places less emphasis on lawfulness.

According to Sutherland and Cressey, if one grows up in a setting in which criminal activity is seen as legitimate, one is more likely to engage in criminal activity. From this perspective criminality is not so much the result of the anomie brought on by thwarted aspiration, but rather is the result of what may be a well-adjusted socialization to a subculture whose values are at variance with the larger society. Obviously this cultural-deviance approach relies heavily on the doctrine of cultural relativism and in some variants denies the very validity of crime; that is, crime may be treated as merely a category or label applied to behaviors that the dominant culture finds objectionable, but that may be perfectly legitimate within a minority subculture. In this view, if someone responds to verbal abuse with a violent assault, it may be because he lives among people who regard such a response as the only honorable course of action. From this perspective underclass youth may adopt norms of manliness that, however alien they may be in middle-class circles, are not uncommon in other, often admirable cultures set in different times and places.

Merton's structural-strain position and the cultural-deviance approach are clearly complementary and were brought together in one of the most influential works in the criminological literature, *Delinquency and Opportunity* by Richard Cloward and Lloyd Ohlin. In this book, published in 1960, the authors argue, following Merton, that thwarted opportunities in lower-class youth drive many into illegitimate activities. Following Sutherland and Cressey, they argue that when many people become engaged in illegitimate pursuits, a criminal subculture often grows up that legitimates those activities. While middle-class youth are exposed to bankers and lawyers and therefore come to aspire to those roles, these "conventional success-models may not be salient" for lower-class youth. Poor young people are more likely to come into daily contact with the successful criminal types who are "intimate" and "personal figure[s] in the fabric of lower class life."[43]

Cloward and Ohlin point out that much criminal activity is pursued in a regular, business-like fashion and may even come to be respected in lower-class communities. Prohibition created many opportunities for criminal entrepreneurs. Today drugs create similar entrepreneurial opportunities. Cloward and Ohlin claim that socially accepted criminal enterprises offer opportunities for respectability that would otherwise be lacking.

They also maintain that these criminal enterprises have the positive side effect of curtailing youthful violence and taming youthful delinquency. Young men recruited into the subculture of organized criminality are socialized into its dominant ethic, and their behavior becomes less violent and random and more opportunistic. Criminal enterprises impose social controls "to suppress undisciplined expressive behavior; there is no place in organized crime for the impulsive, unpredictable individual."[44]

Not all lower-class children who are predisposed to criminal behavior find opportunities in organized criminal activities. According to Cloward and Ohlin, many such youngsters may, owing to the chaotic communities in which they live, have little in the way of socialization in either legitimate or criminal norm structures. Such youngsters may seize "upon the manipulation of violence as a route to status." Such a "warrior adjustment" does not require

'' 'connections,' 'pull' or elaborate technical skills,'' but rather manly ''guts'' and ''heart'' that are often the only ways some young men can demonstrate personal worth. Cloward and Ohlin argue that ''[a]s long as conventional and criminal opportunity structures remain closed, violence remains unchecked.''[45]

Put briefly, this theory argues that American children are raised to believe that worthwhile human beings can get ahead, and all American children in greater or lesser degree come to believe that. When young people find legitimate avenues closed to them, they often resort to those illegitimate activities that meet with the approval of their local neighborhood culture. When even illegitimate means are unavailable, they often resort to violent activities that gain them status among other young people in similar circumstances, even when those activities are frowned upon by their own adult neighbors.

Cloward and Ohlin conclude their compelling and important book by reiterating their faith in social causation. They argue that delinquency cannot be reduced by approaches directed at ''delinquent individuals or groups,'' since delinquency is a ''property of the social systems'' in which these individuals live. ''The target for preventive action, then,'' they write, ''should be defined not as the individual or group that exhibits the delinquent pattern, but as the social setting that gives rise to delinquency.''[46]

The authors do not make it clear how they would recommend changing the social setting that gives rise to delinquency, although it is obvious from their treatment that creating greater opportunities for social ascent through legitimate means would be important. They seem reluctant to acknowledge, however, that some people may be incapable or unwilling to take advantage of those opportunities that are available. They do acknowledge, on the other hand, that delinquency will be less common where opportunities for criminality are limited. According to Cloward and Ohlin:

> If, in a given social location, illegal or criminal means are not readily available, then we should not expect a criminal subculture to develop among adolescents. By the same logic, we should expect the manipulation of violence to become a primary avenue to higher status only in areas where the means of violence are not denied to the young.[47]

This clearly suggests the value of strict law enforcement in preventing crime. Unfortunately, Cloward and Ohlin do not stress the need for a greater police presence in lower-class communities in order to deprive youngsters of the opportunity to engage in criminal activity, even though it follows directly from their comments. Policy makers who used their book as a guide in the sixties and seventies took to heart the need to provide opportunities, but unfortunately failed to take seriously the need to put constraints on the expression of youthful violence.

While the advocates of these prominent positions take pains to distinguish their views from each other, they are hardly incompatible. Rather, they seem to complement one another, and certainly all can be useful in trying to understand underclass criminal behavior. There can hardly be any question that some underclass men engage in aggressive displays to achieve the sort of respect they are unable to obtain through more legitimate activities, as structural-strain theory suggests. It is also the case that when large numbers of people feel the same deprivation, cultural norms may develop that justify and may even glorify criminality, as cultural-deviance theory suggests.

Furthermore, while these sociological theories are usually viewed as incompatible with utilitarian and psychological explanations, even modest reflection reveals no such incompatibility. The utilitarian view, after all, suggests that individuals will attempt to use the means available to them to achieve maximum fulfillment of their desires at minimal cost. If legitimate means are not available, and illegal ones are acceptable, i.e., impose no intolerable psychic cost, then utilitarian theory suggests that illegal means will be used. Likewise, the consideration of individual variables (like academic aptitude) which are known to correlate with delinquency would seem to strengthen the sociological views on crime outlined above.

Not all researchers ignored individual factors. In *Causes of Delinquency*, which reports on the results of a large survey of southern California teenagers, sociologist Travis Hirschi stressed the importance of school aptitude for understanding delinquency. He argued that school failure tends to alienate young people from the educational system and that alienation from school predisposes young people to delinquency. Hirschi's view, known as "control theory," is that young people are likely to deviate from the norms of society if they lack important attachments and commitments to those institutions, such as families and schools, that promulgate social norms. When people are involved with and committed to social institutions, they have much to lose by violating the norms of those institutions. On the other hand, when they are not involved and committed, they lack strong moral inhibitions and are likely to engage in deviant and delinquent behavior.[48]

In America the path to upward mobility is very much tied to schooling, and we would expect that those who do not perform well in school may well be tempted to engage in illegitimate means to achieve their ends, especially if their socialization is such as to make those means acceptable. Furthermore, those who perform less well in school are more likely to reject the values of the institution that casts them in a demeaning and negative light. It is hardly irrational for individuals to reject institutional values that condemn them to failure or very low status at best.

Johns Hopkins sociologist Robert Gordon has presented strong statistical evidence that low IQ may be an important precipitating factor in criminality.

Young people scoring about one standard deviation below the average appear to be at very great risk for delinquency.[49] Perhaps children with learning deficits have more difficulty acquiring basic socialization for the same reasons they have difficulty learning things in general. This may be true independently of whether the learning deficit is acquired or inherited. In their important book *Crime and Human Nature,* James Q. Wilson and Richard J. Herrnstein chastise most criminologists for ignoring the strong evidence for this and other individual factors in attempting to understand criminal behavior. In particular, they point out that, "[d]espite over forty years of confirmation, the correlation between intelligence and crime has yet to penetrate most of the textbooks or the conventional wisdom of criminology."[50] Most theorists clearly preferred, and continue to prefer, to locate the sources of crime in the social conditions surrounding the delinquents rather than in any characteristic of the delinquents themselves. As I have already discussed, this made it difficult for them to explain why the same social conditions predispose a few to criminality, while the great majority remain law-abiding in their behavior.

In retrospect, it is interesting and unfortunate that prominent theories of crime, such as Cloward and Ohlin's, were interpreted by the public and by policy makers in the 1960s to mean that improving economic conditions in lower-class neighborhoods would almost by itself reduce crime. As we saw, that is not what these theorists said. They argued that lower-class areas are prone to the sort of normlessness that Durkheim called anomie and that, to some extent, can be counteracted by organized crime as well as by legitimate avenues to economic advancement. And they argued that it was the weakened norms common among lower-class youth which directly caused delinquency. Poverty was merely a precondition, but neither a necessary nor a sufficient precondition, for anomie and crime.

To say that a community has strong social norms is to say that individuals have internalized those norms and conform their behavior to them. Normlessness can arise if there is an insufficient uniformity in values and young people become confused by conflicting value orientations. In other words, no single set of values gains children's loyalty to the extent necessary to constrain their behavior, which was Cloward and Ohlin's position. On the other hand, normlessness can arise because the children in a community are so alienated from the people (such as parents and teachers) who carry and transmit the community's norms that they have no real incentive to adopt them, which was Hirschi's view. In addition, when criminality becomes very common within a community, large numbers of young people may come to view criminality as normal, which was Sutherland and Cressey's cultural-deviance view.

These views, taken in conjunction, go a long way in explaining the particular patterns common in lower-class communities. The multiethnic character of New York City early in this century, for instance, included many immigrants who embodied various and often conflicting norms and social values. This explains to some extent the delinquency found among the children there. On the other hand, members of immigrant families often found it necessary to look to each other for economic sustenance and psychological support, and this greater family commitment explains why many of the children of immigrant groups did not become delinquent, and in fact struggled to overcome barriers to legitimate means of social ascent.

One thing that is clear from almost all of the prominent theories, perhaps more so in hindsight, is that when children lack, for whatever reason, the internal controls that strong norms provide, delinquency will increase unless additional external restraints are imposed.

In the underclass today, in the absence of those external restraints, criminal violence has become so common that large numbers of young people appear to believe that violence is a normal and acceptable way to obtain their ends. This pattern clearly reflects the kind of cultural deviance to which Sutherland and Cressey alluded. Furthermore, the instability of families and the chaos in underclass schools militates against creation of the sort of institutional commitments which build powerful social norms against criminal behavior. Large numbers of underclasss youth have, therefore, retreated into their own adolescent subculture, which has the features that are to be expected under the principles of sociobiology, such as a glorification of physical prowess and aggressiveness in men.

These theories, taken together, offer some broad guidelines for social policy. In the specific case of blacks in the 1960s, these theories would surely have advised dismantling discrimination against blacks to assure equal opportunities. They would just as surely have advised strengthening the schools and the families which are vital elements in any program of economic advancement and equally vital for the adequate socialization of children.

There is little in these sociological theories of crime, however, which suggests that a less vigorous pursuit of law enforcement was advisable. If anything, the dual goals of increasing opportunities and increasing socialization, as we shall see, are greatly enhanced in communities made safe by an adequate police presence.

Unfortunately, most theories of crime tended not to emphasize the importance of law enforcement. They attempted to explain why crime might be more common in certain social circumstances than in others, but devoted relatively little attention to crime control itself. In fact, as previously discussed, deterrence and law enforcement were out of fashion in the 1960s. James Q. Wilson reports that when he and other social scientists were called upon by government committees in the 1960s and 1970s to offer practical solutions to the burgeoning problem of crime, most social scientists often relied upon their own ideologically favored intuitions rather than the clear implications of criminological theory. Wilson reports that he came to realize "that many of those seated about me, urging in the strongest tones various 'solutions' to crime, were speaking out of ideology, not scholarship."[51] Policy makers, for their part, seemed content with vague assertions that crime was the result of certain "root causes": poverty, racism, and discrimination.

It is important to recall Durkheim's argument that anomie is brought on when traditional norms are challenged by dramatic changes in people's aspirations. Given the new opportunities that were opening to blacks, it was reasonable to expect that the traditional norms within black communities that had enabled them to deal with thwarted opportunities in the past would come to be questioned. Under such circumstances we would expect anomie to increase, especially among the young.

Yet at the very moment when sociological theory would have expected a weakening of internal restraints among black youth, government embarked on programs which greatly weakened the external restraints that normally limit opportunities for the expression of delinquent behavior. In particular, the freedom of action of police and other adult authorities that have traditionally restrained delinquency in poor children was reduced at the very time when theory suggested that they would be more important than ever. It is important to understand why this happened when it did.

V. Crime and the 1960s

There can be no doubt that the nature of crime in urban neighborhoods took a turn for the worse during the 1960s. Most indexes of crime had steadily declined from the end of Prohibition in 1933 until the early sixties when those indexes started a steady climb upward.[52] A crucial factor in this turn for the worse was the changed perception of social disorder that became common-place in the 1960s. This new perception led in time to changes in the criminal justice system and in police behavior that dramatically reduced communities' ability to control delinquency.

The antiwar movement and the civil rights movement had the effect of casting government authority in a negative light among many young people and among many blacks. Civil disobedience was often thought justified in light of the injustices that the government sponsored or tolerated, especially against blacks in the South. When the police were called upon to control crowds or arrest protestors, they were all too easily characterized, even in the North, as the oppressive agents of an oppressive state—which they clearly were in the South. At the time, even simple street crime came to take on a political hue, with many social activists claiming that crime in black lower-class neighborhoods was a species of social protest against the conditions of poverty. In the antiestablishment attitude common at the time, almost all state authority was viewed with suspicion, and none more so than police authority.

The more militant civil rights movement in the South in the 1960s was accompanied by the series of devastating riots in major cities I discussed earlier. Large-scale rioting broke out in black urban enclaves all over the United States. It is worth restating that between 1964 and 1968, there were approximately 329 riots in 247 cities.[53] These riots were no doubt brought on, in part, by the new expectations created among blacks by the civil rights movement, expectations which were in part reflected in a new militancy among black leaders such as Malcolm X. This explanation of the riots in terms of raised expectations is, of course, based in Durkheim's theory of anomie. Other explanations, common at the time, characterized the riots as a justified revolt of the oppressed. Whatever the explanation, however, the impact these riots had on public perceptions can hardly be underestimated.

The reaction of the federal government to these riots was framed in the famous 1968 Kerner Commission Report, which is instructive for what it tells us about the temper of the times.[54] The report in general reiterated the arguments of Myrdal's *An American Dilemma* and interpreted the riots as a response to continued discrimination against blacks. The general tenor of the report is captured in the words of then President Lyndon Johnson (from a speech given in 1967) cited at the beginning of the report:

> The only genuine, long-range solution for what has happened lies in an attack—mounted at every level—upon the conditions that breed despair and violence. All of us know what those conditions are: ignorance, discrimination, slums, poverty, disease, not enough jobs. We should attack these conditions— not because we are frightened by conflict, but because we are fired by conscience. We should attack them because there is simply no other way to achieve a decent and orderly society. . . .[55]

In its conclusion, the report listed three "Objectives for National Action." The first required the "opening up of opportunities to those who are restricted by racial segregation and discrimination. . . ." Second was the need to remove the "frustration of powerlessness among disadvantaged" people. The third objective required "increasing communication across racial lines to destroy stereotypes. . . ."[56]

The report was clearly influenced by the criminological theories I have reviewed. It is interesting that while the report described the detrimental effect of crime on inner-city communities, especially the insecurities it created in black Americans, it did not address crime reduction specifically in its recommendations for national action. Rather, it addressed the need for improvements in employment, education, welfare, and housing, and the need for substantial federal expenditures to improve the lives of black Americans. In an earlier section of the report, considerable space was devoted to crime. But this section dwelled mostly on the relations between police and black urban dwellers: "We have cited deep hostility between police and ghetto communities as a primary cause of the disorders surveyed by the Commission." The report went on to say that "[t]he policeman in the ghetto is a symbol of increasingly bitter social debate over law enforcement." It noted the sharp disagreement between those who demanded tougher responses to urban violence and those who were "inflamed against the police as agents of repression." The report argued that because of the policeman's symbolic role in black communities, "it is of critical importance that the police and society take every possible step to allay grievances that flow from a sense of injustice." It asserted, therefore, that "the police bear a major responsibility for making needed changes."[57] I should add that the commission adduced no evidence that police-community relations were in fact a major cause of riots or of crime, but seemed to take it for granted that such was the case. Neither did the commission highlight the fact that most of the rioting, like most crime, was largely the product of young men.

Among the five changes recommended to improve police-community relations, four addressed the need to reduce police misconduct, to create better policies to decrease tensions between police and community, to create better mechanisms for the expression of citizen grievances, and to develop community support for law enforcement. Only one of the five recommendations concerned greater police protection for inner-city residents.[58]

Not surprisingly, the commission report reinforced the views of those who characterized the police as brutal enforcers of the racial status quo whose actions, therefore, needed to be more closely monitored for racial bias. The net effect, over time, was the imposition of numerous limitations on police actions that had the effect of reducing the latitude with which police could carry out their tasks. Police who in the past had considerable freedom of action, and who were able to maintain order in informal ways, were deprived of that discretion.

James Q. Wilson, who is now James A. Collins Professor of Management and Public Policy at the University of California at Los Angeles, outlines in his influential *Thinking about Crime* the changes in the nature of policing that took place in the sixties.[59] In earlier times a policeman could and did control known troublemakers by threatening summary corporal punishment, sometimes mild, sometimes not so mild. Wilson points out that in communities with a great deal of violence, citizens expected and may even have desired police to act with vigor to control unruly characters. The cop on the beat could make life very unpleasant for those who refused to accept his authority. It was well known that police could administer beatings to those "resisting arrest" for minor "trumped up" offenses such as loitering and that such arrests and beatings could rarely be effectively challenged. No doubt this led to abuse of authority, though just how much is widely disputed. While I certainly do not advocate a return to these tactics, I think it is important to recognize that by utilizing these tactics, the police were able to maintain a high degree of public order simply by their presence in a neighborhood. Such is no longer the case.

In the wake of the Kerner Commission Report all such practices were gradually eliminated by rule changes limiting police discretion. In time, the courts overturned loitering and vagrancy statutes that police had used for routine maintenance of order in urban areas.[60] The upshot was that police conduct that had been common and condoned in prior times became the basis for charges of police brutality and possible punitive action by departmental agencies and the courts. Informal means of social control for the restraint of disruptive youthful misbehavior could no longer be used, since they might bring on charges of brutality or racial bias. In addition, the *Miranda* ruling, requiring police to inform suspects of their rights, including the right to a lawyer during interrogations, made gaining convictions more difficult when police did go so far as to make a formal arrest.[61]

One important policy outcome of this new concern with police misconduct was the demise of the older, proactive model of the ''cop on the beat'' who maintained order in his territory. That model was replaced by the ''crime-response model'' in which officers patrolled in cars and responded to reports of crime or other emergencies. The new crime-response model made it easier to monitor police, but it also made it much more difficult for police to monitor criminals and potential criminals. The cop on the beat was in a far better position to head off crime before it happened, because he knew who was likely to commit crime and could effectively deal with potential wrongdoers informally.

The advantages of having the cop on the beat are of late gaining new recognition, and many police departments are turning to what is now called ''community policing.'' However, the primary purpose of the reintroduced beat cop is often framed in terms of improving community relations and allaying the fear of crime. Without the older freedom of action, the advantages of having a police officer in the neighborhood are considerably diminished, though I think it is a positive development nonetheless.

Wilson suggests that disorderly communities are a little like buildings whose broken windows go unrepaired. The fact that a window is not replaced suggests that nobody cares, and therefore no one is about to punish those who break more windows. Needless to say, very quickly all the rest of the windows will be broken. Similarly, when neighborhoods seem to tolerate general disorder, they evoke even more disorder.[62] This appears to be what happened in the inner cities following the changes of the 1960s. Tolerance of petty crimes like vandalism evoked not-so-petty crimes like drug peddling, prostitution, and mugging.

The unwillingness to grant police modest discretion because of fears of racial discrimination led in time, as I have noted, to the judicial system's overturning of loitering and vagrancy laws and even neighborhood curfews for minors. Everyone *knew* that such laws were designed to harass the poor and especially minority groups. Many, however, overlooked the importance of these laws in maintaining public order and civility. The result was that cities became far more disorderly places than they might otherwise have become. Much disruptive behavior that had in the past been prevented or pushed into dark alleys and hidden corners was now on open public display on main avenues.

The deinstitutionalization movement of the 1960s and 1970s, which led to the wholesale discharge of mental health patients from state hospitals, no doubt added to the general disorder of the urban scene. Large state mental hospitals were depicted at the time as thoroughly unwholesome and inhumane places that could not be made humane. Deinstitutionalization was a movement, thought humanitarian at the time, to exploit the advantages of the new antipsychotic drugs that would have allowed for the management of patient symptoms in smaller halfway houses. It was expected that mental patients would live relatively normal lives during the day and return to the sheltered environment of the halfway homes in the evening. Unfortunately, many of these programs were underfunded, many communities objected to the idea of halfway homes in their residential neighborhoods, and the courts made it difficult to confine people to institutions or require them to take medication against their will. The net result was that many former mental patients gravitated to the inner cities where they served to reinforce the chaotic atmosphere that had grown up there.[63]

The open display of so much antisocial and troubled behavior gives the impression that a community is out of control and that therefore anything is permissible. In such an atmosphere it is only natural for young men to walk the streets with loud radios blaring their favorite music. Many adults are angered and annoyed by what they perceive to be careless and defiant behavior, but few, even among police, are inclined to challenge the right of the young music lover to so rudely disturb his neighbors. Similarly, threatening teenagers gather at traffic bottlenecks at rush hours to wash car windows, demanding payment for their unwanted service. Those who refuse the service do so at their own risk, while police officers viewing these activities from a distance pretend to ignore what is an obvious, though legally unprovable case of petty extortion.

Without informal means at their command, police officers' options are limited to the making of formal arrests. Formal arrest procedures are extremely time-consuming, sometimes taking an officer off the street in New York City, for instance, for many hours of paperwork. Furthermore, many petty offenses require the appearance in court of witnesses, many of whom are unreliable or reluctant to take the time to travel to courts or station houses. It is important to note that many crimes that undermine public order, like defacing property with graffiti, are often treated lightly by public prosecutors and judges inundated with more serious offenses.

The impact of all these changes was particularly significant as it related to the regulation of adolescent males, who no longer had to fear summary judgment from neighborhood police officers. Many things, such as provocative challenges to authority, that are, in themselves, not really criminal, now had to be tolerated by the police, who had, and continue to have, few legal and few informal recourses against them. The problem here is that once young men get into the habit of laughing at police, it is much more likely that they will be tempted to engage in conduct that police are supposed to prevent.

In due course it became apparent to everyone in the inner cities that teenagers could do pretty much as they pleased in the way of transgressing community standards so long as they did not engage in seriously criminal conduct. Even when adolescents overstepped the bounds into serious crime, the penalties meted out by the juvenile justice system were such as to engender little more than contempt. This new leniency was consistent with the common criminological views of the time, which doubted the efficacy of punishment and deterrence.

None of the above is meant to convey the impression that police brutality is not a serious problem or to in any way condone police misconduct, but merely to point out the changed view of the means appropriate to the police. The police officer who manhandled known troublemakers for petty offenses was not, at an earlier time, thought to have been engaging in misconduct; rather, he was doing his job and most citizens were pleased with the result. The cop on the beat was, in earlier times, fully expected to maintain public order and civility and was given considerable latitude in how he went about accomplishing his duties in his own territory.

It was inevitable that as minority populations increased in the cities, more and more minority group children would come within the purview of the criminal justice system. This led to widespread charges of racial bias, which is hardly surprising since most police forces continued to be staffed by whites hired in earlier times. Police officers, given the nature of their work, will invariably make mistakes or overreact in some situations. In addition, police forces have always attracted their share of troubled individuals who abuse their authority. In recent years, however, police infractions of all kinds have come increasingly to be characterized as evidence of racial bias, rather than as the unfortunate but unavoidable concomitants of difficult and trying work.

Black Americans exhibit a great deal of ambivalence on the subject of crime and its control. When legions of police and national guardsmen were deployed in Los Angeles in anticipation of possible riots in the wake of the second Rodney King trial in the spring of 1993, many black residents interviewed on television said they were thrilled that the police were there. Many said that this was the only time they felt safe walking around their neighborhoods at night. Nevertheless, blacks exhibit considerable distrust of the police and the criminal justice system, and they tend in overwhelming numbers to reject conservative political candidates who campaign on law-and-order platforms. When asked in the late eighties whether "the courts in this area deal too harshly or not harshly enough with criminals," 83 percent of blacks and 87 percent of whites thought the courts were not harsh enough.[64] Blacks also think the government spends too little on dealing with crime. Fully 89 percent of middle-class blacks thought too little was spent, as did 80 percent of working-class blacks and 72 percent of poor blacks.[65] Only 29 percent of blacks, compared to 60 percent of whites, were satisfied with the police protection they received.[66]

Clearly, based on the responses to these questions, blacks would seem to favor a much greater police presence in their neighborhoods. Nevertheless, black attitudes toward the police and the criminal justice system are largely negative. For instance, in response to a question asking whether blacks were treated as fairly as whites by the police, approximately 80 percent of middle- and working-class blacks thought blacks were not treated as fairly.[67] Only 17 percent of blacks, compared to 51 percent of whites, thought that "[b]lacks and whites are treated equally by the criminal justice system."[68]

So long as blacks maintain a negative attitude toward the criminal justice system and reject law-and-order platforms, it is hard to see how politicians can be expected to devote the resources to crime control that blacks seem to want. Though one might suppose that these attitudes will change as more blacks come to enter police work in cities controlled by black politicians, this appears not to have been the case in cities like Washington, Detroit, or Atlanta that are now in the stewardship of black leaders. Distrust of the police may be one of the most unfortunate legacies of the South's discriminatory Jim Crow policies. The national attention directed to a few highly publicized police-brutality cases, such as that involving Rodney King, serves, unfortunately, to reinforce black distrust of the criminal justice system. Clearly this a problem that needs to be addressed more effectively than has heretofore been the case.

The upshot of all of the changes in legal and police policy undertaken in the sixties and seventies was that poor urban neighborhoods became more chaotic than they might otherwise have become: there was a dramatic increase in petty crime, vandalism, and disorderly conduct. Children growing up under conditions of civic disorder and general lawlessness came to think of these activities as normal. Not surprisingly, juvenile crime, including serious crime, increased.

Crime increased faster than jail space, and judges became even more reluctant to commit youthful offenders to prisons that, in the prevailing wisdom, would only turn them into hardened criminals. Given the small likelihood of a juvenile being apprehended and the generally lenient sentences imposed, few potential juvenile criminals were deterred by the criminal justice system. The upshot was that by the middle of the 1970s the streets of most inner cities had become *no-man's-lands,* controlled in large measure by young men little restrained by any sort of adult authority.

VI. Crime and Welfare Reform

It was not merely government policies toward crime that produced this result. Welfare policy may also have had a strong negative influence, especially in weakening parental authority over children. Since this topic will be discussed in depth in connection with an analysis of illegitimacy, no thorough analysis will be attempted here. Nevertheless, a few words are in order.

As discussed earlier, the Kerner Commission urged substantial increases in government support to improve the conditions of the inner-city poor. President Johnson's "War on Poverty" did just that, but even earlier, in the 1950s, changing attitudes had led to more liberalized welfare policies, which were also becoming more bureaucratized.

These changes troubled Cloward and Ohlin, especially the tendency of the national welfare state to undercut the power of local political machines that had in earlier decades been the primary distributor of financial assistance to the poor. The demise of the local political machine meant the loss of the "many other functions that the machine performed for lower class persons." Local politicians and ward leaders knew the individuals who received aid, since they often lived in the same neighborhoods with the poor people they helped. Those who received aid became "related to a significant social, financial and power structure" in their communities. Cloward and Ohlin, in their 1960 work *Delinquency and Opportunity,* argued that the "growth of bureaucratically administered welfare services and the decline of the political machine are resulting in a progressive breakdown in the cohesion of urban slums." They thought the result would be increased aggression, since "violence among adolescents comes to be widespread in the unintegrated community that lacks both structures of social control and channels of social ascent."[69]

A related effect of more liberal welfare policies resulted from the greater independence from family and neighbors it provided recipients. When aid was more limited, people had to look to their neighbors and families for assistance and, in turn, took on obligations to them. This is not simply romanticizing the past; poor people did in fact rely on each other more, since they rarely had anywhere else to turn. Mutual assistance always implies mutual obligation, both of which are crucial to community cohesion. Once government assistance became bureaucratized and viewed as an entitlement, this important element of social cohesion was lost, and nothing was put in its place. Cloward and Ohlin wrote in 1960, with considerable prescience: "On the basis of the theory developed in this book, we predict that delinquency will become increasingly aggressive and violent as a result of the disintegration of slum organization."[70]

More liberal welfare policies also increased family instability, one obvious sign of which was an increase in single-parent households. As men became less essential to their families for support, their influence upon and commitment to their families declined, and desertion by fathers became commonplace. This had an important impact on the orderliness of inner-city neighborhoods, for one reason in particular which is rarely acknowledged.

Police are the last line of defense against unruly adolescents; the first line is manned by parents and other adults in the community, who can keep young people in check either because the adults are respected or because they are feared. When men live with their families, they necessarily become involved in the day-to-day, mundane concerns of family life, such as fixing faucets and repairing broken windows, etc. They are also more likely to be concerned over the day-to-day dangers that their wives and children confront, especially from unruly adolescent males.

Young men do not lightly insult, much less assault, women in the presence of their fathers and husbands. Mature men who are deeply concerned about their families' welfare are therefore an important deterrent to certain types of delinquency in poor neighborhoods. When large numbers of men have deserted their families and live in different neighborhoods from them, they cannot provide protection even if they wish to do so. When the men in a community are unrelated to the women and children living there, they are far less likely to be a force for order.

This is because an insult or an assault on a child or a woman that incurs no response or retaliation from a male relative sends out a powerful message to a predatory criminal, just as a broken window that goes unrepaired sends a clear message to the would-be stone-thrower. In the lower classes, many men have little patience to wait for the police to right wrongs done to loved ones, especially if the police are impotent. Often such men make their own justice with those who have offended them, especially if the offender is young and can be manhandled relatively easily.

The point is not whether one approves of personal retaliation or not; lawful societies must outlaw such personal retribution. But in the often lawless and

Hobbesian conditions of inner-city neighborhoods, the threat of personal retaliation may be a powerful deterrent to predatory delinquents. Such fear of retaliation can prevent a great deal of minor crime like vandalism and petty theft that can in time demoralize a community. When strong adult men are not around, predatory adolescents are given an open season, as it were, to prey on the weaker members of their communities.

VII. Some Economic Consequences of Crime

The most serious economic consequence of crime and urban disorder for blacks is its negative impact on educational attainment. It is true that most urban teenagers finish high school, and even among those who leave school, large numbers eventually find useful work. Many of these engage in petty crime and unruly behavior, but few turn into hardened criminals. Nevertheless, for every serious delinquent there are dozens of other youngsters, otherwise perfectly normal—who only occasionally, for instance, engage in serious misconduct—who are nevertheless drawn into the adolescent subculture and drawn away from schools and all they represent. Such children waste their formative years in the honing of skills and the acquisition of traits that have no value in the larger society. At eighteen, they are hopelessly unprepared to compete with those who have managed to navigate adolescence successfully.

Among the many functions of schools, one is certainly the grooming of individuals to take their place in the workforce. Punctuality, reliability, toleration of boredom, and acceptance of unearned authority are among the habits of mind terribly important for success in most jobs. Bravado, daring, respect for charismatic authority, and impatience with routine, while essential for participation in the ''action'' of the inner-city youth culture, are useless and counterproductive when it comes to getting and holding a job. In other words, schools, when successful, socialize young people to smoothly take their place in the workplace, and this socialization is every bit as important as the ability to read and write.

Crime dramatically undercuts future opportunities because it interferes with the education and work experience critical for upward mobility. For the many who manage to overcome these handicaps and eventually enter the workplace, the path is far more arduous than it might otherwise have been. In addition, given the handicaps they carry, the survivors can expect far smaller incomes than they might have achieved if they had committed themselves to their schooling. For that reason, it is often difficult for them to escape the depredations of the inner city and equally difficult for their children to escape the pernicious influence of the street culture that has been allowed to dominate life there.

There are other, less direct consequences of crime for black economic well-being. Crime has an extremely negative impact on business activity. Businesses tend to leave because of the inconvenience and added costs of doing business in high crime areas. Losses from theft, vandalism, and arson are high, and it is difficult and expensive to obtain insurance against such losses. Furthermore, middle-class employees resist commuting into such areas. Not surprisingly, many companies leave areas of urban decay and take with them many jobs that could provide employment for inner-city blacks.

Moreover, middle-class people of all races tend to flee from urban enclaves if crime flourishes. With them leave all sorts of jobs, ranging from those requiring little skill or education to those requiring highly refined training. Middle-class lifestyles require the employment of maintenance personnel, carpenters, furniture repairers, computer repair personnel, first-rate auto mechanics, caterers, gardeners, and a host of other service personnel. Middle-class people eat in restaurants; have groceries, flowers, and wine delivered to them; have their clothes cleaned and repaired; and have their homes painted, repaired, and improved to a much greater extent than do poor people. The middle-class style of life, therefore, is an important source of employment for a wide range of people, and an especially rich source of employment for young people.

Many of the jobs that are created to provide services to the middle class are sometimes referred to as "dead-end" jobs. This is a mistake, however, since many of these jobs are better characterized as entry-level employment for people with little education and few skills. In such jobs, one develops skills, one builds a reputation for reliability, and one develops the frame of mind and demeanor suitable to the workplace. Many of these entry-level jobs are particularly suited for young people, many of whom are pursuing education at the same time. No one in a suburban neighborhood who watches neighborhood youngsters standing behind cash registers, or delivering pizzas, or mowing lawns imagines that these young people will remain in those jobs forever. But such employment is extremely important in allowing adolescents to begin their training for a lifetime of work.

Entry-level jobs, furthermore, can lead to higher positions in many areas. Kitchen staff in fast-food establishments often *do* move up into management positions. Learning to mow lawns can lead to the owning of a lawn maintenance service. Acting as a menial laborer at a construction site can lead to skills in carpentry or electrical work that can lead, in turn, to highly paid employment or to the owning of a home-improvement business or contracting firm. In fact, many immigrants have made and continue to make important economic strides in just this way.

There is an important sidelight here. Since most immigrants who come to the United States come as young adults or middle-aged people, higher education is often not a realistic avenue for economic advancement for them.

Therefore, many pursue and manage to thrive in small businesses. Immigrants work long hours and employ children and other relatives and often, over time, achieve a reasonable level of economic success. Immigrants usually enter businesses that are labor intensive and that are often shunned by native Americans. They furthermore enter businesses requiring little capital and often choose low-rent areas for beginning operations, often in predominantly black areas of major cities.

Immigrant entrepreneurs who locate in impoverished black neighborhoods sometimes face animosity from the poorer blacks living there. Such blacks often express confusion, and sometimes resentment, at the apparent prosperity of the immigrants when compared to their own poverty. This was so in the thirties and forties when immigrant entrepreneurs were often Jewish, and it is so today when many are Korean or from the Indian subcontinent. Blacks have traditionally not taken up small businesses in great numbers, leaving a vacuum to be filled by immigrants. Myrdal pointed out that in the thirties the total sales of Asian-owned stores in America were almost at a par with the total sales of black-owned stores even though blacks outnumbered Asians by fifty to one. Why blacks did not, in the past, avail themselves of opportunities in small business to a greater degree is unclear.[71] As recently as 1987, black Americans, who are four times as numerous as Asian Americans, owned 422,000 businesses, compared to Asian Americans who owned 355,000.[72] At least part of the reason for this is that small businesses rely on the work of family members and black families are very unstable compared to most immigrant families. Crime, as we will see in Chapter 10, is a major factor contributing to black family instability.

In summary, crime in the inner cities drives away manufacturing and service jobs. It drives out the middle classes of all races and with them the myriad employment opportunities that the middle class provides to younger and less skilled people. And to the extent that crime contributes to family instability, as it surely does, it undercuts entrepreneurial opportunities that do exist in black neighborhoods and that are left for immigrants to exploit.

VIII. Conclusion

There can be no doubt that crime has a devastating effect on black communities. The sorts of aimless violence and disorganized mayhem that exist among undersocialized adolescents seem to be on the increase quantitatively and qualitatively. Truly depraved patterns of behavior, which have become increasingly common among adolescents in the inner cities, strike terror in the hearts of those who live there. Most Americans are by now inundated with reports of what appear to be mindless acts of violence. Random "drive-by" shootings claim an increasing number of innocent victims in underclass enclaves. Gratuitous killings are now common in routine robberies, whether the victim submits or not. In New York City the grisly crime of setting homeless people on fire for "thrills" or to demonstrate "macho" has become a common occurrence. Between January and April of 1992, fourteen homeless men were set afire by bands of teenagers in the New York City subway system alone. Adolescents capable of such utter depravity now freely walk the streets and terrorize whole neighborhoods.[73]

As I said in the introductory comments to this chapter, there is nothing that could improve the lives and the economic prospects of black Americans more than crime reduction in black neighborhoods. Furthermore, the task of reducing crime is not something government should shirk, nor is it a task that is beyond the capability of government. However, the task is not easy, especially with the changes in the criminal justice system that have occurred over the past thirty years. What should be abundantly clear and indisputable is that crime will not be reduced by attacking poverty or attempting to reduce prejudice against young blacks by education directed at whites.

One obvious problem is that given the current size of police forces and current levels of crime, most policing has come to involve primarily after-the-fact attempts to arrest perpetrators for criminal acts already committed. Older methods made it easier to prevent crime, especially youthful street crime, from happening in the first place. Crime could be dramatically reduced by, for instance, saturating underclass neighborhoods with police or national guardsmen. If the possibility of getting away with a criminal act were close to negligible, as it would be in such a scenario, street crime, at least, would decline markedly. So would the excitement that the street provides for young men. Since far fewer crimes would occur, the problem of housing criminals would be much reduced. While this approach appears politically unacceptable at the current time, it would, if implemented, pretty much "solve" the problem of juvenile street crime.

The argument being made here is that youthful imperatives, many of which are influenced by biological factors, need not lead in any necessary or deterministic way to antisocial activities. In fact, as has been stressed, most societies are able to channel those youthful imperatives into eminently useful and healthy activities. What is required is sufficient adult supervision to prevent the spontaneous development of a dangerous juvenile subculture. By way of illustrating this point, consider the fact that during the six to twelve months that American troops were in the Gulf War theater, there appear to have been very few cases of violent assaults among the troops in the Gulf area, even though five hundred thousand young men were gathered together in none too comfortable circumstances. When one considers that many of the soldiers in the Gulf area were from impoverished backgrounds, and many in their violence-prone years, and that all were carrying lethal weapons, the contrast to civilian violence is striking. Had the soldiers in the Gulf area experienced the homicide rate of the south Bronx, for instance, there would have been 750 murders there in a year. Moreover, there were few women among the troops, no children, and no older individuals, all of whom have very low murder rates. If one compares the Gulf population, composed primarily of young males, with a comparable group in the south Bronx, the expected number of murders in the Gulf would have numbered in the thousands. Of course, young men who join the armed services are a special sample, and cannot be directly compared to their civilian counterparts. Nevertheless, even when the draft was in effect during earlier wars, criminality among well-supervised troops was relatively uncommon. The point is that young men can, relatively easily, be restrained from expressing violent aggression if they are properly disciplined and under adequate supervision.

The key to crime control appears to be to assure a high enough ratio of people acting to deter crime in relation to those disposed to engage in crime. According to this hypothesis, if the ''active deterrence/potential delinquents'' ratio is high, crime should be low, if the ratio is low, crime should be high. In most middle-class communities, that ratio is relatively high since there are a sufficient number of concerned adult males and police in proportion to young people prone to wrongdoing. The reasons for this are many.

First, since densities are low in suburban areas, with most people living in single-family homes, rather than in multistory apartment buildings, the anonymity common to urban areas is less in evidence. Untoward behavior by adolescents is likely to be noticed and reported, as is the presence of unknown youngsters. In addition, the threshold for troublesome behavior is likely to be lower in suburban communities, and disturbances are therefore more likely to be resented. Second, most middle-class adolescents are required to attend school. Absence from school is quickly noticed and quickly transmitted to parents, who have sufficient authority in most cases to enforce school attendance. In those cases where children can remove themselves from school, they are easily noticed in suburban communities and are not likely to carry off many criminal acts before being arrested.

In small towns in rural and suburban America, adult supervision is so common and thorough that few people realize it is taking place. The lack of anonymity in such places makes the task relatively easy and requires minimum police involvement. In small traditional communities all over the world, property crime is an anomaly. People cannot gain much by stealing from their neighbors and do not do so. Most of the behavior we would call criminal in such settings involves violent behavior resulting from personal disputes among adults that have gotten out of hand. Children and adolescents only rarely are the perpetrators of such violent acts.

In urban underclass neighborhoods, just the opposite is true: crime is predominantly a youth problem, and adult supervision is much more difficult. Children are truant from school with impunity and can wander urban settings and commit wrongdoing almost without fear of arrest or serious punishment. A criminal record is of little account to those who are unconcerned about college or prestige employment. The number of adults, especially males, in a position to deter crime is low for the reasons discussed earlier, leaving the police as the only effective agents of deterrence. Add to this the fact that distrust of the police among underclass blacks is endemic, making their job even more difficult and undoubtedly undermining their motivation to deal with the problem wholeheartedly.

There is no question that a first priority of any policy to restore order to the inner cities must be a major increase in the size of police forces. But given the current levels of crime, it would be necessary to almost saturate underclass neighborhoods with police officers in an attempt to increase the active deterrence side of the "active deterrence/potential delinquents" ratio in large cities. Such a massive police presence would seem politically and fiscally unacceptable, at least at the present time. Perhaps, therefore, the solution lies in an attempt to decrease the "potential delinquents" side of the "active deterrence/potential delinquents" ratio. From this perspective the problem is to reduce the presence of potential wrongdoers on the streets so that criminal behavior could be handled by only moderately larger police forces. This can be achieved in a number of ways. Let me offer two suggestions that might dramatically improve things.

The first and most important of these is to enforce in a serious way the truancy laws that are currently on the books. It certainly seems reasonable to require that all children below the age of eighteen spend the equivalent of the school day in some supervised setting. Urban children who opt out of school are currently free to do what they want beyond the gaze of concerned adults. It is hardly surprising that many of them engage in unproductive or destructive activities.

A student who decides to leave school should be required to find gainful employment or to be otherwise engaged in some activity supervised by adults. Such is the pattern among middle-class adolescents, and were it to become the pattern for underclass adolescents, there is every reason to believe that such supervision would have a salutary effect. Of course, for such a program to be effective, schools and related institutions would have to take attendance very seriously; truancy laws that are often ignored would have to be seriously enforced. If that were done, urban adolescents wandering the streets without any obvious purpose would stand out as much as do suburban teenagers in similar circumstances now.

A second powerful tool for reducing adolescent misconduct can be found in reinstituting the curfews for young people that were common earlier in the century. Curfews have the powerful advantage of taking children off the streets and out of harm's way. They have the secondary effect of allowing police officers to question young people who are on the streets beyond the curfew, so that they can act in a preventative manner. Any visitor to a large American city is likely to be appalled by the fact of adolescents, some hardly in their teens, wandering such places as New York's Times Square in the middle of the night. Many of these children are clearly engaged in prostitution, drug dealing, mugging, and various sorts of criminal conduct. Unfortunately, under current law, unless they are caught in a criminal act, they must be allowed to roam at will. It is hardly surprising that so many of these urban children end up in city morgues and in emergency rooms. It is also not surprising that those who choose to attend school are unlikely to be particularly productive when they do.

Taken together, these two modest suggestions would dramatically reduce youthful misbehavior. Children would simply not have the opportunity to engage in very much criminal activity. These proposals would have the effect of preventing crime before it happens, and as such can be said to be "proactive." The more common strategy today is to wait for crimes to occur and then attempt to find the perpetrator, to deal with crime "reactively." The problem here, besides the fact that in the cities the reactive strategy has largely failed as a deterrent, is that young people may engage in dozens of criminal acts before they are ever apprehended. Even if apprehended, an adolescent without many prior arrests is unlikely to be punished. Understandably, judges are reluctant to mete out harsh punishments to youngsters who appear to have committed only one or two crimes, even though most judges must be aware that a "first arrest" is very unlikely to be a "first crime." For this reason, the reactive strategy has the effect of allowing most young people who are disposed to criminal activity to engage repeatedly in criminal conduct without any discipline at all. It is not surprising that some develop a fairly powerful crime habit. It is also not surprising that the seriousness of the sorts of crimes committed tends to escalate over time.

If adolescents were kept off the streets for most of the day and night, police manpower could be used more effectively than it is now. The value of compulsory daytime supervision of adolescents and nighttime curfews is that they make it possible to achieve an effective "active deterrence/potential delinquents" ratio without the excessive costs and the totalitarian climate that a more massive police presence might create. In other words, to get a similar reduction in crime merely by increasing the number of police would probably require the tripling or quadrupling of police forces. This would be financially difficult, and many would find it socially undesirable. Nevertheless, it is essential to increase the number of police actively on street patrol even with policies designed to keep children off the streets, if only to enforce truancy laws and curfews.

These proposals for increased supervision of adolescents, including aggressive truancy regulation, coupled with curfews and more extensive foot patrolling are fairly practical measures. Such measures were in fact effective when they were used in the past, and given the nature of the problems they address and past experience, are likely to be highly effective today. These strategies would undoubtedly cost a great deal of money, but they would, in fairly short order, save more money than they cost.

Money would be saved directly by government in court and prison expenses. Substantial savings would be realized from reduced medical costs of providing care for the often indigent victims of criminal assault. Money would also be saved by city and state agencies because of reduced maintenance for graffiti removal and damages from other sorts of vandalism. Improved business conditions would increase sales-tax receipts, and increased real-estate values would also produce increased revenues from real-estate taxes. In addition, the cost to businesses and homeowners for insurance and other crime-related costs would be much reduced as rates of burglary, robbery, arson, and physical assault declined. Improved educational attainment, if it were effected, would likely improve overall productivity. And of course, the overall quality of life and well-being of inner-city residents would be immeasurably improved. Being poor and an urban dweller would no longer imply living in wretched circumstances.

The modest proposals I have suggested would, however, meet with a host of objections of the sort that have prevented a serious assault on crime for twenty-five years. These objections have paralyzed policy makers, who have allowed crime and public disorder to reach proportions that are historically unprecedented and of a magnitude unimaginable in any other modern democracy.

The main objection would be the claim, by now twenty-five years old, that attempts to reduce crime and disorder are merely disguised attempts to oppress black Americans—that such policies would be discriminatory and would fall heaviest on the backs of black men. While this argument may have had some merit in the fifties and early sixties, it is wildly off the mark today. Police officers are not killing and maiming large numbers of black people today, black adolescents are. Whites are not burning the homes and businesses of black people in the major cities, black adolescents are doing that in their own neighborhoods. Even the most viciously racist police officer would be hard pressed, today, to hurt as many blacks as can one pathological adolescent.

It is important that the distrust of police by blacks be overcome. If this means greater vigilance over police conduct on the part of city administrations, many now in the hands of black leaders, then such a course must be vigorously pursued. On the other hand, if much of the black distrust of the police is the result of historic perceptions that are now out of alignment with the facts, concerted efforts must be made to change those perceptions. Indeed, an important task for social science is to clarify matters on this issue and find ways to overcome the current doubts about fairness in the criminal justice system expressed by black Americans. Few tasks are more urgent.

A second objection to some of these proposals might come from children's rights advocates who argue that children must be given all the rights and privileges of adults, even if the straightforward result of such a policy is that children destroy their own lives and the lives of those around them. Such advocates have opposed curfews and other laws designed to protect children. They have argued that students in school should be given the same privacy protections as adults, and on that ground have opposed the use of metal detectors in schools to keep out firearms, and locker searches to discourage drug sales on school grounds.[74]

In the case of enforcing current truancy laws, I do not think children's rights advocates have reasonable grounds for objecting. School attendance is an obligation for all American children. Only underclass children regularly avoid that obligation, and that is because we fail to enforce that obligation on poor children. Middle-class suburban children are not entitled to avoid these obligations. Why should poor children be treated differently than middle-class children in this regard? If we believe education is important for children, fairness and decency require that we see to it that all children are put in a position to benefit from it.

In the case of curfews, though many judges have ruled them unconstitutional, it is by no means clear that the U.S. Supreme Court would invalidate well-written statutes.[75] Curfews would have the effect, as would enforcement of truancy laws, of reducing class disparities. Few middle-class children are allowed to wander about late at night. Why should poor children be treated differently and be less carefully protected from harm?

Children who are chronically truant or who continuously violate curfews are very likely to be heading for serious problems. Such behavior also suggests that their parents are unable or unwilling to supervise them adequately. One way to assure that these laws are respected is to impose sure sanctions for their violation. Those sanctions, however, must not be so severe that judges shrink from imposing them. One possible solution for chronic violators of truancy laws and curfews would be to require them to attend residential schools, preferably located in rural areas, until the end of the school year in which they have incurred their infractions. These ought not to be reform schools where children are committed for criminal acts. Rather, these schools should be specifically designed for the purpose of dealing with chronic truants and curfew violators and should not be used to house delinquents who have been convicted of crimes against persons or property.

The advantage of such schools is that they would surely have a deterrent effect, since most students would prefer staying home and going to school in their own neighborhoods. Such a policy would have a secondary effect of bringing under closer social supervision children whose parents have not been able or willing to provide adequate supervision.

These proposals do not preclude other changes in a juvenile justice system that cries out for revision. In her 1988 book *At a Tender Age,* social researcher Rita Kramer has outlined the perverse nature of the way juvenile criminals are treated in most large U.S. cities.[76] In New York City, youngsters with long criminal careers are turned back onto the streets after brief stays in juvenile detention facilities and are left unsupervised to visit terror on their neighborhoods.[77] The problem is that even though the absolute failure of this system is apparent to most of those familiar with it, there seems little or no political will to change it. It should be changed, but many of its features are dictated by federal and state court rulings which in many ways take the shaping of criminal justice out of the hands of popularly elected legislators. The virtue of the above proposals is that they can succeed in preventing criminal acts by juveniles, independently of any major changes in the current criminal justice system, changes that are unlikely to be soon forthcoming. They can be enacted swiftly and can begin to show benefits almost immediately.

Similarly, legislation limiting the access of minors to handguns would likely have a salutary effect. Unfortunately, in most major cities which already have such laws, they go largely unenforced—for the simple reason that court rulings make it extremely difficult for police to randomly search youngsters likely to possess guns. Ironically, court rulings designed to protect black children from discriminatory harassment and unwarranted searches have made it impossible for the police to thwart armed adolescents who, in alarming numbers, murder each other as well as a multitude of innocent people. Seeing that children are in school where they can be legally required to pass through metal detectors would more effectively disarm them than any new legislation. Similarly, keeping children off the streets late at night with curfews would dramatically reduce the need for or the value of gun possession. There is also the possibility, rarely taken seriously among social scientists, that removing from the law-abiding citizenry the right to carry arms may in fact increase the incidence of certain kinds of crimes. Indeed, armed adolescents, today, can pick and choose victims with near certainty that few will be in a position to actively protect themselves.

Furthermore, efforts to reduce drug abuse among youngsters are to be applauded, but so far seem to have had only very modest effects. How can they be effective, when so many youngsters are free to roam the streets without adequate supervision, and are therefore easy prey for those who would entice them, for pecuniary or sexual ends, into drug use.

These proposals rest on a fundamental rule that should and does govern decent societies—namely, that all of a society's children should be cared for and nurtured so that they can make their way into adulthood with as few scars and limitations as possible. Societies cannot prevent the accidents of birth from making childhood easier for some children than for others, but they can surely attempt to ameliorate the more damaging influences to which some children are exposed. Under any understanding of decency there is no justification whatsoever for a society to actively foster differential treatment between the children of the poor and the children of the affluent as we currently do in the United States.

Poor children should not be treated differently from middle-class children in the amount of supervision they receive, on the simple grounds that they need at least as much if not more supervision. The fact that poor black children now receive far less supervision than their white middle-class counterparts is clearly the main reason poor black children have so much difficulty in coming to terms with adolescence. If poor children were treated more like their middle-class counterparts, more would approximate middle-class patterns of behavior.

In the most fundamental sense, effective societies have only as much crime as they tolerate. We have a great deal of crime in America because we tolerate a great deal of crime. Greece and Spain have far more poor people than does the United States, but they tolerate crime less and therefore have more peaceful societies. If the United States wishes to help blacks achieve social and economic parity with whites, it can powerfully forward that goal by tolerating less crime in the inner cities of America. The obfuscation of this simple truth has done great harm to the social fabric of the United States and inflicted needless damage and suffering, not least of all on black Americans.

9

Education

I. Introduction

Because of the strong relationship between educational achievement and economic success, and because blacks have lagged behind whites in education, a primary emphasis of government strategies to overcome inequalities has been an attempt to improve the education of black Americans. Whether as a result of these efforts, or due to a general improvement in the circumstances facing black Americans, there have been notable gains in this area. The gap between the proportion of blacks and whites who complete high school has been steadily reduced over the years. In 1940, only 11 percent of blacks in the 25 to 34 year age range had completed four years of high school or more, compared to 39 percent of whites. In 1960, a large gap remained, with 33 percent of blacks and 61 percent of whites in that age range completing four or more years of high school. In the sixties the gap began to close, and in 1970, 52 percent of blacks aged 25 to 34 had completed four years of high school, compared to 74 percent of whites. In 1991, the comparable figures were 81.9 percent for blacks and 86.7 for whites.[1]

It should be noted that, on average, black students take longer to finish high school and are more likely to obtain high school diplomas through the nontraditional route of the General Education Development Certificate, designed for students who fail to finish high school in the usual time. In 1991, among those in the 18 to 21 age range, 79.1 percent of whites had completed high school, while only 69.3 percent of blacks had done so. In that age range, only 6.9 percent of whites were still in high school, whereas 14.2 percent of blacks were still attending.[2] The situation is particularly troubling in the cities.

In New York City, for instance, only 39 percent of the students graduate in four years. Only 57 percent complete high school by age twenty-one, after which age they must leave and obtain their diploma through other means. But these figures are for all students. In predominantly black and minority high schools the situation is much worse. Four-year graduation rates as low as 17 and 18 percent are reported for some inner-city high schools, and many have rates in the 25 percent range.[3]

Such students, even if they eventually graduate, are likely to fall behind others who graduated on time. In addition, there is reason to believe many of these students lack basic skills necessary for higher education and the advanced training necessary for skilled jobs. Their prospects have not been good in recent years due to the continuing decline in industrial jobs resulting from increased automation and the increasing internationalization of trade. These trends are unlikely to be reversed, and in the future even more emphasis will be placed on the need for individuals prepared for advanced training and education.

Nevertheless, it is clear that, today, blacks nationwide have, at least by the age of thirty-five, made considerable progress and have achieved near parity with whites in the attainment of the high school diploma, a significant employment credential.

There have also been important gains for blacks in academic achievement. On the National Assessment of Educational Progress (NAEP) tests on reading and mathematics proficiency given to seventeen-year-olds, for example, the gap between black and white students has been almost halved in the last ten years. These tests, which are administered to a representative sample of students in public and private schools, show that in 1980 the average score in reading for whites was 293, while blacks achieved an average score of 243 out of a maximum of 500. This represented a black-white gap of 50 points. By 1990, black seventeen-year-olds had raised their reading scores to an average of 267, while whites had remained almost the same at 297, closing the gap to 30 points. This is a significant improvement in a proficiency essential for academic advancement. Gains in basic mathematical proficiency were even greater. In 1980, white seventeen-year-olds had an average score of 306, and blacks an average score of 268, a gap of 38 points. By 1990, whites scored 310 and blacks 289, having reduced the gap to 21 points.[4]

The impressive gains in high school completion rates and gains in basic proficiencies have not been fully translated into gains at more advanced levels. While there have been striking increases in the number of blacks completing four or more years of college during the last thirty years, these have been matched by equally dramatic increases among the general population. In 1960, for instance, 12 percent of whites between the ages of twenty-five and thirty-four had completed college, while only 4 percent of blacks in that age range had done so. In 1991, the figures had doubled for whites to 24.9, and trebled to 12.2 for blacks. This represents substantial educational progress, but the fact that blacks currently obtain four-year college degrees at only half the rate for whites is disturbing. This difference accounts for the considerable disparities that continue to exist in professional and managerial employment and accounts for a substantial amount of the differential in black and white wages.[5]

David Armor has suggested that the NAEP gains can best be explained by the rising socioeconomic status of black parents, since higher socioeconomic status is usually reflected in better school performance.[6] However, while blacks have made striking progress in closing the gap in high school reading and mathematics proficiency, they have made no such gains in science proficiency and much less progress on tests of preparedness for higher education such as the Scholastic Aptitude Test (SAT).[7] One possible explanation for this is that reading and mathematics fundamentals are usually inculcated before high school, while more sophisticated education usually takes place in high school. This interpretation is strengthened by widespread reports of disorder in inner-city high schools, where large numbers of black students complete their education. Inner-city elementary schools and middle schools do not seem as troubled as the high schools. Furthermore, truancy, which is an exceedingly serious problem in the inner cities, is predominantly a problem for high school students.

In other words, blacks are showing major improvements in achieving the basic skills that are usually mastered in the lower grades where an orderly school climate is the rule, but do not seem to be gaining at the same rate in the advanced grades where, by all reports, a significant degree of disorder is common. Perhaps the increased socioeconomic status of blacks is effective in improving performance in the early grades, but is undercut at the high school level by the problems in the high schools. This hypothesis will be taken up more thoroughly in a later section. The problems of inner-city high schools may help explain the growing disparities between underclass blacks who attend those schools and middle-class blacks who more often attend suburban and private schools.

Since academic performance has become so critical to economic success, it is crucial that we have a clear and accurate understanding of why blacks have more difficulties in this area than whites. This has, needless to say, been one of the more vexing problems confronting social scientists and policy analysts in recent years. It has been particularly vexing because of the controversies surrounding the meaning of standardized tests of intelligence such as the IQ test.

II. The IQ Controversy

The IQ controversy is really three controversies. The first has to do with whether IQ is, in part, inherited. The second is whether IQ is important for social and economic success—in other words, whether IQ tests really measure what we mean when we talk about intelligence. The third controversy deals with whether meaningful racial differences in IQ exist or whether the test-score differences that currently exist merely reflect a bias in the tests themselves. The first question, dealing with the heritability of IQ, is not really very controversial anymore, at least among psychologists. Almost all introductory psychology texts report with some confidence that IQ is, to a considerable degree, inherited. Studies of adopted children, for instance, indicate a closer correlation with the biological parents of children who had been adopted at an early age than with the children's adoptive parents.[8] While environment has an effect, nature is now seen as at least as important as nurture in determining adult IQ.

There is somewhat less agreement among psychologists on the second controversy, dealing with the significance of IQ differences for social and economic success—do the tests in fact measure intelligence—but not much less. Large numbers of studies have shown a reliable relationship between IQ and educational attainments, occupational status, criminal activity, etc. The relationship between IQ and socioeconomic status or "class" is clear and consistent. Whatever it is that IQ actually measures, it clearly appears to reflect one or more of the traits or predispositions valued in modern societies, and significantly affects a person's chances for success.[9]

The third controversy, about the meaning of racial differences in IQ, is somewhat confused. There is general agreement that a considerable gap in IQ test scores between blacks and whites exists; there is somewhat less but still considerable agreement that the gap is important; but there is widespread disagreement about what causes it, with many arguing that it is merely an artifact of the test's bias favoring middle-class whites. Arthur Jensen brought a storm of criticism upon himself when, in 1969, he argued that IQ was important and that heredity played an important role in average racial differences in IQ.[10] In general, Jensen's view was rejected as racist and inaccurate by a number of well-known social scientists whose critiques were featured in the popular media, and few social scientists came to Jensen's defense.[11] In 1989, however, Mark Snyderman and Stanley Rothman reported that when they surveyed social scientists with expertise in the field, a considerable number appeared to agree with Jensen. Snyderman and Rothman used an extensive questionnaire in their survey of over six hundred social scientists who were selected on the basis of their likely familiarity with IQ and the controversies surrounding it. The respondents included psychologists, sociologists, statisticians, professional psychometricians, etc. On the question dealing with black-white IQ differences, 45 percent of respondents thought that the difference was a product of both genetics and environment. That was Jensen's thesis. Fifteen percent thought it was environment alone and 1 percent thought it was genetics alone. Interestingly, 24 percent thought there was insufficient data upon which to base a reasonable answer to the question, and 14 percent chose not to answer the question at all.[12]

Snyderman and Rothman conclude that the political climate is such that social scientists are reluctant to criticize the popular view that there is strong evidence supporting an exclusively environmentalist explanation for IQ differences between the races. This reluctance on the part of social scientists reinforces the popular view that the only legitimate explanation of black educational problems is one which attributes those problems to discrimination.

I cite the Snyderman and Rothman findings here, not in support of the genetic hypothesis on IQ differences, but rather to highlight the fact that this important question is not a settled one. The assumption that the question has been settled has, unfortunately, made the exploration of alternative explanations that depend on neither genetics nor discrimination somewhat suspect in the public eye, since such explorations clearly imply that the issue is unresolved.

Whatever the final resolution of the argument over the sources of the IQ difference, there can be no doubt as to the significance of the difference. The difference between the mean score for whites and the mean score for blacks is quite large. On IQ tests, whites score on average about 100, and the scores are normally distributed in the familiar bell-shaped curve. On such a curve, approximately two-thirds of the population falls within one standard deviation on either side of the mean, and about 95 percent of the population falls within two standard deviations. IQ tests usually have a standard deviation of fifteen points, so that about two-thirds of the white population falls between the scores of 85 and 115, and 95 percent of the white population falls between 70 and 130.

The black population, on the other hand, has a mean IQ of about 85, with a standard deviation also of about fifteen points, which means that about two-thirds of the black population falls between the scores of 70 and 100, and 95 percent between 55 and 115. The difference between the races of fifteen points, a difference of approximately one standard deviation, has remained fairly constant since IQ measures were first taken earlier in the century. A similar disparity exists in the Scholastic Aptitude Test (SAT) which is used in college admissions. The SAT includes a verbal and a mathematics section, with possible scores falling between 200 and 800 on each section. The nationwide average in 1992 for all test takers was 423 on the verbal portion and 476 on the math portion. For whites, the average was 442 and 491 on the verbal and math sections, respectively. The average score for blacks in 1992 was 352 on the verbal and 385 on the math section. The standard deviations for all test takers were 112 for the verbal and 123 for the math section, so that the differences represent about 80 percent of a standard deviation between blacks and whites on the verbal section and 85 percent of a standard deviation on the math section.[13]

In the past, the difference in SAT performance for blacks and whites was even greater. In 1976, for instance, whites had a combined score of 944 and blacks a combined score of 686, a difference of 258 points. Since then, blacks have narrowed the gap by 25 percent to 196 points, a marked improvement. The narrowing of the gap is only partly due to a decline in white scores. White scores declined only 10 points between 1976 and 1992; black scores rose 51 points.[14] This improvement is indeed heartening, especially when taken together with the previously discussed reduction in the gap in NAEP scores.[15] Having said that, it is important to stress that the remaining gap of almost 200 points in SAT scores between the races indicates a major difference in academic preparedness.

III. Standardized Tests and Affirmative Action Goals

Differences in academic preparedness of almost a standard deviation between two groups is bound to have an important effect on the groups' occupational placement and income. For instance, an IQ of 115 (about one standard deviation above the national mean of 100) is considered a threshold for most professions, such as law, medicine, and college teaching. Prestige universities generally accept only people who score above 600 on both the verbal and math SAT exams, which is even more than a full standard deviation above the mean. Of course, the SAT is taken only by those who hope to attend college, so that a 600 on the SAT places one considerably above the average of all people, if one includes those who did not take the exam.

These disparities mean that, hypothetically, approximately *16* percent of whites should obtain IQ scores greater than 115, since that is one standard deviation above the white mean of 100, whereas only about 2.28 percent of blacks should attain a score of 115, since that score is *two* standard deviations above the black average of 85. Since whites outnumber blacks by about seven to one in the United States, the upshot is that the ratio of whites to blacks who would be expected to surpass this generally acknowledged threshold for professional careers is approximately fifty to one. In other words, if recruitment were based solely on IQ scores, blacks would come to represent only about 2 percent of those in the elite professions.[16]

The above hypothetical reasoning is confirmed by an analysis of SAT scores above the 600 range on each portion of the exam (or a 1200 combined score), which most elite colleges expect in their applicants. In 1992, over a million students took the SAT, of whom approximately seventy-five thousand (or about 7.5 percent) scored over 600 on the verbal portion. Among the ninety-nine thousand blacks taking the test (almost 10 percent of the test takers) only fifteen hundred black students (or about 1.5 percent) scored above 600 on the verbal section in that year. Among the approximately 680,000 whites who took the exam, 55,224 (or about 8 percent) scored above 600 on the verbal portion.[17]

This means that blacks represented only 2 percent of those scoring above 600, while whites represented about 73 percent of those scoring above 600. For purposes of comparison, among the approximately seventy-eight thousand Asians who took the test, over eight thousand surpassed the 600 score on the verbal section. This means that 11 percent of those who scored over 600 on the verbal portion were Asians, even though they are only one-fourth as numerous as blacks in the general population. Since a larger proportion of Asians take the SAT than do blacks, this means they are far more numerous as a group among those qualifying by virtue of verbal test scores for admission to the most prestigious colleges and universities.[18]

Similar disparities exist for math scores. Among blacks about 3 percent (3,404 students) scored above 600 in math. Among whites about 13 percent (132,847 students) scored over 600. Among the seventy-eight thousand Asians who took the test, approximately 35 percent (27,207 students) scored above 600 on the math section.[19]

If these tests are valid measures of academic aptitude, which they appear to be, then the disparity in performance between blacks and other groups creates enormous problems for any sort of affirmative action program geared toward proportional representation for blacks in the professions and in the universities.

Dinesh D'Souza in his *Illiberal Education* outlined the tensions on campuses created by universities attempting to have a black presence at parity with the black population in general. There are simply too few highly qualified blacks (as measured by the SAT) to achieve parity based on academic criteria, and therefore colleges, under affirmative action guidelines, dip deeper into the SAT pool of black applicants. Not surprisingly, blacks admitted on the basis of affirmative action do not perform as well, and drop out of college at much higher rates than whites or Asians.[20]

John Bunzel, past president of San Jose State University, reports that in its attempts to meet affirmative action goals, the Berkeley campus of the University of California established different admissions criteria for different ethnic groups. He reports that among students admitted to Berkeley, the mean combined SAT score in 1986 was 952 for blacks, 1014 for Chicanos, 1232 for whites, and 1254 for Asians. It is unreasonable to expect that the almost 300 point difference between blacks and whites (and Asians) would not be reflected in their performance. Bunzel reports that in the 1985–86 academic year, 90 percent of all regularly admitted students had a grade point average of at least 2.0 (a straight C average) on a 4.0 scale, an average below which a student is normally placed on academic probation. Ninety-three percent of whites, but only 72 percent of blacks, managed to maintain that average. Among blacks admitted under the auspices of affirmative action, only 54 percent managed to maintain a 2.0 average. The net result is not surprising. While 66 percent of the white students graduate within five years of admission, the figure is only 27 percent for black students.[21]

The noted black economist Thomas Sowell has made the point that affirmative action has the perverse effect of creating a misalignment between black students and universities. Under affirmative action, black students are admitted into universities a rung or two above those in which they might have performed well among equally prepared students. They are placed in settings where they face much stiffer competition and tend to drop out at higher rates than would be expected if they were better matched with their institutions.[22]

Similar problems are evident in the professional schools. The Law School Admissions Test (LSAT), for instance, had a scoring system in the 1980s in which the top score was 48. The mean score of those admitted to all law schools was about 36 for whites and 28 for blacks. Elite law schools generally accepted only students who scored above 40, and the average of those accepted was generally higher. At Georgetown University Law Center and at the University of Texas School of Law, the average was approximately 42. Very few black applicants obtained scores in that range. Timothy Maguire reported in *Commentary* that in 1989 the average LSAT for white students admitted to Georgetown University Law Center was 42, while for black students it was 32. Maguire, a student at Georgetown when he made this data available to the public, was threatened with disciplinary action for doing so, a threat that was eventually withdrawn. Universities that engage in these sorts of admissions practices, as many do, are clearly not anxious to advertise these disparities.[23] Similar problems have arisen in medical school admissions.[24] It should be pointed out that the academic difficulties that blacks admitted under affirmative action guidelines experience cannot be hidden from their classmates. Affirmative action policies in this case tend to create negative impressions of black academic ability, whereas race-neutral policies would not, since black students who were admitted to elite institutions would be favorably prepared to compete with whites. But of course there would be far fewer blacks on elite campuses. The effort to approach proportional representation for blacks, therefore, has its costs. Not only are blacks less likely to excel and more likely to drop out when placed in universities with students who are better prepared, but they are bound to be demoralized by the experience. Needless to say, these policies also generate considerable resentment among those whites and Asians who were denied admission to make room for blacks with far weaker academic credentials than their own.

IV. Explanations of the Aptitude-Test Gap

The gap in standardized measures of academic aptitude is therefore very important, and it is important to know what causes it. This is especially true in the case of the SAT, which is a good measure of preparation for advanced education. The consensus among social scientists, which was formed during the early thirties and forties, was that the aptitude-test gap was caused by the impoverished conditions among blacks produced by years of discrimination. As that discrimination abated, it was thought, so would the poverty and, in time, the gap in test performance. In the sixties the view of blacks as a sort of new immigrant group became common. This view seemed especially applicable to blacks who had migrated in large numbers to the major cities of the North during and after World War II. It was expected that they would eventually, barring overt discrimination, follow the paths of other immigrant groups.

Among earlier immigrant groups, various social pathologies, in greater or lesser degree, had been common in the past. Immigrants often lacked skills and credentials, and had to take the least desirable and most insecure jobs. Unemployment and underemployment were common, especially among men, who often relied on their wives to supplement family income. In such circumstances, frustrated men often turned to drink, sometimes engaged in criminal conduct, and commonly abandoned families. Children from immigrant homes, lacking the normal advantages of security and of parents familiar with American culture, exhibited more school failure than others. But the children of past groups had shown remarkable resilience and within a generation or two, at most, had found themselves in the mainstream.

It was expected that blacks, newly migrating from the rural South into southern and northern cities, would face similar difficulties, but it was generally assumed that they too would, given real equality of opportunity, make steady strides toward parity with whites. It was also assumed that a more generous social policy than had prevailed for earlier groups would ease the necessary pain of the transition. It was in this spirit that social scientists encouraged and contributed to the civil rights movement and to strenuous educational efforts to reduce prejudice and racial hostility. It was assumed that over time the IQ gap would disappear.

Probably the most convincing argument for the environmentalist position has been made by Thomas Sowell. Sowell studied old school records and discovered that earlier ethnic minorities exhibited apparent intellectual deficits, but that these tended to disappear as the various groups became acclimated to urban American society. In his justly famous *Ethnic America,* Sowell explains:

> Like fertility rates, IQ scores differ substantially among ethnic groups at a given time, and have changed substantially over time—reshuffling the relative standings of the groups. As of about World War I, Jews scored sufficiently low on mental tests to cause a leading "expert" of that era to claim that the test score results "disprove the popular belief that the Jew is highly intelligent." At the time IQ scores for many of the more recently arrived ethnic groups—Italians, Greeks, Poles, Portuguese, and Slovaks—were virtually identical to those found today for blacks, Hispanics, and other disadvantaged groups. However, over the succeeding decades, as most of these immigrant groups become more acculturated and advanced economically, their IQ scores have risen by substantial amounts.[25]

Sowell's "cultural-assimilation" argument is consistent with the recent improvement in NAEP reading and math scores and the improvement in SAT performance among blacks. David Armor, in fact, offers convincing evidence that the best explanation of the improvement in NAEP scores is the rising socioeconomic status of the generation of blacks whose children are currently in school.[26]

Additional support for the cultural-assimilation hypothesis is provided by the widely reported research of Sandra Scarr and Richard Weinberg showing that mixed-race and black children adopted into above average (socioeconomically) white homes had IQs five to ten points higher than the black average, though not as high as the biological children of the adoptive parents. Black adoptees had average IQs of 98, and mixed-race adoptees averaged 106. Furthermore, the study also found that those adopted earlier had the higher IQs.[27]

These results are impressive because most research indicates that adoptees are generally more similar to their biological parents than to their adoptive parents. The difference between this study and most others could be accounted for by the fact that the environmental differences between biological and adoptive families in the Scarr and Weinberg study may have been much larger than is normally the case. Generally, if environmental factors are not greatly dissimilar, differences between children are likely to be caused by genetic factors. However, if environmental differences are large, they may overwhelm genetic factors. For instance, adult height is likely to be more closely related to biological parents than adoptive ones, for obvious reasons. However, if there is a major nutritional difference between the diets in biological versus adoptive homes, the genetic factors may be swamped by the environmental factor of diet.[28]

Another explanation of the difference between this and most other studies is related to the fact that the biological parents in this study were not randomly selected, and data on the biological parents' IQs was not obtained. Scarr and Weinberg made the assumption that the biological parents were in the average range for their racial group, on the basis of their schooling. The biological parents had an average educational level of twelve years. It is possible that the biological parents, who were relatively young, may have included some who were continuing with their education, suggesting that they may have had higher than average IQs. Without knowledge of the actual IQs of the biological parents, one cannot dismiss the possibility that in the Scarr and Weinberg study, the average IQ of the adoptees would have been higher than average due to inheritance from their parents.

It may well be that the relative importance of nature and nurture in shaping IQ is so complicated a question as to be unresolvable by statistical studies. Sometime early in the next century, the current attempt to map the human genome may begin to provide definitive answers to this and related questions. Whatever the answer, it should not markedly affect educational policy. Children need the best education that can be provided, whatever their native abilities and talents. What seems clear is that poor black children are not now getting very good educations in their schools, so that it is extremely difficult to gauge the actual potential of many black children. Changing that reality ought to be our major concern.

It should be stressed that those who argue that genetic factors play a part in explaining black-white IQ differences almost never argue that cultural and environmental factors are unimportant. Rather, the argument has always been about whether the gap is completely explained by culture or partially explained by culture. Put another way, the question was never whether IQ could or could not be substantially raised by an enriched family experience and enriched educational experiences, but rather how much it could be raised. Would total assimilation eliminate the gap, or would a gap (smaller but still important) remain after total assimilation into the dominant culture?

The cultural-assimilation view is not without its critics. Many point out that IQ tests were new early in the century, and were often little understood and poorly administered. The low scores of many immigrant children might have resulted from difficulties with the English language. Jews may well have performed poorly on IQ tests at the time, but they were generally regarded as able students and performed well in school from the very beginning. In addition, Japanese and Chinese children never exhibited an IQ gap relative to whites. Carl Degler, commenting on the debates about IQ and ethnicity in the 1920s, points out that some researchers, while moving away from biological explanations, continued to have mixed feelings on the nurturist explanation. Psychologist Thomas Garth, for instance, writing in the 1920s and generally opposed to genetic explanations, was nevertheless troubled by the performance of Asian children, since (in Degler's words) their "social backgrounds surely differed dramatically from those of native whites, yet Japanese and Chinese children almost invariably achieved scores on a level with native whites."[29]

Despite misgivings such as Garth's, the general consensus since the thirties has been that the economic and cultural conditions of black children account for their weaker showing on IQ. That consensus was, of course, reflected in Myrdal's report and gave powerful impetus to the demand for greater equality of treatment for blacks. It was widely assumed that the difficulties black children had with school and standardized tests were the product of the sort of culture and home environment produced by poverty.

Few social scientists saw locating the problem in black homes as denigrating blacks per se in any way. Black militants, however—especially those preaching separatism—expressed strong disagreement with the cultural explanation. These separatist groups, which became fairly influential in the 1960s, argued that the cultural explanation was merely an attempt to excuse the past injustices of forced migration and slavery by equating the black experience with that of other immigrant groups whose migration was voluntary. Black militants rejected this equation out of hand. From their perspective there was nothing wrong with black families or black communities, and black poverty was the direct result of past and continuing racism. Denying this was "blaming the victim." The issue came to a head in the furor over the Moynihan Report, which warned of the dangers of the increasing prevalence of single-parent families among blacks (see above, Chapter 4, Section VI).

The Moynihan episode was particularly disturbing to the psychologists. It was, after all, psychologists who had developed the IQ test and who had done the research on the black-white disparity that was first detected when the tests were initially used on a wide scale during World War I. Most psychologists argued strenuously that the black-white difference was produced by environmental factors, and accepted the idea that racism was the ultimate source of the problem. However, few psychologists could reasonably discard the thesis that between white racism and black children's school problems, the conditions in black homes and communities played an important mediating role. Indeed, how could one explain the difficulties of a black child in an all-black school in a black community in terms of the attitudes of whites, whom such a child rarely encountered? In fact, the whole movement to desegregate the schools was premised, at least in part, on the salutary effects that were thought to derive from the acculturation to the larger society thought more likely to occur in integrated settings. If there were no problems in black communities affecting black IQ, why was desegregation expected to improve black IQ?

Furthermore, while psychologists were quick to adopt a cultural explanation for IQ differences, few were prepared to say that IQ was an unimportant factor in educational success. Most research suggested it was very important. In 1969, when Arthur Jensen challenged the prevailing view and argued that a genetic explanation for much of the IQ difference was more consistent with the facts, most psychologists found themselves caught in a bind.[30] Most disagreed with Jensen that genetic factors were important, and "Jensenism" soon became synonymous, unfairly, with racism. But, on the other hand, to suggest that the difference was a function of deficits in the black home was, after the Moynihan affair, also condemned as racist. Most serious professionals found themselves in a very uncomfortable situation, and found it easiest to simply avoid the subject.[31] The issue is, today, so sensitive that some introductory psychology texts, which in the past almost always discussed racial differences in IQ, simply exclude the whole topic in their most recent editions. As psychologist Richard Herrnstein has suggested, discussion of racial differences has become an "obscenity" among social scientists.[32] And no decent person wishes to be caught uttering obscenities. The comments by Sandra Scarr, cited in Chapter 1, on the dangers of pursuing "suspect research" are worth remembering.[33]

The consequence of the retreat by many social scientists from these controversial matters was a general decline in the level of discourse and analysis on black educational problems. In the place of serious discussion about how to overcome the differences in IQ, a major effort was launched by the critics of IQ testing to explain them away. The tests themselves came under attack as culturally biased and therefore invalid in predicting the skills they claimed to predict.

Arguments about the validity of IQ tests have a long history in psychology, and those arguments took on a new urgency. Numerous ingenious explanations were put forward in the late sixties and early seventies to demonstrate the bias in standardized testing, or to demonstrate that they failed to predict what they were designed to predict. By and large, such efforts were unconvincing. A major study sponsored by the National Research Council of the National Academy of Sciences reported that widely used ability tests are unbiased and valid predictors of performance.[34] After reviewing the relevant data, researcher Robert Linn concluded in that report: "Contrary to what is often supposed, the bulk of the evidence shows either that there are essentially no differences in predictions based on minority or majority group data, or that the predictions based on majority group data *give some advantage to minority group members*" (emphasis added).[35]

By the early eighties the claim of bias in testing, and the claim that the tests lacked validity, while still being made, lacked substance and empirical support. Nevertheless, many, usually those unfamiliar with the research on test validity, continued to claim that ability tests are biased. The biased-test assertion is still being used by affirmative action advocates who claim that any test that detects group differences is, by virtue of detecting such differences, necessarily biased and discriminatory. Similar logic leads affirmative action advocates to claim that a test that detects, say, differences between males and females in (for instance) engineering aptitude, must be biased. The assumption they make, of course, is that human groups cannot exhibit real differences in any important ability.

In any case, it is not at all clear why blacks lag behind whites in tests of scholastic aptitude. Henry Gleitman, in his respected introductory psychology text, sums up the position on the issue that had become common by the early eighties:

> Perhaps the fairest thing we can say is that there is no single study whose results or interpretations cannot be challenged, nor is there a single argument (whether genetic or environmental) for which there is no counter-argument. Under the circumstances, no conclusion can be anything but tentative. Even so, the weight of the evidence seems to tilt toward the environmentalist side, especially when one's intuitions about the effects of three hundred years of slavery and racist oppression are thrown into the balance.[36]

By the 1990s, this statement, which fairly summarized much expert opinion, would likely be characterized as racist, since Gleitman did not flatly and strongly deny the possibility of genetic factors in black-white IQ differences. In any case, since tests like the SAT are highly correlated with academic performance, the differences between blacks and whites cannot be dismissed as unimportant. Until the gap is reduced it is unreasonable to expect blacks to achieve parity with whites, especially in the professions and upper-management positions, which are highly dependent on educational success.

Since serious psychologists were reluctant to offer empirically sound explanations as to why blacks have educational difficulties, the field was left open to a variety of assertions that possessed a certain plausibility but that have either not been tested or have been found inadequate when put to scientific test. Some have argued that black educational difficulties are the result of underfunding of inner-city schools. Others maintain that northern schools have become segregated because of white flight, and that this causes problems. Many invoke the ''self-fulfilling prophecy,'' which posits that white teachers have low expectations for black students and thus create student failure, since students are said to perform up to the level expected of them. Some argue that white teachers cannot provide effective *role models* for black children. More recently, some have claimed that the schools fail to teach black history and culture and so deprive black children of the ethnic pride necessary for learning. New Afrocentric curricula must therefore be developed to overcome the

"Eurocentric bias" in American schools. And so on. By now the arguments are well known to most Americans. What is interesting is that so few in the social sciences openly challenge these assertions, even though just about all of them are contradicted by well-published data. An examination of each of the various charges will demonstrate that they are, by and large, lacking in substance.

V. School Funding and Educational Achievement

In the 1960s, sociologist James Coleman led a major research effort funded by the federal government to study the sources of educational inequality. This research led to a 1966 report entitled *Equality of Educational Opportunity,* or more commonly, the Coleman Report. Among other things, the study examined the effects of differential funding on academic achievement. The charge that white communities shortchanged black schools had been one of the primary arguments for integrated education. There can be no doubt that segregated black schools, especially in the South, were woefully underfunded compared to white schools prior to the civil rights movement. Whether the underfunding of black schools was the primary reason for black educational problems had never been clearly tested.[37]

Coleman's extensive analysis revealed that the funds available to schools had, at least by the 1960s, little impact on educational outcomes. Coleman was unequivocal in asserting, based on the data, that "per pupil expenditure, books in the library, and a host of other facilities and curricular measures show virtually no relation to achievement" when other factors are held constant. The report found that such things as the attitudes of students, the education of parents, the stability of the family, and parents' concern about education were far more important than school funding. Not surprisingly, the composition of the student body was also found to be important. Students who came from similar backgrounds and shared a concern with education performed better than those in environments where such concern was lacking. The single most important factor about the schools themselves was the quality of teachers, as measured by teachers' education, and this factor was more important for the education of blacks and other minorities than for whites.[38] One can reasonably infer that well-educated teachers seemed able to overcome some of the differences in family background which accounted for the differences between blacks and whites.

Student attitudes were also very important. The report assessed students' interest in learning, their self-image in terms of academic ability, and their sense of control over their environment. According to the authors of the report, "[o]f all the variables measured in the survey, including all measures of family background and all school variables, these attitudes showed the strongest relation to achievement. . . ."[39] Germane to our discussion, there were important differences between blacks and whites. Interest in education, for instance, bore no relation to school achievement for blacks and other minorities, while it was moderately related to achievement for whites. Among whites and Asians, self-concept was very closely linked to school performance, but was unrelated to performance for blacks and other minorities. This suggests that there is a realistic feedback between school performance and beliefs in one's abilities among whites and Asians, but this realistic feedback seems to be lacking among many black students.[40]

Strikingly, the most important attitudinal variable for blacks was their sense of control over their environment, and this variable was more important than any other in its relation to black school achievement. A student's sense of control over his environment was measured by responses to three statements. The first was that "good luck is more important than hard work for success." The second was "every time I try to get ahead, something or someone stops me." The third was "people like me don't have much of a chance to be successful in life."[41] It is worth repeating that the way children answered these questions turned out to be the most important correlate of black educational success. Put another way, black children who in 1965 believed that their efforts would be rewarded performed better in school than those who took a more fatalistic attitude.

In a paper published a few years after the report came out, Coleman summarized the basic findings of his study this way: "A simple general statement of the major result is that the closest portions of a child's social environment—his family and fellow-students—affect his achievement most, the more distant portion of his social environment—his teachers—affect it next most, and the non-social aspects of his school environment affect it very little."[42]

In general, cultural and psychological factors seem to far outweigh material conditions in promoting educational attainment. New buildings, up-to-date science labs, and well-furnished athletic facilities, all of which are no doubt worthwhile, pale in importance to student and parent social background and school atmosphere, when it comes to promoting educational excellence. The point is not that money doesn't matter, but rather that it matters much less than other factors.

Coleman's research suggests that children's success depends very much on their communities' attitudes toward education. In communities where parents are well educated and are concerned with education, children perform well. A factor here surely is that children with parents who have the desire and ability to help them with homework, and take the effort to assure that homework is done, tend to perform better than children lacking parental involvement. Equally important, especially for minority children, is the world-view that parents inculcate in their children. The attitudes of self-reliance and a faith that hard work, rather than luck or birth, determine one's position in life seem to promote the effort necessary for success. Fatalistic attitudes seem to be self-fulfilling.

Community standards and attitudes also play an important role in reinforcing important family values. When outstanding academic performance is valued and provides status for children, children strive to perform well. In communities that value education, highly qualified teachers are likely to be sought after and retained, and children benefit, especially minority group children. On the other hand, communities in which superior school performance is held up to ridicule, and in which teachers are neither respected nor valued, are likely to find that students do not take education seriously and consequently do not perform very well.

I think it is important to emphasize the fact that children, especially minority children, who are taught the "old-fashioned" American values of self-reliance and the belief that effort counts—values associated with the "Protestant work ethic"—do better than those who feel their fate is not in their own hands. A conclusion one may draw is that the attempt to explain the difficulties of black students in terms of white racism, if it promoted fatalistic attitudes in black children, may have been a very serious impediment to the achievement of those children.

Head Start, though not based in Coleman's research, was conceived on similar premises. Begun in 1965, Head Start seeks to provide additional early educational enrichment to children from impoverished social backgrounds. By providing young children with preparation prior to kindergarten, it seeks to provide poorer children with the sorts of early advantages common in middle-class homes. Unfortunately, the results of the Head Start program have not been very promising. On some measures such as high school drop-out rates, Head Start seems to have modest benefits. On academic and standardized test performance, however, Head Start produces very limited long-term effects. In general, children show improvement for a few years after enrollment in the program, but then fall back to the level of children who had not participated in it. The authors of the authoritative *A Common Destiny: Blacks in American Society* summarized the research on Head Start this way: "Thus, while early intervention at an early age can have a positive impact on achievement, it appears to lose much of its impact over time because of the increasing influence of other factors."[43] It seems that the schools attended by poor blacks are so deficient and their neighborhoods so disordered that they are unable to capitalize on programs such as Head Start. Perhaps it would be wiser to try to make these schools more effective by more directly dealing with the schools themselves. In addition, making poor urban neighborhoods more conducive to educational pursuits might well have an equally positive effect.

VI. Integration and Academic Achievement

The Coleman Report made it very clear that schools reflect the social backgrounds of the students who attend them. Well-educated and concerned parents create conditions for their children's success, and that includes creating good schools for their children. Parents lacking in education often cannot create those conditions, and when the children of many such parents go to school together, they tend to reinforce each other's weaknesses. The lack of widespread advanced education among black parents and other problems common in black communities suggested to Coleman and others that any attempt to create good schools in those communities would be hopelessly handicapped. Integration of black children into white schools seemed the most effective way to bring these children into school environments that Coleman found correlated with academic achievement. White classmates would provide the sort of social environment so often lacking in black schools. Coleman found that black children in middle-class white schools seemed to show higher achievement, although it was difficult to determine if integration was the reason since many of those children may have come from middle-class backgrounds themselves. Nevertheless, Coleman clearly felt that his research supported integration. "The results," Coleman asserted, "clearly suggest that school integration across socioeconomic lines (and hence across racial lines) will increase black achievement."[44]

Coleman's work seemed to confirm the early arguments for school integration in the South that relied heavily on the notion that segregation itself and not unequal funding was detrimental to black education. Psychologist Kenneth Clark had been influential in these arguments. He argued that segregation fostered negative self-images in black children, and that these negative self-images hindered educational success and had other detrimental effects. Clark testified in a 1947 school-desegregation case that "[t]he essence of this detrimental effect is a confusion in the child's concept of his own self-esteem—basic feelings of inferiority, conflict, confusion in his self-image, resentment, hostility towards himself, hostility toward whites." In Clark's view integration was essential to raising self-esteem, and improved self-esteem was essential to improving education.[45]

The Supreme Court, in its famous 1954 *Brown v. Board of Education of Topeka* decision, rejected the doctrine of "separate but equal" and asserted that "modern authority" had "amply supported" the argument that separate education retards the education of black children. Among those cited under the rubric of "modern authority" were Kenneth Clark and Gunnar Myrdal. The argument made was that segregation implied that blacks were inferior and that this, in turn, led to low self-esteem among black children. It was furthermore assumed that low self-esteem undercut educational achievement.[46]

Perhaps Clark's most influential work on this issue was the research he had conducted with his wife, Mamie Clark, showing that black children seemed to prefer white dolls to black ones. The Clarks asserted that this reflected the low self-esteem that racism engendered in black children. The Clarks had found that approximately 60 to 67 percent of the black children they interviewed preferred to play with white dolls rather than black ones, if given the option. These children, when asked, indicated that they thought the white doll was the ''nice doll,'' and thought it a ''nice color.'' Furthermore, the Clarks found that 59 percent of the black children thought the black doll ''looked bad.''[47]

It is extremely difficult to determine just what these results mean. It certainly seems to suggest, as the Clarks claimed, that black children held lower opinions of blacks than they did of whites. It should be pointed out that more-recent studies of this phenomenon produce conflicting results. In some studies black children indicate a preference for black dolls, in other studies they continue to show a preference for white dolls.[48]

Even if we grant that black children who dislike black dolls think poorly of their own race, it is unclear whether holding people in one's own race in low esteem implies that one has lower esteem for oneself. In fact, a study of attitudes sponsored by the U.S. Department of Education in 1988 indicated that of all groups, blacks reported the highest degree of self-esteem. Only 19.2 percent of blacks, compared with 40.4 of whites, were characterized as having a low self-concept. Fully 49.4 percent of blacks, but only 32.8 percent of whites, reported high self-concept. These data suggest that whatever may have been true in the past, it does not appear today that black children suffer low self-esteem in greater proportions than white children; quite the reverse seems to be true.[49]

Furthermore, it is not clear what the relationship is between self-esteem and educational success. Considerable research over the years has failed to clarify this issue. As we saw, Coleman's findings suggested a fairly low correlation between self-esteem and academic achievement among blacks. Nevertheless, most educators have taken it almost for granted, without evidence, that positive self-image is critical for academic success.

Some thought on this issue ought to give one pause. Recently the Mattel Corporation tried to sell its Barbie doll in Japan and thought it would succeed if the doll were given slightly less Western features. The doll flopped. Mattel is thinking of introducing the Western version and hopes to do better in the belief that Japanese girls admire and prefer Western styles and features.[50] Whether Mattel is right on this issue is less important than the fact that few would suggest Japanese schoolchildren's preference for Western things has much to do with their academic performance.

Consider also the fact that in America considerable emphasis is placed on rather idealized images of women, most of which depict women who are unusually slim. Chubby teenage dolls are uncommon in the American market, presumably because young children prefer slender Barbie-type dolls. Considering the popularity of weight-loss programs and books on the topic, it is apparent that most young women in America would rather be slim than obese, and those who are obese may indeed suffer to some extent a negative self-image as a result of their obesity. While it is certainly worthy of examination, there is at present no evidence that obesity is an important factor in, for example, SAT performance.

This is not to denigrate the importance of self-esteem, or to deny the unhappiness caused to those who suffer from poor self-images. Rather, it is to question the relevance of self-esteem to academic success. The point is that while such a relation is certainly plausible, the relation lacks substantive empirical support and on its face seems to contradict everyday experience.

If the idea that heightened self-esteem would improve educational achievement was on shaky ground from the start, the idea that integration would lead to heightened self-esteem was on even shakier ground. Given the educational and social differences between the average black student and the average white student, integration should, logically, have allowed for more, not fewer, bases for unfavorable comparisons between blacks and whites. Gordon W. Allport, in his widely read *The Nature of Prejudice,* had argued that integrating individuals of equal status could improve race relations. "Prejudice . . . may be reduced by equal status contact between majority and minority groups in the pursuit of common goals."[51] However, he also argued that integration of people of unequal status might make things worse.[52] The hoped-for beneficial effect of school integration depended, at least from Allport's perspective, upon the bringing together of black and white children who could compete equally, and this condition was rarely met in integrated public schools.

Whatever the theoretical basis, by the late 1960s the federal government committed itself to massive efforts to integrate education. While these efforts were often successful, more often they led to the common phenomenon of white flight that left the schools in the largest cities of America even more segregated, in many cases, than they had been before the efforts were attempted. Since the original thinking that promoted integration as a solution to black educational problems is still widely accepted, strenuous efforts to increase integration continue to be made, sometimes at the expense of alternative methods to improve black performance.

Unfortunately, the bulk of research on the effects of integration where it has taken place suggest that by itself integration does not contribute much to black school achievement. In a report to the state legislature of Massachusetts in 1976, Coleman concluded that his earlier optimistic hopes for the effects of integration had been misdirected, since surveys of integrated schools could find no appreciable improvement in black achievement. Furthermore, improved overall social integration, an important goal thought to be aided by school integration, was in fact hindered by it. Coleman argued, based on a study of integration during the period from 1968 to 1973, that the massive busing in large cities had only served to drive whites into suburbs to avoid sending their children to majority-black schools. The net effect was less school integration, and less social integration as well, since the center cities came to be increasingly black enclaves surrounded by growing white suburbs. Only in the South did school integration actually increase during this period. Coleman urged the legislature to adopt noncoercive means to encourage educational integration in such a way as not to increase general social segregation between the races. In recent years many communities have followed Coleman in this regard. One of his suggestions, the creation of what we now call "magnet schools," has been widely implemented.[53] These are regional schools with special programs, such as programs in science or the arts, designed to be attractive to students with special interests or abilities from all races and social classes.

In any case, even where integration was successfully achieved it did not seem to have an important effect on black achievement or self-esteem. Walter G. Stephan reviewed a large number of studies on the impact of integration in a well-regarded 1978 report. He found that integration did not, as had been predicted, increase black self-esteem. In ten published studies that he reviewed, seven reported no difference in the self-esteem of black students in segregated as opposed to integrated schools. In the remaining three studies, however, black self-esteem was in fact reported to be lower in the integrated schools. It is instructive that not one study (including ten additional unpublished reports he reviewed) reported higher black self-esteem in integrated settings.[54]

Stephan also found that integration had little effect on white attitudes toward blacks. The effect of integration on black attitudes toward whites, however, was sometimes to make them more positive, but just as often to make them more negative.[55]

Black academic performance did seem to benefit from integration, but only on occasion and only modestly. Stephan reported that in nine of the fifteen studies he reviewed in which performance was assessed, there was no improvement stemming from integration. Six of the studies reported some improvement, but in many of these studies the results were ambiguous.[56]

More recently, in 1984, the National Institute of Education commissioned a report on desegregation to specifically study its impact on black academic achievement. Thomas D. Cook and six other respected scholars took part and analyzed nineteen studies selected for their value in addressing the issue of the impact of integration on black academic performance. Cook concluded that while there appeared to be no negative effects on achievement, integration had only very modest positive effects. He found no measurable improvement in mathematics performance, for instance. There did seem to be an improvement in reading performance, but based on the empirical data, this improvement amounted to only "somewhere between .06 and .16 of a standard deviation."[57] Herbert J. Walberg, who contributed to the study, concluded in his section of the report that "school desegregation does not appear to prove promising in the size or consistency of its effects on the learning of black students . . ." when compared to other strategies.[58] While even the small improvement in black performance in integrated schools is important, it seems woefully inadequate when compared to the effort, expenditure, and social disruption that desegregation caused, especially in the major cities of the North, which in the end, left those schools more segregated than they had been at the outset. Had those energies gone into the simpler task of attempting to improve the education of black children directly, more success might have been achieved.

This is not to suggest that integration is not an important goal. In a pluralistic nation it is. It is to suggest, rather, that integration cannot, by itself, overcome other obstacles to academic success. The key to better achievement, following Coleman, seems to be the social climate of the school created by a middle-class student body and not the race, per se, of the student body. If the social climate of the school is determined by children from lower-class backgrounds, as is often the case in urban schools, education is likely to deteriorate, and middle-class parents, both black and white, will desert such schools. Research which will be reviewed shortly suggests that an effective school climate can be achieved for lower-class children, but that it has to be implemented from above. Too often the climate of urban schools is set by the children who attend them, and as a consequence, these schools cannot overcome the deficits such children bring from their homes and neighborhoods.

This is consistent with the findings of Thomas Sowell, who has documented many cases where assimilation into middle-class values and outstanding academic performance occurred in completely segregated black schools. He attributes this to the serious academic climate fostered in these schools.[59] David Armor's argument concerning the recent rise in black NAEP test scores (discussed earlier, in Section I) also reinforces this interpretation. He found that black children in integrated schools did not gain more than those in segregated schools. In fact, those in segregated settings actually gained more relative to whites than did those in integrated schools. As I noted earlier, Armor concluded that these improvements are best explained by the gains in black parents' socioeconomic status that put them in a better position to assist their children to achieve academically.[60] As more blacks enter the middle class, one can expect that this will translate into more-favorable social climates in schools attended by blacks, whether those schools are segregated or not. If Armor is correct, it follows that as more blacks enter the middle class, whatever value integration has for academic performance will in time diminish.

Before leaving the topic of school desegregation, it is worthwhile to review an intensive observational study of an integrated school so as to better understand why integration often fails to produce more desirable results. Janet Ward Schofield, of Columbia University Teachers College, spent three years studying the workings of a new school set up in such a way as to create a favorable setting for integration. Her interest focused on the impact of integration on interpersonal relations rather than on academic achievement.[61]

The study began during the first year of the school's operation in 1975. The school, referred to by the fictitious name of Wexler Middle School (to protect the anonymity of the participants) was located in a large, industrial city in the northeast. This city had, according to Schofield, "a rich variety of ethnic groups." One-quarter of the city's population was black. The school itself was designed to attract students and was extremely well-appointed physically. Students applied to the school voluntarily and were admitted on a first-come, first-served basis within guidelines to assure that about equal numbers of blacks and whites attended.[62]

A problem that Schofield detected fairly early in her study was the wide gap in academic preparation between the races. Black students on average fell about one standard deviation below the whites on standardized ability tests. Schofield writes: "This difference was clearly reflected in the students' grades." She reported that on a typical math test in a class that was "routinely observed, almost fifty percent of the white students received A's, compared with about seven percent of the black students." She also reports that of the sixty-eight students who were honored for obtaining straight A averages during the first year, only eight were black, while sixty were white.[63]

The obvious disparities in performance were well known by black and white students alike and created considerable tension between the races. The performance gap tended to foster, according to Schofield, "the belief that whites are brighter and more interested in learning than blacks." These beliefs were held by black and white students alike. In addition, blacks sometimes resented the superior performance of whites, whom they sometimes viewed as arrogant and conceited. Some blacks expressed the opinion that whites performed well merely to impress others and sometimes to humiliate blacks. Fairly early, according to Schofield, "whiteness became associated with success."[64]

A second source of difficulty was that blacks were seen by both races as more disruptive in class and more physically aggressive than whites, while whites were viewed as more rule-abiding and more physically restrained.

Blacks developed the reputation of being more willing to use force to intimidate others, while whites were seen as weak and unwilling to defend themselves when threatened. Schofield reports that white males had an especially difficult time and expressed a considerable amount of fear in their day-to-day activities at the school. Schofield suggests that blacks may have been more aggressive in their relations with whites as a way of compensating for their inferior academic performance.[65]

Whatever the motives, both black and white students came to see "blacks as physically tougher than whites and inclined to use this toughness to defend themselves and to dominate others."[66] These attitudes reflected behavioral differences between the races. Over 80 percent of the suspensions at Wexler involved black students. Schofield makes the point that even when black students engaged in what they thought were acts of friendly teasing, white students often interpreted these actions as intimidating.

Because of these achievement and behavioral differences, there was relatively little social mixing in nonacademic activities. Blacks and whites tended to choose friends from among their own race. Very little mixing took place, for instance, in the school cafeteria. It is interesting to note that Schofield found less social integration among the girls than among the boys. Girls tended to engage in intimate discussions with friends and were therefore less likely to cross racial lines during their free time. Boys more often engaged in team sports, which by their nature tend to foster greater interracial interaction.[67]

It should be stressed that Wexler was designed to create good conditions for integrated schooling. Teachers and administrators were anxious for the school to succeed. Since attendance at the school was voluntary, it seems reasonable to assume that parents were in general supportive of the school's goals. Over time, during the three years the school was observed, there did appear to be an overall improvement in racial relations, reflected, according to Schofield, in a greater number of interracial friendships. Surprisingly, the improved atmosphere did not result from changed perceptions. Attitudes, in fact, hardly changed at all.[68] Whites still tended to see blacks as more aggressive, and blacks continued to think of whites as conceited. Schofield thinks that better relations came about because both races became more sensitive to individual differences over time, and came to know and like particular individuals. She also says that relations improved because the fears among whites of blacks declined as "they developed techniques for reducing or handling their fear."[69] Whites came, in time, to know which blacks were truly hostile and which were merely having fun in a physical way. Whites also learned to avoid confrontations with blacks by, for instance, avoiding areas like washrooms that were unsupervised by adults. In some cases more-timid whites learned the value of standing up to intimidation.[70]

One interesting sidelight here is that during the three-year period of the study, the television miniseries *Roots* was aired. The miniseries, which traces the history of blacks in America, tended to exacerbate racial tensions since, according to Schofield, "black children who saw the series tried to get back at whites for the historical oppression of blacks which it demonstrated."[71]

The conclusion one must reach from Schofield's observations and from a fairly large literature on the effects of desegregation is that integration, by itself, does not appear to dramatically improve race relations or change negative attitudes about out-groups, especially when those attitudes are confirmed by experience. White students who attended Wexler developed a set of attitudes toward blacks, often negative, even if they held no such attitudes at the outset. If they already had such attitudes, their experience at Wexler merely reinforced them. It could hardly be otherwise when even black students' attitudes reflected the actual behavior and performance of the black students. The experience of Wexler also makes clear why black children's self-esteem is not likely to improve through integration. Blacks performed less well than whites, and blacks and whites both thought this reflected less ability on the part of blacks.

Integration does appear to be correlated with modest improvements in black educational performance, but it is unclear whether far greater improvements could not be achieved by simply trying to improve the educational climate in all schools, whether integrated or not.

VII. Effective Schools

The Coleman Report suggested that academic achievement depended more on the social background of students than on any particular characteristic of the schools themselves. It was certainly the case that good schools tended to have a different atmosphere than ineffective schools, but this climate in turn seemed merely to reflect the values and abilities of the students attending them. This in turn seemed to imply an insoluble conundrum. Good education was a prime ingredient for black socioeconomic advancement, but how could schools be created to provide effective education so long as black parents languished socioeconomically? The dilemma was only heightened by the fact that schools were extremely difficult to integrate and, when integrated, did not seem to produce better outcomes for blacks.

A consequence of this pessimistic assessment was a concerted effort on the part of educational researchers to see if more effective schools could in fact be created for children from impoverished backgrounds. One of the earliest efforts in this regard was undertaken by Coleman himself, who examined the differences between Catholic and public schools.[72]

In one report authored by Thomas Hoffer and Andrew Greeley, together with Coleman, the authors found that Catholic school students performed significantly better than public school students, especially among minority children and those from disadvantaged backgrounds. The Catholic schools were more effective in spite of the fact that, according to the authors, the Catholic schools "had larger classes, less professional teacher training, more limited resources, smaller per-pupil costs and religious narrowness. . . ." Hoffer, Greeley, and Coleman attributed the advantage of the Catholic schools to a more disciplined and more highly structured school environment, to the greater demands placed on children attending Catholic schools, and to the higher expectations for their achievement. The authors concluded that these factors are especially important for minority youngsters. Public schools, they asserted, are especially harmful to the least-advantaged students because of "their lack of structure, lower demands and lower expectations."[73]

A growing body of literature has, over the last decade, tended to confirm in a general way the views of Coleman and his coauthors. This "effective-schools" literature was analyzed in an important review by Stewart Purkey and Marshall Smith.[74] The authors comment rather ironically that what emerges from this literature is a new respect for older "tried and true" methods of education, and they suggest that a "partial return to yesteryear may be more than an exercise in nostalgia." They go on to say that "[i]ndeed, there is a remarkable and somewhat disturbing resemblance between the traditional view of schools as serious, work-oriented, and disciplined institutions where students were supposed to learn their three R's and the emerging view of the modern effective school."[75]

Among those characteristics that seem important in creating an effective school are clear goals and high expectations for students, and an orderly school and a disciplined student body. Purkey and Smith point out that "common sense alone suggests that students cannot learn in an environment that is noisy, distracting or unsafe." A positive school climate is usually correlated with collegial relations among staff and a sense of community among all those involved in school activities. It is also correlated with stable staff, clearly articulated goals for the school, parental involvement, and an emphasis on and recognition of academic excellence.[76]

It follows directly from the above that rules and regulations that make it difficult to discipline children or remove disruptive students from schools make it much more difficult to create an effective school environment. Ironically, many of the regulations governing school authorities and teachers, especially in inner-city schools, were put in place as a result of charges that effective disciplinary measures unfairly targeted black youngsters. Whether the charges were true or not, the net result has been that urban black schools have become increasingly disorderly places.

A study sponsored by the liberal Brookings Institution and carried out by John Chubb and Terry Moe resulted in the 1990 report *Politics, Markets, and America's Schools.*[77] The authors undertook a major review of the effective-schools literature and echo most of the conclusions of the other authors I have discussed. Chubb and Moe emphasize, as did earlier researchers, that effective schools have a high degree of local autonomy. It is the greater autonomy and freedom from central bureaucracies, in their view, that enable private and parochial schools to establish the sort of educational environment and school organization best suited to the student bodies they serve.

Chubb and Moe found that the bureaucratic control common to large urban school districts hampers administrators and teachers from applying the experience they have gathered regarding what is effective for their own students. The net result is that the students in these schools fail to benefit from that experience. The point is that not all student bodies are the same and that trying to treat them the same is a great hindrance to successful education. The authors acknowledge that in smaller suburban school districts, local public schools often have a high degree of autonomy, and that is why, along with an often highly motivated and capable student body, they tend to perform well.[78]

Chubb and Moe conclude that since school autonomy is so important, no significant improvement in education, especially in inner-city education, is likely without it. They also conclude that such autonomy is impossible to achieve in centrally controlled, bureaucratically administered school systems. Such systems must satisfy such a broad range of parents and teachers and students, that they cannot possibly allow individual schools to tailor an environment that is most likely to be effective for the particular students they are trying to educate. As a consequence, Chubb and Moe urge an almost unrestricted policy of school choice based on educational vouchers or scholarships to be applied to any public or private school a child wishes to attend. In addition, they believe that schools should be free to select students on any set of criteria as long as they do not practice illegal discrimination.[79]

An interesting innovation they suggest is that disadvantaged students be given larger scholarships to make them more attractive to the schools to which they apply. Some schools may specialize in "gifted" children, but some may spring up to deal with slower learners, or those with behavioral problems.[80] In the Chubb and Moe plan, parents would have the freedom to choose those schools that prove they can work with their children, that is, provide them with the skills and habits parents wish their children to obtain. Of course, some parents may not much care where their children attend school, and as a consequence those children may not be well served, but they will hardly be any worse off than they are in urban schools today.

Furthermore, older youngsters themselves are likely to have a say in where they choose to apply their scholarships or vouchers. Older children may make wiser choices than uncaring parents or parents who are unfamiliar with educational practices, a not uncommon phenomenon among recent immigrants. Chubb and Moe's plan has much to recommend it, not least of which is that it is well-reasoned and based on solid empirical grounds, something that cannot be said for the many other proposals to improve the nation's educational performance, especially its dismal performance with many minority children.

It is worth reiterating that a universal finding in this literature is that effective schools must be orderly schools. In suburban school districts serving largely middle-class youngsters, the means necessary to maintain order are likely to be very different from the means necessary in an urban school inhabited by youngsters from underclass backgrounds. Chubb and Moe recognize these differences and the different responses that may be required. In the typical suburban school, merely threatening a student with citing an infraction on his school record may be a devastating threat to the future aspirations of a college-bound student. In an inner-city school, such a threat may be all but meaningless, especially to an unruly adolescent who may already have a record at the police department, let alone in the principal's office. To insist that disciplinary methods be uniform in both circumstances is to guarantee that the urban child who wishes to learn and move upward is thwarted by those who have the desire for neither and who, because of lax discipline, are allowed to interfere with the learning of everyone around them.

VIII. Teacher Expectations

Most research on effective schools has found, as we have seen, that such schools place high demands on and have high expectations for their students. This is sometimes interpreted to mean that any realistic assessment of student ability is likely to harm the education of those thought to possess lower ability. On such grounds "tracking" according to ability is often disparaged. But what the effective-schools literature, in fact, reveals is that in better schools teachers have higher expectations and make greater demands on all students, whatever their ability. Such an attitude does not at all imply a belief that children do not differ in ability.

Often there is a confusion in the meaning of "expectations." The effective-schools literature defines expectations in terms of the work expected or demanded of students, not in the sense of a teacher's "predictions" about student performance. This second definition is the one meant in the claim that black children lag behind whites because teachers, especially white teachers, have lower expectations for their black students. This argument could not, of course, explain the problems in southern schools where black children are most commonly taught by black teachers, unless black teachers also have lower expectations.

The idea that teacher expectations, in the sense of predictions of future performance, greatly affect student outcomes is based in large measure on a famous experiment conducted in the 1960s by Robert Rosenthal and Lenore Jacobson and reported, among other places, in an oft-quoted *Scientific American* article "Teacher Expectations for the Disadvantaged" and in their influential book *Pygmalion in the Classroom.*[81] This research seemed to answer in the affirmative the question posed by the researchers: "Have the schools failed the children by anticipating their poor performance and thus in effect teaching them to fail?"[82] As will become clear, the authors' assertion that teachers' expectations have an important impact on children's performance comes perilously close to being a scientific hoax.

The research took place in an elementary school serving a lower socioeconomic neighborhood in San Francisco. An IQ test was administered to all children in grades one through six in the spring before the start of the next school year. In each grade there were three classes, so that there were eighteen classes in all. At the beginning of the school year teachers were given the results of the test taken in the spring and were told that it was a test that detected children expected to "spurt" academically. In each class, 20 percent of the students, chosen at random, were identified as "spurters," who the teachers were told "would show considerable academic improvement during the year."[83]

Rosenthal and Jacobson reported that at the end of the year all the students were retested for IQ and those who had been labeled spurters showed an improvement in IQ greater than the others. Since the only difference between the spurters and the other students was in their faked likelihood of showing growth, the improvement was attributed to teacher expectations. The improvement, however, was quite small, amounting to a difference between the two groups, overall, of four IQ points.[84] Rosenthal and Jacobson did not report on this modest overall difference in their *Scientific American* article, but instead highlighted the sizable improvement in the two lowest grades.

In fact, all of the improvement in IQ was accounted for by the difference in grades one and two; there was no statistically significant difference between experimental and control students in grades three and four or five and six.[85] Furthermore, a year later the effect had evaporated. Rosenthal and Jacobson speculate that "[p]erhaps the younger children, who by then had different teachers, needed continued contact with the teachers who had influenced them in order to maintain their improved performance.[86]

Richard Snow, a research psychologist then at Stanford University, in reviewing Rosenthal and Jacobson's full-length report in their book *Pygmalion in the Classroom,* was very direct in his analysis of the problems with the research. Quoting Snow:

It is the considered opinion of this reviewer that the research would have been judged unacceptable if submitted to an APA [American Psychological Association] journal in its present form. Despite its award-winning experimental design, the study suffers from serious measurement problems and inadequate data analysis. Its reporting, furthermore, appears to violate Rosenthal's own earlier admonitions to experimenters and stands as a casebook of many of Darrell Huff's (*How to Lie with Statistics*) admonitions to data analysts.[87]

Among the problems Snow cited was the use of a particular test of intelligence that, according to Snow, "does not have adequate norms for the youngest children, especially for children from lower socioeconomic backgrounds." Furthermore, the teachers administered the test themselves, which "adds considerable uncertainty about standardization of procedure." Indicative of the test's problems was the fact that the first-grade students who had been tested in kindergarten had an average reasoning IQ of 58, far below the expected average of 100. Snow asks if it is reasonable to suppose that "these children were functioning at imbecile and low moron levels?" "More likely," suggests Snow, "the test was not functioning at this age level." For children to score that low, according to Snow, suggests that they answered the questions in "a random or systematically incorrect" way.[88] In other words, the test was in all likelihood not a valid measure of IQ for young children. Not surprisingly, the children's individual scores changed enormously from one year to the next. One student's scores rose from 17 to 148, another's from 18 to 122.[89] In other words, the variation in the lower grades could easily have been explained by the fact that the test, in being invalid with young children, was not reliably measuring anything. Since all the supposed teacher-expectation effect occurred among the first and second graders, one must conclude that there probably was no effect at all.

Today, some introductory psychology texts do not even discuss the teacher-expectation effect, even though the phenomenon was widely discussed and praised at the time in the popular media and continues to be used to bolster the claim that low expectations, especially of white teachers for black students, can hold children down. The public would probably have been more cautious if reporting in the media had made clear just how weak the case for the phenomenon was and that it failed to last into the second year. The kindest thing one can say of the original finding was that it may have been a fluke. It is, however, hard to be kind about the way the study was reported. Snow charges Rosenthal and Jacobson with performing a disservice to teachers and schools for "inadequately and prematurely" reporting their results in the popular media.[90]

According to respected social psychologist Roger Brown, there have been over a hundred studies conducted in an effort to replicate the original effect. By and large, these studies have demonstrated that teachers' expectations can be unwittingly communicated to students, but that the impact of such expectations appears to be very limited. Brown does allow that they seem to "produce modest effects," but goes on to say:

> Teachers' expectancies are not shaped once and for all by a single test score. ... The most important limitation on what can be accomplished by manipulating expectancies is, of course, the day-to-day reality of student performance. Teachers adjust their expectancies in response to student performance, and prior performance affects the credibility of attempts to create new expectancies.[91]

Put another way, teachers may have low expectations for a child but readily adjust those estimates depending on what the child actually does. In other words, it is primarily the student's actual performance that shapes the teacher's expectations and not the other way around. In any case, it is clear that the effect of teacher expectations is woefully inadequate to explain the problems black students face in school.

It is interesting in this context to point out that when children are themselves asked about their relationships with teachers, black children respond more favorably than do whites. Among eighth graders asked in 1988 whether "[t]eachers praise my efforts when I work hard," 72.1 percent of black students responded affirmatively, compared to 60.3 percent of white students. When asked whether "[t]eachers listen to what I have to say," 73.2 percent of black students and 67.1 percent of white students responded in the affirmative.[92]

IX. Afrocentric Education

Part of the widespread, but misguided, appeal of the Rosenthal/Jacobson findings was the common assumption that white teachers, in particular, had low expectations for black children. It is commonly argued, for that reason, that black children are best taught by black teachers. The premise that black children need black teachers is highly suspect on its face and is unsupported by research findings. Why black children cannot learn from white instructors but Asian children, for instance, seem to flourish under those same teachers is an important question that is rarely addressed by those who make the criticism.

Sometimes the argument in favor of black teachers for black children takes the form of an argument that black children need black role models. Closely related is the argument that American education is Eurocentric and fails to provide black children with the ethnic pride needed for academic success. The argument rests on the notion that self-esteem is essential for academic success, and in addition makes the claim that ethnic pride is essential to individual self-esteem. The evidence reviewed earlier (in Section VI) suggests that black children do not suffer from low self-esteem, and in fact seem to fare far better in that regard than do white children.

Pulitzer prize winning historian Arthur Schlesinger, Jr., in *The Disuniting of America,* discusses the movement to inculcate an Afrocentric perspective in the education of urban black children.[93] This movement has gained momentum in recent years in the school systems in some large cities. One of the primary assertions of the Afrocentrists is that ancient Egypt was a black African civilization and Egypt was in turn the source of most Western ideas. The West is said to have stolen its most important ideas from Africa.[94] Afrocentric education, as commonly promulgated, fails to make the distinction between North African Semitic cultures and sub-Saharan African black cultures. Black children are thus taught that Egyptian culture is their true ethnic and cultural heritage.[95]

The idea behind this movement seems to be that black children's self-esteem will be improved by the knowledge that most great ideas are of black African origins. A corollary to this notion is that traditional ''Eurocentric'' education has a stifling effect on black children since it denies the role of black Africans in world history.

In New York State these ideas were introduced into the curriculum under the guise of multiculturalism. This doctrine argues that the older melting-pot model of assimilation cannot work with blacks and other nonwhite ethnic groups, and that therefore all ethnic groups must be taught to value and preserve their own cultural heritage. Schlesinger sat on the New York State task force on curricular revision that made this recommendation. Schlesinger cites the task force for its view that ''the systematic bias toward European culture and its derivatives has a terribly damaging effect on the psyche of young people of African, Asian, Latino and Native American descent.'' This Eurocentric bias is thought to explain ''why large numbers of children of non-European descent are not doing as well as expected.''[96] Of course, it ignores the fact that children of Asian descent are doing quite well in New York schools.

The idea that Egypt was a black African society is supported by very little accepted scholarship. Schlesinger asks, reasonably, if the self-esteem of black children will be improved when they ''grow up and learn that many of the things the Afrocentrists have taught them are not true.''[97] There is no scholarly evidence that instructing people in an inflated and erroneous image of their ancestors will help them to do better in today's world. Schlesinger points out that knowledge of Roman glory seemed to have no positive effect on the academic achievement of children of Italian descent, even though Roman glory was highlighted in history texts.[98] In fact, Italians lagged behind other ethnic groups in educational attainment in the first half of this century.[99]

If anything, logic suggests that the emphasis on Afrocentric education may be thoroughly counterproductive, at least insofar as education is concerned. If Sowell is right that academic progress for the children of ethnic parents is fostered by assimilation into the larger culture, anything that impedes black assimilation into middle-class culture also impedes the normal improvement in academic aptitude that is the expected byproduct of that assimilation. That, of course, was why Coleman and others urged the integration of the schools.

Of course, Sowell may be wrong and the academic improvement of earlier ethnic groups may not have been a product of their assimilation into mainstream culture. Perhaps the causation was the other way around; as academic performance improved (for whatever reason) assimilation was the natural result. Perhaps the causation works both ways. Certainly, to the extent that assimilation implies adoption of American middle-class values, it also implies an increased emphasis on education as a means for advancement.

If, as so much of the literature on schooling suggests, parental and community attitudes are crucial to children's success, the current black interest in emphasizing ''blackness'' and ''African identity'' in children, while understandable as a means of bolstering group pride, may have unexpectedly negative consequences for black education. This is especially the case if black children come to associate ''white'' with ''middle class,'' and if in their desire to be truly and authentically ''black,'' they feel it necessary to reject white attitudes and values—in particular, middle-class attitudes and values.

That there is an association in the minds of some black children between being white and being middle class is illustrated in a very disturbing report in *Time* on the social difficulties black inner-city children face when they take education seriously, work hard, and show above-average performance. *Time* reports that these children sometimes face ostracism, intimidation, ridicule, and harassment from their schoolmates for ''acting white.'' Some black gangs purposely target superior students with physical violence for ''betraying their race.''[100]

Such attitudes are not so surprising when in many militant black circles ''middle-class values'' are often disparagingly equated with ''white'' values. To the extent that the black separatist agenda postpones assimilation, it may have taken the place of racial discrimination as the most potent enemy, today, of the educational advancement of black children.

An additional unfortunate consequence of the new concern with Afrocentric education is the concomitant tendency to disparage European history and science, philosophy and literature. The disparaging of Western culture is at best merely gratuitous; one can point to successful members of one's own group and the virtues of one's own ethnicity without explicitly denigrating others. At worst, the attack on Western culture by black activists, reinforced by various disaffected academics, has the effect of further alienating white Americans from black Americans.

Harmony between the races is not improved by teaching black children that whites harbor a centuries-old animus toward Africans. Nor is racial harmony aided by teaching black children that Americans and Europeans continue to exploit blacks, although more subtly than in the days of slavery, and that whites consciously distort African intellectual contributions in order to deny blacks their rightful place in history.

If large numbers of blacks come to accept these distortions of history, racial harmony and racial integration will be further postponed. The educational prospects of black children are likely to suffer if their understanding of history diverges from what is generally accepted. What is one to make of the education of a black child who is taught that the conquest of Egypt, first by the Macedonians and later by the Romans, and more recently by the British, was motivated by the same anti-black attitudes that produced apartheid in modern-day South Africa? On the inculcation of such false ideas, Schlesinger says: "If some Kleagle of the Ku Klux Klan wanted to devise an educational curriculum for the specific purpose of handicapping and disabling black Americans he would not be likely to come up with anything more diabolically effective than Afrocentrism."[101]

It is hard to know how seriously the arguments for Afrocentric education are taken by those who put them forward. There can be no doubt that some believe, mistakenly, that these ideas will build black pride and thereby improve their children's education. On the other hand, it may also be the case that some use the false claim of historical deceptions about African contributions for the demagogic purpose of fanning racial animosity. Whatever the case, these ideas have no prospect of improving black educational attainment or the self-esteem, in the long run, of those who are misled.

X. Conclusion

The educational problems that blacks face and that are accurately reflected in standardized tests are vexing indeed. The truth of the matter is that nobody has the definitive answer or answers as to why black children have these problems with education. It is critical to stress, however, that even if we knew the answers, it would little change the strategies necessary for optimally educating black children. All children, if they are to perform at their best, require orderly families, orderly communities, and orderly schools. Things that create disorder in children's lives make it less likely that they will perform at their best.

While I noted earlier that black children express positive feelings toward their teachers, they are considerably less positive about their schools. According to the U.S. Department of Education, 18 percent of black eighth graders reported that they did not feel safe at their schools, while only 9.9 percent of white children felt that way. Fully 54.9 percent of black students and 35.7 percent of white students felt that "[d]isruptions by other students interfere with my learning." This response was most common among poorer children. This is a powerful reason why inner-city black children do not perform as well as their middle-class white counterparts.[102]

The continuing charge of white racism has the effect of obscuring the truly debilitating effects of the conditions of underclass life and of inner-city schools. It has the unfortunate effect of undercutting efforts to help improve these conditions. Even if in some fundamental sense it could be demonstrated that white racism is at the root of these problems, what strategies does that knowledge provide? After assigning blame, we are still left with children in jeopardy. All too many people seem to take the position that once blame has been assigned, the situation requires no further attention—or that assigning blame will somehow, by itself, solve things.

By now it should be abundantly clear that such is not the case. Whatever level of racism still exists in American society, we may have reached the point of diminishing marginal return in trying to stamp it out. However important or unimportant racism continues to be, there are no new tactics on the horizon that are likely to be effective in further diminishing it. Social policy designed to improve black education by targeting racism is, today, a policy of despair. It wastes resources on a goal unlikely to be achieved while ignoring extremely important factors that are achievable and that are likely to have a profound and salutary effect.

We should not forget Coleman's finding that while black children's self-esteem did not seem important to educational success, black children's belief in the efficacy of their own efforts was very important indeed. The continual claim that educational failure is the fault of white racist society is a lesson in fatalism and, for the children who take it seriously, a recipe for personal failure.

Orderly schools and neighborhoods are obviously not the only important avenues to pursue in the attempt to improve the education of black children. But it is most emphatically the case that no improvement is possible without these things. Whatever new and fruitful ideas are brought forward by educational research, none of them can possibly have any impact until they can be implemented in safe and orderly schools in safe and orderly neighborhoods. In the concluding chapter of this book, I will attempt to outline how such goals might be achieved. For now, it is enough to point out that the failure to address the issues of order and discipline in schools has the effect of making it impossible for most black underclass children, no matter how much they might struggle, to climb out of the disabling circumstances to which they are currently consigned.

10

Illegitimacy

I. Introduction

Disordered communities beset by crime create other problems that feed back synergistically to increase the magnitude of the disorder in those communities. A sort of behavioral whirlpool develops out of which it is difficult for any single individual to extricate himself and even more difficult for individuals or even groups to take corrective actions to reverse the downward spiral.

As outlined in the last chapter, educational failure is one result of neighborhood disorder that serves to further exacerbate the problems found there. This chapter discusses illegitimacy, which I argue is also an effect of the chaotic conditions of underclass life, and it too is part effect and part cause of those conditions. Unwed motherhood, as a byproduct of underclass turmoil, is the most important proximate cause of the wide income disparities between black and white families. It is simply not possible for single-parent, one-earner families, on average, to achieve the same degree of economic well-being as more conventional two-parent, two-earner families. It is the thrust of what follows that one of the salutary effects of establishing order in the inner cities would be a marked decline in single parenthood and a consequent decline in the poverty that so often accompanies it.

The focus of this chapter is on the sources of illegitimacy rather than the larger phenomenon of single parenthood, which results from divorce and widowhood as well as unwed motherhood. The reason for this is that rates of divorce and widowhood as sources of single-parent families among blacks are not much in excess of what they are among whites. In 1990, 11.2 percent of black women and 8.6 percent of white women were divorced. Exactly the same percentage, 11.6 percent, of white and black women were widowed. These statistics clearly indicate that the much greater percentage of single-parent families among blacks when compared to whites is primarily produced by markedly higher rates of illegitimacy among blacks than among whites. Furthermore, as will become clear, single parenthood is most damaging for young women, especially those who have not completed their schooling or who have failed to obtain steady employment. Divorce and widowhood are inconsequential causes of single parenthood for young black and white women alike. Only 1.7 percent of white women and 0.9 percent of black women between fifteen and twenty-five years old were divorced in 1990. Widowhood in this age group is too low to be reported for black women and is 0.1 percent for white women. Clearly if white and black women had similar rates of unwed motherhood, differences between the composition of black and white families would be very limited. Single parenthood would still be a problem, but it would be of limited usefulness in explaining the differences (such as differences in income) between whites and blacks.[1]

Family breakdown as a major source of black economic and social difficulties is no longer seriously in dispute. Social scientists as ideologically diverse as the conservative Charles Murray and the liberal William Julius Wilson are in agreement on this point, though they differ in their explanations for the dissolution of the underclass family.[2]

While there is considerable disagreement about the impact of father absence per se on children's development, there is widespread agreement that communities that contain many families lacking male providers eventually evolve into those we have come to label "underclass." The glaring absence of fathers in the homes of poor underclass families is perhaps the most telling indicator of their underclass status. Neighborhoods in which biological fathers are present and contribute to the care of their children rarely exhibit the sorts of social pathology so common in underclass areas.

If black marriage patterns were more similar to white patterns, it is safe to say that the "race problem" would be cast in an altogether different light, and might in fact cease to be a problem that needed explaining. Black families would have incomes similar to white families, as two-parent black families currently do. Crime would probably be reduced and educational deficiencies would certainly be less severe. Whatever difficulties blacks as a statistical group now have, almost all would greatly diminish if black families exhibited the stability common in the larger population.

It is important to note the extraordinary degree of black family dissolution and the degree to which it has worsened in recent years. Black families have traditionally been less stable than white families, but very high rates of illegitimacy and single-parent families among blacks are a relatively recent development. The relative instability of black families earlier in this century is most easily explained in terms of historically high poverty rates among blacks. Poor families are in general less stable than those better off.

Some have argued that the slave system, in which husbands, wives, and children were sometimes taken from each other and sold off to new owners in distant places, may be partially a cause of this instability. This cruel practice, however, did not appear to reduce the commitment of blacks to the family as an institution. Historian Herbert Gutman argues that there is "no evidence whatsoever" that black family instability was a legacy of slavery. Based on data for blacks in the South in 1900, he found that the length and stability of black marriages were hardly different from whites in similar areas. After reviewing data from the rural South and urban North, he concluded that between 1880 and the 1930s, "the typical Afro-American family was lower-class in status and headed by two parents." Gutman analyzed data for Harlem in 1905 and 1925 and found that the single-parent home headed by a woman with many children "was relatively insignificant." In fact, he found that only 3 percent of all families "were male-absent and headed by a woman under thirty."[3] Clearly the current instability of black families is a recent development.

According to census data, in 1950 approximately 17 percent of all black births were to single women. That figure has risen rather steadily since then and reached 64 percent by 1989. Illegitimacy rates have been rising among whites as well, but from a much lower level. Between 1950 and 1989, the illegitimacy rate among whites rose from 6 percent to 19 percent in 1989.[4] It is instructive to note that the current figure for white illegitimate births is almost the same as was the black figure in 1950. Had black illegitimacy remained constant, in other words, it would be at a par with the white rate today. The point is that while an illegitimacy rate of 19 percent is surely a cause of concern, it is in no sense a comparable cause of concern as the current black rate of 64 percent.

Illegitimacy is most common among young women. Thirty-two percent of out-of-wedlock births are to women under twenty years of age, and 67 percent are to women under twenty-five.[5] The dramatic rise in out-of-wedlock births does not appear to be the result of any major change in sexual activity. Fertility rates for black women have actually declined over the years.[6] This decline is, of course, partly the effect of the availability of abortion and oral contraception. In 1988, for every 1,000 live births there were 638 abortions among blacks and other nonwhites (compared to 335 per 1,000 live births for white women).[7] The major change producing high illegitimacy rates is in the marital behavior of black men and women. In the past, young black women who gave birth to children usually were married; today they rarely are. No doubt many of these women married while pregnant. Nevertheless, it appears that it is not so much that sexual behavior has changed, but rather that there has been a decline in the tendency for young men and women (black and white) to marry as a consequence of pregnancy.

Many women who give birth to children out of wedlock do eventually marry, but not nearly in the numbers of those who take a more conventional route to childbearing, especially those who bear out-of-wedlock children in their teens. Furthermore, more women are likely to be divorced today than in the past. The net result of these trends is a striking increase in single-parent families. Census figures indicate that in 1960, only 6 percent of white families and 20.7 percent of black families with children under eighteen were headed by a single woman.[8] By 1991, the number of female-headed families with children had grown to 19.3 percent for whites and 53.8 percent for blacks. In fact, in 1991, only 37.4 percent of black families with children contained two parents, while the comparable figure for white families was 77 percent.[9]

Had rates of single parenthood for blacks not grown, they would be comparable with that of whites today, and would represent a problem of comparable magnitude. The social dilemmas posed by the one-in-five white families without male wage-earners are serious enough, but pale in comparison to those posed by the more than one-in-two black families so constituted.

William Julius Wilson, in his important book *The Truly Disadvantaged,* outlined the magnitude of the problem for the poor urban blacks among whom illegitimacy and single parenthood are almost universal. According to Wilson, in the Robert Taylor Homes, a large public-housing project in Chicago, home to over twenty thousand people, 69 percent of the inhabitants were children under eighteen and 93 percent of the families with children were headed by a single parent, almost always the mother. Wilson reports that this project, which houses less than 1 percent of Chicago's three million people, accounted for approximately 10 percent of the murders, rapes, and aggravated assaults in the city. He also reports that unemployment in the project was close to 50 percent and that 83 percent of the families with children were on the welfare rolls. Similar problems exist in the Cabrini Green housing project, the second largest in Chicago, where 92 percent of families with children are headed by a single parent. Wilson makes the point that single parenthood and welfare dependency are not unique to residents of public housing. According to Wilson, "[t]he projects simply magnify these problems, which permeate ghetto neighborhoods and to a lesser extent metropolitan areas generally."[10]

Most black women do eventually marry, but they marry at a later age and are more likely never to marry than white women. In 1992, only 28.5 percent of white women aged twenty-five to twenty-nine had never married. Among black women the comparable figure was 60.4 percent. Among women thirty to thirty-five years old, only 15.1 percent of white women, but fully 41 percent of black women, had never been married. This is a dramatic change since 1970, when only 5.5 percent of white women and 10.8 percent of black women aged thirty to thirty-five had not married.[11] Furthermore, black women have a somewhat greater tendency to be divorced and unmarried than do white women. As I've noted, 11.2 percent of black women were divorced and unmarried in 1990, compared to 8.6 percent of white women.[12]

A consequence of all of these trends, according to the authors of *A Common Destiny,* a major 1989 report on the status of blacks in America, is that "[o]n average, black women spend 16 of their expected 73 years of life with a husband; white women spend 34 of an expected 77 years of life married."[13] The upshot is that a majority of black children are born into homes without fathers. Most of their mothers were unmarried when they were born, and of those who were married, a good number were later divorced. The result is that most black children, and almost all children in the underclass, live for extended periods without a male in the home, and not many live with their own biological fathers. Among all children under eighteen years old, only 31 percent of black children, but 67 percent of white children, are living with both biological parents. These figures include very young children, many of whose fathers will leave their families through divorce. The result is that a very small percentage of black children compared to white children will grow to adulthood with their own biological father in the home. It must be emphasized that these figures include children from all social classes. Father absence is more common among poorer families. For underclass black children, therefore, father absence is near universal.[14]

It is important to be reminded how unusual this marital and family pattern is and how divergent it is from common experience in other cultures and other times. The extraordinarily high rates of illegitimacy and single parenthood in the black underclass are in fact without precedent.[15] In almost all known cultures, the fertility of women of childbearing age is a valuable resource that is vigorously protected. Women of childbearing age are sought after, fought over, and protected from sexual assault or seduction. There are two important reasons why this is so. First, in many cultures, the sexual favors of women are the highest values men can attain. The offspring of fertile women are often equally valued; sometimes even more valued. To take someone's wife or daughter without just compensation was, in almost all times and places prior to industrialization, the vilest and most flagrant sort of theft and was punished accordingly.

Second, since offspring require care, a man who engages a women sexually is almost everywhere responsible for assisting in the upbringing of any children that should result from their union. Fathers are, in addition, often crucially important in the training of their children, especially their sons. Where substantial wealth accumulation is possible, patrilineality is the rule and fathers take a special interest in the legitimacy of sons and in their sons' social and economic success and their ability to carry on the family fortune.

In most societies, in fact, an illegitimate child is held in varying degrees of contempt. To be a bastard is, in most places, a cause of shame and embarrassment (however unfair it is to visit the sins of the father on the son). Furthermore, it is usually an indication of serious social disintegration when men in great numbers abandon the children they have fathered. This is obvious in times of social unrest, during wars and civil strife, when, if the social order collapses, rape and abandonment are common. In all ordered societies, however, men are expected to care for their offspring, and most societies see to it that they do.

It is important to note that illegitimacy is not merely a result of social disorder, it is a primary source of social disorder as well. In early industrial societies, children without fathers often were orphaned due to the death of their mothers or abandoned by women who simply could not provide for their needs. Such orphaned or abandoned children, as we saw in our discussion of crime in nineteenth-century London (in the introduction to Part IV), were quite likely to drift into unsavory occupations and, depending on their numbers, contributed considerably to general mayhem and disorder. Similarly, in our own time, illegitimacy, especially among the poor, is a concomitant of crime and educational failure, for reasons we shall shortly discuss.

A similar pattern of maternal abandonment exists in underclass communities today, often as a result of drug addiction on the part of young mothers. Jane Gross reported in the *New York Times* about the problems of an inner-city school in Oakland, California, where it is estimated that more than half of the youngsters live in homes without a biological mother or father.[16] In 1991, census figures indicate that for all black children nationwide, 7 percent lived in such ''zero-parent'' homes.[17] This figure probably understates the problem, since children in such circumstances are among the most likely to be missed by census workers. Also, according to Gross, teachers indicate that children in such straits are deeply shamed by their condition and therefore they, and often their equally shamed caretakers, are likely to conceal their true status from strangers and census workers. But whatever the true numbers, these children are an especially vulnerable group. Quoting Gross:

> Scarred by years of abuse and neglect, many of these children are angry and disruptive, even after they settle in loving foster homes or with doting grandmothers. They are distrustful of adults, greedy for attention and convinced that they must be worthless. . . . They are unresponsive to threats that their misbehavior will land them into trouble, because things already seem as bad as they can get.[18]

II. The Sources of Illegitimacy

How are we to understand the divergent marriage patterns of blacks and whites, especially the very large differences in out-of-wedlock births? Surely part of the answer is given by psychologist Kenneth Clark in his book *Dark Ghetto:*

> In the ghetto, the meaning of the illegitimate child is not ultimate disgrace. There is not the demand for abortion or for surrender of the child that one finds in more privileged communities. In the middle-class, the disgrace of illegitimacy is tied to personal and family aspirations. In lower-class families on the other hand, the girl loses only some of her already limited options by having an illegitimate child; she is not going to make ''a better marriage'' or improve her economic and social status either way. On the contrary, a child is a symbol of the fact that she is a woman, and she may gain from having something of her own. Nor is the boy who fathers an illegitimate child going to lose, for where is he going? The path to any higher status seems closed to him in any case.[19]

Clark's point is well taken and certainly explains the higher rates of illegitimacy among blacks in earlier decades. But it is difficult to understand why the situation deteriorated so rapidly in the quarter-century since Clark penned that passage. Why do young black people continue to believe their situation is hopeless in the face of the new opportunities that have been provided in recent decades? Why were illegitimacy rates so much lower in the 1950s, when discrimination surely made conditions for blacks more difficult than they are today? Perhaps racial discrimination is not now a primary determinant of marital choice, and perhaps other factors are now more important.

The two most prominent explanations of the trends in black marital behavior are offered by Charles Murray in his *Losing Ground* (1984) and William Julius Wilson in his *The Truly Disadvantaged* (1987).[20] Murray points the finger at the new attitude toward welfare engendered by the Johnson Administration's War on Poverty. In the 1960s, the welfare rolls grew dramatically and poor people were encouraged to view government assistance as an entitlement rather than as charity which they should be ashamed to receive. By most accounts that effort has been successful. Anecdotal reports on the attitudes of welfare recipients suggest that while they do not particularly like the welfare system, they are not ashamed to receive aid. Along with this changed attitude came a dramatic increase of welfare dependency. In the two years between 1966 and 1968, in New York City, for instance, the number of people on welfare doubled to over one million.[21]

Murray's argument is buttressed by powerful statistical evidence that the changed economic and social incentives created by the War on Poverty launched by President Johnson were mirrored in the behavior of all poor people, not only blacks. When welfare became easier to obtain and carried less social stigma, men and women became less prudent in their behavior. The easy availability of welfare, in Murray's view, makes it less painful to have children out of wedlock than if government support is hard to obtain and carries a heavy dose of social disapproval.[22]

Wilson challenges this explanation. He relies on a number of studies which show that single parenthood and illegitimacy rates seem unrelated to benefit levels over time or across state lines. Furthermore, even though benefit levels have remained relatively constant during recent years, when corrected for inflation, illegitimacy has continued to climb. But these studies are hardly definitive, as Wilson acknowledges: since "all states have AFDC [Aid to Families with Dependent Children] and food stamp programs, there can be no true test of the effects of welfare on family structure; there is no 'control' population that has not been exposed to these welfare programs."[23]

A major weakness in these studies is a failure to consider the possibility of a threshold effect. Perhaps any welfare support that is sufficient to allow a mother and child to survive in minimally adequate circumstances is the primary factor rather than the level of support. A recent (1989) study lends some support to this view. Robert Plotnick of the University of Washington found that for black teenagers the eligibility requirements of state welfare programs were related to nonmarital births. Where it was more difficult to qualify for welfare, illegitimacy was lower.[24]

Another point made by Plotnick is that until recently women married to unemployed men were not eligible for AFDC grants, and this acted to deter some young couples from marrying. Plotnick studied the effect of a new AFDC-UP (unemployed parent) program that allows women to marry without being disqualified from AFDC. He found that in states with such a program, illegitimacy among teenagers was lower.[25]

Wilson's hypothesis is that illegitimacy is not the result of welfare policies, but is rather the result of the marked increase in joblessness among young males during recent years. In the past, young men with jobs were in a position to marry girlfriends who became pregnant, whereas today they are far more likely to be unemployed and therefore incapable of supporting families. This argument is bolstered by the fact, cited earlier, that fertility rates for black women are lower today than they were in 1960, while illegitimacy has surged since then. His argument is further strengthened by strong statistical evidence that during this period the number of employed young black men declined sharply, and was not matched by a decline in the employment of young white men.[26]

Further support for Wilson's argument comes from a study, published in 1989, demonstrating that employed men were about twice as likely as unemployed men to legitimate the birth of their offspring by marrying the child's mother, either before she gave birth or within three years of the birth of their child. This was true for all the ethnic groups included in the sample.[27]

Many seem to believe that Wilson's economic explanation of illegitimacy and Murray's welfare explanation are mutually exclusive, but I think it is a mistake to think these explanations are incompatible. Rather, they complement each other. If men lack the means to support families, they are less likely to marry the women they make pregnant. But absent any means of support, black women are likely to act with caution before becoming pregnant. The availability of welfare support, if it approximates what a potential marriage partner can provide, reduces the economic advantages of marriage. The availability of welfare acts to cushion the economic consequences of an out-of-wedlock birth that might well be devastating without it. Of course, such a cushion would not be very attractive if many men were in a position to support families. In other words, Murray and Wilson are both correct, they merely emphasize different aspects of what motivates young women to choose to become mothers without husbands rather than postpone motherhood.

University of Pennsylvania sociologist Elijah Anderson, who reports on an ethnographic survey of poor inner-city blacks, points out that in poor communities "with the dearth of well-paying jobs, public assistance is one of the few reliable sources of money." If men have difficulty finding work, and if marrying their pregnant girlfriends will disqualify their children for AFDC, as it did in the past, then it makes economic sense in many cases to avoid marriage.[28]

This is not to suggest that poor women in substantial numbers have children *in order to* obtain benefits, which is clearly not what is being said. What is being said is that many young women want children, and are more likely to act on their desire if, all other things being equal, they can afford to do so. The argument made is that if having children out of wedlock is very costly, both financially and socially, fewer young women will act on their desire. If the economic burden and the social stigma of illegitimacy are reduced, however, the illegitimacy rate should go up, all other things being equal.

In most historical periods economic factors have been of paramount importance in determining suitability for marriage and family life. Any familiarity with the life of peasant populations everywhere points to the fact that sexuality is severely restricted in young people for largely economic reasons. Parents living at the margin of survival are simply not about to allow an irresponsible daughter to burden them with an additional mouth to feed, when plain prudence can prevent such an outcome.

Whatever the reality on this issue, the question of the impact of welfare is something of a dead issue, since it is very unlikely that anyone will recommend a draconian move such as its total elimination. Consequently, a true test of the link between welfare and illegitimacy is unlikely to be made any time soon. Even the suggestion that young women who have children out of wedlock should be required to stay in their parental homes or take some outside work are usually shunned as inhumane. It is hard to understand why work requirements are viewed as unjust for poor women when middle-class women are encouraged to get on with their careers as soon as possible after their babies are born. Also hard to understand is the provision, common in many states, which allows the mother of an illegitimate child to move into her own apartment, even if she is herself a minor. Of all the pains that illegitimacy might imply for a sixteen-year-old, the opportunity to set up house independent of her parents is not likely to be one of them.

While women do not appear to have children to obtain welfare, it is equally difficult to explain the very large number of illegitimate births by black women that are carried to term when birth control and abortion are readily available. Of course, many pregnancies may result from carelessness and ignorance about birth control. Some unwed mothers are, after all, quite young. It should be noted, however, that only 1 percent of births to unmarried women are to girls younger than 15 years of age. Perhaps black women may be more reluctant to avail themselves of abortion than white women, but this explanation is inconsistent with the data cited earlier on the use of abortion by black and white women.

In New York and other major cities, condoms are for sale in supermarkets and convenience stores (and, in some cities, are distributed free of charge in schools), sex education is mandatory, and birth control pills are freely distributed to needy women at public health clinics. Much public commentary notwithstanding, to suggest that black girls fifteen years and older do not understand birth control as well as white girls, and that they have children outside of marriage because of ignorance, contradicts everyday experience and is somewhat demeaning to black women. More persuasive is the argument that women in black underclass communities, because of the social mores common in those communities, have fewer qualms than white women about becoming pregnant in the first place and carrying to term the unintended pregnancies that result. An additional factor may be that unmarried black males seem to attach a greater value, and to attach less stigma, to becoming fathers than do unmarried white males. Some young men may pressure young women into ignoring sound birth control practices out of selfish desires.[29]

This interpretation is given support by a survey of ten thousand never-married females which found that the incidence of out-of-wedlock births was totally unrelated to a young woman's knowledge about birth control. Researchers Sandra Hanson, David Myers, and Alan Ginsburg found that having taken a sex education course and reporting knowledge about birth control did not correlate with reduced illegitimacy at all among young women.

What they found was that attitudes were more important than knowledge. In particular, black girls who responded positively to the question of whether they "would consider having a child out-of-wedlock" were 80 percent more likely to subsequently have had an illegitimate child than those who responded negatively to that question.[30] Somewhat surprisingly, these researchers found that black girls who had taken sex education courses were more likely to be of the opinion that it was acceptable to have a child out of wedlock than were girls who had taken no such courses.[31] These findings, taken in conjunction, suggest that black women understand contraception but are somewhat less concerned about the consequences of failing to employ it effectively than are white women.

The large number of women who give birth to illegitimate children, when free or subsidized abortion is readily available, and when there is no strong social stigma against it, suggests that a substantial number of women give birth to children without husbands out of a conscious desire to do so. Elijah Anderson, who interviewed many inner-city residents, argues that some young women may purposely become pregnant in the hope that their boyfriends will marry them as a result. This strategy is not usually successful. But Anderson suggests that in addition some young women may become pregnant in order to "establish their households on their own, without the help or burden of a man." He points out that babies in underclass neighborhoods "have become a sought-after symbol of status, of passage to adulthood, of being a 'grown woman.' In such circumstances babies can become valued emblems of womanhood."[32]

While unemployment among young black men is very high, most eventually do obtain jobs. Why do not young black women merely postpone childbearing until their prospective mates are in a position to support families, which is the pattern common among white women? It is important to note that while joblessness among young men in the black community is extremely high, by the time these men reach their late twenties approximately 90 percent are employed. Labor force participation rates for black men aged twenty-five to thirty-four were about 95 percent in the 1960s and fell to about 90 percent in the 1970s, and have not changed much since then.[33] Even if it is true that many black men in their late twenties and early thirties earn fairly low salaries, that does not fully explain why a black woman would choose to handicap her lifelong marital opportunities by bearing an out-of-wedlock child in her late teens or early twenties.

White women have been postponing marriage and maternity in increasing numbers over the years.[34] There is no reason to believe young white women are remaining chaste while waiting for marriage; quite the opposite is the case, but they are postponing parenthood. Why are white women willing to postpone parenthood until their potential husbands are in a position to support them, while black women are much less likely to do so? Perhaps young black women act as they do because they have come to believe that no adequate mate will ever become available to them. But why should they come to have so pessimistic a belief?

III. The Sex Ratio

A possible answer to this question is provided by social scientists Marcia Guttentag and Paul Secord in their book *Too Many Women: The Sex Ratio Question*.[35] Guttentag and Secord argue that for a good part of this century there has been a marked shortage of black men relative to black women, and that this shortage has been especially acute in the large urban areas of the North. They argue that this imbalance has had an impact on black marital patterns irrespective of unemployment rates. In fact, the imbalance may help to explain those high unemployment rates.

Guttentag and Secord argue that it is not merely marriage patterns which are influenced by the balance of men and women in society, but rather the whole social climate. That climate, in turn, can create conditions which magnify the impact of the sex imbalances themselves.

Their thesis is that men, who everywhere dominate the institutions of society, tend to shape those institutions, in important ways, to take account of the supply of women available as potential mates. When the ratio of men to women is low, men will be less willing to indulge individual women to win them over, since there are so many available alternatives. When men confront an oversupply of women, therefore, they will tend to be less loyal and faithful, and generally to exhibit less graciousness toward women, because it is relatively easy for them to find replacements for their current wives and consorts. Societies experiencing a shortage of men are referred to as low sex ratio societies.[36]

When conditions are reversed and there is a scarcity of women relative to men (high sex ratio conditions), Guttentag and Secord argue that women will be highly valued and very much protected. Women will be expected to stay at home and care for the domestic tasks of housekeeping and childbearing. Men will be more loyal and loving toward their wives and extremely jealous of potential interlopers. Women will have less need to seek work and consequently be less concerned about equality of treatment outside the home.[37] Unequal sex ratios can result from many circumstances. Differential birth and infant-mortality rates can create unequal ratios. More males are usually born, but males also suffer higher mortality rates, so that in many societies by the age of marriage there may be a shortage of males. Wars take a heavier toll on men than on women, as do some epidemics such as plague.[38] Migration may, because of differential rates for men and women, create imbalances. In most cases men migrate and create low ratios in the places they leave and high ratios in the places to which they migrate.

Guttentag and Secord think the feminist movement gained strength in nineteenth-century New England because of the low sex ratio created by the many men who traveled West in search of better circumstances.[39] The "Roaring Twenties" may have had its origins in the low sex ratio among people in their twenties in the aftermath of World War I, especially in Europe.

Guttentag and Secord argue that many of the social conditions associated with the 1960s and 1970s fit those associated with low sex ratio societies. In the 1960s, the baby boom came of age and the population of people in their twenties climbed rapidly. This would not, of course, affect sex ratios in any particular age cohort—of, say, men and women in their early twenties. Women, however, in most times and places, tend to seek mates a few years older than themselves. In a rapidly rising population, more people coming into the demographic pipeline create imbalances between the women in one age cohort and the men in the age cohort a few years older than them. As the ranks of younger women swelled from the baby boom, they found themselves in greater than usual competition for the males of the most desirable age for marriage. Guttentag and Secord argue that what they call the "marriage squeeze" contributed to the sexual revolution and the feminist movement during the 1960s. The marriage squeeze came to an end as the baby boom aged, and it is impossible now to determine if women would have changed their ideas as to the appropriate age of men they view as desirable mates.[40]

A related squeeze developed for highly educated women and those in preferred occupations. Women have traditionally not only preferred to marry up in age, but also in status. Perhaps the difficulty which high-status women have in finding even higher status males has contributed to the appeal of feminism among many educated women. It will be interesting to see if women's attitudes in this regard will, over time, adjust to this marriage squeeze that, unlike the marriage squeeze created by the baby boom, is likely to remain permanent.

Guttentag and Secord cite orthodox Jews as an example of a very high sex ratio society with a considerable excess of men over women. They believe this high sex ratio helps to explain the high degree of protectiveness toward women, the high expectation of domesticity on women's part, as well as a concern with sexual propriety on the part of men and women. Women are not treated as equals in public life and seem not to demand such equal treatment. On the other hand, they are treated with great respect within the home. Orthodox Jewish marriages are extremely stable. Orthodox Jewish women have large numbers of children and devote a great deal of care to their upbringing.[41]

This care is reflected, according to Guttentag and Secord, in extremely low infant-mortality rates historically among orthodox Jews compared to others in similar environments. It is this low infant-mortality rate which helps explain the large number of orthodox men relative to women. Since boys are more vulnerable to infant death, fastidious maternal care tends to benefit male children to a greater degree than female children, and thereby tends to drive up the sex ratio. In addition, Guttentag and Secord suggest that the unusual sexual practices prescribed for orthodox Jews may predispose them to having male offspring. In particular, the extended period of abstinence following menstruation in women may create conditions favorable to sperm carrying the male chromosome.[42]

Sex imbalances create special problems for the sex in greater supply. When there are too many men chasing too few females, as among orthodox Jews, men will "bid up the price" of females, and many men may simply be unable to secure a mate. Not only are men likely to be more indulgent to individual women in such circumstances, but they will also be inclined to work harder and exhibit more ambition to acquire financial resources in order to impress women they wish to marry or, in traditional societies, to obtain the approval of families of women they wish to marry. Likewise, when there are too many women for eligible men, women find themselves at a severe disadvantage. If many young women have difficulty finding suitors, many will come to feel insecure and to wonder if they will ever marry. Desirable young men, on the other hand, should find that women seem easy to attract, and some men may become callous in their relations with women, treating them as sexual trophies, as it were. In low sex ratio conditions, men will tend to put off marriage, and when they marry will be less likely to remain in marriages which become unsatisfying.

According to Guttentag and Secord, social norms which are usually enforced by men should reflect their relative advantage or disadvantage in the mating game. The authors argue that in low sex ratio conditions, "[s]exual libertarianism would be the prevailing ethos," and would favor males who would "have opportunities to move from woman to woman or to maintain multiple relationships with different women." These cultural patterns "would not emphasize love and commitment, and a lower value would be placed on marriage and the family."[43] Such a pattern is of course common in underclass circles. Guttentag and Secord think it follows from the sexual imbalances among blacks. They report that "[a]side from postwar shortages of men in various countries, American blacks present us with the most persistent and severest shortage of men in a coherent subcultural group that we have been able to discover during the era of modern censuses."[44]

Guttentag and Secord examined census records and found that in most major cities the ratio of black males to black females is remarkably low, much lower than in rural areas. They also discovered that the sex ratio, which was already low in 1930, fell steadily after that, reaching a low point in the 1970s, after which things started to improve. To some extent, these imbalanced sex ratios can be explained in terms of the higher infant-mortality rate of black males and a higher mortality rate among black males of all ages. But the major factor, according the authors, was the differential rates of migration of men and women during the massive movement of blacks out of the rural South into southern and northern cities during the thirties, forties, and fifties. The authors cite census data indicating that there was greater northward migration by black women than black men: "The Northeast gained almost two nonwhite/black females for every male, the North Central region gained about three nonwhite/black females for every two males." In New York City in 1970, for instance, the authors' figures indicate that there were only 72 nonwhite males for every 100 nonwhite females in the 20 to 24 year age cohort. Even in the South there was a shortage of men in urban areas, since more women than men moved into cities. The average for the 20 to 25 year age cohort in six large cities, including Atlanta and Baltimore, was 75 males for every 100 females. It was even lower in 1940, when in those same cities there were only 71 men for every 100 women in that age range.[45]

The authors offer no explanation for this imbalanced migration pattern to the North and into cities. Perhaps it is explained by the greater employment opportunities for unskilled black women in the unregulated and nonunion occupation of domestic service. Black men were often kept out of the job market by discriminatory labor practices. Perhaps also there was less work in rural areas for unskilled black women in domestic and other sorts of work as rural families moved to the cities.

It is important to be aware that the actual shortage of black men is somewhat exaggerated due to census undercounting of black underclass men, especially those without permanent addresses. However, this undercounting does not substantially change the problem confronting black women, since men without permanent residences are unlikely to be prime candidates for matrimony.

The authors contend that this shortage of males goes a long way in explaining the social conditions common in the inner cities. Today, the massive black migration to northern cities has ended and sex ratios among blacks are now more balanced. In 1989, according to census data, there were 98.2 black males per 100 black females in the 14 to 24 year age group, as compared to 103.3 white males per 100 white females. However, among adults in the 25 to 44 year age range, there were, in 1989, only 87 black men per 100 black women nationwide. Among whites of those ages, there were 101 men per 100 women.[46]

Even more telling, perhaps, is the ratio of unmarried men to unmarried women. In 1991, among those in the 15 to 24 year age range, there were 114 unmarried white men for every 100 unmarried white women. Among blacks there were only 96 unmarried men per 100 unmarried women in that age range.

More striking were the differences for the 30 to 34 year age range, where there were 136 unmarried white men for every 100 unmarried white women, but only 77 unmarried black men for every 100 unmarried black women. These figures may explain why young black women are pessimistic about finding husbands if they wait until men mature and are able to support families.[47]

The present situation, while better than in the past, is still very troublesome. This is especially so since unemployment and incarceration rates have increased substantially among young men in urban areas and have severely depleted the pool of men eligible for marriage and, in particular, the pool of men in a position to provide income significantly greater than can be gotten from welfare. Intermarriage, while hardly substantial, nevertheless adds to the problem. Three-quarters of interracial marriages involve black men marrying white women; it is much less common for white men to marry black women.[48] Furthermore, those black men who marry white women are often socially and financially successful, and are generally the sort of men usually sought after by both black and white women.

It is important to note that social patterns tend to exhibit a sort of behavioral inertia. It may well be that attitudes toward marriage, and patterns of marital behavior, among urban black women today are still affected by the experiences of their mothers, who faced a severe shortage of men in the fifties, sixties, and seventies. Such attitudes are reinforced by the less severe but continuing shortage of men available to black women today.

The situation is most severe for black women in the underclass. Large numbers of middle-class blacks flee the inner cities. Middle-class blacks are often middle class because they manage to maintain stable marriages and draw on two incomes. The sons of middle-class couples are unlikely to look for girlfriends or wives among underclass females. People tend to choose mates of similar status to themselves, a phenomenon sociologists refer to as ''assortative mating.'' Within any racial or ethnic group this tends to limit the opportunities available to poor young women for upward mobility through marriage. Young black women in the underclass are therefore at a double disadvantage. In being black, they face a general shortage of men. In being poor and in the underclass, they are limited to men whose numbers are further diminished (to a far greater degree than middle-class men) by murder, AIDS, and incarceration, and whose suitability for marriage is diminished by high rates of chronic drug addiction, inadequate schooling, and unemployment. In light of the realistic alternatives available to them, the choices of underclass women to raise families without men is considerably less irrational than first appearances suggest.

A good deal of research has been undertaken in an attempt to assess the thesis that the shortage of eligible men accounts for the marriage patterns and high rates of single parenthood among black Americans. Sociologists Mark

Fossett and K. Jill Kiecolt, for instance, examined a wide variety of factors which might contribute to these patterns. Their analysis, based on 1980 census data, produced results which "suggest that mate availability has dramatic implications for African American family structure." They found that moderate differences in sex ratios produced important differences in marriage rates, nonmarital births, and single-parent families among blacks. Furthermore, the economic status of black men and women was also influential in determining the prevalence of marriage among blacks. Where black men had better economic prospects, marriage was more common and illegitimacy less common. Conversely, where local conditions favored black women economically, marriages were less common and nonmarital births more so. This latter finding suggests that black women are more likely to forgo marriage if they can afford to do so, especially if the men available as mates are not economically attractive.[49]

Researchers Daniel Lichter, Felicia LeClere, and Diane McLaughlin also found that "the local supply of economically 'attractive' males plays an especially large role in the marital behaviors of U.S. black and white women." Based on 1980 census data, they found that the "economic opportunities (including welfare) for women" also influenced local variations in marriage rates. They concluded that the increasing economic independence of women has "eroded a fundamental basis for marriage." In addition, they concluded that a woman's likelihood of marrying "has been greatly affected by the deteriorating economic condition of young men," and that racial differences in marriage rates were clearly influenced by the availability of economically desirable mates.[50]

While the relationship between marriage rates and the availability of marriageable men seems relatively clear, the relationship between mate availability and illegitimacy is less so. For instance, sociologists Scott South and Kim Lloyd, of the State University of New York at Albany, studied the effects of local marriage market conditions and other factors on nonmarital births. Their analysis of 1980 and 1981 census data produced results suggesting only a modest effect of mate availability on illegitimacy. In addition, they found that the extreme differences in illegitimacy between blacks and whites could not be explained adequately in terms of mate availability.[51]

In other words, while South and Lloyd seem to confirm the Guttentag and Secord hypothesis that low sex ratios drive up the illegitimacy rate, their data indicate that other factors must be at work to make the black rate of single parenthood so much higher than the white rate. One possible explanation for this negative finding is that national sex ratios have an impact on the overall cultural climate affecting relations between the sexes, and this climate may affect local markets which have sex ratios divergent from those found nationally.

White women, even if confronted by a local shortage of men, are living in a national environment where there is no overall shortage. White American society is not a low sex ratio society, and we would not expect white men and women to exhibit the sorts of attitudes common to low sex ratio societies. Black American society, on the other hand, *is* a low sex ratio society, and therefore we would expect black attitudes to reflect that fact. Put another way, white women who confront a local shortage of men are confronting an unusual situation and can remedy that situation by turning to the national "market," where they face better prospects; they can, in effect, cast their marriage net in wider waters. Black women, on the other hand, have no such option, since their local market shortage of marriageable men is likely to reflect the national one.

The mirror image of this situation holds for black and white men. Eligible black men are almost everywhere in short supply and therefore in high demand. For white men, such a condition is likely to be a local and often transient circumstance. It is reasonable to expect that these differences in the national marriage "market" will have a differential effect on the attitudes of whites and blacks. It should be recalled that Guttentag and Secord argued that where men were in demand, they would become reluctant to marry, would tend to be less faithful, and would tend to be cavalier and even callous toward the women with whom they interact. That would produce in women a tendency to view men with greater suspicion and would create motivation for greater economic independence on the part of women.

Sociologist Scott South, in another study, reviewed questionnaire data gathered in 1987 and 1988 from over two thousand respondents which seems to confirm Guttentag and Secord's hypothesis. He reports that "[b]lack men and women are significantly less desiring of marriage than their white counterparts," and that the difference between white and black men was significantly greater than that between white and black women.[52] Among unmarried men between the ages of nineteen and thirty-five, black males view marriage as less desirable than do white or Hispanic males. Fully 22.8 percent of black men in that age range reported no desire to marry, compared to 12.6 percent of white men and only 6.8 percent of Hispanic men.[53]

South explains this difference in terms of the perceived benefits of marriage to black men, especially in terms of their access to the sexual favors of women. Black men, in much greater proportions than whites, do not believe that marriage will improve their opportunities for sexual gratification. South reports that once this factor is taken into account, the racial differences in desire to marry disappear. In other words, black men who expect as great a sexual benefit from marriage as do white men are equally desirous of marriage as their white counterparts.

Interestingly, although the desire for marriage among black males declines slightly as they age, it declines sharply for black women. Black women in their early twenties see marriage in a much more positive light than do black women in their thirties.[54] This may reflect a realistic analysis of the market, since there is, as we saw earlier, a considerable shortage of unmarried men relative to unmarried women among over-thirty blacks.

These survey data are consistent with the ethnographic report of sociologist Elijah Anderson on inner-city black youth. He reports that poor young black women have a very romantic image of marriage and hope to find a man who will allow them to raise a family in a middle-class manner. According to Anderson, inner-city young men, on the other hand, are driven by a peer culture which views relations between the sexes as a game of sexual exploitation. Women are thought of as prizes to be picked off by enterprising young men. Young men who can seduce many young women are held in high esteem by their peers. Fatherhood is deemed confirmation of a young man's sexual prowess, but he is considered foolhardy to allow himself to be dragged into marriage. Anderson depicts the underclass male as callous and indifferent to the pain he causes young women and as almost exclusively motivated by the desire to gain the approval of his male peers.[55]

This callousness toward women is confirmed by the personal experiences of Shawn Sullivan. Sullivan, writing in the *Wall Street Journal,* is identified as a student intern and an undergraduate at Amherst College. He argues that growing up in the inner-city neighborhood of Bedford-Stuyvesant exposed him to an extremely misogynist culture. It is, according to Sullivan, ''an atmosphere in which young men are 'taught' by their fathers, if they have one [*sic*], and older brothers to refer to women as 'ho's' ('whores') who need abuse; where physical violence is a common means of ending verbal disputes; and where women are mistrusted and detested.'' Given the accounts of Anderson and Sullivan, it is hardly surprising that black women become less enamored of marriage as they grow older and more experienced.[56]

Black women also become more conscious of economic realities. Richard and Kris Bulcroft, sociologists from Western Washington University, also analyzed survey data gathered in 1987 and 1988 on black and white attitudes toward marriage. They report that ''black women perceive more economic benefits from marriage than white women in early adulthood, but the difference disappears and reverses slightly in the later years.'' The authors suggest that ''black women adjust their perceptions downward, reflecting, perhaps, a more realistic view of their marriage market options.''[57] The authors report, however, that black women expect potential mates to provide economic resources and that ''marriage rates for black females are most likely declining because of a lack of available black males who can meet black women's'' high economic expectations.[58]

It is hard not to come to the conclusion that black sexual and marital behavior is conditioned by the historical imbalance between the sexes, and the continuing shortage of eligible men. The flamboyant teenage male who proudly boasts to the television interviewer that he has had numerous children by many women is reflecting a widespread and accepted cultural pattern. The young women who conceive children and show relatively little anger toward the men who made them pregnant likewise reflect this pattern. Similarly, the very young girls who feel they need to provide sexual favors to older boys in order to maintain their loyalty strongly suggest an insecurity based on the knowledge that females are in oversupply.

Our discussion of the evolution of courtship strategies in Chapter 6 suggests that as women come to believe that help from men in rearing children is not to be expected, they are likely to be more motivated to look for masculine characteristics that will benefit their own children; they will, in Richard Dawkins's terms, tend to discount men as resource providers and value them more as contributors of positive genetic characteristics for their children. The flamboyance of young men, it will be recalled, may be influenced by this attitude on the part of women, so that the attitudes and behavior may create a pattern that is self-reinforcing. Once men begin to recognize that women do not look to them as primary providers, they are likely to reduce their investment in acquiring the habits and skills which would enable them to be good providers. This, in turn, makes women even less likely to expect provision from them.

IV. The Poor and the Sexual Revolution

In trying to come to grips with the factors contributing to black family dissolution, it is important not to overlook the impact of the culture-wide sexual revolution of the 1960s, since it was then that the current problems began to evidence themselves. The sexual revolution was in large measure fueled by the introduction of the birth control pill in the mid-sixties and the relaxation of abortion laws in many states at about the same time. *Roe v. Wade,* of course, made abortion legal throughout the U.S. in 1973. These developments allowed women for the first time in history to engage in sexual activity without running the risk of unwanted children. In effect, sex became for many women what it had always been for many men, namely a source of pleasurable gratification with limited risk. Not surprisingly, social values changed. Behavioral psychologist B. F. Skinner argued that social values are codifications of the actual consequences of behavior; when actual conditions change, so will social values.[59] Skinner's thesis gains confirmation from the case of premarital sex, which ceased to carry the moral and social stigma it had in earlier times. Sex became more casual and, for some, even a form of social entertainment requiring no lasting commitment. It was not until the 1980s that AIDS cast some doubt on the notion that sex was a risk-free enterprise.

One obvious consequence of these changes was that the moral taint associated with premarital sexual relations was severely lessened in almost all classes in society. In addition, oral contraceptives and legal abortion tended to shift the responsibility of preventing pregnancy from men onto women. One consequence was that the moral imperatives that encouraged many men to marry pregnant girlfriends in the past were much diminished. As fewer pregnant females were able to induce their boyfriends into marriage, the rate of illegitimacy shot up in all racial groups and in all social classes.

The feminist movement also had an impact, even though its rhetoric seemed largely aimed at middle-class white women. Much feminist rhetoric emphasized the importance of personal self-fulfillment and argued that women should not stay in stifling marriages merely for the sake of children. Such rhetoric was supported by social scientists who, in the sixties and seventies, argued that the children of troubled couples would be better off in single-parent homes than in homes disrupted by marital conflict. Since feminists tend to diminish the significance of sex differences, it was natural for them to deny the significance of fathers in children's healthy development. Given the difficulty black women had in finding suitable husbands, this sort of talk had the effect, whether intended or not, of making black women somewhat less reluctant than they might have been to try to manage families on their own. Put another way, in a circumstance where single parenthood already had many justifications, the argument that children didn't really need fathers added one more.

V. Illegitimacy—Consequences for Children

While common sense suggests that the absence of fathers ought to have an important effect on the development and adjustment of children, there has been rather surprising disagreement on this point among social scientists. The problem in large measure is the result of the fact that illegitimacy is usually interrelated with so many other problems, especially in underclass communities, that it is often difficult to determine what causes what. For instance, many illegitimate babies are born to mothers with inadequate schooling. If these children perform poorly in school, is it due to a lack of fathers, to the lack of education on the part of mothers, or is it the result of inherited similarities between mother and child? In other words, maybe these children would do poorly in school even if their mothers were married. Nevertheless, the evidence seems fairly strong that illegitimate children have more difficulties in school even after controlling for the influence of factors like mother's income and educational attainment. The effects of illegitimacy on children's delinquency, as we will see, are considerably less clear than are its effects on education.

Perhaps the best recent data on the effects of illegitimacy on children's education and welfare are provided in a major study undertaken by Deborah Dawson, a researcher at the U.S. Department of Health and Human Services. She studied the impact of family status on the health and welfare of a sample of over seventeen thousand children whose parents or guardians were interviewed in 1988.[60] Dawson broke down her data on children into four categories: children living with both biological parents; those living with a formerly married but now single mother; those living with a mother and stepfather; and those living with a never-married mother. (Other cases—e.g., children living with their fathers only, or in other arrangements—occurred too infrequently to be used in Dawson's analysis.)

School problems experienced by children were assessed by questions relating to whether a child repeated a grade, whether he was ever suspended or expelled from school, and whether he was ever the subject of a parent-teacher conference. On all measures, children living with both biological parents had the fewest incidents of problems with school, while children living with never-married mothers had the most. Interestingly, children living with divorced women and those living with stepfathers reported intermediate levels of school problems and did not differ much from each other in that regard.

Dawson found, for instance, that among school-age children, 12 percent of those living with both biological parents had repeated a grade. In contrast, she reports that "the figure was 22 percent for children living with formerly married mothers or with mothers and stepfathers, and 30 percent for those living with never-married mothers." Dawson found furthermore that "[t]his general pattern was maintained for all age, race, and ethnic categories."[61]

Similar patterns prevailed in the figures for expulsions and suspensions from school. Only 4 percent of children living with both biological parents had ever been expelled or suspended, whereas the figure was 15 percent for those living with never-married mothers. The likelihood of having been the subject of a parent-teacher conference (a common indicator of school difficulties) was also much higher for children in single-parent homes than for those living with both biological parents, even controlling for other important factors. The pattern for education was quite clear and was consistent across class and race lines.[62]

The evidence is quite convincing, therefore, that children of single mothers cope less well with the institutional setting of the school. Unfortunately, Dawson did not have data on actual school performance like grade averages, although being held back a grade in school certainly indicates poor academic achievement.

It is important to note that Dawson's data relate to the whole population. The impact of illegitimacy on black children's school performance is magnified, however, since black children exhibit more school problems in general than white children and the number of illegitimate children is much greater in black communities. For instance, 8.5 percent of black children living with both biological parents reported having been expelled or suspended from school, whereas the comparable figure for white children was 4.1 percent, or less than half as many. For children living with never-married mothers, this ratio stays roughly the same, but the outcome is that 18.2 percent of black children, as opposed to 9.1 percent of white children, were subject to such disciplinary procedures.[63]

It is important to emphasize that repeating a grade (reported for over 30 percent of black children living with never-married mothers) and being suspended or expelled from school are very serious indices of school difficulty. In black underclass communities, such as those in the Chicago housing projects described earlier, where approximately 90 percent of children live in single-parent homes, such problems are probably worse than these figures indicate. Inner-city schools are known to tolerate behavior that would result in automatic suspension in middle-class suburban schools. Furthermore, inner-city schools are more likely to have lower academic standards and to practice "social promotion," so that many youngsters in inner-city schools are passed along, whereas in more rigorous schools they might have been held back.

Part of the problem for illegitimate children is that their mothers often gave birth as young women whose education may have been prematurely terminated or compromised by their pregnancies. It is widely known that parents' education is among the more powerful predictors of children's school success. In addition, educated parents tend to involve themselves more in school activities, understand education better, and are more likely to assist their children when they have problems with school. In neighborhoods with large concentrations of poorly educated parents, there is likely to be considerably less parental involvement and less social pressure on children to perform well.

The difficulties children without fathers confront are not limited to school performance. Dawson also reports on indices of emotional and behavioral problems unrelated to school. The evidence is clear that children living with both biological parents reported the fewest emotional problems. Somewhat surprisingly, there were no differences among the other three categories of children who, after controlling for important factors, all had considerably more emotional difficulties than those living with both biological parents.[64]

A similar pattern emerged when Dawson examined evidence of behavioral problems. She found that children living with both parents had fewer behavioral problems, as indicated by antisocial behavior and peer conflict, than did children from broken homes. After controlling for other important factors, she found no differences among children living with never-married mothers, those living with unmarried, divorced women, and those living with mothers and stepfathers.[65]

These data suggest that a key factor in inoculating children against behavioral and emotional problems may not so much be the presence of a male provider, but rather the specific presence of the child's biological father. A child born to a married woman whose husband subsequently leaves the family seems to fare no better behaviorally than a child born to an unmarried woman. Likewise, the subsequent marriage of a woman who has borne a child out of wedlock, unless the husband is the biological father of her child, seems to benefit the child's emotional well-being little if at all.

In fact, the marriage of a woman who earlier bore an illegitimate child may create problems, at least in one area. Dawson presents rather extraordinary data indicating that children living with never-married mothers were almost half as likely (9.1 percent versus 17.7 percent) to have suffered an accident, injury, or poisoning compared to those living with stepfathers. In fact, children living with never-married mothers were even less likely to have suffered these mishaps than children living with both biological parents (13.4 percent). Although this relationship was not significant for black and Hispanic children or for children under the age of five, it did hold up for white children even after controlling for demographic and socioeconomic factors.[66]

Dawson attributes the greater probability of such harm to the climate and tension generated by divorce. She does not argue, though the data are suggestive, that part of the problem may be the presence of stepfathers. This is, of course, consistent with our discussion of the evolution of parental behavior. Perhaps men are more conscientious in the care of their own children than they are with stepchildren?

Given these findings, it is hard not to imagine that children without fathers are also more prone to delinquency. It seems reasonable to suppose that children who lack warm and loving fathers, and the discipline such fathers enforce, should be more prone to delinquency and criminal activity as well. There can be no doubt that there is a correlation between illegitimacy and delinquency, but the interpretation of that correlation is highly debated. Social scientists Lawrence Rosen and Kathleen Neilson report that there is considerable disagreement in the field over the effect of broken homes on adolescent criminality. They point out that although the belief that family instability contributes to delinquency was widely assumed in earlier decades, in more recent years this is no longer the case. According to Rosen and Neilson, a review of the literature revealed that "[t]he predominant position among contemporary criminologists seems to be that broken homes are of *secondary* importance for understanding juvenile delinquency."[67]

Rosen and Neilson reviewed fifteen studies on delinquency conducted from 1932 to 1975 which had purported to show a strong relationship between family instability and delinquency. These studies, according to Rosen and Neilson, suffer from such serious conceptual and methodological problems that it is simply not possible to draw any firm conclusions from them. The authors conclude that the broken home "has little explanatory power in terms of delinquency."[68]

This somewhat surprising conclusion is echoed by respected scholars James Q. Wilson and Richard J. Herrnstein, in their important book *Crime and Human Nature*. They also reviewed the literature on the relationship between delinquency and broken homes and, in addition, examined the effect of abusive homes on future delinquency. They report that "when we look for evidence of a direct connection between abusive or broken homes and subsequent criminality, we find that it is less clear-cut than we had supposed." They conclude that, at best, broken and abusive homes are only "an imperfect indicator of the existence of a complex array of factors that contribute to criminality."[69]

One should note that most of the important studies on this question were undertaken before the recent meteoric rise of illegitimacy had taken its full effect. The studies run from 1932 to 1975, a period when illegitimacy and single-parent families were still relatively uncommon, even among blacks. Nevertheless, the case that illegitimacy in underclass communities is a major contributor to the criminality found there is at least questionable.

It is important not to misunderstand what these authors mean when they suggest that illegitimacy is a weak contributor to delinquency, especially in regard to the meaning of "statistical contribution." To say that something contributes little to a final outcome, as is being said about the contribution of illegitimacy to crime, is to say that when all other important factors are held constant, illegitimacy per se does not add very much in the way of predictive or explanatory power.

The inability to demonstrate a causal relationship between single parenthood and criminality may result from the fact that so many other important contributors to criminality co-vary with illegitimacy, especially among blacks in the inner cities. For instance, problems in school are related to delinquency. As we have seen, illegitimacy is more common among women who themselves have difficulty with school and often pass on that difficulty, by example or by inheritance, to their children. In addition, illegitimacy, in that it correlates with poverty, makes it much more likely that illegitimate children will live in disorderly, crime-ridden neighborhoods and attend disordered and troubled schools, known contributors to delinquency. Furthermore, neighborhoods that contain large numbers of unwed mothers are unlikely to have substantial numbers of responsible adult males who, by their mere presence, tend to inhibit youthful indiscretions.

Once one controls for factors such as school failure and disorderly neighborhoods, etc., it may not be all that apparent how much illegitimacy or father absence, by itself, adds to the probability of delinquency. In other words, it is unclear whether an adolescent living with a divorced, but financially secure woman, and attending a good school in a safe middle-class neighborhood, will be any more likely to become delinquent than if his mother had remained married. As Rosen and Neilson argue, the evidence suggests a moderately increased susceptibility to delinquency, but not much more than that.

It is possible that illegitimacy among blacks may increase delinquency in an indirect way. Illegitimacy among whites is relatively uncommon, and therefore white illegitimate children generally grow up in neighborhoods where most children have biological fathers in the home. Such neighborhoods are not commonly prone to high levels of delinquency, for all the reasons discussed in Chapter 8. On the other hand, illegitimacy among black children, especially in underclass neighborhoods, is almost universal. A black child without a father is very likely, therefore, to find himself in a neighborhood where most children live without biological fathers. Such neighborhoods are prone to a host of ills known to act as precipitating factors which increase delinquency.

Put another way, the evidence suggests that children born out of wedlock are not, due to their birth status alone, much more likely to fall into delinquency, but the community in which a child grows up is important in this regard. Since most white children grow up in orderly communities, delinquency among whites is relatively low. Among blacks, however, illegitimacy often implies poverty and life in underclass neighborhoods. The data suggest that for a child exposed to the full panoply of the conditions of underclass life, his birth to an unmarried woman may not be of particular importance in determining whether or not he succumbs to delinquency.

VI. Illegitimacy—The Impact on Men

Often overlooked in discussions of illegitimacy in the black community are its effects on black men. In the inner city, black men in very large numbers have become economically superfluous for the support of women and children. It is unreasonable to suppose that this economic marginality does not have an impact on the morale and well-being of black men.

On a wide variety of measures of emotional stress—alcoholism, suicide, mortality, psychiatric problems, and overall unhappiness—unmarried men evidence a considerable disadvantage when compared to men who are married.[70] Sociologists Peter and Brigitte Berger, in their book *The War over the Family,* argue that family life offers a haven from the "tenuousness and fragmentation" of modern life, the conditions of which often make personal identity "unstable, unreliable and therefore full of anxiety." The Bergers argue that "it is a vital necessity for the individual's sanity and emotional well-being that there be some relationships that are stable, reliable and unfragmented." They suggest that if the modern marriage did not exist we would probably invent it, so well suited is it to "satisfy this need for stable identity affirmation."[71]

In other words, a person's sense of his own worth is very much dependent upon other people's actual assessment of that worth. Very few people in this or any age can expect the world to hold them in high esteem and thereby confirm their personal significance. Few people can hope for high salaries to confirm their value or hope to attain satisfying or challenging careers in which to validate their excellence and their significance. For all sorts of reasons, many people, perhaps most, will always have to work at jobs that convey minimal status, modest income, and minor psychic reward. Doing a job to the best of one's ability is an important and admirable goal and is, in the final analysis, its own reward, but few can sustain rich and meaningful lives with that reward alone.

In most societies and in most times, men in even the meanest circumstances could at least lay claim to respect and dignity by their honest support of families. A society or subculture that denigrates the virtues of the "self-respecting man" is a society likely to breed a sizable number of "good for nothing" men. That both of these phrases are antiquated today has profound implications for the moral temper of our time.

Self-respecting men do not allow their families to go without provision, even if it means taking on the lowest and least-respected tasks. Such men neither ask for nor expect the world to show them respect, but are satisfied if they can gain the appreciation of those closest to them. For many men, perhaps most, this is their surest and most gratifying source of self-respect and self-esteem.

Government support of women in the underclass has had the unfortunate consequence of making the economic contributions of underclass men, especially those who are young and unskilled, of marginal significance. Many such men are thereby deprived of one of few significant roles in life to which they can reasonably aspire, and not surprisingly, a great many have fallen into the status of being "good for nothing" and pay a high moral and emotional price for their failure.

To the extent that men come to believe that they are superfluous, they are likely to make fewer efforts to obtain the training and discipline needed to attain jobs adequate for the support of families. In a sense, the high illegitimacy that is fostered by the poor prospects black women confront in finding husbands may, in turn, as discussed earlier, foster the attitudes that make so many men unsuitable to be husbands in the first place.

To state the problem in another way, it is a near-universal characteristic of people to seek some sort of personal transcendence. People everywhere hunger for participation in something more lasting and more meaningful than they can achieve by virtue of their own individual existence. Participation in something that is lasting and important makes one's own contribution important and worthy of respect. In Christian societies the desire for transcendence can be satisfied by following God's dictates, in the faith that even the efforts of the humblest will be recognized and respected in an everlasting state of grace. In Confucian societies the transcendental impulse is satisfied through efforts on behalf of an extended patriarchal lineage that will be honored by lasting remembrance after one has died.

In all societies, whatever their dominant religions, the family unit provides, albeit on a small scale, a means to satisfy the transcendent impulse. The family as a vehicle for transcendence makes up for its lack of grandeur and permanence with its widespread availability. No matter how otherwise insignificant a person's life may seem, if he is responsible for the care and support of children, he can take satisfaction that his contribution is needed and important.

Men without meaningful family roles, without real religious faith, or without profoundly absorbing work, can all too easily drift into a disaffected state. Such men, if they are young, are especially prone to demagogic appeals promising transcendence in violent nationalisms or tribalisms. Some find less grandiose meaning in local gangs and gang activities. Others merely descend into the stupefying and self-destructive nihilism of drugs and other base gratifications. But whatever their response, such young men represent a real danger to the fabric of civic order, a danger all too evident today on the streets of America's inner cities.

VII. Conclusion

In the 1960s, the illegitimacy rate in America began a steep and steady climb that continues to this day. The black rate is over 60 percent nationwide and is over 90 percent in many inner-city neighborhoods. The upshot is that in the period since the passage of the Civil Rights Act and the resulting improvements in opportunities for blacks, income for black Americans, taken in the aggregate, has stagnated. Those intact families with two wage-earners have begun to approximate similar white households, while at the very same time, single-parent families, which constitute over one-half of all black families with children, are mired in poverty. It is now abundantly clear that single parenthood is the most important single proximate cause of poverty among black families. If black marital behavior mirrored white marital behavior, there would hardly be any income gap at all, especially if one holds constant such factors as education, age, and inherited wealth.

In addition, it is clear that single-parent families create conditions that impede educational success and that such families contribute heavily to the concentration of young men in the sort of environments that foster high rates of delinquency. Furthermore, the superfluity of black men for the support of families seems to have a demoralizing effect on black men that surely contributes to many of the problems they have.

Of the many reasons offered to explain the rise in unwed motherhood among black women, the most compelling is that which cites the relative scarcity of black men in underclass communities. There is an absolute shortage of men in general and, more importantly, a shortage of men who represent desirable marriage partners.

Black women seem to have adopted a fatalism with regard to their marital chances. They seem to assume that the men around them will never be in a position to serve as adequate husbands or fathers to their children. Rather than give up on childbearing, however, they give birth to children and support them as well as possible with aid from the government. Current welfare policies allow them to do so in a condition of, at least to them, tolerable impoverishment. There is reason to believe that these young women are somewhat too pessimistic about the prospects of the young men around them. The census data reviewed earlier in the chapter indicate that the overwhelming majority of these young men will gain useful employment by their late twenties. In the 25 to 34 year age group of black men, about 90 percent are in the labor force, and of those in the labor force approximately 90 percent are employed at any given time.[72] These figures are not dramatically lower than employment data for white men and suggest that the marriage prospects of women who postpone motherhood are not as bleak as first appearances suggest. By having out-of-wedlock children at an early age, however, black women seriously harm their own marital prospects, since black men are even more reluctant than white men to marry women with children.[73] Of course, the absolute shortage of black men would still pose a problem for black women, but would be less of a problem for women without offspring. Finally, it is important not to ignore the misogynist culture that has developed among underclass males, a development which certainly seems to diminish black women's desire to marry.

One clear-cut goal of any policy to reduce illegitimacy should be an enlargement of the pool of males prepared to take on the responsibilities of marriage. That task clearly relates to the other two prongs of the debilitating triad, namely crime and educational failure. If order were restored to the inner cities, crime would be reduced and educational outcomes would be improved. One consequence would be that black men in far greater numbers and at far earlier ages would be in a position to support families. In addition, restoring adult authority to inner-city neighborhoods would greatly reduce the impact of the destructive adolescent subculture currently shaping the values of many young men and women in the underclass. Those values reward masculine bravado and shortsighted, often criminal behavior among young men. Those values often instill a disdain, almost a contempt, for women, fostered in part by the low sex ratios created by the male casualties of youthful criminal behavior. The absence of adult authority, in turn, allows young women to participate in that adolescent subculture and suffer inevitably the pain of male betrayal and all too often the burden of childbirth at tragically young ages.

The survey discussed earlier (in Section II) of ten thousand young women, which found that the acceptance of illegitimacy predisposes young women to have babies out of wedlock, bolsters these conclusions. One of the most important factors leading to unwed motherhood among young women was being in a steady relationship with a boy. It also found that parental concerns about their daughters reduced illegitimacy.[74] These two findings, taken together, suggest that women who are more closely supervised by parents are less likely to succumb to illegitimacy. Many parents, through concerned supervision, are able to effectively overcome their daughters' desires to involve themselves in steady relationships, especially those with daughters who are very young.

These findings suggest, in addition, that the sort of strategies designed to reduce male criminality, such as improved truancy enforcement and reasonable curfews, would reduce unwed motherhood in adolescent girls, for much the same reasons they would reduce delinquency among boys: namely, by reducing the opportunity for children to engage in behaviors that lead them into trouble. That, of course, was the reasoning behind most of the customs designed to keep females chaste in earlier times.

However important these strategies are, it would be a mistake to ignore the contribution of current welfare policies that make out-of-wedlock motherhood seem a reasonable option. Welfare reform is therefore essential if we are to induce young black women to postpone motherhood until such time as responsible men become available to them. Unfortunately, most proposals for welfare reform are not radical enough to actually modify ingrained perceptions and behavior patterns. Since few Americans, understandably, are prepared to let children starve or go homeless because of their parents' behavior, most proposals for welfare reform lack the sort of powerful disincentives to premature pregnancy that served as deterrents in earlier centuries. Welfare reform, if it is to have an effect, must create powerful disincentives to bearing children out of wedlock, but must also be protective of the out-of-wedlock child.

Earlier in the century this set of conditions was met by charitable homes for unwed mothers, to which young women could go, have their babies, and be provided with a nurturing and safe atmosphere where they could complete their education or learn skills useful for employment. Perhaps since pregnancy often meant that girls had to leave their communities and take up residence in supervised settings away from home, fewer opted to bear children out of wedlock. A virtue of this earlier practice was that babies were not penalized for being born illegitimately, and many benefited by being removed from what were in many cases unwholesome environments.

In today's intellectual climate, the treatment of unwed mothers in earlier times seems harsh and uncaring. Part of the difficulty we face in finding solutions in this area is an altogether proper reluctance today to impose similarly harsh consequences on young women who become pregnant outside of marriage. It is important to recognize, however, that today's more liberal attitudes and policies are producing consequences that, while different, are in many ways as cruel and tragic as were produced by earlier practices. Unfortunately, few proposals currently under discussion are in any sense adequate for dealing with the problem.

As with the other problems plaguing the underclass, illegitimacy results from the inadequate supervision of adolescents, of children really. No thoughtful parent would allow a child of his or her own to engage in clearly self-destructive behavior if it were in any way possible to stop it. I do not think underclass parents are different in their hopes for their children, but far too many lack the resources and the capabilities to keep their children out of harm's way. Any society that abandons large numbers of its children to their own devices and thereby allows them to destroy their opportunities for future productivity and personal fulfillment is one which has lost its moral compass. Such a society, in giving children too much freedom, is not generous and liberal as many seem to think, but is simply callous and uncaring.

Until black illegitimacy approximates the white rate it will be impossible to appreciably narrow the economic and social disparities which currently differentiate blacks from whites in our society. It has been a failure to recognize this indisputable fact which has undermined all current efforts to reduce income disparities and social inequalities. Even more tragically, this failure has led to policies which have deprived countless children of relationships with their fathers, relationships that can be as profoundly gratifying as any they will come to know. It seems hardly necessary to add that their fathers are equally bereft.

Conclusion

The populating of the New World was a momentous social phenomenon with vastly important human consequences which continue to this day. For the great majority of Europeans and their heirs it represented a bold leap into a future with wonderful opportunities and freedoms. For Africans it represented a cataclysmic loss of homeland, of culture, and of freedom; for Africans it was a descent into an almost impossibly unhappy and miserable condition. The African slave trade was perhaps the darkest episode in human history if only because of its long duration and the sheer number of people involved. Untold numbers of Africans died or were enslaved in a brutal and callous subjugation that has few if any parallels in human history.

It took a bloody four-year war to bring that system to an end. Hundreds of thousands of Americans, both black and white, died in the Civil War that took place almost a century after the American nation was founded. But the condition of black Americans living in the South was hardly improved as a consequence, and economically many may have been left worse off than before the war. For decades after the Civil War, southern blacks were subjugated by an unfair and brutal regime of racial separation and discrimination, and white Americans, for the most part, remained indifferent to the plight of their black countrymen.

That indifference became harder to sustain as more blacks migrated north and began to play a more important economic role in the North's economy, especially during World War II. Furthermore, the increased mobility of Americans and improved communications also started to break down regional differences, and these changes also tended to undermine northern ignorance of the plight of southern blacks. Gunnar Myrdal synthesized in his book the dilemma that decent whites faced in the aftermath of World War II. The stark contrast between the values Americans had championed during World War II and the facts of America's treatment of its black citizens could no longer be ignored. The generation that had fought World War II set about the task of redressing the hypocrisy and the historical wrong of white America's treatment of its black citizens. All Americans today owe a debt of gratitude to that generation for the honesty and energy with which they undertook that task. It would be a scandal if the sons and daughters and grandchildren of that generation failed to see this task to a satisfactory conclusion.

The debate over race today is not about the rightness of that cause, but rather about the most effective way to carry it out. As I think the preceding pages have made clear, many of the policies that were initiated thirty and forty years ago were sound and have borne fruit in black progress and in racial harmony. Many policies, however, have not been so successful, and some have caused serious harm.

Broadly speaking, it is possible to distinguish those policies which were successful from those which were not. Policies that attempted to provide blacks with equal opportunities within the bounds of traditional American values and that relied on modest changes in important institutions seem to have been, in the main, successful. Those policies, such as barring discrimination in the workplace, in education, and in public accommodations, rested on the assumption that blacks were no different from other ethnic groups and, if treated like others, would come in time to resemble them in behavior and achievement. These policies also rested on the assumption that American institutions were fundamentally sound, except in their discriminatory practices, and could be made fully sound by ridding them of discrimination.

On the other hand, those policies that attempted to transform important institutions in the hope of improving the lot of black Americans have had a less salutary effect. Many institutional changes were implemented in the belief that white Americans were so racist that they would resist and thwart the attempts of blacks to achieve equality. Out of a concern that police could not be trusted to treat blacks fairly, for instance, criminal justice procedures were altered so as to make discriminatory behavior by police less likely. Similarly, out of a concern that white teachers could not deal fairly with black students, educational practices and standards were altered. Out of a sense that whites' objections to welfare were really motivated by a lack of understanding of black difficulties, new theories of welfare entitlement were developed and used to justify more-liberal support for the poor. Because so many whites were thought incapable of judging blacks fairly, the principle that reward should be based on demonstrated merit was partially replaced with the principle that reward should be based on group membership. These policies, taken as a whole, have had serious effects on all the major institutions of American life.

In few cases do these institutions perform better today than they did in the past; in most cases they perform less well. As important, perhaps, is that in few cases have these policies improved the lot of black Americans. In fact, the lives of many black Americans are bleaker now than at any time since World War II. Nowhere is this more apparent than in the deterioration of black neighborhoods in every major city in the United States where blacks live in substantial numbers.

I. The Growth of the Underclass

It is by now plain to all thoughtful Americans that life in many of the nation's inner cities has descended into a state of near anarchy. It might well be a cause for war if a foreign power threatened the physical destruction and human suffering that has been visited on underclass enclaves during the last thirty years. This human catastrophe, furthermore, is no natural disaster like a hurricane over which human beings had no control. Rather, it was brought about by the decisions of numerous people who were in a position to act differently from the way they did. It is essential to recognize that human beings were responsible for what has happened and that, if they choose to do so, they can begin to correct the errors that have led to the current impasse.

As is abundantly clear from the evidence put forward in the preceding pages, the problems of black Americans are largely the problems of adolescents who have been set adrift by misguided policies and allowed to set their own agenda. The economic and social disparities between whites and blacks will not be seriously addressed until this truth is recognized. Assuring domestic order and socializing children may appear monumental tasks in America in the late twentieth century, but however difficult these tasks may appear, they are the *sine qua non* of civil society. Any society that cannot do these things is civilly and morally bankrupt. Since it was bad ideas that led us to the current condition, it is only by throwing off those bad ideas that we can hope to make things right.

In order to deal with the problems of adolescents, one idea that must be cast aside is that which holds that children should be provided the same sort of rights as adults. Children are rightly treated as a protected class and their freedom is therefore properly limited. They are treated differently because it cannot be assumed that they have the sort of judgment and competence that we routinely expect in adults. We do not allow children to drive cars and it is well that we do not. Likewise, we do not think children below a certain age are competent to decide whether they should receive an education, sign contracts, engage in sexual activities, or use alcohol or firearms. Some children are, of course, exceptional and could handle some of these decisions responsibly. But most cannot. When we grant children freedoms they are ill equipped to handle, we should hardly be surprised when many of them misuse those freedoms and make a mess of their own lives and the lives of those among whom they live. Nor should we be surprised that when young men are not restrained by adult authority, a small but not insignificant number will kill, rape, and wreak havoc in their own communities.

It is important to rethink in hard terms the costs and benefits of various policy options in the way we deal with young people. Strong medicine can be painful, but failure to apply strong medicine when it is needed can be lethal. It has become clear, for instance, that there are a substantial number of young men in the underclass who are a serious threat to themselves and those around them. We cannot hope to create a better environment for the majority until these young men are deterred from expressing violent behavior. If that requires that we reinvent the reform school, we cannot continue to reject that option, as we now do, because more black than white delinquents would probably be placed in reform schools. There can be no doubt that, given current conditions, reform schools would have a disparate impact on black and white adolescents, but the continuing failure to act vigorously in this case has a much more serious impact: namely, the murder and rape and mayhem visited disparately on black citizens. It is simply an error to think that society performs a kindness toward blacks when it sets free among them adolescents, convicted of violent crime, who are palpable threats to their safety. Setting such adolescents free out of sympathy for their poverty or wretched family conditions is no favor to the community in which they live, nor is it a favor in the long run to those set free, but just the opposite. In this case, as in so many others, there is no free lunch.

For too long, policy makers have put off hard choices about adolescents in inner cities because they have acquiesced in the false belief that there was no need for direct action. They have indulged themselves with the palliative that the problems of black adolescents would somehow disappear if American society were made less racist or if black poverty were reduced. This does not appear to be true, and social scientists have a responsibility to make clear just how weak is the scientific basis for this idea. It is not easy to say things that may be unpopular, or may be misinterpreted, or used by some for evil ends. But failure to say what needs to be said is, in the current circumstance, a gross dereliction of professional responsibility. No engineer would be happy to declare that his design for a bridge was flawed and that the bridge must, therefore, be dismantled, but it would be criminal were he not to speak plainly in such a case. Similarly, social scientists who come to believe that current social policies are leading to personal and social tragedies must also speak plainly.

The failures of social policies are far more wide-ranging and tragic than are those of civil engineering. Approximately two thousand people are murdered every year in New York City, many of whom would be alive if we had more-effective criminal justice policies. Over fifty people died in the riot in Los Angeles in 1992, all of whom would be alive if we had more honest explanations for the economic and social problems of black Americans. The number of people killed and injured in hurricanes and tornadoes is minuscule compared to those killed and maimed by crime and civil disorder. Social scientists have been far too cavalier about the potential costs of the policies they champion. We can hardly prevent all the tragedies that life inevitably produces, but we cannot avoid responsibility for seriously engaging those about which we claim professional knowledge. Doctors, lawyers, engineers, and military leaders who act imprudently cause great harm, and so do social scientists.

II. Policy Considerations

I have already outlined a number of steps that could be taken that would immeasurably improve life in inner-city neighborhoods and that would improve the chances that black children would gain the tools needed to enter middle-class life and achieve economic prosperity. Let me repeat briefly the proposals that seem most likely to reduce crime, improve education, and reduce single parenthood.

Since crime is the most serious problem, it must be confronted directly and vigorously. If life for blacks is to improve and race relations are to grow more cordial, a major attack on crime must be mounted. That will cost a great deal, but the costs that such an attack might incur pale beside the economic and social costs of continuing on the present course. As I outlined earlier, it is absolutely necessary to see that the number of police on the streets of the inner cities relative to potential lawbreakers be sufficiently great to deter criminal activity at the outset. In some places, that will require more police than in others, but in no case should the numbers be allowed to fall below those necessary to restore order. This may not be as costly or as difficult as is sometimes imagined. In the ten days following the earthquake in Los Angeles in January 1994, the police markedly increased their presence on the streets. They did this by, among other things, moving police from desk jobs to street work. Normally, seven hundred officers patrol the streets of Los Angeles, one of the nation's largest and most crime-plagued cities. In the aftermath of the earthquake, the city deployed about two thousand officers. Crime declined to only 10 percent of what it had averaged during the previous months. Obviously other factors were involved in this dramatic decline, such as the presence of several hundred National Guard troops, but the temptations to commit crimes such as looting were also much greater than normal after the quake. The point is that the cost of deploying two thousand street patrol officers for a sprawling metropolis like Los Angeles with a large underclass population appears a very reasonable price to pay for a major reduction in crime and crime's attendant costs, especially in relation to the costs of other, far less critical, city services.[1]

Moreover, as I argued earlier, strict enforcement of truancy laws would be very useful in reducing the number of adolescents in a position to engage in criminal conduct. Chronic truants must be removed to special schools designed specifically for that purpose. Equally useful would be the imposition and strict enforcement of curfews for school-age children. In addition, inner-city schools must be made as safe and orderly as are those in suburban communities.

The point of these strategies is to prevent crime among young people before it is actually committed. This is a deterrence strategy, but different from the sort usually envisioned where crime is deterred by swift and severe punishment. The notion of deterrence advocated here is one in which there are a sufficient number of police to deter wrongdoing by their mere presence.

One virtue of these proposals is that they merely attempt to reintroduce common policies that worked in the past and currently work wherever they are employed. I think these policies would meet with widespread approval by the general public. Polls indicate that crime is a major concern of most Americans, both black and white, and blacks, in particular, express a need for greater police protection.[2] In the case of truancy curtailment, the proposal merely calls for the enforcement of current laws. Almost all parents, black and white, place great emphasis on the education of their children; few are likely to oppose efforts to assure that their children attend school, especially if schools are made safe and secure. In the case of curfews, few people seem to think it is well for school-age children to be on the streets late at night.

Another virtue of these proposals is that they do not require a major overhaul of the criminal justice system. In fact, if the actual number of crimes committed by adolescents were markedly reduced, as I think would be the case, then the current system could probably be returned to effective functioning. It is now overwhelmed by the sheer number of defendants that need to be processed. With fewer criminals being prosecuted, jails would be less crowded, and judges would have greater latitude to incarcerate those they felt required incarceration.

The main obstacles to these proposals would be political. These policies would be opposed by those who claim that they will serve to damage black children, since black children will be unfairly charged with wrongdoing, will be unfairly relegated to inferior schools, and will be targeted by authorities for minor truancy and curfew violations. But this argument is less than convincing, since the failure in recent decades to control crime and adolescent misbehavior has led to damage to black children far more grievous than could have been inflicted by discriminatory whites. White middle-class children rarely die because their classmates roam the streets carrying handguns; black underclass children die in appalling numbers because of such behavior.

Such objections rest on the idea that white authorities are so endemically racist that they would use whatever means possible to thwart the advancement of black children. While there was some merit to this charge, especially in reference to the Deep South thirty years ago, today it is hard to sustain. Why should city officials and police forces that are increasingly composed of blacks discriminate against black children in cities which are themselves made up of black majorities? Have we become so distrustful of civil servants that we do not believe that appropriate safeguards can be devised to prevent abuse? There is something seriously wrong with the thinking that allows such fears to forestall policies to prevent a violent minority of adolescents from destroying their communities and crippling the opportunities of the children living there.

It should be clear by now that those who oppose efforts to reduce crime are not, whatever they may claim or believe, acting in the best interest of black children, but rather are, by their opposition, compelling black children to continue in a way of life that is killing them and destroying their chances for productive futures. The claim that any politician raising the issue of crime is pandering to white racism must be shown to be the false charge it usually is. People in positions to influence public opinion, not least of all social scientists, must make clear to the general public, and especially to blacks, just how vital orderly communities are for the healthy development of children.

A more fully developed proposal to curtail crime in the inner cities cannot reasonably be presented here. It is enough to point out that few societies are unable to perform the basic function of maintaining domestic tranquility. It is simply not credible to maintain that the United States is incapable of finding ways of dealing with this problem if it musters the political and moral will to do so.

A reduction in crime would serve, in addition, an important role in an overall strategy to reduce illegitimacy among young women. The most effective way to encourage black women to postpone pregnancy would be to increase the supply of suitable marital prospects. A direct effect of curtailing crime among black adolescent males would be to improve their educational performance and their chances of finding employment and earnings sufficient to support families. This, in turn, might induce more black women to postpone motherhood.

The enforcement of truancy laws and curfews would also go a long way toward reducing illegitimacy. In recent years ever-younger children are becoming pregnant. It is not uncommon for fifteen- and sixteen-year-old girls to be mothers. Many educators argue that this proves the need for greater sex education and for the distribution of contraceptives in schools, even though these strategies have little likelihood of success. The polling data reviewed in Chapter 10 suggests that sex education may in fact increase the rate of illegitimacy among young women.[3] As is proved the world over, however, the best prophylactic for youthful sexual indiscretions is the watchful eyes of concerned parents and other caretakers who can regulate the activities of young people. Curfews and truancy laws make that task easier.

Such an approach to adolescent sexuality is sometimes said to be unrealistic and an attempt to "turn back the clock." People who say such things seem to believe that human patterns of behavior are directed by a sort of unalterable historical process having a life of its own. Of course one cannot go back in time, but one can most assuredly rethink social policies and reinstate those that have worked in earlier times. History does not just *happen,* it is made to happen by human beings who act in more or less responsible, and more or less reasonable, ways.

If, in addition, the government were to change the way it assists unmarried mothers, it might add further incentives to postpone pregnancy. Under current policies the incentives tend to operate in the wrong direction. No policy should be cruel to children or callous toward the special difficulties of women, but an effective policy to reduce illegitimacy must nevertheless create a system of incentives that promotes the postponement of motherhood until a woman is in a position to provide for her children. In most cases that implies postponing pregnancy until marriage. In no case should a policy be maintained that creates positive incentives for unwed motherhood, such as that which allows young women to set up their own independent households once they have given birth to a child.

Of course, any program to curtail illegitimacy is likely to be attacked by some as an attempt to limit black population growth. Such a charge ignores the demographic data. Black women today are not raising especially large numbers of children compared to white women, but rather are giving birth to children at young ages without the assistance of husbands. An effective policy to encourage black women to postpone motherhood need not have any effect on black population growth, but would marvelously improve black economic prospects.

If crime and illegitimacy were brought down to more manageable levels, it is reasonable to suppose that black educational performance would show marked improvement, for all the reasons outlined in earlier chapters. The simple expedient of enforcing truancy laws would by itself have a positive effect. However, the single most important requirement for improved education for black children is restoring order in the schools they attend. Schools can only be made orderly if administrators and teachers are in a position to enforce rules and regulations and to remove those who continually violate them. Children who disrupt the education of others, who threaten and assault others, have no place in a normal school and must be removed to special settings until it is clear that they can behave appropriately.

No middle-class parent in suburbia would allow a child to attend the sort of schools to which the urban poor are condemned. Politicians and educators who tell parents they must accept disorder and violence in schools are professionally bankrupt. Probably the clearest argument for school choice is that poor inner-city parents would no longer be captive to school administrators who refuse to deal effectively with these problems.

Those who oppose school choice argue that the public schools would become the "dumping grounds" for all those thought undesirable by private and parochial schools. This argument ignores the fact that these undesirable students are currently dumped into the public schools. The public schools, due to the policy restrictions placed on them, cannot adequately deal with these children. The effect is that these troubled children are failed by the current system, as are the nondisruptive students whose education is undermined by the presence of troubled children in their midst.

Perhaps if public schools became the schools of last resort, the people who run them could turn to more effective ways to deal with disruptive students. Perhaps in such circumstances, children's rights advocates would be more understanding of the need for revised measures to enforce school regulations—measures that would be somewhat less restrictive than those necessary in criminal proceedings.

One advantage of these proposals for educational improvement is that most recommend a return to policies that were effectively employed in this country in the past and are currently employed to good effect all over the world. The United States appears to be the only modern society where people are expected to send children to schools that are disorderly and dangerous. The simple fact, recognized worldwide, is that schools cannot function unless education is treated as a serious business that must be conducted in a disciplined and orderly environment.

A primary advantage of most of the proposals made here is that they deal with problems in a preventative rather than in a remedial way. This is not the case with many of the proposals discussed in the popular media, which are designed to solve problems that never should have been allowed to develop in the first place. This is especially misguided in light of the fact that many of these problems involve habits of thought and behavior that, in normal circumstances, take years to inculcate and are rarely amenable to quick or easy solutions.

For instance, we often hear of the need for job training programs to prepare the poor for useful employment. Yet the most successful job training program ever developed, the public school, is deprived of its ability to carry out its task because of debilitating and restrictive regulations. The educational systems in most advanced countries are able to prepare almost all students for useful employment or for more-advanced training. We should attempt to emulate countries that are successful in this regard, rather than attempting to create new methods out of whole cloth.

Job training programs are likely to be effective with displaced workers who already possess basic skills and fundamental work habits. They are not likely to be effective with young people who have never worked and who lack the rudimentary skills they should have learned in school. How is remedial training likely to produce employable workers in six months when the schools have failed to produce them in twelve years?

Similarly, some have urged an expansion of the Head Start program to overcome the deficits poor children bring to their first years in school. But the evidence indicates that Head Start has only short-run effects on academic achievement and only modest effects on things like drop-out rates and being held back in school.[4] This should surprise no one. How can a year or two in pre-kindergarten be sufficient to overcome the debilitating and demoralizing conditions in black neighborhoods and schools that doom so many black children to failure? If the schools were made more effective, efforts like Head Start might be unnecessary or, if found necessary, might begin to show more-promising results.

In a similar vein, we are told of the need for drug treatment programs, even though the evidence is clear that such programs are only fitfully effective. All the while, the most effective way of preventing drug abuse, namely employing the watchful eyes of concerned adults over children, is dismissed as unrealistic, even though where this remedy is employed, it almost always works.

Other common policy proposals are unpromising on other grounds. An example is the recent proposal to curtail single parenthood by limiting welfare payments to two years, after which a work requirement would be imposed. The problem with this proposal is that Americans are not likely to support a policy that allows a child to go hungry or homeless because a mother is irresponsible and refuses to take a job. As a consequence, it is difficult to see how a work requirement could be realistically imposed.

Another example is the proposal for enterprise zones to attract businesses and jobs to the inner cities, which on its face seems a reasonable idea. Yet it is ironic to be forced to think this way because we have squandered, and continue to squander, the richest source of jobs for unskilled young people in the city, which is the presence of a vibrant middle class. A return of the middle class to the nation's cities, which can only be effected by safe and agreeable neighborhoods, would be a far greater boon than the few businesses that could be lured into locating there by government tax relief.[5]

It is true that the cities have lost large numbers of industrial jobs to the suburbs and to foreign competition, as William Julius Wilson has maintained.[6] But it is not clear whether we could or should attempt to reverse the economic trends that have led to those job losses. Why should children in the inner cities be trained for jobs that are increasingly becoming obsolete, while their suburban counterparts are being made ready for more skilled advanced-technology occupations? Of course, so long as inner-city schools fail in their most rudimentary tasks, we can hardly expect them to prepare students for advanced training.

The proposals outlined here are race-neutral: children of all races need orderly schools and communities, and all are entitled to these things. The implementation of these proposals would go a long way toward reducing the wide disparities in the difficulties confronting black and white children as they struggle to make their way to maturity. These proposals also benefit from the fact that they involve local concerns. Communities can tailor police forces, truancy laws, and curfews to meet local needs and conditions. In fact, states and local communities should be encouraged to experiment with different mixes of strategies to restore order to troubled neighborhoods.

It would be naive to imagine that these proposals would be readily accepted and easily implemented. The current cultural, political, and legal climate militate against their adoption. But it is a mistake to imagine that the status quo can be maintained. Conditions in the inner cities are growing worse, and none of the widely discussed ideas to correct the spiral of violence and despair are likely to be even minimally effective. It is well for those in positions of influence to begin a reevaluation of current policies and their consequences.

III. Social Policy and the Rise of Black Ethnocentrism

Current social policy, by words and actions, conveys to underclass blacks the understanding that other people are responsible for their problems. It should not surprise us that as a consequence some blacks take these admonitions seriously. Neither should it surprise us that some blacks express hostility and bitterness toward those they have been led to believe cause them so much harm.

A common explanation of the riot in Los Angeles in the spring of 1992 was that the young people who rioted there were expressing their rage at the injustices of American society. This of course is similar to the explanation offered by the Kerner Commission Report about the riots of the 1960s.[7] If, however, the conventional explanation of black difficulties is wrong, then these young rioters attacked and killed dozens of innocent people and destroyed thousands of businesses out of the mistaken belief that others were responsible for their distressed circumstances. False explanations of people's problems cannot provide them with solutions and can cause great harm. It is not unreasonable to characterize the many victims of the Los Angeles riot, and especially the Koreans whose businesses were destroyed and whose loved ones were maimed and killed, as scapegoats for black grievances based on false explanations.[8]

The animosity expressed by some blacks against the Koreans in Los Angeles reflects a similar pattern in other large cities with substantial numbers of recent immigrants. This is especially the case where new immigrants come to dominate various retail trades, as is common in New York and other cities where Koreans, for instance, dominate the small grocery business and people from the Indian subcontinent dominate newspaper and magazine stores. Ugly demonstrations against these immigrant enterprises have become a common tactic of black demagogues who claim that immigrants succeed by exploiting black citizens. These attacks are reminiscent of similar charges made in the 1940s and 1950s against Jewish merchants, who often dominated retail trade in black communities at the time. Myrdal commented on a certain anti-Semitism among blacks in the larger cities in those decades but explained it as "rather natural," since Jews often had more contact with blacks than other whites in their roles as businessmen and landlords and were easy targets for black frustrations.[9]

It is hard to believe that the constant message to young blacks that the problems of their people are brought on by the machinations of the larger society, or by specific groups such as Jews or Asians, will have no effect. Many black youth may come to be filled with racial resentment that can only lead to a poisoning of race relations.

A sad case in point was the recent outbreak of anti-Semitic rioting in August 1991 in New York's Crown Heights neighborhood. In Crown Heights some 15,000 Hasidic Jews live in an enclave surrounded by some 100,000 blacks. The rioting was triggered by an automobile accident in which a car driven by a Hasidic driver jumped the sidewalk and killed a black child and injured another. Within minutes, a false rumor spread that a Hasidic ambulance service refused to assist the injured children, one of whom died as a consequence of this callous behavior. The incident was followed by an orgy of violence and looting by black adolescents that lasted for four days and resulted in the death of a Jewish man and numerous injuries to others. Throughout this period the black community was exhorted by a host of people who characterized the rioting as the justifiable response to the injustices perpetrated by the Hasidic community.[10]

What were the injustices claimed? It was argued that the Jews had more police protection and better community services than did blacks. A second charge was a somewhat updated version of the old claim that Jews are excessively clannish.

Both of these assertions about Hasidic Jews are in large measure true, but utterly beside the point when it comes to explaining black problems. The Hasidic Jews are an insular community, as are many people belonging to religious sects. They are well organized and hence are better able to demand needed city services. The claim, however, that they obtain better police protection than blacks, while probably true, is somewhat hypocritical when uttered by leaders who regularly attack the police in the most unmeasured tones for insensitivity and brutality in their dealings with blacks.

The Hasidic community is virtually free of crime, drug abuse, and illegitimacy. Hasidic children do well in school and are generally hardworking. For black children to be taught that the disarray in which they live is somehow produced by the machinations of their religious neighbors is hardly conducive to racial harmony and understanding. Nor is it likely to improve the circumstances of black underclass children.

Similar charges are also regularly leveled against Korean merchants, who are subject to black boycotts in many large American cities. One particularly ugly boycott in New York City dominated the news for months in 1990. A Korean merchant was said to have assaulted a black customer, a charge that was never filed with the police and was, in all likelihood, fraudulent. Boycotters chanted that blacks should only shop at stores owned by "people who look like us," and threatened customers who entered the store. Sadly, even though ordered by the court to keep the boycotters some distance from the store, the city administration callously refused to enforce the order. The consequence was that the Korean couple who ran the store were eventually forced out of business and lost their life savings in the process.[11]

It is not really all that strange that some blacks should harbor resentment against successful ethnic groups living side-by-side with them. After all, they have been told by various authoritative figures that their difficulties really do stem from white conspiracies to keep blacks down and that white economic advantage accrues from discrimination against blacks. It is a simple extension of that logic to imagine that any group that exhibits economic success and that has contact with blacks must likewise achieve its success by exploiting them. The sad fact is that few black leaders in New York attempted to point out the error of this way of thinking during the attacks on the Jews and the Koreans.

The expression of open hostility among many in the black community toward other ethnics is extremely unfortunate. Social scientists who seek to excuse and justify such violent reactions on the part of blacks are, of course, free to continue to do so. But they can no longer seriously maintain that in so doing they are holding the moral high ground; there are far too many innocent victims strewn about to make that claim sustainable.

IV. The Consequences of Temporizing

If we do not consciously set about to correct the status quo, we may find current conditions generating an unexpected and unfortunate chain of circumstances that may be difficult to reverse. The reason is plain. Societies are not static in nature, but rather are dynamic systems in which trends that continue for any period of time almost always create new realities that modify those trends. American society is particularly dynamic and fluid, marked by large-scale immigration and great social and geographic mobility. It is, in fact, very unlikely that the current uneasy accommodation of most Americans to the deteriorating conditions in the inner cities will continue unchallenged.

Consider the impact of immigration as only one factor that may produce unexpected changes. America is clearly becoming more racially and ethnically heterogeneous. While the focus of attention on racial matters during the past forty years has been on relations between blacks and whites, this may not be the case in the future. It is true that political control of many major cities has shifted to blacks, who are likely to remain in control for many years to come. In some cities, however, new ethnic alignments may arise, and control may well shift to new coalitions.

New York City, for instance, which until recently had a black mayor, is less than 30 percent black. As Asians and Hispanics increase in numbers, all sorts of new alignments are possible. Furthermore, it is quite possible that these alignments may be based as much on class or value orientations as on race or ethnicity. It is not at all clear, for instance, that upwardly mobile Asians and Hispanics will align themselves with underclass blacks on the grounds that they are all oppressed by whites, a dubious proposition in cities with increasingly less-visible white populations.

Needless to say, the open attacks by blacks against successful immigrants in major cities that we have witnessed recently, and the failure of city officials to respond vigorously to them, are unlikely to promote ethnic harmony between blacks and other ethnics. It is by no means certain that the newer ethnic groups will react passively to such attacks, especially as their numbers grow. The clear breakdown of police protection for Korean store-owners during the Los Angeles riot led many to arm themselves for their own protection.[12] If future riots find the police equally impotent, we should not be altogether surprised were a minor race war to break out. Anyone who thinks this cannot happen has not learned much from recent history.

It is a great mistake to dismiss the growing stridency and separatist rhetoric of black leaders with its openly ethnocentric content. The political value of demagogic hate-mongering aimed at disaffected young men is too well known to belabor. To the extent that underclass blacks represent the largest segment of disaffected urban dwellers, we can expect to see even more of these appeals, especially if they are left unchallenged. The problem is compounded by social scientists and political leaders who, for all manner of reasons, seek to excuse the excesses of black criminals and gang members, as was apparent in the discussions following the riot in Los Angeles.[13]

It is important to acknowledge forthrightly that many of those who raise objections to dealing effectively with black crime are simply old-fashioned demagogues who benefit from the existence of a large disaffected urban underclass. If life among the urban poor were orderly and free of crime and physical decay, and if urban schools were effective, to whom would such leaders direct their appeals? If black neighborhoods had rates of crime and social pathology similar to Asian neighborhoods, white Americans would exhibit no more fear of blacks than they currently exhibit of Asians or other ethnics. Who benefits from the fears (often confused with racism) of whites engendered by underclass pathologies?

There are obvious dangers in appeals to ethnic resentment. At the very least, such appeals undercut support among whites who have in the past been supportive of black aspirations. A much worse possibility is that intemperate posturing among black leaders will spawn a counter-movement among disaffected whites, who are unlikely to distinguish between middle-class blacks and the angry demonstrators appearing nightly on the evening news.

Perhaps as disturbing as what is transpiring in the inner cities are parallel trends in higher education, where the next generation of middle-class blacks is being groomed for roles of leadership and responsibility. Unfortunately, instead of fostering assimilation, current trends in higher education may be doing just the opposite.

These trends can be traced in part to affirmative action policies practiced by colleges and universities. The beneficiaries of affirmative action are often the children of middle-class blacks or those already on the road to middle-class status; few children from the underclass are in a position to take advantage of college educations. The sense of unfair advantage with which these programs are viewed creates resentment in those who feel harmed by them. Not least among these are the ambitious sons and daughters of immigrant groups, Asians in particular, who are unlikely to continue to accept quietly the disadvantages that affirmative action programs impose on them.

At the University of California at Berkeley, for instance, Asians must score over two hundred points higher than blacks on the SAT to gain admission. Understandably, Asians have protested this discrimination. The Chinese children of parents working long hours in their own small businesses, for example, are not likely to be persuaded that they somehow have advantages that are unavailable to the sons and daughters of black accountants and school teachers. It is difficult to deny that the Asian students have logic on their side.[14]

These policies have, as discussed earlier, the perverse effect of placing black students in settings where they are at a competitive disadvantage and consequently perform less well than their white and Asian counterparts. An unfortunate but common reaction is for black students to insulate themselves from others. Black students often retreat into segregated black enclaves in their social contacts and in their housing. Some retreat into black studies programs to gain refuge from the problems they face in college settings. Unfortunately, many of the courses offered under the rubric of black studies encourage racial chauvinism and frequently espouse separatist positions.[15] The dominant themes on many ''politically correct'' campuses reinforce these separatist teachings. Popular theories in the social sciences and the humanities promote highly critical views of American values and institutions, which serve to alienate young people from the American mainstream. White students who come out of that mainstream and who hope to return to it are not likely to be permanently harmed by exposure to such ideas. Black students, many of whom are not yet at home in the mainstream, may be discouraged from efforts to gain acceptance.

The upshot is that instead of preparing the future black middle-class to take its place beside the white middle-class, many colleges are acting to make that more difficult. It is possible that many of these students may come to feel as alienated from the dominant ethos of American society as have many of their counterparts in the underclass.

It is unwise to ignore the possibility that current trends have already set in motion dynamic changes whose future course is difficult to gauge. If conditions in the inner cities do not improve, and instead continue to grow more pathological, blacks, including those in the middle class, may find themselves facing increased hostility from whites who are fearful of under-class behavior and less sympathetic to blacks in general. To the extent that a black separatist rhetoric is increasingly endorsed by blacks, including middle-class college graduates, the less likely are blacks to have common grounds of discourse with whites or with the growing ranks of new immigrant groups, who seem anxious to follow the assimilationist example of earlier groups. It may well be that the current consensus on race will start to unravel, and with it public support for current civil rights policies. What this augurs for America is difficult to judge.

If the problems plaguing underclass black neighborhoods continue un-abated, we can expect middle-class Americans of all races and ethnic groups to attempt to quarantine the inner cities and to build protective walls around their own communities. This of course has already happened in many areas. Walled private communities where entry is barred to all but residents have sprung up in various parts of the country. Shopping malls, especially those in large cities, are clear responses to the inability of police to provide protection on public thoroughfares. Such malls, being private property, can enforce their own rules with their own private police forces.[16] If these trends continue, we may witness the beginnings of a new system of racial segregation and isolation. This is all the more likely if public opinion comes to accept segregationist actions as legitimate responses to the threat of violent crime.[17]

A scenario in which the major cities of America come to take on the nightmarish cast of Detroit would mean that America has lost its way. To abandon the inner cities and deliver their impoverished inhabitants into the hands of a violent criminal subculture would be an admission of utter moral bankruptcy. But that is where present policies are inexorably leading. In such a grim scenario, preachments of racial tolerance would fall on deaf ears, especially if the cities rang with preachments of racial hatred and racial retribution.

American institutions earlier in the century, while committed to the idea of pluralism, were even more committed to the idea of assimilation and were willing to impose assimilation—in language and fundamental values—even when it was resisted, which it rarely was. That willingness was fortified by a profound sense of the rightness of the American experiment and an almost reverential respect for its values and its history. The most glaring and repugnant exception was the enslavement and subsequent segregation of black Americans that was finally repudiated some four decades ago by the generation of Americans whose moral vision was fixed by the barbarities of World War II.

It is considerably less clear whether American institutions, today, have either the commitment or the will necessary to break the spiral of ethnic and racial disharmony that we are currently witnessing. A reluctance to defend the American ethos is all too common today. It arises out of the mistaken belief that to require Americans of different backgrounds to acquire mainstream values is to denigrate their own cultural heritage. This is a false and pernicious idea.[18]

It would be ironic and tragic if American institutions, out of a desire to demonstrate respect for the painful black experience in this country, failed to act vigorously to reverse the current trends toward separation. It is folly to continue to allow the cities to spiral out of control. A failure now to set things right may set in motion a dynamic and unexpected series of social changes that may be impossible to reverse. Far better to confront the problems of the black underclass now while there is still a powerful desire for racial harmony and considerable sympathy for efforts to assist blacks on the part of most Americans. To squander that sympathy or to imagine it is boundless is to betray a profound lack of historical and ethical imagination.

It is well to recall that Gunnar Myrdal, in the conclusion to his monumental *An American Dilemma,* expressed the belief that the driving force behind social science was a "faith that institutions can be improved and strengthened and that people are good enough to live a happier life."[19] In the 1960s, far too many people, including social scientists, forgot the fundamental message Myrdal delivered, which was that it was the essential decency of American democracy, of its values and institutions, which would form the moral basis for the attack on the unjust practices under which black Americans suffered. It was in the traditional American values of fair play, of hard work and self-reliance, of optimism and open opportunity that Myrdal saw the antidote to narrow prejudice and discrimination. He urged a strengthening of American values and institutions, not their wholesale revision.

The alterations, and consequent weakening, of American institutions and of traditional values that began in the 1960s were premised on the belief that they would quicken the attainment of racial equality. In retrospect, it is understandable why things went awry. Social institutions and moral values evolve organically over generations to cope with fundamental human problems. If they function well, it is because they serve human needs and accommodate themselves to those aspects of human nature which cannot be easily altered. It is not always possible for individuals living at a specific moment in history to understand fully why those institutions and values take the forms they have or to see clearly what might be the consequences of changing them.

Two centuries ago, Edmund Burke, in reflecting on the tragic consequences of the French Revolution, understood this well. He pointed out that it is difficult to assess the outcomes of social change. As Burke wrote:

> [V]ery plausible schemes, with very pleasing commencements, have often shameful and lamentable conclusions. . . . The science of government being . . . a matter which requires experience, and even more experience than any person can gain in his whole life, however sagacious and observing he may be, it is with infinite caution that any man ought to venture upon pulling down an edifice which has answered in any tolerable degree for ages the common purposes of society. . . .[20]

The fundamental values and institutions of American society were not in need of the changes that they underwent beginning in the 1960s. What they needed instead was to be broadened to accommodate all Americans, including black Americans who for so long had been excluded. Once included, however, black Americans had every reason to hope and believe that those values and institutions would serve their aspirations as well as they had served the aspirations of white Americans for generations. Such hopes and beliefs were well founded, and as the data reviewed in earlier chapters indicates, blacks made great progress in the twenty-five years following World War II. It is because those values and institutions were too often altered or abandoned since the late 1960s that we now face such serious difficulties.

America owes the children growing up in the inner cities the same opportunities and hopes for a better life that it now extends to those who flock to our shores from every corner of the earth. The surest and finest way to meet that obligation is by restoring the institutions and values and orderly communities that enable families and children to thrive and prosper. If we can manage to do that, I think it is reasonable to assume that black children will complete the task of securing racial equality that America began with so much hope almost a half-century ago.

Notes

Introduction

1. Arnold Rose, "Postscript: Twenty Years Later," in Gunnar Myrdal, with Richard Sterner and Arnold Rose, *An American Dilemma: The Negro Problem and Modern Democracy,* 20th anniversary ed. (New York: Harper & Row, 1962), p. xliv. Rose went on to say: "These changes would not mean that there would be equality between the races within this time, for the heritage of past discriminations would still operate to give Negroes lower 'life chances.' But the dynamic social forces creating inequality will, I predict, be practically eliminated in three decades."
2. Langston Hughes, *Selected Poems of Langston Hughes* (New York: Alfred A. Knopf, 1959), pp. 252–54.
3. See S. Robert Lichter, Stanley Rothman, and Linda Lichter, *The Media Elite: America's New Powerbrokers* (Bethesda, MD: Adler and Adler, 1986).
4. See Carl N. Degler, *In Search of Human Nature: The Decline and Revival of Darwinism in American Social Thought* (New York: Oxford University Press, 1991), pp. 32–55, for a useful discussion of these arguments. See also Ernest R. Hilgard, *Psychology in America: A Historical Survey* (New York: Harcourt Brace Jovanovich, 1987), pp. 455–73.
5. It is necessary to point out here that the social scientists may have been overreaching in this; ethnic and religious murder on a massive scale are hardly historical curiosities, and it is a mistake to blame Darwin's *Origin of Species* for ethnocentrism and xenophobia, which may be near-universal propensities among human groups. This point is taken up at length below, in Chapter 7. For a chilling discussion of the state-sponsored mass murder of civilians in the Vendée region of western France in the years immediately following the Revolution of 1789, a relatively recent pre-Darwinian case in point, see Simon Schama, *Citizens: A Chronicle of the French Revolution* (New York: Alfred A. Knopf, 1989), pp. 787–92.
6. See, for example, Thomas Sowell, *Civil Rights: Rhetoric or Reality?* (New York: William Morrow and Company, 1984).

7. James S. Coleman, "On the Self-Suppression of Academic Freedom," *Academic Questions,* vol. 4, no. 1 (Winter 1990–91), p. 20.

8. See, for example, Mark Snyderman and Stanley Rothman, *The IQ Controversy: The Media and Public Policy* (New Brunswick, NJ: Transaction Books, 1988). This book offers a well-researched and well-documented case study of the sort of suppression under discussion.

9. See Lichter, Rothman, and Lichter, *The Media Elite,* esp. pp. 20–92.

10. "Woman Forced to Watch as 2 Friends Are Killed," *New York Times,* December 1, 1992, p. B8.

11. The four men were apprehended shortly after the murders. One pled guilty and agreed to testify against the other three, who were put on trial for murder. See Henry Pierson Curtis, "Teen Could Get Life after Guilty Plea in Carjacking," *Orlando Sentinel,* February 3, 1993, p. B1.

12. David O. Sears, Letitia Anne Peplau, Jonathan L. Freedman, and Shelley E. Taylor, *Social Psychology,* 6th ed. (Englewood Cliffs, NJ: Prentice Hall, 1988), p. 413.

13. *Brown v. Board of Education of Topeka,* 74 S. Ct. 686 (1954); the quoted material is drawn from Kenneth B. Clark, "Blacks' S.A.T. Scores," *New York Times,* October 21, 1982, p. 31.

14. Abigail Thernstrom, "Beyond the Pale," *New Republic,* December 16, 1991, p. 22.

15. Myrdal, Sterner, and Rose, *An American Dilemma,* 20th anniversary ed., pp. 800–801.

16. U.S. Bureau of the Census, *Statistical Abstract of the United States 1992,* 112th ed. (Washington, DC), p. 69.

17. U.S. Bureau of the Census, *Statistical Abstract of the United States 1982–83,* 103d ed. (Washington, DC), p. 66.

18. Seymour P. Lachman and Barry A. Kosmin, "Black Catholics Get Ahead," *New York Times,* September 14, 1991, p. 19. Barry Kosmin is identified as the director of the City University of New York's survey of religious identification, from which this information was obtained.

19. Sowell, *Civil Rights,* p. 77.

20. Gunnar Myrdal, with Richard Sterner and Arnold Rose, *An American Dilemma: The Negro Problem and Modern Democracy,* 2 vols. (New York: Harper & Brothers Publishers, 1944).

21. T. W. Adorno, Else Frenkel-Brunswik, Daniel J. Levinson, and R. Nevitt Sanford, *The Authoritarian Personality* (New York: Harper & Row, 1950).

22. See William Tucker, "Is Police Brutality the Problem?" *Commentary,* vol. 95, no. 1 (January 1993), pp. 23–28. Tucker argues that crime has grown more violent in recent years, and also that the number of young men in the crime-prone eighteen- to twenty-four-year-old age cohort is going to increase in coming years.

23. Sam Roberts, quoting Senator Bradley, in "Race Meets Race, But Fear Is Faster," *New York Times,* April 13, 1992, p. B3.

24. See Tucker, "Is Police Brutality the Problem?"; and Arch Puddington, "Is White Racism the Problem?" *Commentary,* vol. 94, no. 1 (July 1992), pp. 31–36.

25. See Harold Meyerson, "Fractured City: How the Riots Will Change L.A.," *New Republic,* May 25, 1992, pp. 23–25; Midge Decter, "How the Rioters Won," *Commentary,* vol. 94, no. 1 (July 1992), pp. 17–22; Edward Norden, "South-Central Korea: Post-Riot L.A.," *American Spectator,* vol. 25, no. 9 (September 1992), pp. 33–40; and Philip Gourevitch, "The Crown Heights Riot and Its Aftermath," *Commentary,* vol. 95, no. 1 (January 1993), pp. 29–34.

26. Jason DeParle, "Talk Grows of Government Being Out to Get Blacks," *New York Times,* October 29, 1990, p. B6.

Part I. The Current Scene

1. Gunnar Myrdal, with Richard Sterner and Arnold Rose, *An American Dilemma: The Negro Problem and Modern Democracy,* 2 vols. (New York: Harper & Brothers Publishers, 1944).

Chapter 1. Social Science and Social Responsibility

1. See William R. Beer, "Sociology and the Effects of Affirmative Action: A Case of Neglect," *American Sociologist,* vol. 19, no. 3 (1988), pp. 218–31; Sandra Scarr, "Race and Gender as Psychological Variables: Social and Ethical Implications," *American Psychologist,* vol. 43, no. 6 (1988), pp. 56–59; Richard J. Herrnstein, "Still an American Dilemma," *Public Interest,* no. 98 (Winter 1990), pp. 3–17; and Jan H. Blits and Linda S. Gottfredson, "Employment Testing and Job Performance," *Public Interest,* no. 98 (Winter 1990), pp. 18–25.
2. Thomas Sowell, *Civil Rights: Rhetoric or Reality?* (New York: William Morrow and Company, 1984); Charles Murray, *Losing Ground: American Social Policy 1950–1980* (New York: Basic Books, 1984); William Julius Wilson, *The Truly Disadvantaged: The Inner City, the Underclass, and Public Policy* (Chicago: University of Chicago Press, 1987). Useful collections of writings on these issues are found in Sheldon H. Danziger and Daniel H. Weinberg, eds., *Fighting Poverty: What Works and What Doesn't* (Cambridge, MA: Harvard University Press, 1986); and Christopher Jencks and Paul E. Peterson, eds., *The Urban Underclass* (Washington, DC: Brookings Institution, 1991).
3. Thomas Sowell, *Ethnic America* (New York: Basic Books, 1981).
4. *Ibid.,* pp. 155–79.
5. See, e.g., Stephen Jay Gould, *The Mismeasure of Man* (New York: W. W. Norton and Company, 1981).
6. Maureen C. McHugh, Randi Daimon Koeske, and Irene Hanson Frieze, "Issues to Consider in Conducting Nonsexist Psychological Research: A Guide for Researchers," *American Psychologist,* vol. 41, no. 8 (1986), pp. 879–90.
7. Mill is very clear on the importance of the free exchange of ideas:

> [T]he peculiar evil of silencing the expression of an opinion is that it is robbing the human race, posterity as well as the existing generation—those who dissent from the opinion, still more than those who hold it. If the opinion is right, they are deprived of the opportunity of exchanging error for truth; if wrong, they lose, what is almost as great a benefit, the clearer perception and livelier impression of truth produced by its collision with error.

See John Stuart Mill, *On Liberty* (New York: Bobbs-Merrill, 1956), p. 21.
8. See, e.g., Peter L. Berger and Thomas Luckmann, *The Social Construction of*

Reality: A Treatise in the Sociology of Knowledge (Garden City, NY: Doubleday Anchor Books, 1967).

9. See, e.g., Thomas S. Szasz, *The Myth of Mental Illness: Foundations of a Theory of Personal Conduct* (New York: Harper and Row, 1970); and R. D. Laing, *The Divided Self: An Existential Study of Sanity and Madness* (Baltimore, MD: Penguin Books, 1965). This approach is sometimes referred to as "labeling theory." It played a prominent role in the movement to "deinstitutionalize" mental patients.

10. Charles Wellford, "Labeling Theory," in Leonard D. Savitz and Norman H. Johnston, eds., *Crime in Society* (New York: John Wiley and Sons, 1978), pp. 186–97.

11. See, e.g., "Critical Legal Studies Symposium," *Stanford Law Review,* vol. 36, no. 1 (January 1984); "A Symposium of Critical Legal Studies," *American University Law Review,* vol. 34, no. 4 (Summer 1985); and "Symposium: A Critique of Rights," *Texas Law Review,* vol. 62, no. 8 (May 1984).

12. See, e.g., Christopher Norris, *Deconstruction: Theory and Practice,* rev. ed. (New York: Routledge, 1986); John Ellis, *Against Deconstruction* (Princeton, NJ: Princeton University Press, 1989); and John R. Searle, "Is There a Crisis in American Higher Education?" *Partisan Review,* vol. 60, no. 4 (Fall 1993), pp. 693–709.

13. Of course, few scientists as scientists embrace the full logic of this view: namely, that all science serves some class interest. To do that would undercut their own claim to objectivity. Instead, they argue that the scientific theories with which they disagree serve such interests, and therefore deserve to be debunked. Consider the following attack on evolutionary thinking: "[T]hese theories operate as powerful forms of legitimation of past and present social institutions such as aggression, competition, domination of women by men, defense of national territory, individualism, and the appearance of a status and wealth hierarchy." See Sociobiology Study Group of Science for the People, "Sociobiology—Another Biological Determinism," *BioScience,* vol. 26, no. 3 (March 1976), signed by three dozen scholars; reprinted in Arthur L. Caplan, ed., *The Sociobiology Debate* (New York: Harper and Row, 1978), pp. 280–81.

14. See, e.g., Susan Chira, "Bias against Girls is Found Rife in Schools, with Lasting Damage," *New York Times,* February 12, 1992, p. 1; and Rita Kramer, "Are Girls Shortchanged in School?" *Commentary,* vol. 93, no. 6 (June 1993), pp. 48–49.

15. Edward O. Wilson, *Sociobiology,* abridged ed. (Cambridge, MA: Harvard University Press, 1980). Unless otherwise indicated, the institutional affiliation of an author refers to his or her affiliation at the time the cited work was published.

16. See Sociobiology Study Group of Science for the People, "Sociobiology—Another Biological Determinism."

17. Elizabeth Allen et al., "Against 'Sociobiology'," Letter to the Editor of the *New York Review of Books,* November 13, 1975, signed by a group of scholars heavily overlapping with the membership of the Sociobiology Study Group of Science for the People; reprinted in Caplan, ed., *The Sociobiology Debate,* p. 260.

18. *Ibid.,* p. 264.

19. Arthur Fisher, "Sociobiology: Science or Ideology?" *Society,* vol. 29, no. 5 (July/August 1992), p. 74.

20. Harvard psychologist Richard J. Herrnstein has correctly pointed out that not all traits and talents are equally distributed in all groups; some groups have more people with certain traits, others fewer. He points out that raising this issue is currently "taboo in polite company." He goes on to say that discussing

differences between blacks and whites which may exist and be unrelated to racial discrimination is now "our obscenity, much as public discussion of sexuality was the Victorian obscenity" (Herrnstein, "Still an American Dilemma," p. 7).

21. Arthur R. Jensen, "How Much Can We Boost I.Q. and Scholastic Achievement?" *Harvard Educational Review,* vol. 39 (1969), pp. 1–123.
22. Scarr, "Race and Gender as Psychological Variables," p. 57.
23. Ernest R. Hilgard, *Psychology in America: A Historical Survey* (New York: Harcourt Brace Jovanovich, 1987), p. 484.
24. Scarr, "Race and Gender as Psychological Variables," p. 56.
25. Sowell, *Civil Rights,* p. 123.
26. Sandra Scarr and Richard A. Weinberg, "IQ Test Performance of Black Children Adopted by White Parents," *American Psychologist,* vol. 31 (1976), pp. 726–39.
27. Chester W. Oden, Jr. and W. Scott MacDonald, "The RIP in Social Scientific Reporting," *American Psychologist,* vol. 33 (1978), p. 954.
28. *Ibid.,* p. 953.
29. Stephen Ceci, Douglas Peters, and Jonathan Plotkin, "Human Subjects Review, Personal Values, and the Regulation of Social Science Research," *American Psychologist,* vol. 40, no. 9 (1985), pp. 994–1002.
30. *Ibid.,* p. 1000.
31. *Ibid.,* p. 1001.
32. Sandra Graham, "Most of the Subjects were White and Middle Class: Trends in Published Research on African Americans in Selected APA Journals, 1970–1989," *American Psychologist,* vol. 47, no. 5 (1992), p. 636.
33. *Ibid.,* p. 637.
34. *Ibid.*
35. See Byron M. Roth, "Social Psychology's 'Racism'," *Public Interest,* no. 98 (1990), pp. 26–36.
36. See Arch Puddington, "Clarence Thomas and the Blacks," *Commentary,* vol. 93, no. 2 (February 1993), pp. 28–33.
37. William Ryan, *Blaming the Victim* (1971; New York: Vintage, 1976), pp. 27–28.
38. *Ibid.,* pp. 28–29.
39. *Ibid.,* p. 29.
40. *Ibid.,* p. 30.
41. James S. Coleman, "On Self-Suppression of Academic Freedom," *Academic Questions,* vol. 4, no. 1 (Winter 1990–91), p. 21.
42. *Ibid.*
43. *Ibid.*
44. A dated, but still excellent, introduction to decision theory is found in Duncan R. Luce and Howard Raiffa, *Games and Decisions* (New York: Wiley, 1957). For more-recent introductions, see Martin Shubik, *Game Theory in the Social Sciences: Concepts and Solutions* (Cambridge, MA: MIT Press, 1982); and John D. Mullen and Byron M. Roth, *Decision Making: Its Logic and Practice* (Savage, MD: Rowman and Littlefield, 1991).
45. See Donald R. Kinder, "The Continuing American Dilemma: White Resistance to Racial Change Forty Years after Myrdal," *Journal of Social Issues,* vol. 42, no. 2 (1986), pp. 151–71.
46. Sophfronia Scott Gregory, "The Hidden Hurdle," *Time,* March 16, 1992, pp. 44–46.
47. Thomas Sowell, quoted in the editorial "A Source of Ideas," *Wall Street Journal,* September 13, 1991, p. A10.

48. See Sowell, *Civil Rights.*
49. See Gunnar Myrdal, with Richard Sterner and Arnold Rose, *An American Dilemma: The Negro Problem and Modern Democracy,* 20th anniversary ed. (New York: Harper & Row, 1962), pp. 524–25.
50. Recent polls suggest that suspicion of the police and courts is common among blacks. For instance, only 17 percent of blacks, compared to 51 percent of whites, thought that ''[b]lacks and whites are treated equally by the criminal justice system'' (''A Portrait in Black and White,'' *American Enterprise,* January/ February 1991, p. 97). This topic is taken up in Chapter 8.
51. See Walter E. Williams, *The State against Blacks* (New York: McGraw-Hill, 1982).

Chapter 2. White Attitudes and Black Economic Status Today

1. Gunnar Myrdal, with Richard Sterner and Arnold Rose, *An American Dilemma: The Negro Problem and Modern Democracy,* 2 vols. (New York: Harper & Brothers Publishers, 1944). This book is discussed extensively in Chapter 3.
2. Thomas Sowell, *Preferential Policies: An International Perspective* (New York: William Morrow and Company, 1990).
3. Thomas Sowell, *Ethnic America* (New York: Basic Books, 1981), pp. 155–79.
4. Linda Chavez, *Out of the Barrio: Toward a New Politics of Hispanic Assimilation* (New York: Basic Books, 1991), p. 104.
5. *Ibid.,* pp. 104–7.
6. *Ibid.,* pp. 139–59.
7. *Ibid.,* pp. 150–51.
8. Thomas Sowell, *Civil Rights: Rhetoric or Reality?* (New York: William Morrow and Company, 1984), pp. 77–78.
9. For a recent report on the experience of Haitian New Yorkers, see Joel Dreyfuss, ''The Invisible Immigrants,'' *New York Times Magazine,* May 23, 1993, p. 20.
10. See, e.g., Daniel Benjamin, ''Cracking Down on the Right,'' *Time,* vol. 140, no. 24 (December 14, 1992), pp. 43–45; and Jacob Heilbrunn, ''What German Crisis?'' *New Republic,* vol. 207, no. 26 (December 21, 1992), pp. 21–23.
11. *Oxford English Dictionary,* 2d ed. (Oxford: Clarendon Press, 1989).
12. Gerald David Jaynes and Robin M. Williams, Jr., eds., *A Common Destiny: Blacks and American Society* (Washington, DC: National Academy Press, 1989), p. 566.
13. James Allan Davis and Tom W. Smith, *General Social Survey, 1972–1989: Cumulative Codebook* (Chicago: National Opinion Research Center, 1989). The compilation of this data is part of the National Data Program of the Social Sciences, supported by the National Science Foundation. The General Social Survey includes a fair number of questions on race, some asked regularly, but not necessarily in every year. Howard Schuman and Lawrence Bobo (both on the Board of Overseers of the General Social Survey), along with Charlotte Steeh, compiled an extremely useful summary of the raw data on racial questions gathered by the General Social Survey from 1942 to 1983 in their book *Racial Attitudes in America* (Cambridge, MA: Harvard University Press, 1985). They also included data from other national polling organizations such as the Institute

of Social Research at the University of Michigan and the Gallup organization. Much of the data cited on trends in racial attitudes comes from their analysis and from more-recent General Social Surveys.

14. Schuman, Steeh, and Bobo, *Racial Attitudes in America,* pp. 123–25.

15. David Krech, Richard S. Crutchfield, and Egerton L. Ballachey, *The Individual in Society: A Textbook of Social Psychology* (New York: McGraw-Hill, 1962), p. 194.

16. Allen C. Johnson, *Human Arrangements: An Introduction to Sociology* (New York: Harcourt Brace Jovanovich, 1989), p. 334. Johnson performed a breakdown by race for this question from the raw data of the General Social Survey for 1986.

17. James R. Kluegel, "Trends in Whites' Explanations of the Black-White Gap in Socioeconomic Status, 1977–1989," *American Sociological Review,* vol. 55 (August 1990), p. 519.

18. Blacks and whites, on average, differ by about 15 IQ points and by about 200 points on the combined verbal and math SAT. These differences are discussed in depth in Chapter 9. See also the works cited in notes 9 and 13 of Chapter 9.

19. Schuman, Steeh, and Bobo, *Racial Attitudes in America,* pp. 74–76.

20. *Ibid.*; Davis and Smith, *General Social Survey, 1972–1989: Cumulative Codebook,* p. 284.

21. Schuman, Steeh, and Bobo, *Racial Attitudes in America,* pp. 74–76.

22. Davis and Smith, *General Social Survey, 1972–1989: Cumulative Codebook,* p. 179.

23. *Ibid.*, p. 182.

24. Schuman, Steeh, and Bobo, *Racial Attitudes in America,* pp. 74–76.

25. Davis and Smith, *General Social Survey, 1972–1989: Cumulative Codebook,* p. 177.

26. *Ibid.*, p. 284.

27. *Ibid.*, p. 285.

28. Schuman, Steeh, and Bobo, *Racial Attitudes in America,* pp. 130–31.

29. *Ibid.*, pp. 78, 91.

30. Charlotte Steeh and Howard Schuman, "Young White Adults: Did Racial Attitudes Change in the 1980s?" *American Journal of Sociology,* vol. 98, no. 2 (1992), p. 340.

31. See "Race on Campus," a special issue of *New Republic,* February 18, 1991, for an important and enlightening group of articles on this issue.

32. See Byron M. Roth, "Social Psychology's 'Racism'," *Public Interest,* no. 98 (1990), pp. 26–36.

33. Rodney Stark, *Sociology,* 3d ed. (Belmont, CA: Wadsworth Publishing Company, 1989), p. 296.

34. U.S. Bureau of the Census, Current Population Reports, Series P-20, No. 464, *The Black Population in the United States: March 1991* (Washington, DC: U.S. Government Printing Office, 1992), p. 2.

35. U.S. Bureau of the Census, *Statistical Abstract of the United States 1982–83,* 103d ed. (Washington, DC), p. 432.

36. U.S. Bureau of the Census, *Statistical Abstract of the United States 1991,* 111th ed. (Washington, DC), p. 169.

37. See, e.g., Sowell, *Ethnic America*; Sowell, *Civil Rights*; and Sowell, *Preferential Policies.*

38. U.S. Bureau of the Census, Current Population Reports, Series P-20, No. 458,

Household and Family Characteristics: 1991 (Washington, DC: U.S. Government Printing Office, 1991), p. 8.

39. *Ibid.*, p. 9.
40. U.S. Bureau of the Census, *Statistical Abstract of the United States 1991*, p. 455.
41. U.S. Bureau of the Census, *The Black Population in the United States: March 1991*, pp. 8–9.
42. *Ibid.*, pp. 25–26.
43. U.S. Bureau of the Census, *Statistical Abstract of the United States 1992*, 112th ed. (Washington, DC), p. 54. These percentages were calculated by the author from statistics given in table no. 68. A similar pattern emerges for white families with children, but with the important difference that poverty is not so powerfully related to family composition for whites. Forty-two percent of white families, but only 12 percent of black families (with children), who reported incomes below $15,000 were two-parent families.
44. U.S. Bureau of the Census, *The Black Population in the United States: March 1991*, p. 17.
45. *Ibid.*, p. 21.
46. *Ibid.*, p. 74.
47. Sam Roberts, "Blacks Reach a Milestone in Queens: Income Parity," *New York Times,* June 6, 1992, p. 1.
48. U.S. Bureau of the Census, Current Population Reports, Series P-20, No. 448, *The Black Population in the United States: March 1990 and March 1989* (Washington, DC: U.S. Government Printing Office, 1991), p. 33.
49. *Ibid.*, p. 11.
50. U.S. Bureau of the Census, Current Population Reports, Special Studies Series P-23, No. 80, *The Social and Economic Status of the Black Population in the United States: An Historical View, 1790–1978* (Washington, DC: U.S. Government Printing Office, 1980), p. 48.
51. U.S. Bureau of the Census, *The Black Population in the United States: March 1990 and March 1989,* p. 9.
52. It should be noted that black and white women are equally likely to participate in the labor force. Approximately 58 percent of both groups are working or actively seeking work (*ibid.*, p. 8).
53. *Ibid.*, p. 10.
54. *Ibid.*, p. 31.
55. *Ibid.*, p. 12.
56. *Ibid.*, p. 11.
57. U.S. Bureau of the Census, *The Social and Economic Status of the Black Population in the United States: An Historical View, 1790–1978,* p. 48.
58. U.S. Bureau of the Census, *The Black Population in the United States: March 1990 and March 1989,* p. 9.
59. *Ibid.*, p. 8. The labor participation rate is the proportion of people who are currently working or seeking work and excludes those not seeking work, such as full-time students.
60. *Ibid.*, p. 10.
61. *Ibid.*, p. 31.
62. *Ibid.*, p. 12.
63. *Ibid.*, p. 61.
64. The SAT gap will be taken up in Chapter 9.

65. Sowell, *Civil Rights,* p. 45.
66. Anthony DePalma, "While Number of Black Ph.D.'s Falls, Some Ask if Foreigners are Favored," *New York Times,* April 21, 1992, p. 18.
67. U.S. Bureau of the Census, *Statistical Abstract of the United States 1991,* p. 402.
68. Jason DeParle, "Young Black Males in Capital: Study Finds 42% in Courts," *New York Times,* April 18, 1992, p. 1.
69. U.S. Bureau of the Census, *Statistical Abstract of the United States 1991,* p. 139.
70. *Ibid.,* p. 415.
71. U.S. Bureau of the Census, *The Black Population in the United States: March 1990 and March 1989,* p. 70.
72. U.S. Bureau of the Census, *Statistical Abstract of the United States 1991,* p. 65.
73. *Ibid.,* p. 18.
74. *Ibid.,* p. 138. These figures are for median educational attainment, which is the educational level at the 50th percentile level. Medians are insensitive to differences at the extremes. As we will see in Chapter 9, whites are more likely than blacks to have training beyond the high school level, and in consequence the gap in *mean* educational level between whites and blacks is greater than indicated here.
75. William Julius Wilson, *The Truly Disadvantaged: The Inner City, the Underclass, and Public Policy* (Chicago: University of Chicago Press, 1987), p. 26.
76. Ze'ev Chafets, *Devil's Night: And Other True Tales of Detroit* (New York: Random House, 1990).
77. Roger Brown, *Social Psychology,* 2d ed. (New York: Free Press, 1986), p. 587.
78. The *New York Times* reports that Dale W. Lick, "a finalist for the presidency of Michigan State University has run into trouble for a remark he made in 1979." Mr. Lick had said: "A black athlete can actually outjump a white athlete on the average, so they're better at the game. All you need to do is turn to the N.C.A.A. playoffs in basketball to see that the bulk of the players on those outstanding teams are black." One may disagree with the conclusion Mr. Lick drew from his watching N.C.A.A. teams, but the point is that his remark was taken as evidence, on its face, of potential racism ("Racial Remark Stalls Job Seeker," *New York Times,* July 22, 1993, p. A18).
79. Anne Locksley, Christine Hepburn, and Velma Ortiz, "Social Stereotypes and Judgments of Individuals: An Instance of the Base-Rate Fallacy," *Journal of Experimental Social Psychology,* vol. 18 (1982), pp. 23–42.
80. *Oxford English Dictionary,* 2d ed. (Oxford: Clarendon Press, 1989).
81. William James, *The Principles of Psychology,* vol. 2 (New York: Dover Publications, 1950), pp. 345–48.
82. DeParle, "Young Black Males in Capital," p. 1.
83. James Dao, "A Living, Barely, Behind the Wheel," *New York Times,* December 6, 1992, p. 49.
84. According to the expected-value rule, widely applied in decision theory, the value of a choice or a gamble is a product of the probability and the value of the resulting outcome of the choice. For instance, in a gamble decided by the toss of a coin that results in a winning of $5.00, the choice of "heads" is said to have an expected value of $2.50. See John D. Mullen and Byron M. Roth, *Decision Making: Its Logic and Practice* (Savage, MD: Rowman and Littlefield, 1991), pp. 157–80.
85. Dao, "A Living, Barely, Behind the Wheel," p. 49.

Part II. The Formation of Current Thought on Race Relations

1. Gunnar Myrdal, with Richard Sterner and Arnold Rose, *An American Dilemma: The Negro Problem and Modern Democracy,* 2 vols. (New York: Harper & Brothers Publishers, 1944).
2. U.S. Bureau of the Census, Current Population Reports, Special Studies Series P-23, No. 80, *The Social and Economic Status of the Black Population in the United States: An Historical View, 1790–1978* (Washington, DC: U.S. Government Printing Office, 1980), p. 13.
3. T. W. Adorno, Else Frenkel-Brunswik, Daniel J. Levinson, and R. Nevitt Sanford, *The Authoritarian Personality* (New York: Harper & Row, 1950).
4. See, e.g., John B. McConahay and Joseph C. Hough, Jr., "Symbolic Racism," *Journal of Social Issues,* vol. 32, no. 2 (1976), p. 24.
5. Thomas Byrne Edsall and Mary Edsall, *Chain Reaction: The Impact of Race, Rights, and Taxes on American Politics* (New York: W. W. Norton, 1991), pp. 55–56. The overwhelming identification of blacks with the Democratic party took shape in the 1960s. Prior to that time, neither party was seen as especially supportive or opposed to blacks on civil rights issues. Southern Democrats were often hostile to black interests.

Chapter 3. Gunnar Myrdal and An American Dilemma

1. Gunnar Myrdal, with Richard Sterner and Arnold Rose, *An American Dilemma: The Negro Problem and Modern Democracy,* 2 vols. (New York: Harper & Brothers Publishers, 1944); 20th anniversary ed. (New York: Harper & Row, 1962). The pagination is the same for both editions, except for the front matter; references to pages of the front matter are keyed to the twentieth-anniversary edition.
2. *Ibid.,* pp. 75–78.
3. *Ibid.,* pp. 1016–18.
4. *Ibid.,* p. xxiii.
5. U.S. Bureau of the Census, *Statistical Abstract of the United States 1992,* 112th ed. (Washington, DC), p. 8; John A. Garraty, *The American Nation: A History of the United States* (New York: Harper & Row, 1966), p. 424.
6. Garraty, *The American Nation,* pp. 427–28.
7. *Ibid.,* pp. 430–32.
8. *Ibid.,* pp. 441–43.
9. *Ibid.,* pp. 444–47.
10. *Ibid.,* pp. 482–83.
11. U.S. Bureau of the Census, Current Population Reports, Special Studies Series P-23, No. 80, *The Social and Economic Status of the Black Population in the United States: An Historical View, 1790–1978* (Washington, DC: U.S. Government Printing Office, 1980), pp. 13, 17.
12. Nathan Glazer and Daniel Patrick Moynihan, *Beyond the Melting Pot: The Negroes, Puerto Ricans, Jews, Italians, and Irish in New York City* (Cambridge, MA: MIT Press, 1963), p. 26.
13. U.S. Bureau of the Census, *The Social and Economic Status of the Black Population in the United States: An Historical View, 1790–1978,* p. 13.

14. Myrdal, Sterner, and Rose, *An American Dilemma*, p. 183.
15. *Ibid.*, p. 192.
16. U.S. Bureau of the Census, *Statistical Abstract of the United States 1992*, pp. 33–36.
17. Herbert G. Gutman, *The Black Family in Slavery and Freedom* (New York: Pantheon Books, 1976), p. 543.
18. Thomas Sowell reports that the residential segregation of blacks in the North was limited in the late nineteenth century, but that segregation grew in response to the migration north of uneducated rural blacks early in the twentieth century. See Thomas Sowell, *Ethnic America* (New York: Basic Books, 1981), p. 210.
19. Immigration Act of 1924. There has been much debate on the role of psychologists and IQ testing in leading to the passage of this act. See, e.g., Mark Snyderman and Richard J. Herrnstein, "Intelligence Tests and the Immigration Act of 1924," *American Psychologist*, vol. 38 (1983), pp. 987–1000.
20. Quoted in Carl N. Degler, *In Search of Human Nature: The Decline and Revival of Darwinism in American Social Thought* (New York: Oxford University Press, 1991), p. 50.
21. *Ibid.*, pp. 42–45.
22. *Ibid.*, pp. 48–49.
23. Ernest R. Hilgard, *Psychology in America: A Historical Survey* (New York: Harcourt Brace Jovanovich, 1987), p. 470.
24. See Degler, *In Search of Human Nature*, pp. 59–83; Derek Freeman, *Margaret Mead and Samoa: The Making and Unmaking of an Anthropological Myth* (Cambridge, MA: Harvard University Press, 1983), pp. 1–64; and Franz Boas, *Race, Language, and Culture* (New York: Macmillan, 1940), pp. 3–59.
25. John B. Watson, *Behaviorism* (New York: People's Institute Publishing Company, 1925). Watson's famous statement on this is: "Give me a dozen healthy infants, well-formed, and my own special world to bring them up in and I'll guarantee to take any one at random and train him to become any type of specialist I might select—doctor, lawyer, artist, merchant-chief and, yes, even begger-man and thief, regardless of his talents, penchants, tendencies, abilities, vocations, and race of his ancestors" (p. 82).
26. Margaret Mead, *Coming of Age in Samoa: A Psychological Study of Primitive Youth for Western Civilization* (New York: William Morrow, 1928).
27. Degler, *In Search of Human Nature*, pp. 187–90.
28. David W. Southern, *Gunnar Myrdal and Black-White Relations: The Use and Abuse of An American Dilemma* (Baton Rouge: Louisiana State University Press, 1987), pp. 1–6.
29. Myrdal, Sterner, and Rose, *An American Dilemma*, 20th anniversary ed., p. xxv.
30. Southern, *Gunnar Myrdal and Black-White Relations*, pp. 49–54.
31. *Ibid.*, pp. 50–51.
32. *Ibid.*, p. 6; Allan Carlson, "Forward to the Past: Rebuilding Family Life in Post-Socialist Sweden," *Family in America*, vol. 6, no. 7 (July 1992), pp. 1–7, published by the Rockford Institute Center on the Family in America.
33. F. P. Keppel, "Foreword," in Myrdal, Sterner, and Rose, *An American Dilemma*, 20th anniversary ed., p. xlviii.
34. Southern, *Gunnar Myrdal and Black-White Relations*, pp. 71–76.
35. Myrdal, Sterner, and Rose, *An American Dilemma*, 20th anniversary ed., p. lxxxii.
36. *Ibid.*, p. lxxvi.
37. *Ibid.*, p. lxxv.

38. *Ibid.*
39. *Ibid.*, pp. 30–40.
40. *Ibid.*, pp. 3–4, italics omitted.
41. *Ibid.*, p. 48.
42. *Ibid.*, pp. 1011–15.
43. *Ibid.*, pp. 1015–21.
44. *Ibid.*, pp. 1022–23.
45. *Ibid.*, p. 24.
46. *Ibid.*, p. 54.
47. *Ibid.*, pp. 84–86.
48. Degler, *In Search of Human Nature,* p. 179. Degler points out that Klineberg was a student of, and heavily influenced by, the Columbia University anthropologist Franz Boas, the leading figure in the movement to replace hereditarian explanations with cultural explanations.
49. *Ibid.*, p. 186. Degler went on to argue that social scientists rejected hereditarian explanations largely for ideological reasons, and not because the evidence was particularly convincing. They rejected such explanations, in the thirties, for the same reason they have continued to do so, namely because they are seen as antidemocratic, inegalitarian, and veiled attempts to justify racism.
50. Myrdal, Sterner, and Rose, *An American Dilemma,* 20th anniversary ed., p. 59.
51. *Ibid.*, p. 58.
52. *Ibid.*
53. *Ibid.*, p. 75.
54. *Ibid.*
55. *Ibid.*, p. 76.
56. *Ibid.*, pp. 1008–11.
57. *Ibid.*, pp. 60–61.
58. *Ibid.*, p. 61.
59. *Ibid.*, pp. 58–59.
60. *Ibid.*, pp. 78–80.
61. *Ibid.*, pp. 77–78; italics omitted.
62. *Ibid.*, p. 91.
63. *Ibid.*, p. 92.
64. *Ibid.*
65. *Ibid.*, p. 1024.
66. *Ibid.*, p. xxvii.
67. Southern, *Gunnar Myrdal and Black-White Relations,* pp. 127–50.
68. Myrdal, Sterner, and Rose, *An American Dilemma,* 20th anniversary ed., pp. xliii-xliv.
69. Thomas Byrne Edsall and Mary Edsall, *Chain Reaction: The Impact of Race, Rights, and Taxes on American Politics* (New York: W. W. Norton, 1991), pp. 35–36. The 1964 election result offers some validation of the positive response to equal rights found in the General Social Survey data reviewed in Chapter 2.
70. *Ibid.*, p. 61. The Democratic party at the time had not completely broken from its past position as a supporter of southern autonomy on racial matters.
71. *Ibid.*, p. 48.
72. *Ibid.*, p. 109.
73. Nathan Glazer, *Affirmative Discrimination: Ethnic Inequality and Public Policy* (New York: Basic Books, 1975), p. 5.
74. *Brown v. Board of Education of Topeka,* 347 U.S. 483 (1954).

75. Myrdal, Sterner, and Rose, *An American Dilemma,* p. 1066.
76. *Ibid.*
77. Edsall and Edsall, *Chain Reaction,* p. 51.
78. *Ibid.*, p. 75.
79. *Ibid.*, p. 62.

Chapter 4. The Authoritarian Personality

1. T. W. Adorno, Else Frenkel-Brunswik, Daniel J. Levinson, and R. Nevitt Sanford, *The Authoritarian Personality* (New York: Harper & Row, 1950).
2. Herbert H. Hyman and Paul B. Sheatsley, " 'The Authoritarian Personality'—A Methodological Critique,'' in Richard Christie and Marie Jahoda, eds., *Studies in the Scope and Method of "The Authoritarian Personality"* (Glencoe, IL: Free Press, 1954), p. 50.
3. Roger Kimball, who identifies Adorno as a "Frankfurt School Marxist," reports that Adorno and Max Horkheimer launched an attack on the Enlightenment in the midst of the Second World War, claiming that the "Enlightenment is totalitarian" while "safely ensconced in Los Angeles," having found asylum from Nazi Germany in the U.S. See Roger Kimball, "The Treason of the Intellectuals and 'The Undoing of Thought'," *New Criterion,* December 1992, p. 13. It is necessary to point out that one of the most important legacies of the Enlightenment was the importance of free markets. See also John Ray, "Eysenck on Social Attitudes: An Historical Critique," in Sohan Modgil and Celia Modgil, eds., *Hans Eysenck: Consensus and Controversy* (Philadelphia: Falmer Press, 1986), pp. 158–59.
4. Ernest R. Hilgard, *Psychology in America: A Historical Survey* (New York: Harcourt Brace Jovanovich, 1987), p. 643.
5. Paul F. Lazarsfeld and Wagner Thielens, Jr., *The Academic Mind: Social Scientists in a Time of Crisis* (Glencoe, IL: Free Press, 1958), pp. 3–34.
6. Karl Marx and Friedrich Engels, *The Communist Manifesto,* ed. Samuel H. Beer (Arlington Heights, IL: AHM Publishing Corporation, 1955), p. 29.
7. Adorno et al., *The Authoritarian Personality,* pp. 151–52.
8. *Ibid.*, p. 152.
9. *Ibid.*, p. 156.
10. *Ibid.*
11. Thomas Byrne Edsall and Mary Edsall, *Chain Reaction: The Impact of Race, Rights, and Taxes on American Politics* (New York: W. W. Norton, 1991), p. 41.
12. See John Gray, *Liberalism* (Minneapolis: University of Minnesota Press, 1986), for an informative treatment of classical liberalism.
13. Friedrich A. von Hayek, *The Road to Serfdom* (London: Routledge, 1944).
14. Karl R. Popper, *The Open Society and Its Enemies,* vol. 2, *The High Tide of Prophecy: Hegel, Marx, and the Aftermath* (1945; New York: Harper & Row, 1966), p. 31.
15. G. W. F. Hegel, *The Philosophy of History* (New York: Dover, 1956), p. 30.
16. *Ibid.*, p. 32.
17. See H. R. Trevor-Roper, "The Phenomenon of Fascism," in S. J. Woolf, ed., *European Fascism* (New York: Random House, 1968), pp. 18–38. Trevor-Roper, a noted British historian, made the important point that while anti-Semitism was for centuries "endemic in Europe," it was in modern times "only in Germany that it assumed a rabid form." Without the power of Germany, he argued, "the

systematic destruction of the Jews, even by native 'fascist' governments, would have been unthinkable'' (pp. 36–37). It is important to note that Italian Army officers went to great lengths to frustrate efforts to deport Jews out of areas occupied by the Italians. See Jonathan Steinberg, *All or Nothing: The Axis and the Holocaust* (New York: Routledge, 1990).

18. Don Vittorio Segre, *Memoirs of a Fortunate Jew* (New York: Adler and Adler, 1987), pp. 46–47.
19. Adorno et al., *The Authoritarian Personality,* p. 145.
20. *Ibid.,* p. 207.
21. *Ibid.,* pp. 225–41.
22. *Ibid.,* p. 287.
23. *Ibid.,* p. 385.
24. *Ibid.,* p. 387.
25. John A. Garraty, *The American Nation: A History of the United States* (New York: Harper & Row, 1966), p. 766.
26. Adorno et al., *The Authoritarian Personality,* p. 709.
27. William Ryan, *Blaming the Victim* (1971; New York: Vintage, 1976).
28. A classic, and still valuable, introduction to this research is found in Jerome D. Frank, *Persuasion and Healing: A Comparative Study of Psychotherapy,* rev. ed. (New York: Schocken Books, 1974).
29. Thomas F. Pettigrew, ''Personality and Sociocultural Factors in Intergroup Attitudes: A Cross-National Comparison,'' *Journal of Conflict Resolution,* vol. 2 (1958), pp. 39–40.
30. Roger Brown, *Social Psychology* (New York: Free Press, 1965), p. 479.
31. Roger Brown, *Social Psychology,* 2d ed. (New York: Free Press, 1986), p. 575.
32. See Hilgard, *Psychology in America* (*supra* note 4).
33. Hyman and Sheatsley, '' 'The Authoritarian Personality'—A Methodological Critique,'' pp. 54–69.
34. Adorno et al., *The Authoritarian Personality,* p. 171.
35. *Ibid.,* p. 128.
36. Many of the items were so clear (i.e., transparent to the respondent) in the attitudes they were tapping that the researchers might just as well have asked, ''Do you dislike blacks?'' For instance, the five-item version of the ethnocentrism scale is given below:

> 1. Zootsuiters prove that when people of their type have too much money and freedom, they just take advantage and cause trouble.
> 2. Negroes have their rights, but it is best to keep them in their own districts and schools and to prevent too much contact with whites.
> 3. The worst danger to real Americanism during the last 50 years has come from foreign ideas and agitators.
> 4. It would be a mistake ever to have Negroes for foremen and leaders over whites.
> 5. If and when a new world organization is set up, America must be sure that she loses none of her independence and complete power in matters that affect this country. (Adorno et al., *The Authoritarian Personality,* p. 128)

In this version of the scale, only three items deal directly with blacks (zoot suits could, by the late 1940s, have been worn by any ethnic group, but were originally a style associated with blacks), and quite obviously tap anti-black feelings. The problem is that if the range of responses to these three items were limited (as appears to have been the case), then a person's score on the overall scale would have been very much influenced by how he responded to the political items, number 3 and number 5. In other words, if two people expressed identical opinions with regard to the anti-black statements, but one respondent agreed with the political statements, while the other disagreed, then the person agreeing would have been classified as ethnocentric while the other would have been classified as tolerant. Thus, the scale of ethnocentrism clearly confounded political views with intolerant views.

37. Adorno et al., *The Authoritarian Personality*, pp. 134–35.
38. Hyman and Sheatsley, " 'The Authoritarian Personality'—A Methodological Critique," pp. 89–96.
39. Adorno et al., *The Authoritarian Personality*, p. 169.
40. *Ibid.*, p. 171.
41. *Ibid.*
42. Hyman and Sheatsley, " 'The Authoritarian Personality'—A Methodological Critique," pp. 72–73.
43. *Ibid.*, p. 76.
44. David Krech, Richard S. Crutchfield, and Egerton L. Ballachey, *The Individual in Society: A Textbook of Social Psychology* (New York: McGraw-Hill, 1962), p. 209; Herbert McCloskey, "Conservatism and Personality," *American Political Science Review,* vol. 42 (1958), p. 37.
45. Krech, Crutchfield, and Ballachey, *The Individual in Society,* pp. 209–10; Herbert McCloskey, "Conservatism and Personality," pp. 27–45.
46. Herbert McCloskey, quoted in Krech, Crutchfield, and Ballachey, *The Individual in Society,* p. 208.
47. McCloskey, quoted in *ibid.*, pp. 209–10.
48. Stanley Rothman and S. Robert Lichter, *Roots of Radicalism: Jews, Christians, and the New Left* (New York: Oxford University Press, 1982), p. 53.
49. Daniel P. Moynihan, *The Negro Family: A Case for National Action* (Washington, DC: Office of Policy Planning and Research, U.S. Department of Labor, March 1965); Ryan, *Blaming the Victim.* See also Lee Rainwater and William L. Yancey, eds., *The Moynihan Report and the Politics of Controversy* (Cambridge, MA: MIT Press, 1967).
50. See, e.g., Tamar Lewin, "Black Churches: New Mission on Family," *New York Times,* August 24, 1988, p. A1.

Chapter 5. Racism and Traditional American Values

1. For reviews of the evolution of civil rights policy, see Nathan Glazer, *Affirmative Discrimination: Ethnic Inequality and Public Policy* (New York: Basic Books, 1975); Thomas Sowell, *Civil Rights: Rhetoric or Reality?* (New York: William Morrow and Company, 1984); and Thomas Byrne Edsall and Mary Edsall, *Chain Reaction: The Impact of Race, Rights, and Taxes on American Politics* (New York: W. W. Norton, 1991). Among those who reacted most strongly to this new policy were Jews who had familiarity with the "number clauses" commonly used in Europe to deny Jews entrance to universities and professions. Quotas were also imposed on Jews in university admissions in the 1920s and 1930s to overcome what was thought to be "overrepresentation" of Jews in elite institutions and

professions. This was a main point of contention which put strains on the historical Jewish-black alliance in America.

2. *Griggs v. Duke Power Company,* 91 S. Ct. 849 (1971).
3. See Jared Taylor, *Paved with Good Intentions: The Failure of Race Relations in Contemporary America* (New York: Carrol and Graff, 1992); Howard Glickman, Tim Smart, Paula Dwyer, Troy Segal, and Joseph Weber, ''Race in the Workplace,'' *Business Week,* no. 3221 (July 8, 1991), pp. 50–63; Dinesh D'Souza, *Illiberal Education: The Politics of Race and Sex on Campus* (New York: Free Press, 1991); and Chester E. Finn, ''Quotas and the Bush Administration,'' *Commentary,* vol. 92, no. 5 (November 1991), pp. 17–23.
4. *Wards Cove Packing Company, Inc. v. Atonio,* 109 S. Ct. 2115 (1989).
5. *City of Richmond v. J. A. Croson Company,* 109 S. Ct. 706 (1989); see also Terry Eastland, ''Racial Preference in Court (Again),'' *Commentary,* vol. 87, no. 1 (January 1989), pp. 32–38.
6. President Bush signed the Civil Rights Act of 1991 on November 21, 1991. See Andrew Rosenthal, ''President Tries to Quell Furor on Interpreting Scope of New Law,'' *New York Times,* November 22, 1991, p. A1.
7. Glickman et al., ''Race in the Workplace,'' p. 56.
8. Seymour Martin Lipset and William Schneider, ''The Bakke Case: How Would It Be Decided at the Bar of Public Opinion?'' *Public Opinion,* March/April 1978, p. 41.
9. *Ibid.*
10. *Ibid.,* p. 42.
11. *Ibid.,* p. 39.
12. Linda S. Lichter, ''Who Speaks for Black America?'' *Public Opinion,* August/September 1985, p. 42.
13. Lipset and Schneider, ''The Bakke Case,'' p. 41.
14. ''Blacks and Whites Hand Down Opinions,'' *American Enterprise,* September/October 1991, p. 83.
15. Donald R. Kinder, ''The Continuing American Dilemma: White Resistance to Racial Change Forty Years after Myrdal,'' *Journal of Social Issues,* vol. 42, no. 2 (1986), pp. 151–52.
16. Howard Schuman, Charlotte Steeh, and Lawrence Bobo, *Racial Attitudes in America* (Cambridge, MA: Harvard University Press, 1985), p. 77.
17. *Ibid.,* p. 88.
18. *Ibid.,* p. 74.
19. *Ibid.,* p. 91.
20. *Ibid.,* p. 197.
21. The polling data reviewed by Lipset and Schneider, and by Linda Lichter, indicated that only a minority of blacks approved of racial preferences in the late seventies and early eighties. The most recent poll in 1991, on the other hand, found that 64 percent of blacks approved.
22. There were behaviorists, such as Edward Chase Tolman, who rejected this sort of mindless view of man; see Edward C. Tolman, *Purposive Behavior in Animals and Men* (New York: Appleton-Century, 1932). B. F. Skinner in his later writings, especially in his *Beyond Freedom and Dignity* (New York: Bantam Books, 1971), seems to give up the ghost (although he denies doing so), since in that book he writes a good deal about culture and values in a way which clearly implies acceptance of an active mind.

23. Paul F. Lazarsfeld and Wagner Thielens, Jr., with David Riesman, *The Academic Mind: Social Scientists in a Time of Crisis* (Glencoe, IL: Free Press, 1958).
24. *Ibid.*, p. 14.
25. *Ibid.*, p. 16.
26. *Ibid.*, p. 17.
27. *Ibid.*, p. 23.
28. Everett Carll Ladd, Jr. and Seymour Martin Lipset, *The Divided Academy: Professors and Politics* (New York: McGraw-Hill, 1975).
29. *Ibid.*, p. 369.
30. *Ibid.*, p. 368.
31. *Ibid.*, p. 231.
32. *Ibid.*, p. 145.
33. "Politics of the Professoriate," *American Enterprise,* July/August 1991, p. 87.
34. *Ibid.*, p. 86.
35. T. W. Adorno, Else Frenkel-Brunswik, Daniel J. Levinson, and R. Nevitt Sanford, *The Authoritarian Personality* (New York: Harper & Row, 1950), p. 156.
36. *Ibid.*, p. 155.
37. *Ibid.*
38. Paul M. Sniderman and Michael Gray Hagen, *Race and Inequality: A Study in American Values* (Chatham, NJ: Chatham House, 1985), p. 97.
39. *Ibid.*
40. *Ibid.*, p. 93.
41. *Ibid.*, p. 96.
42. *Ibid.*, pp. 91–93.
43. *Ibid.*
44. "A Portrait in Black and White," *American Enterprise,* January/February 1990, p. 100.
45. James Kluegel and Eliot Smith, "Affirmative Action Attitudes: Effects of Self-Interest, Racial Affect, and Stratification Beliefs on Whites' Views," *Social Forces,* vol. 6, no. 3 (March 1983), p. 801.
46. See Kinder, "The Continuing American Dilemma" (*supra* note 15); Donald R. Kinder and David O. Sears, "Prejudice and Politics: Symbolic Racism versus Racial Threats to the Good Life," *Journal of Personality and Social Psychology,* vol. 40, no. 3 (1981), pp. 414–31; David O. Sears and Donald R. Kinder, "Whites' Opposition to Busing: On Conceptualizing and Operationalizing Group Conflict," *Journal of Personality and Social Psychology,* vol. 48, no. 5 (1985), pp. 1141–47; David O. Sears, Carl P. Hensler, and Leslie K. Speer, "Whites' Opposition to 'Busing': Self-Interest or Symbolic Politics?" *American Political Science Review,* vol. 73 (1979), pp. 369–84; John B. McConahay, "Self-Interest versus Racial Attitudes as Correlates of Anti-Busing Attitudes in Louisville: Is It the Buses or the Blacks?" *Journal of Politics,* vol. 44 (1982), pp. 692–720; John B. McConahay, "Modern Racism and Modern Discrimination: The Effects of Race, Racial Attitudes, and Context on Simulated Hiring Decisions," *Personality and Social Psychology Bulletin,* vol. 9, no. 4 (1983), pp. 551–58; John B. McConahay, Betty B. Hardee, and Valerie Batts, "Has Racism Declined in America? It Depends on Who is Asking and What is Asked," *Journal of Conflict Resolution,* vol. 25, no. 4 (1981), pp. 563–79; John B. McConahay and Joseph C. Hough, Jr., "Symbolic Racism," *Journal of Social Issues,* vol. 32, no. 2 (1976), pp. 23–45; Cardell K. Jacobson, "Resistance to Affirmative Action: Self-Interest

or Racism?'' *Journal of Conflict Resolution,* vol. 29, no. 2 (1985), pp. 306–29; Sheri Lynn Johnson, ''Unconscious Racism and the Criminal Law,'' *Cornell Law Review,* Spring 1989, pp. 1016–37; Thomas F. Pettigrew and Joanne Martin, ''Shaping the Organization Context for Black American Inclusion,'' *Journal of Social Issues,* vol. 43, no. 1 (1987), pp. 41–78; and Russell H. Weigel and Paul W. Howes, ''Conceptions of Racial Prejudice: Symbolic Racism Reconsidered,'' *Journal of Social Issues,* vol. 41, no. 3 (1985), pp. 117–38.

For critiques of the symbolic-racism theory, see Lawrence Bobo, ''Whites' Opposition to Busing: Symbolic Racism or Realistic Group Conflict?'' *Journal of Personality and Social Psychology,* vol. 45, no. 6 (1983), pp. 1196–1210; Byron M. Roth, ''Symbolic Racism: The Making of a Scholarly Myth,'' *Academic Questions,* vol. 2, no. 1 (Summer 1989), pp. 53–65; Byron M. Roth, ''Social Psychology's 'Racism','' *Public Interest,* no. 96 (Winter 1990), pp. 26–36; Paul M. Sniderman and Philip E. Tetlock, ''Symbolic Racism: Problems of Motive Attribution in Political Analysis,'' *Journal of Social Issues,* vol. 42, no. 2 (1986), pp. 129–50; and Paul M. Sniderman and Philip E. Tetlock, ''Reflections on American Racism,'' *Journal of Social Issues,* vol. 42, no. 2 (1986), pp. 173–87.

47. Kinder and Sears, ''Prejudice and Politics,'' p. 416.
48. *Ibid.*
49. *Ibid.,* p. 420.
50. *Ibid.,* p. 418.
51. Edsall and Edsall, *Chain Reaction,* p. 49.
52. *Ibid.,* pp. 62–64.
53. Kinder and Sears, ''Prejudice and Politics,'' p. 416.
54. *Regents of the University of California v. Bakke,* 98 S. Ct. 2733 (1978); Edsall and Edsall, *Chain Reaction,* pp. 126–27.
55. Kinder and Sears, ''Prejudice and Politics,'' p. 416.
56. Schuman, Steeh, and Bobo, *Racial Attitudes in America,* pp. 144–46.
57. Kinder and Sears, ''Prejudice and Politics,'' p. 417.
58. *Ibid.*
59. McConahay and Hough, ''Symbolic Racism,'' p. 35.
60. Kinder and Sears, ''Prejudice and Politics,'' pp. 419–20. The term ''Jensenism'' refers to the argument of Arthur Jensen attributing black-white IQ differences, in part, to genetic differences. This topic is taken up extensively in Chapter 9, which deals with the educational problems confronting black children. For citations of Jensen's work on this subject, see Chapter 9, notes 9 and 10.
61. Kinder and Sears, ''Prejudice and Politics,'' p. 414.
62. Sniderman and Tetlock, ''Reflections on American Racism'' (*supra* note 46), pp. 182–83; C. Wright Mills, ''Situated Actions and Vocabularies of Motives,'' *American Sociological Review,* vol. 5 (1940), pp. 904–13.
63. Sniderman and Tetlock, ''Symbolic Racism: Problems of Motive Attribution in Political Analysis'' (*supra* note 46), pp. 144–45.
64. Sniderman and Hagen, *Race and Inequality*; Schuman, Steeh, and Bobo, *Racial Attitudes in America*; James R. Kluegel and Eliot R. Smith, *Beliefs about Inequality* (New York: Aldine De Gruyter, 1986).
65. Sniderman and Hagen, *Race and Inequality,* p. 93.
66. Schuman, Steeh, and Bobo, *Racial Attitudes in America,* pp. 106–8.
67. Gerald David Jaynes and Robin M. Williams, Jr., eds., *A Common Destiny: Blacks and American Society* (Washington, DC: National Academy Press, 1989), p. 133.

68. *Doe v. University of Michigan,* 721 F. Supp. 852, 856 (E.D. Michigan 1989); Joseph D. Grano, "Free Speech v. the University of Michigan," *Academic Questions,* vol. 3, no. 2 (Spring 1990), pp. 10–11.
69. *Doe v. University of Michigan,* 721 F. Supp. 852, 860 (E.D. Michigan 1989).
70. *Ibid.,* p. 860.
71. Sowell, *Civil Rights,* pp. 88–90.
72. Gunnar Myrdal, with Richard Sterner and Arnold Rose, *An American Dilemma: The Negro Problem and Modern Democracy,* 20th anniversary ed. (New York: Harper & Row, 1962), p. 759.
73. *Ibid.,* p. 760.

Part III. Evolution and Human Nature

1. Edward O. Wilson, *Sociobiology* [1975], abridged ed. (Cambridge, MA: Harvard University Press, 1980); Richard Dawkins, *The Selfish Gene* [1976], new ed. (New York: Oxford University Press, 1989).
2. Pierre L. van den Berghe, *Human Family Systems: An Evolutionary View* (New York: Elsevier, 1979).
3. Charles J. Lumsden and Edward O. Wilson, *Promethean Fire: Reflections on the Origins of Mind* (Cambridge, MA: Harvard University Press, 1983), p. 15.

Chapter 6. Evolution and Adolescent Behavior

1. Charles Darwin, *The Origin of Species by Means of Natural Selection* (1859; New York: Avenel Books, 1979); Charles Darwin, *The Descent of Man, and Selection in Relation to Sex* (1871; Princeton, NJ: Princeton University Press, 1981).
2. David Barash, *The Whisperings Within: Evolution and the Origin of Human Nature* (New York: Penguin Books, 1979), pp. 20–21.
3. Richard Dawkins, *The Selfish Gene* (New York: Oxford University Press, 1978), p. iii. This comment appears in the preface to the original paperback edition and does not appear in the revised new edition (1989). Note that other references to this book are to the new edition.
4. Derek Freeman, "Paradigms in Collision: The Far-Reaching Controversy over the Samoan Researches of Margaret Mead and Its Significance for the Human Sciences," *Academic Questions,* vol. 5, no. 1 (Winter 1991–92), p. 29.
5. Daniel Janzen has argued that microorganisms create unpleasant tastes and odors in carcasses so as to keep larger animals away from devouring an important source of nutrition for the microorganisms. As Janzen put it: "Fruits rot, seeds mold, and meat spoils because that is the way microbes compete with bigger animals"; see Daniel Janzen, "Why Fruits Rot, Seeds Mold, and Meat Spoils," *American Naturalist,* vol. 111, no. 980 (July-August 1977), pp. 691–713.
6. Claude A. Villee, *Biology,* 4th ed. (Philadelphia: W. B. Saunders, 1962), pp. 174, 418–19.
7. Edward O. Wilson, *Sociobiology* [1975], abridged ed. (Cambridge, MA: Harvard University Press, 1980), p. 156.
8. *Ibid.*

9. *Ibid.*, p. 47.
10. *Ibid.*, pp. 47–48.
11. *Ibid.*, p. 162.
12. Barash, *The Whisperings Within*, pp. 39–41.
13. Alan P. Bell, Martin S. Weinberg, and Sue Kiefer Hammersmith, *Sexual Preference: Its Development in Men and Women* (Bloomington: Indiana University Press, 1981).
14. Roger Brown, *Social Psychology,* 2d ed. (New York: Free Press, 1986), pp. 351–53.
15. Lee Ellis and M. Ashley Ames, "Neurohormonal Functioning and Sexual Orientation: A Theory of Homosexuality-Heterosexuality," *Psychological Bulletin,* vol. 101, no. 2 (1987), p. 251.
16. *Ibid.*, p. 240.
17. *Ibid.*
18. *Ibid.*, p. 241.
19. *Ibid.*, pp. 248–49.
20. J. Michael Bailey and Richard C. Pillard, "A Genetic Study of Male Sexual Orientation," *Archives of General Psychiatry,* vol. 48 (December 1991), pp. 1089–96.
21. Marcia Barinage, "Is Homosexuality Biological?" *Science,* vol. 253 (August 30, 1991), pp. 956–57.
22. Eleanor Gibson and Richard D. Walk, "The 'Visual Cliff'," *Scientific American,* vol. 202 (1960), pp. 2–9.
23. Tiffany M. Field, Robert Woodson, Reena Greenberg, and Debra Cohen, "Discrimination and Imitation of Facial Expressions in Neonates," *Science,* vol. 218 (October 8, 1982), pp. 179–81.
24. Barash, *The Whisperings Within,* p. 83.
25. Richard Dawkins, *The Selfish Gene* [1976], new ed. (New York: Oxford University Press, 1989), p. 141.
26. *Ibid.*, pp. 141–42. Dawkins's speculation in this matter is based in part on the important paper by G. A. Parker, R. R. Baker, and V. G. F. Smith, "The Origin and Evolution of Gamete Dimorphism and the Male-Female Phenomenon," *Journal of Theoretical Biology,* vol. 36 (1972), pp. 529–53.
27. J. Maynard Smith, "The Theory of Games and the Evolution of Animal Conflicts," *Journal of Theoretical Biology,* vol. 47 (1974), pp. 209–21.
28. Wilson, *Sociobiology,* pp. 158–62.
29. Gerald Borgia, "Sexual Selection in Bowerbirds," *Scientific American,* vol. 254, no. 6 (1986), pp. 92–98.
30. Pierre L. van den Berghe, *Human Family Systems: An Evolutionary View* (New York: Elsevier, 1979), pp. 65–67.
31. David G. Myers, *Psychology,* 3d ed. (New York: Worth Publishers, 1992), p. 580.
32. Napolean A. Chagnon, *Yanomamo: The Fierce People,* 2d ed. (New York: Holt, Rinehart, and Winston, 1977), p. 75; van den Berghe, *Human Family Systems,* pp. 145–46.
33. Jean-Louis Flandrin, *Families in Former Times: Kinship, Household, and Sexuality in Early Modern France* (New York: Cambridge University Press, 1979), pp. 184–86.
34. *Ibid.*, p. 184.
35. Edmund S. Morgan, *The Puritan Family: Religion and Domestic Relations in*

Seventeenth-Century New England (New York: Harper & Row, 1966), pp. 143–46.

36. John Demos, *A Little Commonwealth: Family Life in Plymouth Colony* (New York: Oxford University Press, 1970), p. 78.

37. Van den Berghe, *Human Family Systems,* p. 91.

38. Hugh D. R. Baker, *Chinese Family and Kinship* (New York: Columbia University Press, 1979), pp. 176–82.

39. Van den Berghe, *Human Family Systems,* p. 103.

40. *Ibid.*, pp. 149–58.

41. Robin Fox, *Kinship and Marriage* (Harmondsworth, England: Penguin, 1967), pp. 97–103.

42. Roland Oliver and Anthony Atmore, *Africa since 1800,* 2d ed. (New York: Cambridge University Press, 1967), p. 13.

43. Fox, *Kinship and Marriage,* pp. 101–2.

44. *Ibid.*, p. 101.

45. Van den Berghe, *Human Family Systems,* pp. 102–9.

46. Fox, *Kinship and Marriage,* p. 101.

47. *Ibid.*, p. 100.

48. Van den Berghe, *Human Family Systems,* p. 108.

49. *Ibid.*, p. 106.

50. *Ibid.* Van den Berghe relies on Gwen J. Broude and Sarah J. Green, "Cross-Cultural Codes on Twenty Sexual Attitudes and Practices," *Ethnology,* vol. 15, no. 4 (1976), pp. 409–29.

51. This is not to deny that parents should be equally concerned with the behavior of their adolescent sons. The age-old double standard in the treatment of sons and daughters is to be deplored not least because it suggests that people are driven more by the economic impact of children's behavior on themselves than by the impact of that behavior on their children's well-being.

52. Charles Murray, "The British Underclass," *Public Interest,* no. 99 (Spring 1990), pp. 4–28.

53. After reviewing data on illegitimacy and income, researchers Greg Duncan and Saul Hoffman conclude: "Our descriptive work on the consequences of teenage behavior shows that one rule does not appear to have changed: national data still support the claim that schooling and delayed childbearing are sufficient conditions for most women, black and white, to avoid poverty as adults." See Greg J. Duncan and Saul D. Hoffman, "Teenage Behavior and Subsequent Poverty," in Christopher Jencks and Paul E. Peterson, eds., *The Urban Underclass* (Washington, DC: Brookings Institution, 1991), p. 172.

Chapter 7. The Evolutionary Roots of Ethnocentrism

1. Eckhard H. Hess, " 'Imprinting' in a Natural Laboratory," *Scientific American,* August 1972; reprinted in Rita L. Atkinson and Richard C. Atkinson, eds., *Mind and Behavior: Readings from the Scientific American* (San Francisco: W. H. Freeman, 1980), pp. 45–53.

2. Edward O. Wilson, *Sociobiology* [1975], abridged ed. (Cambridge, MA: Harvard University Press, 1980), pp. 175–76.

3. Richard Dawkins, *The Selfish Gene* [1976], new ed. (New York: Oxford University Press, 1989), pp. 248–51.
4. Michael P. Ghiglieri, "The Social Ecology of Chimpanzees," *Scientific American,* vol. 252, no. 6 (June 1985), p. 110.
5. Wilson, *Sociobiology,* pp. 59–60.
6. Dawkins, *The Selfish Gene,* new ed., pp. 21–45.
7. *Ibid.*
8. Hugh D. R. Baker, *Chinese Family and Kinship* (New York: Columbia University Press, 1979), pp. 26–27.
9. William D. Hamilton, "The Genetical Evolution of Social Behavior," *Journal of Theoretical Biology,* vol. 7 (1964), pp. 1–53; reprinted in James H. Hunt, ed., *Selected Readings in Sociobiology* (New York: McGraw-Hill, 1980), pp. 7–30.
10. The fact that most members of a species share the overwhelming majority of genes with each other could lead to the incorrect interpretation of inclusive fitness that all species members should be powerfully concerned with each other. As is discussed somewhat later in this chapter, such an interpretation overlooks the fact that the members of most species are very much in competition with each other for the same resources and mates. It is only in the case of very close relatives that genes benefit more from mutual altruism than they suffer from the increased competition such altruism creates. As Dawkins explains: "There is a kind of baseline relatedness, shared by all members of a species; indeed to a lesser extent, shared by members of other species. Altruism is expected toward individuals whose relatedness is higher than the baseline, whatever that happens to be" (Dawkins, *The Selfish Gene,* new ed., p. 288).
11. Ghiglieri, "The Social Ecology of Chimpanzees," pp. 111–12.
12. J. Maynard Smith and G. R. Price, "The Logic of Animal Conflict," *Nature,* vol. 246 (November 2, 1973), p. 1518.
13. Brian C. R. Bertram, "The Social System of Lions," *Scientific American,* vol. 232, no. 5 (May 1975), pp. 54–65.
14. *Ibid,* p. 65.
15. David Barash, *The Whisperings Within: Evolution and the Origin of Human Nature* (New York: Penguin Books, 1979), p. 103; Sarah Hrdy, *The Langurs of Abu* (Cambridge, MA: Harvard University Press, 1974).
16. See Hamilton, "The Genetical Evolution of Social Behavior."
17. Andrew R. Blaustein and Richard K. O'Hara, "Kin Recognition in Tadpoles," *Scientific American,* vol. 254, no. 1 (January 1986), pp. 108–16.
18. Dawkins, *The Selfish Gene,* new ed., pp. 293–94.
19. Alison Jolly, *The Evolution of Primate Behavior* (New York: Macmillan, 1972), pp. 91–132.
20. Wilson, *Sociobiology,* p. 264.
21. Pierre L. van den Berghe, *Human Family Systems: An Evolutionary View* (New York: Elsevier, 1979), pp. 132–40.
22. *Ibid.,* pp. 129–49.
23. Baker, *Chinese Family and Kinship,* pp. 136–61.
24. *Ibid.,* p. 146.
25. Johan Huizinga, *Homo Ludens: A Study of the Play Element in Culture* (Boston: Beacon Press, 1950).
26. Wilson, *Sociobiology,* pp. 84–86.
27. Robert L. Trivers, "The Evolution of Reciprocal Altruism," *Quarterly Review of*

Biology, vol. 46 (1971), pp. 35–57; reprinted in Hunt, ed., *Selected Readings in Sociobiology (supra* note 9), pp. 38–68.

28. Henri Tajfel, M. G. Billig, R. P. Bundy, and Claude Flament, "Social Categorization and Intergroup Behavior," *European Journal of Social Psychology,* vol. 1 (1971), pp. 149–77.

29. *Ibid.*

30. Henri Tajfel, "Social Psychology of Intergroup Relations," *Annual Review of Psychology,* vol. 33 (1982), p. 24.

31. For authoritative reviews of the minimal group literature, see David M. Messick and Diane M. Mackie, "Intergroup Relations," *Annual Review of Psychology,* vol. 40 (1989), pp. 45–81; Marilynn B. Brewer and Roderick M. Kramer, "The Psychology of Intergroup Attitudes and Behavior," *Annual Review of Psychology,* vol. 36 (1985), pp. 219–43; and Tajfel, "Social Psychology of Intergroup Relations."

32. Anne Locksley, Vilma Ortiz, and Christine Hepburn, "Social Categorization and Discriminatory Behavior: Extinguishing the Minimal Intergroup Discrimination Effect," *Journal of Personality and Social Psychology,* vol. 39, no. 5 (1980), pp. 773–83.

33. Tajfel, "Social Psychology of Intergroup Relations," pp. 24–25.

34. Messick and Mackie, "Intergroup Relations," p. 59.

35. *Ibid.,* p. 61.

36. *Ibid.,* p. 62.

37. Erving Goffman, *The Presentation of Self in Everyday Life* (New York: Doubleday Anchor Books, 1959). Of course, team spirit is encouraged through socialization, but that socialization fits in nicely with our hypothesized genetic tendency to divide the world into an "us" and a "them."

38. Locksley, Ortiz, and Hepburn, "Social Categorization and Discriminatory Behavior," pp. 773–83.

39. Norbert Vanbeselaere, "The Effects of Dichotomous and Crossed Social Categorizations upon Intergroup Discrimination," *European Journal of Social Psychology,* vol. 17 (1987), pp. 143–56.

40. *Ibid.,* pp. 149–53.

41. *Ibid.,* p. 146.

42. Messick and Mackie, "Intergroup Relations," p. 70.

43. Jill Smolowe, "Intermarried . . . With Children," *Time,* Special Issue, vol. 142, no. 21 (Fall 1993), p. 64.

Part IV. The Debilitating Triad: Crime, Illegitimacy, and Inadequate Education

1. J. J. Tobias, *Urban Crime in Victorian England* (New York: Schocken Books, 1972), pp. 244–55.

2. *Ibid.,* pp. 251–52.

3. *Ibid.,* p. 252.

4. *Ibid.*

5. Claude Brown, "Manchild in Harlem," *New York Times Magazine,* September 16, 1984, p. 40.

6. Jason DeParle, "Young Black Males in Capital: Study Finds 42% in Courts," *New York Times,* April 18, 1992, p. 1.

7. See Elijah Anderson, "Sex Codes and Family Life among Inner-City Youths,"

Annals of the American Academy of Political and Social Science, vol. 501 (January 1989), pp. 59–78.

Chapter 8. Crime

1. Anne Parrella, "Industrialization and Murder: Northern France, 1815–1904," *Journal of Interdisciplinary History,* vol. 22, no. 1 (Spring 1992), pp. 627–54.
2. Allen C. Johnson, *Human Arrangements: An Introduction to Sociology* (New York: Harcourt Brace Jovanovich, 1989), p. 255.
3. U.S. Bureau of the Census, *Statistical Abstract of the United States 1992,* 112th ed. (Washington, DC), p. 182.
4. *Ibid.*
5. *Ibid.*
6. *Ibid.*
7. *Ibid.*
8. U.S. Department of Justice, *Criminal Victimization in the United States, 1990* (Washington, DC), p. 103.
9. *New York Times,* March 31, 1992, p. B1.
10. *New York Times,* April 1, 1992, p. B1.
11. U.S. Bureau of the Census, *Statistical Abstract of the United States 1992,* p. 183.
12. Jonathan Greenberg, "All about Crime," *New York Magazine,* vol. 23, no. 34 (September 3, 1990), p. 29.
13. U.S. Bureau of the Census, *Statistical Abstract of the United States 1992,* p. 182.
14. *Ibid.,* p. 197.
15. U.S. Bureau of the Census, *Statistical Abstract of the United States 1991,* 111th ed. (Washington, DC), p. 194.
16. Greenberg, "All about Crime," pp. 29–30.
17. U.S. Department of Justice, *Criminal Victimization in the United States, 1990,* p. 62.
18. *Ibid.,* p. 61.
19. U.S. Bureau of the Census, *Statistical Abstract of the United States 1992,* p. 180.
20. *Ibid.,* p. 187.
21. Jason DeParle, "Young Black Males in Capital: Study Finds 42% in Courts," *New York Times,* April 18, 1992, p. 1.
22. U.S. Bureau of the Census, *Statistical Abstract of the United States 1965,* 86th ed. (Washington, DC), p. 146; U.S. Bureau of the Census, *Statistical Abstract of the United States 1976,* 97th ed. (Washington, DC), p. 153; U.S. Bureau of the Census, *Statistical Abstract of the United States 1982–83,* 103d ed. (Washington, DC), p. 174; U.S. Bureau of the Census, *Statistical Abstract of the United States 1992,* p. 180.
23. U.S. Bureau of the Census, *Statistical Abstract of the United States 1965,* p. 146; U.S. Bureau of the Census, *Statistical Abstract of the United States 1976,* p. 153; U.S. Bureau of the Census, *Statistical Abstract of the United States 1982–83,* p. 174; U.S. Bureau of the Census, *Statistical Abstract of the United States 1992,* p. 180.
24. Edward Shorter, *The Making of the Modern Family* (New York: Basic Books, 1977), pp. 120–36.
25. *Ibid.*

26. See *ibid.*; and Philippe Aries, *Centuries of Childhood: A Social History of Family Life* (New York: Alfred A. Knopf, 1962).

27. See Elijah Anderson, "Sex Codes and Family Life among Inner-City Youths," *Annals of the American Academy of Political and Social Science,* vol. 501 (January 1989), pp. 59–78.

28. Erving Goffman, *Interaction Ritual: Essays on Face to Face Interaction* (New York: Anchor Books, 1967), pp. 181–94.

29. Emile Durkheim, *Suicide: A Study in Sociology,* ed. George Simpson, trans. J. A. Spaulding and George Simpson (New York: Free Press, 1951), pp. 51–52.

30. See James Q. Wilson and Richard J. Herrnstein, *Crime and Human Nature* (New York: Simon and Schuster, 1985), pp. 69–103.

31. Marvin E. Wolfgang, Robert M. Figlio, and Thorsten Sellin, *Delinquency in a Birth Cohort* (Chicago: University of Chicago Press, 1972).

32. Marvin E. Wolfgang, Terence P. Thornberry, and Robert M. Figlio, *From Boy to Man, From Delinquency to Crime: The Follow-up Study to Delinquency in a Birth Cohort* (Chicago: University of Chicago Press, 1987), p. 2.

33. *Ibid.,* pp. 1–6.

34. Rodney Stark, *Sociology,* 3d ed. (Belmont, CA: Wadsworth, 1989), p. 218.

35. Durkheim, *Suicide,* pp. 241–76.

36. *Ibid.,* pp. 254–58.

37. Robert K. Merton, "Social Structure and Anomie," in Leonard D. Savitz and Norman Johnston, eds., *Crime in Society* (New York: John Wiley and Sons, 1978), p. 115.

38. *Ibid.,* pp. 120–21.

39. *Ibid.,* pp. 121–22.

40. *Ibid.,* p. 121.

41. *Ibid.,* p. 117.

42. Edwin H. Sutherland and Donald R. Cressey, *Criminology,* 9th ed. (New York: J. B. Lippincott, 1974), p. 75.

43. Richard A. Cloward and Lloyd E. Ohlin, *Delinquency and Opportunity* (New York: Free Press, 1960), p. 163.

44. *Ibid.,* p. 164.

45. *Ibid.,* p. 175.

46. *Ibid.,* p. 211.

47. *Ibid.,* pp. 151–52.

48. Travis Hirschi, *Causes of Delinquency* (Berkeley: University of California Press, 1969).

49. Robert A. Gordon, "Scientific Justification and the Race-IQ-Delinquency Model," in Timothy F. Hartagel and Robert A. Silverman, eds., *Critique and Explanation: Essays in Honor of Gwynne Nettler* (New Brunswick, NJ: Transaction Books, 1986).

50. Wilson and Herrnstein, *Crime and Human Nature,* p. 155.

51. James Q. Wilson, *Thinking about Crime,* rev. ed. (New York: Vintage Books, 1985), p. 56.

52. *Ibid.,* pp. 15–16.

53. Thomas Byrne Edsall and Mary Edsall, *Chain Reaction: The Impact of Race, Rights, and Taxes on American Politics* (New York: W. W. Norton, 1991), p. 51.

54. National Advisory Commission on Civil Disorders, *Report of the National Advisory Commission on Civil Disorders* (New York: Bantam Books, 1968).

55. *Ibid.*, p. xv.
56. *Ibid.*, p. 413.
57. *Ibid.*, pp. 299–300.
58. *Ibid.*, p. 301.
59. Wilson, *Thinking about Crime*, pp. 61–74.
60. See, e.g., *Sawyer v. Sandstrom*, 615 F.2d 311 (5th Cir. 1980).
61. *Miranda v. Arizona*, 86 S. Ct. 1602 (1966).
62. Wilson, *Thinking about Crime*, pp. 75–90.
63. Daniel Patrick Moynihan, "Defining Deviancy Down," *American Scholar* (Winter 1993), pp. 19–21.
64. "A Portrait in Black and White," *American Enterprise*, January/February 1990, p. 103.
65. Franklin D. Gilliam, Jr., "Black America: Divided by Class?" *Public Opinion*, February/March 1986, p. 54.
66. "A Portrait in Black and White," p. 96.
67. Gilliam, "Black America: Divided by Class?" p. 56.
68. "A Portrait in Black and White," p. 97.
69. Cloward and Ohlin, *Delinquency and Opportunity*, pp. 208–9.
70. *Ibid.*, p. 203.
71. Gunnar Myrdal, with Richard Sterner and Arnold Rose, *An American Dilemma: The Negro Problem and Modern Democracy*, 20th anniversary ed. (New York: Harper & Row, 1962), p. 310.
72. "Asian-American Demographics," *American Enterprise*, November/December 1991, p. 90.
73. "Youths Set Homeless Man Afire in Subway," *New York Times*, October 5, 1992, p. B3. This article appeared in the Early City Edition, but not in later editions.
74. The ACLU is in the forefront of these efforts. See, e.g., *New Jersey v. T.L.Q.*, 105 S. Ct. 733 (1985).
75. A good example of the logic used to overturn curfew ordinances is found in *Waters v. Barry*, 711 F. Supp. 1125 (D.D.C. 1989). This was a case in which the court invalidated a Washington, D.C., curfew designed to keep children off the streets from 11 P.M. to 6 A.M., even though it allowed for all sorts of exceptions for work, religious attendance, community service, those traveling in cars, buses, and subways, etc. Judge Charles R. Richey expressed concern that "every juvenile in the District of Columbia would be arrested if he or she sought to wander the monuments at night, or if he or she sought to gaze at the stars from a public park." Judge Richey also held that the desire to protect children from the dangers of urban life was not a sufficient justification for treating children differently from adults. He reasoned so: "[I]t is obvious that the plague afflicting the District poses no peculiar danger to children; those thousands of children who engage in wholly legitimate nocturnal activities are no more endangered in the current climate than are the District's adults. The violence is ubiquitous; it afflicts all of us" (p. 1137).
76. Rita Kramer, *At a Tender Age: Violent Youth and Juvenile Justice* (New York: Holt, Rinehart, and Winston, 1988).
77. Craig Horowitz, "Law and Disorder: How the Juvenile Justice System is Letting Kids Get Away with Murder," *New York Magazine*, vol. 27, no. 2 (January 10,

1994), pp. 18–27; Jonathan Greenberg, "All about Crime," *New York Magazine,* vol. 23, no. 34 (September 3, 1990), pp. 20–32.

Chapter 9. Education

1. U.S. Bureau of the Census, Current Population Reports, Special Studies Series P-23, No. 80, *The Social and Economic Status of the Black Population in the United States: An Historical View, 1790–1978* (Washington, DC: U.S. Government Printing Office, 1980), p. 85; U.S. Bureau of the Census, Current Population Reports, Series P-20, No. 464, *The Black Population in the United States: March 1991* (Washington, DC: U.S. Government Printing Office, 1992), p. 42.
2. U.S. Bureau of the Census, *Statistical Abstract of the United States 1992,* 112th ed. (Washington, DC), p. 161.
3. David Seifman, "More Staying in HS . . . and Staying . . . and Staying," *New York Post,* February 3, 1993, p. 2.
4. U.S. Bureau of the Census, *Statistical Abstract of the United States 1992,* p. 160.
5. U.S. Bureau of the Census, *The Social and Economic Status of the Black Population in the United States: An Historical View, 1790–1978,* p. 75; U.S. Bureau of the Census, *The Black Population in the United States: March 1991,* p. 91.
6. David Armor, "Why is Black Educational Achievement Rising?" *Public Interest,* no. 108 (Summer 1992), pp. 65–80.
7. U.S. Bureau of the Census, *Statistical Abstract of the United States 1991,* 111th ed. (Washington, DC), pp. 155–56.
8. N. D. Henderson, "Human Behavior Genetics," *Annual Review of Psychology,* vol. 33 (1982), pp. 407–11; Sandra Scarr and Richard A. Weinberg, "The Influence of 'Family Background' on Intellectual Attainment," *American Sociological Review,* vol. 42 (1978), pp. 674–92.
9. Linda S. Gottfredson, "Societal Consequences of the g Factor in Employment," *Journal of Vocational Behavior,* vol. 29, no. 3 (1986), pp. 379–410; Richard J. Herrnstein, "Still an American Dilemma," *Public Interest,* no. 98 (Winter 1990), pp. 3–17; Lloyd G. Humphreys, "Commentary," *Journal of Vocational Behavior,* vol. 29, no. 3 (1986), pp. 421–37; Arthur R. Jensen, *Straight Talk about Mental Tests* (New York: Macmillan, 1981); Mark Snyderman and Stanley Rothman, *The IQ Controversy: The Media and Public Policy* (New Brunswick, NJ: Transaction Books, 1988).
10. Arthur R. Jensen, "How Much Can We Boost I.Q. and Scholastic Achievement?" *Harvard Educational Review,* vol. 39 (1969), pp. 1–123.
11. Ernest R. Hilgard, *Psychology in America: A Historical Survey* (New York: Harcourt Brace Jovanovich, 1987), pp. 482–85.
12. Snyderman and Rothman, *The IQ Controversy,* pp. 128–29.
13. The College Board, *College Bound Seniors: 1992 Profile of SAT and Achievement Test Takers* (New York: The College Board, 1992). The detailed breakdown by ethnic groups (not appearing in the public release) was obtained by request from the College Board.
14. *Ibid.,* p. v.
15. It is too soon to tell if these improvements in SAT and basic proficiencies are

reflected in changes in actual IQ test scores. According to Arthur Jensen, SATs measure the same abilities measured by IQ tests; see Arthur R. Jensen "'g: Artifact or Reality?'" *Journal of Vocational Behavior,* vol. 29, no. 3 (1986), pp. 304–12. Black-white IQ test score differences have remained relatively constant for the period from 1921 to 1980; see Robert A. Gordon, "Scientific Justification and the Race-IQ-Delinquency Model," in Timothy F. Hartagel and Robert A. Silverman, eds., *Critique and Explanation: Essays in Honor of Gwynne Nettler* (New Brunswick, NJ: Transaction Books, 1986), p. 118. The issue is complicated because some states, such as California, have banned the use of IQ tests, making it difficult to get recent information on differences in the general population.

16. See Gottfredson, "Societal Consequences of the g Factor in Employment." This hypothetical example is based on Gottfredson's more comprehensive analysis. In her analysis, she used slightly different assumptions and produced results suggesting even greater disparities than in the hypothetical example here.

17. The College Board, *College Bound Seniors: 1992 Profile of SAT and Achievement Test Takers.* The detailed breakdown by ethnic groups (not appearing in the public release) was obtained by request from the College Board.

18. *Ibid.*

19. *Ibid.*

20. Dinesh D'Souza, *Illiberal Education: The Politics of Race and Sex on Campus* (New York: Free Press, 1991), pp. 38–39.

21. John H. Bunzel, "Affirmative-Action Admissions: How It 'Works' at UC Berkeley," *Public Interest,* no. 93 (Fall 1988), pp. 111–32.

22. Thomas Sowell, *Preferential Policies: An International Perspective* (New York: William Morrow, 1990), pp. 107–12.

23. Timothy Maguire, "My Bout with Affirmative Action," *Commentary,* vol. 93, no. 4 (April 1992), p. 51.

24. Robert A. Gordon, "Thunder from the Left," *Academic Questions,* vol. 1, no. 3 (Summer 1988), p. 92.

25. Thomas Sowell, *Ethnic America* (New York: Basic Books, 1981), pp. 8–9; citations omitted.

26. See Armor, "Why is Black Educational Achievement Rising?" (*supra* note 6).

27. Sandra Scarr and Richard A. Weinberg, "IQ Test Performance of Black Children Adopted by White Parents," *American Psychologist,* vol. 31 (1976), pp. 726–39.

28. Snyderman and Rothman, *The IQ Controversy,* pp. 127–28.

29. Carl N. Degler, *In Search of Human Nature: The Decline and Revival of Darwinism in American Social Thought* (New York: Oxford University Press, 1991), p. 178.

30. Jensen, "How Much Can We Boost I.Q. and Scholastic Achievement?" (*supra* note 10).

31. Hilgard, *Psychology in America,* pp. 482–85; Snyderman and Rothman, *The IQ Controversy,* pp. 217–34.

32. Herrnstein, "Still an American Dilemma," p. 7. See note 20 in Chapter 1.

33. Sandra Scarr, "Race and Gender as Psychological Variables: Social and Ethical Implications," *American Psychologist,* vol. 43, no. 6 (1988), pp. 56–59. I discuss Scarr in Section II of Chapter 1.

34. The National Research Council was established by the National Academy of Sciences. Its members are drawn from the National Academy of Sciences, the National Academy of Engineering, and the Institute of Medicine. The report states that "'[t]he members of the Committee responsible for the report were chosen for

their special competences and with regard to appropriate balance." See Alexandra K. Wigdor and Wendell R. Garner, eds., *Ability Testing: Uses, Consequences, and Controversies* (Washington, DC: National Academy Press, 1982), p. ii.

35. Robert Linn, "Ability Testing: Individual Differences, Prediction, and Differential Prediction," in Wigdor and Garner, eds., *Ability Testing,* Part II, p. 384.

36. Henry Gleitman, *Basic Psychology* (New York: Norton, 1987), p. 462.

37. James S. Coleman, Ernest Q. Campbell, Carol J. Hobson, James McPartland, Alexander M. Mood, Frederic D. Weinfeld, and Robert York, *Equality of Educational Opportunity* (Washington, DC: U.S. Government Printing Office, 1966); reprinted in James S. Coleman, *Equality and Achievement in Education* (Boulder, CO: Westview Press, 1990), pp. 75–120.

38. *Ibid.*, p. 105.

39. *Ibid.*, p. 109.

40. *Ibid.*, pp. 107–19.

41. *Ibid.*, p. 113.

42. *Ibid.*, p. 74.

43. Gerald David Jaynes and Robin M. Williams, Jr., eds., *A Common Destiny: Blacks and American Society* (Washington, DC: National Academy Press, 1989), p. 348. See also Nathan Glazer, "Education and Training Programs and Poverty," in Sheldon H. Danziger and Daniel H. Weinberg, eds., *Fighting Poverty: What Works and What Doesn't* (Cambridge, MA: Harvard University Press, 1986), pp. 154–61 (the comment by Christopher Jencks on Glazer in the same volume is instructive, pp. 173–79); Douglas Besharov, "A New Head Start for Head Start," *American Enterprise,* March/April 1992, pp. 52–57; and Armor, "Why is Black Educational Achievement Rising?" pp. 75–77.

44. Coleman, *Equality and Achievement in Education,* p. 74.

45. James Kluger, *Simple Justice: The History of Brown vs. Board of Education and Black America's Struggle for Equality* (New York: Knopf, 1976), p. 353.

46. *Brown v. Board of Education of Topeka,* 74 S. Ct. 686, 691–92 (1954).

47. Kenneth B. Clark and Mamie P. Clark, "Racial Identification and Preference in Negro Children," in Eleanor E. Maccoby, Theodore M. Newcomb, and Eugene L. Hartley, eds., *Readings in Social Psychology,* 3d ed. (New York: Holt, Rinehart, and Winston, 1958), p. 608.

48. Roger Brown, *Social Psychology,* 2d ed. (New York: Free Press, 1986), pp. 559–60.

49. Carrell Peterson Horton and Jessie Carney Smith, *Statistical Record of Black America* (Detroit, MI: Gale Research, Inc., 1993), p. 47.

50. Pauline Yoshihashi, "Now a Glamorous Barbie Heads to Japan," *Wall Street Journal,* June 5, 1991, p. B1.

51. Gordon W. Allport, *The Nature of Prejudice* (New York: Addison Wesley, 1979), p. 281.

52. *Ibid.*, p. 274.

53. Coleman, *Equality and Achievement in Education,* pp. 198–210.

54. Walter G. Stephan, "School Desegregation: An Evaluation of Predictions Made in Brown v. Board of Education," *Psychological Bulletin,* vol. 85, no. 2 (March 1978), pp. 226–28.

55. *Ibid.*, p. 217.

56. *Ibid.*, pp. 228–33.

57. Thomas D. Cook, David Armor, Robert Crain, Norman Miller, Michael Carlson, Walter G. Stephan, Herbert J. Walberg, and Paul M. Wortman, *School Desegre-*

gation and Black Achievement (Washington, DC: National Institute of Education, 1984), p. 9.

58. *Ibid.*, p. 187.
59. Thomas Sowell, "Patterns of Black Excellence," *Public Interest,* no. 43 (Spring 1976), pp. 26–58.
60. Armor, "Why is Black Educational Achievement Rising?" pp. 77–80.
61. Janet Ward Schofield, *Black and White in School: Trust, Tension, or Tolerance?* (New York: Teachers College Press, 1989).
62. *Ibid.*, pp. 2–3.
63. *Ibid.*, p. 76.
64. *Ibid.*, pp. 93–97.
65. *Ibid.*, pp. 108–13.
66. *Ibid.*, p. 108.
67. *Ibid.*, pp. 106–7.
68. *Ibid.*, pp. 157–59.
69. *Ibid.*, p. 164.
70. *Ibid.*, pp. 164–65.
71. *Ibid.*, p. 169.
72. Coleman, *Equality and Achievement in Education,* pp. 250–306.
73. *Ibid.*, p. 302.
74. Stewart Purkey and Marshall Smith, "Effective Schools: A Review," *Elementary School Journal,* vol. 83, no. 1 (March 1983), pp. 427–52.
75. *Ibid.*, p. 440.
76. *Ibid.*, pp. 443–45.
77. John Chubb and Terry Moe, *Politics, Markets, and America's Schools* (Washington, DC: Brookings Institution, 1990).
78. *Ibid.*, p. 183.
79. *Ibid.*, pp. 215–19.
80. *Ibid.*, pp. 221–23.
81. Robert Rosenthal and Lenore F. Jacobson, "Teacher Expectations for the Disadvantaged," *Scientific American,* April 1968; reprinted in Richard C. Atkinson, ed., *Contemporary Psychology: Readings from the Scientific American,* pp. 448–52. See also Robert Rosenthal and Lenore F. Jacobson, *Pygmalion in the Classroom: Teacher Expectations and Pupils' Intellectual Development* (New York: Holt, Rinehart, and Winston, 1968); and Robert Rosenthal, "On the Social Psychology of Self-Fullfilling Prophecy: Further Evidence for Pygmalion Effects and Their Mediating Mechanisms" (New York: MSS Modular Publications, 1974), Module 53, pp. 1–28.
82. Rosenthal and Jacobson, "Teacher Expectations for the Disadvantaged," p. 448.
83. *Ibid.*
84. Rosenthal, "On the Social Psychology of Self-Fullfilling Prophecy," p. 6.
85. *Ibid.*
86. Rosenthal and Jacobson, "Teacher Expectations for the Disadvantaged," p. 452.
87. Richard E. Snow, "Unfinished Pygmalion," *Contemporary Psychology,* vol. 14, no. 4 (April 1969), p. 197; citations omitted.
88. *Ibid.*, p. 198.
89. *Ibid.*
90. *Ibid.*, p. 199.
91. Brown, *Social Psychology,* 2d ed., pp. 517–18.

92. U.S. Department of Education, *Digest of Education Statistics, 1991* (Washington, DC: National Center for Education Statistics, 1991), p. 132.

93. Arthur M. Schlesinger, Jr., *The Disuniting of America: Reflections on a Multicultural Society* (New York: W. W. Norton and Company, 1992).

94. See Molefi Kete Asante, *The Afrocentric Idea* (Philadelphia, PA: Temple University Press, 1987); and Maulana Karenga, *Introduction to Black Studies* (1982; Los Angeles: University of Sankore Press, 1989). For critical comments, see Anne Wortham, "Errors of the Afrocentrists," *Academic Questions,* vol. 5, no. 4 (Fall 1992), pp. 36–50; and Midge Decter, "E Pluribus Nihil," *Commentary,* vol. 92, no. 3 (September 1991), pp. 25–29.

95. Many of these claims rely on Martin Bernal, *Black Athena: The Afroasiatic Roots of Classical Civilization,* 2 vols. (New Brunswick, NJ: Rutgers University Press, 1991). For critical comments, see Mary Lefkowitz, "The Afrocentric Myth," *New Republic,* February 10, 1992, pp. 29–36; and Mary Lefkowitz, "Ethnocentric History from Aristobulus to Bernal," *Academic Questions,* vol. 6, no. 2 (Spring 1993), pp. 12–20.

96. Schlesinger, *The Disuniting of America,* p. 88. The report cited is "One Nation, Many Peoples: A Declaration of Cultural Independence," a proposal for a New York State social studies "curriculum of inclusion."

97. Schlesinger, *The Disuniting of America,* p. 94.

98. *Ibid.*, p. 89.

99. Sowell, *Ethnic America,* pp. 119–21.

100. Sophfronia Scott Gregory, "The Hidden Hurdle," *Time,* March 16, 1992, pp. 44–46.

101. Schlesinger, *The Disuniting of America,* p. 94.

102. U.S. Department of Education, *Digest of Education Statistics, 1991,* p. 132.

Chapter 10. Illegitimacy

1. U.S. Bureau of the Census, *Current Population Reports,* Series P-20, No. 448, *The Black Population in the United States: March 1990 and 1989* (Washington, DC: U.S. Government Printing Office, 1991), p. 25.

2. Charles Murray, *Losing Ground: American Social Policy 1950–1980* (New York: Basic Books, 1984); William Julius Wilson, *The Truly Disadvantaged: The Inner City, the Underclass, and Public Policy* (Chicago: University of Chicago Press, 1987).

3. Herbert G. Gutman, *The Black Family in Slavery and Freedom, 1750–1925* (New York: Pantheon Books, 1976), pp. 449–56.

4. U.S. Bureau of the Census, *Statistical Abstract of the United States 1982–83,* 103d ed. (Washington, DC), p. 66; U.S. Bureau of the Census, *Statistical Abstract of the United States 1992,* 112th ed. (Washington, DC), p. 69.

5. U.S. Bureau of the Census, *Statistical Abstract of the United States 1992,* p. 69.

6. *Ibid.*, p. 65.

7. *Ibid.*, p. 74.

8. U.S. Bureau of the Census, *Statistical Abstract of the United States 1982–83,* p. 51.

9. U.S. Bureau of the Census, *Current Population Reports,* Series P-20, No. 458,

Household and Family Characteristics: 1991 (Washington, DC: U.S. Government Printing Office, 1991), p. 9.

10. Wilson, *The Truly Disadvantaged*, pp. 25–26.

11. U.S. Bureau of the Census, *Current Population Reports*, Series P-20, No. 468, *Marital Status and Living Arrangements: March 1992* (Washington, DC: U.S. Government Printing Office, 1992), p. viii.

12. U.S. Bureau of the Census, *Current Population Reports*, Series P-20, No. 448, *The Black Population in the United States: March 1990 and 1989*, p. 25.

13. Gerald David Jaynes and Robin M. Williams, Jr., eds., *A Common Destiny: Blacks and American Society* (Washington, DC: National Academy Press, 1989), p. 512.

14. These percentages were calculated by the author from data presented in Deborah Dawson, *Family Structure and Children's Health,* Series 10: Data from the National Health Survey, No. 178, DHHS Publication No. (PHS) 91–1506 (Hyattsville, MD: National Center for Health Statistics, 1991), p. 16.

15. The illegitimacy rates in Sweden and Denmark of 48 percent and 44 percent, respectively, are the highest national rates in the industrialized world; see U.S. Department of Education, *Youth Indicators 1991* (Washington, DC: U.S. Government Printing Office, 1991), p. 24. For a discussion of the case of Sweden, see Allan Carlson, "Forward to the Past: Rebuilding Family Life in Post-Socialist Sweden," *Family in America,* vol. 6, no. 7 (July 1992), published by the Rockford Institute.

16. Jane Gross, "Collapse of Inner-City Families Creates Orphans," *New York Times,* March 29, 1992, p. 1.

17. U.S. Bureau of the Census, *Statistical Abstract of the United States 1992,* p. 55.

18. Gross, "Collapse of Inner-City Families Creates Orphans," p. 1.

19. Kenneth B. Clark, *Dark Ghetto: Dilemmas of Social Power* (New York: Harper & Row, 1965), p. 72.

20. See note 2 above.

21. Thomas Byrne Edsall and Mary Edsall, *Chain Reaction: The Impact of Race, Rights, and Taxes on American Politics* (New York: W. W. Norton, 1991), p. 68.

22. See Murray, *Losing Ground,* pp. 154–66.

23. Wilson, *The Truly Disadvantaged*, p. 78.

24. Robert D. Plotnick, "Welfare and Out-of-Wedlock Childrearing: Evidence from the 1980s," *Journal of Marriage and the Family,* vol. 52 (August 1990), p. 742.

25. *Ibid.*

26. Wilson, *The Truly Disadvantaged*, pp. 39–45.

27. Mark Testa, Nan Marie Astone, Marilyn Krogh, and Kathryn M. Neckerman, "Employment and Marriage among Inner-City Fathers," *Annals of the American Academy of Political and Social Science,* vol. 501 (January 1989), p. 79.

28. Elijah Anderson, "Sex Codes and Family Life among Inner-City Youths," *Annals of the American Academy of Political and Social Science,* vol. 501 (January 1989), p. 77.

29. *Ibid.*, pp. 61–67.

30. Sandra L. Hanson, David E. Myers, and Alan L. Ginsburg, "The Role of Responsibility and Knowledge in Reducing Teenage Out-of-Wedlock Childbearing," *Journal of Marriage and the Family,* vol. 49 (May 1987), p. 248.

31. *Ibid.*, p. 251.

32. Anderson, "Sex Codes and Family Life among Inner-City Youths," p. 69.

33. Wilson, *The Truly Disadvantaged*, p. 42.

34. U.S. Bureau of the Census, *Statistical Abstract of the United States 1992*, pp. 91, 65.
35. Marcia Guttentag and Paul F. Secord, *Too Many Women: The Sex Ratio Question* (Beverly Hills, CA: Sage, 1983).
36. *Ibid.*, pp. 20–21.
37. *Ibid.*, pp. 19–20.
38. Stephen R. Ell, "Iron in Two Seventeenth-Century Plague Epidemics," *Journal of Interdisciplinary History*, vol. 25, no. 3 (Winter 1985), pp. 445–57. Ell argues that women more often suffer iron deficiencies, which gives them partial protection against a variety of pathogens including those causing plague, which require iron to grow.
39. Guttentag and Secord, *Too Many Women*, p. 147.
40. *Ibid.*, pp. 173–79.
41. *Ibid.*, pp. 79–111.
42. *Ibid.*, pp. 95–110.
43. *Ibid.*, pp. 20–21.
44. *Ibid.*, p. 199.
45. *Ibid.*, pp. 199–212. The census category "nonwhite" included, at the time, other groups besides blacks, but for the northern cities discussed, the category was comprised largely of blacks.
46. U.S. Bureau of the Census, *Statistical Abstract of the United States 1991*, 111th ed. (Washington, DC), p. 117.
47. U.S. Bureau of the Census, *Current Population Reports*, Series P-20, No. 461, *Marital Status and Living Arrangements: March 1991*, p. 6.
48. U.S. Bureau of the Census, *Statistical Abstract of the United States 1991*, p. 44.
49. Mark A. Fossett and K. Jill Kiecolt, "Mate Availability and Family Structure Among African Americans in U.S. Metropolitan Areas," *Journal of Marriage and the Family*, vol. 55 (May 1993), pp. 297–98.
50. Daniel T. Lichter, Felicia B. LeClere, and Diane K. McLaughlin, "Local Marriage Markets and the Marital Behavior of Black and White Women," *American Journal of Sociology*, vol. 96, no. 4 (January 1991), pp. 864–65.
51. Scott J. South and Kim M. Lloyd, "Marriage Markets and Nonmarital Fertility in the United States," *Demography*, vol. 29, no. 2 (May 1992), pp. 247–64.
52. Scott J. South, "Racial and Ethnic Differences in the Desire to Marry," *Journal of Marriage and the Family*, vol. 55 (May 1993), p. 357.
53. *Ibid.*, p. 362.
54. *Ibid.*, p. 366.
55. Anderson, "Sex Codes and Family Life among Inner-City Youths," pp. 61–67.
56. Shawn Sullivan, "Wife-Beating N the Hood," *Wall Street Journal*, July 6, 1993, p. A12.
57. Richard A. Bulcroft and Kris A. Bulcroft, "Race Differences in Attitudinal and Motivational Factors in the Decision to Marry," *Journal of Marriage and the Family*, vol. 55 (May 1993), p. 344.
58. *Ibid.*, p. 352.
59. B. F. Skinner, *Beyond Freedom and Dignity* (New York: Bantam Books, 1972), pp. 108–12.
60. See Dawson, *Family Structure and Children's Health* (*supra* note 14).
61. *Ibid.*, p. 9.
62. *Ibid.*
63. *Ibid.*, p. 25.

64. *Ibid.*, p. 9.
65. *Ibid.*, p. 10.
66. *Ibid.*, p. 7.
67. Lawrence Rosen and Kathleen Neilson, "The Broken Home and Delinquency," in Leonard D. Savitz and Norman H. Johnston, eds., *Crime in Society* (New York: John Wiley and Sons, 1978), p. 407.
68. *Ibid.*, p. 414.
69. James Q. Wilson and Richard J. Herrnstein, *Crime and Human Nature* (New York: Simon and Schuster, 1985), p. 261.
70. Robert H. Coombs, "Marital Status and Personal Well-Being: A Literature Review," *Family Relations,* vol. 40 (January 1991), pp. 97–102.
71. Peter Berger and Brigitte Berger, *The War over the Family: Capturing the Middle Ground* (Garden City, NY: Anchor Press/Doubleday, 1983), p. 166.
72. Wilson, *The Truly Disadvantaged*, p. 42; U.S. Bureau of the Census, *Statistical Abstract of the United States 1992*, p. 389.
73. Bulcroft and Bulcroft, "Race Differences in Attitudinal and Motivational Factors in the Decision to Marry," p. 345.
74. Hanson, Myers, and Ginsburg, "The Role of Responsibility and Knowledge in Reducing Teenage Out-of-Wedlock Childbearing," p. 249.

Conclusion

1. Drummond Ayres, Jr., "Earthquake Sends Crime on Vacation," *New York Times,* January 27, 1994, p. A18.
2. "A Portrait in Black and White," *American Enterprise,* January/February 1990, pp. 96–98.
3. Sandra L. Hanson, David E. Myers, and Alan L. Ginsburg, "The Role of Responsibility and Knowledge in Reducing Teenage Out-of-Wedlock Childbearing," *Journal of Marriage and the Family,* vol. 49 (May 1987), p. 251.
4. See note 43 in Chapter 9.
5. According to the *New York Times,* a growing number of blacks from the Caribbean are leaving New York City once they have acquired middle-class status. A prime destination of these people is Florida. The *Times* reports that thousands of Caribbeans left during the late 1980s. It reports that they are leaving for the same reasons other middle-class people leave: for better schools and safer streets. See Garry Pierre-Pierre, "For Caribbean New Yorkers, Palmy Life in Florida is Alluring," *New York Times,* July 13, 1993, p. B3.
6. See William Julius Wilson, *The Truly Disadvantaged: The Inner City, the Underclass, and Public Policy* (Chicago: University of Chicago Press, 1987).
7. National Advisory Commission on Civil Disorders, *Report of the National Advisory Commission on Civil Disorders* (New York: Bantam Books, 1968).
8. Harold Meyerson, "Fractured City," *New Republic,* May 25, 1992, pp. 23–25; Midge Decter, "How the Rioters Won," *Commentary,* vol. 94, no. 1 (July 1992), pp. 17–23.
9. Gunnar Myrdal, with Richard Sterner and Arnold Rose, *An American Dilemma: The Negro Problem and Modern Democracy,* 20th anniversary ed. (New York: Harper & Row, 1962), p. 1331.

10. Philip Gourevitch, "The Crown Heights Riot and Its Aftermath," *Commentary,* vol. 95, no. 1 (January 1993), pp. 29–34.

11. Louis Winnick, "America's Model Minority," *Commentary,* vol. 90, no. 2 (August 1990), pp. 26–27; Arch Puddington, "The Question of Black Leadership," *Commentary,* vol. 91, no. 1 (January 1991), pp. 22–28.

12. John R. Emshwiller, "Riot Fallout Lingers in L.A.'s Koreatown," *Wall Street Journal,* October 26, 1992, p. B1.

13. Puddington, "The Question of Black Leadership," pp. 22–28.

14. Vincent Sarich, "The Institutionalization of Racism at the University of California at Berkeley," *Academic Questions,* vol. 4, no. 1 (Winter 1991), pp. 72–81.

15. See Dinesh D'Souza, *Illiberal Education: The Politics of Race and Sex on Campus* (New York: Free Press, 1991), pp. 50–53; Jacob Weisberg, "The Skins," *New Republic,* February 18, 1991, pp. 22–24; Tamar Jacoby, "Psyched Out," *New Republic,* February 18, 1991, pp. 28–30; Fred Siegel, "The Cult of Multiculturalism," *New Republic,* February 18, 1991, pp. 34–40; Mwangi S. Kimenyi, "Rent-Seeking in the Academy: The Political Economy of Specialty Programs," *Academic Questions,* vol. 5, no. 2 (Spring 1992), pp. 41–54; Thomas Short, "A 'New Racism' on Campus?" *Commentary,* vol. 86, no. 2 (August 1988), pp. 46–50; and Edward Alexander, "Race Fever," *Commentary,* vol. 90, no. 5 (November 1990), pp. 45–48.

16. For a discussion of the importance of safety in the appeal of shopping malls, see Joel Garreau, *Edge City: Life on the New Frontier* (New York: Doubleday, 1991).

17. Social scientist Amitai Etzioni, editor of *Communitarian Quarterly,* argues that this is an understandable response to the fact that the government has shown that it is "unwilling or unable to discharge its most elementary duty—to protect citizens from violent crime." He reports that in Los Angeles there are thirty-five neighborhoods that have asked permission to put up protective gates on streets in their communities. He says that figure includes African-American communities. See Amitai Etzioni, "Do Fence Me In," *Wall Street Journal,* December 1, 1992, editorial page.

18. See Arthur M. Schlesinger, Jr., *The Disuniting of America: Reflections on a Multicultural Society* (New York: W. W. Norton and Company, 1992).

19. Myrdal, Sterner, and Rose, *An American Dilemma,* p. 1024.

20. Edmund Burke, *Reflections on the Revolution in France* [1790], published in one volume along with Thomas Paine, *The Rights of Man* (Garden City, NY: Dolphin Books/Doubleday and Company, 1961), p. 74.

Index

Class warfare, 102–3
Classical liberalism, 104. *See also* Free-market economics
Cloward, Richard, 233–34, 236, 245, 246
Coleman, James, 6, 38–39, 273–80 *passim*, 283–84, 291, 293
Coleman Report, 273–74, 276, 283
Coming of Age in Samoa (Mead), 83
Common Destiny, A (Jaynes and Williams), 48, 275, 299
Communities: and education, 274–75; and welfare reform, 245–46
Community policing, 241
Competition: athletic, 198–99, 282; for mates, 163–66, 186. *See also* Courtship
Compromise of 1877, 79, 89
Conduct, and rationality, 39–41
Conflict: and altruism, 179–88; ethnic, 188–93; intergroup, 179, 194–99, 204–5
Conservatism, 74, 103–4, 112–15, 117, 137
Continuum of Descent, 183
Contraception, 168, 304–5, 315
Cook, Thomas D., 279–80
Courtship, 159–61, 165; in the underclass, 173–77. *See also* Mates
Cressey, Donald, 232, 233, 236, 237
Crime, 17–18, 214–16, 219–21, 241–42; and black Americans, 42, 69–70, 223–25; consequences of, 61–62, 247–49; and educational failure, 235–36, 247; explanations of, 229–38; and the nineteen-sixties, 238–45; in nineteenth-century London, 211–13, 300; organized, 109, 233; policies on, 220–21, 250–51, 331–33; and poverty, 220, 230; racially motivated, 7–8; and sociobiology, 226–29; statistics on, 221–26; subculture of, 232–33; and welfare reform, 245–47. *See also* Delinquency
Crime and Human Nature (Wilson and Herrnstein), 236, 319
Criminal justice system, 332; attitude of black Americans toward, 240, 244, 254–55, 352 n. 50. *See also* Law enforcement

"Criminal type," 229
Criminology (Sutherland and Cressey), 232
Critical legal studies, 31
Crown Heights, 338–39
Crutchfield, Richard, 114
Cubans, 46
Cuckoo birds, 181
Cultural determinism, 82–83
Cultural practices, 28, 34
Curfews, 242, 253, 255, 324, 332–34, 372 n. 75

Dancing, 165
Dark Ghetto (Clark), 301
Darwin, Charles, 149–50, 347 n. 5
Darwinian fitness, 149–50, 182–83
Dawkins, Richard, 145, 150, 162, 182–85 *passim*, 189, 314, 366 n. 26, 368 n. 10
Dawson, Deborah, 316, 317–18
Decision theory, 39–40, 355 n. 84
Deconstruction, 31
Degler, Carl, 82, 88, 269, 270, 358 nn. 48 and 49
Deinstitutionalization, of mental health patients, 242
Delinquency, 227–28, 230, 234; and illegitimacy, 318–20. *See also* Crime
Delinquency and Opportunity (Cloward and Ohlin), 233, 245
Delinquency in a Birth Cohort (Wolfgang, Figlio, and Sellin), 230
Demagogues, 107, 197–98
Democratic party, and black Americans, 356 n. 5 (of Part II), 358 n. 70
DePalma, Anthony, 60
Deterrence, 332
Devil's Night (Chafets), 64
Dickens, Charles, 211
Discipline, in schools, 284, 286
Discrimination, 2, 10, 25, 42, 46–47, 52–53, 57, 63, 69–70; by government, 79, 94–95; and immigrants, 80–82; and law enforcement, 254–55; varieties of, 90, 206, 208. *See also* Affirmative action; Quotas
Disparate impact, 121–22
Disuniting of America, The (Schlesinger), 290

About the Author

Byron M. Roth is Professor of Psychology at Dowling College in Oakdale, New York, and has served as Academic Chair of the College's Social Science Division. He received his Ph.D. in Psychology from the New School for Social Research and is the coauthor, with John D. Mullen, of *Decision Making: Its Logic and Practice,* published in 1991 by Rowman and Littlefield.